MARINA CVETAEVA

HER LIFE AND ART

Marina Cvetaeva with her daughter, Ariadna.

MARINA CVETAEVA
Her Life and Art

SIMON KARLINSKY

University of California Press
BERKELEY AND LOS ANGELES 1966

University of California Press
Berkeley and Los Angeles, California
Cambridge University Press
London, England

Note on Transliteration

This book deals with a Russian poet whose last name occurs in at least half a dozen different transcriptions: Tsvetaeva, Tsvetayeva, Tzvetayeva, Tzvetaéva, Zwetajewa, and so forth. Despite some acceptance gained by the Library of Congress system of transliterating the Cyrillic alphabet, transcriptions of Russian names in this country remain in a state describable only as chaotic. New and unscholarly systems of transliterations are being introduced each year by various hands, adding further to the confusion and creating for the Cyrillic alphabet the reputation of being extremely difficult and esoteric. In fact, the contemporary Russian alphabet is quite simple and adequate to its purpose. There has been in existence for decades a logical system of transcribing Russian names into Latin characters, a system which is based on the spelling of a related Slavic language, Czech, which uses Latin letters. In the United States this system has been long used by the Slavicists and in such publications as The Slavic and East European Journal. It has now gained a wide general acceptance in Germany, Italy, and the Western Slavic countries. This is the only system so far devised which makes possible a transcription not only from the Cyrillic but also back into Cyrillic, thus making cross-reference easy and factually reliable. French, German, and even Polish writers retain the spelling of their names in all Western languages, but Pushkin turns out to be Puschkin in Germany and Pouchkine in France. With the acceptance of the scholarly, Czech-based system of transliteration, he becomes Puškin and remains so in all countries.

The objections to this system from the point of view of the English spelling are its use of diacritics and the use of *j* for the phonetic *yod*. The prospect of the names traditionally spelled Tolstoy and Dostoevsky ending in a *j* seems particularly frightening to certain critics—yet these same critics would never dream of replacing the *j* in German of Scandinavian names with a *y,* or of adopting a new spelling for such a name as Rimbaud to make sure that English and American readers unversed in French give it a properly French pronunciation. Futhermore, the *y* in Tolstoy and that in Dostoevsky by no means represent the same Russian sound; in fact, the *y* that we encounter in various Russian names in our current press may represent any of at least four Russian sounds or combinations, transcribed in the scholarly system as *y, j, yj,* or *ij.* There is really no reason why the glide at the end of *Tolstoj* and the two different vowel-plus-glide combinations in *Dostoevskij* and *Belyj* should all be represented by the same ubiquitous *y.* The clarity and logic inherent in the scholarly transliteration system seem well worth the minor initial inconvenience of the unfamiliar diacritics and *j*'s. Its universal acceptance is undoubtedly only a matter of time; it seemed to me only sensible to use this system in the present book.

Those accustomed to the more traditional methods of transcription need be concerned only with the transliteration of the few characters given in the table below; the rest of the Latin characters retain their traditional values in major Western languages.

Cyrillic	Scholarly Transliteration	Library of Congress and other traditional systems	Approximate sound
ж	ž	zh	*s* in measure
й	j	i or y	*y* in boy
х	x	kh or h	a guttural *h* (as in German a*ch* or Spanish *J*orge)
ц	c	ts	*ts* in boots
ч	č	ch	*ch* in church
ш	š	sh	*sh* in shoe

Cyrillic	Scholarly Transliteration	Library of Congress and other traditional systems	Approximate sound
Щ	šč	shch	fi*sh* *ch*urch
Ъ	”	” or omitted	(the "hard sign")
Ы	y	y or omitted in certain combinations	*i* in bit
Ь	’	’ or omitted	(the "soft sign," palatalizes the preceding consonant)
Э	è	ė or e	*e* in them
Ю	ju	yu or iu	*you*
Я	ja	ya or ia	*yah*

It remains to be added that *ë* is pronounced as *yaw* in yawn. After familiarizing themselves with these few characters, those who do not read Russian will no longer have to worry whether the Russian critic and poet Khodasevich is the same man they saw spelled elsewhere as either Chodasewitsch or Hodasevitch; they will instead see his name transcribed, logically and precisely, from its Russian spelling as Xodasevič. Those who do read Russian will be able to reconstruct the original Russian spelling of any name with precision and fidelity, which other, more traditional systems would not enable them to do. To those who already know the Cyrillic and are bored by the whole issue, it is suggested that an occasional touch of pedantry is the price one pays for clarity and logic.

S.K.

Contents

Note on Transliteration, v
Introduction, 1

PART ONE: HER LIFE

I "Her Mother and Poetry," 15
II Marriage. Revolution. (1912–1922), 35
III Exile (1922–1929), 52
IV Last Decade in Paris (1929–1939), 79
V Elabuga and After (1939–1941 and on to 1965), 101

PART TWO: HER ART

VI Technical Aspects: Language, Versification, Poetic Devices, 123
VII Lyric Poetry, 171
VIII Longer Poems, 207
IX Dramatic Works, 237
X Prose, 266
Conclusion, 283
Bibliography, 290
Index, 311

Introduction

Russian Poetry In The Twentieth Century and Marina Cvetaeva

As the earlier decades of the present century gradually recede into history, it is becoming more and more evident that between approximately 1895 and 1930 poetry in Russia went through one of the most glorious bursts of flowering that any poetry has experienced in modern history. Until now, literary historians have traditionally called the years 1810–1840 the "Golden Age of Russian Poetry." That period is dominated by the greatest and most momentous figure in *all* Russian literature, Aleksandr Puškin, and his age was indeed a time when poetry in Russia attained a high artistic and technical level, produced a number of excellent poets, and was enjoyed by an appreciative audience. Yet the time has perhaps come to state that in the early twentieth century (usually dubbed "a period of decadence" in Soviet criticism and, with greater justice, the "Second Golden Age" or the "Silver Age" of Russian poetry by the Russian émigré critics) the total achievement of Russian poetry is greater in scope and magnitude, deeper and more varied than that of Puškin's time.

If we were to apply to Russian poets of the first half of the nineteenth century an imaginary mechanical device which measured relative literary magnitude, only four of them would cause the indicator arrow to reach the notch marked "major" and to fluctuate between it and the next one, marked "great": Žukovskij, Baratynskij, Tjutčev, and Lermontov. The numerous other poets of the period, as fine or even delightful as some of them are, would not quite bring the indicator to the "major" mark, while Puškin himself is, of course, beyond the reach of our device and would jam the mechanism hopelessly.

The age of Puškin was followed by a rapid decline of poetry. The loss of style, taste, and craftsmanship is painfully evident even in the work of the finest poets of the second half of the nineteenth century, such as Fet, Nekrasov, and A. K. Tolstoj. This loss reached catastrophic proportions in the verse of their imitators and lesser contemporaries. The great feat of the early Symbolists of the eighteen-nineties was to revive the art of writing good verse (all but lost by the end of the century) and to liberate Russian poetry temporarily from the "narrow prison of ideology and prejudice" (as Nikolaj Gumilëv put it) to which it had been confined since the eighteen-forties through the efforts of a succession of influential and civic-minded critics who had fatally assumed that poetry, beauty, and imagination are incompatible with enlightenment and social progress. After about 1895, every few years bring new groups of poets of whom astonishing numbers qualify for the "major-to-great" category.

The older generation of Symbolists which entered literature at the end of the nineteenth century is remarkable for the richness and variety of the poetry it produced: Valerij Brjusov, more Parnassian than Symbolist in his cool detachment; the melodious Konstantin Bal'mont, equally capable of being banal or sublime; Zinaida Gippius with her self-centered philosophical and tragic poetry; the morbid and fantastic Fëdor Sologub; and the most authentic Symbolist in the whole of Russian poetry, even though he was never affiliated with the movement and considered himself its opponent— Innokentij Annenskij. In less than ten years, these poets were joined by the second Symbolist generation in the person of three poets who, while differing profoundly from each other in many ways, were united in their view of poetry as a mystical, metaphysical, visionary experience. These were Aleksandr Blok, Andrej Belyj, and Vjačeslav Ivanov. There was also Mixail Kuzmin, a contemporary of the younger Symbolists, who was one of the first in his poetry to turn from the Symbolist visions and metaphysical depths to the joys and pleasures of this world. Kuzmin's example of preferring real and immediate poetic values to symbolic and mystical ones was followed around 1910 by two new literary movements, Acmeism and Futurism, which ostensibly revolted against Symbolism, but which in fact carried on the high standards of literary culture attained by that movement.

The sane and sensible poetic theories of Acmeism, which insisted on primacy of reality and everyday life, formed the early poetry of Anna Axmatova, Nikolaj Gumilëv and Osip Mandel'štam; eventually all three outgrew Acmeist poetics. Futurism emphasized the verbal aspects of poetic expression and developed poetic styles closely patterned on the current developments in the visual arts, especially Cubism, with its unexpected shifting of planes and its use of elementary shapes and primary colors. The great Futurist poets were Velimir Xlebnikov and Vladimir Majakovskij; the young Boris Pasternak began his literary career as an adherent of one of the minor trends within Russian Futurism. Simultaneously with the emergence of Acmeism and Futurism there appeared three other important poets who did not participate in movements, but whose individualities blend in various ways into the poetic abundance that characterized the period: Vladislav Xodasevič, whose poetry can be better described as a fusion of the classical and the romantic, rather than in terms of one of the then-current trends; Marina Cvetaeva, whose lonely poetic path only remotely paralleled the general drift of Russian poetry from the late nineteenth-century romanticism to Symbolism and then to Futurism; and Georgij Ivanov, a proficient and slickly elegant versifier when he began to write, who attained true greatness in the bitter, nihilistic, and surrealistic poetry he wrote in his old age in the nineteen-fifties. Adding further to the incredible variety are the two major peasant poets, Nikolaj Kljuev and Sergej Esenin, called "peasant" not because of their origin, but because this origin and the fate of Russian village life in the twentieth century were the central obsessive themes in their poetry.

The condensed survey above concentrates only on the undoubtedly first-rate figures. A slightly greater degree of leniency in evaluation could easily have resulted in a listing three times as long. If we now bring back the metaphorical magnitude meter that was applied to early nineteenth-century poets (an imprecise and approxi-

mate device, to be sure) and insist on applying it to Russian poetry
of the early twentieth century, we see that around 1910 there lived
and wrote in Russia no less than nineteen poets who easily fit into
the "major-to-great" category (as compared to four in Puškin's
time), every single one of whom could easily qualify as the central
national figure in some less richly endowed literature.

The reasons that the world at large is not sufficiently aware of this
early twentieth-century miracle are to be sought in the Russians'
own neglect that stems in turn from certain traditions in the
treatment of poets by the Russian state in almost all periods and by
the so-called "progressive" literary critics after the eighteen-forties.
These traditions were revived, broadened, and intensified in the
decades following the October Revolution, but their roots are in the
past. From the caning of Vasilij Trediakovskij by a cabinet minister
for failure to produce a desired poem on time (in the seventeen-
forties) to the sentencing of Iosif Brodskij to forced labor for failure
to write the kind of poetry the state approves (in the nineteen-
sixties), it has been the same dismal story, on and off. Few nations
have been granted the abundance and variety of important poets
that Russia has produced in the last hundred and fifty years; no
nation, ancient or modern, has persecuted its poets so repeatedly,
relentlessly, and in so many different ways. Nineteenth-century
Russian poets were killed in duels, banished to remote provinces,
and forced to serve as common soldiers in the tsar's army. Later in
the century, the physical persecution of the overly-independent poets
by the imperial government abated, to be replaced by savage literary
hounding of the powerful utilitarian-minded critics, who opposed
the government and were ostensibly on the side of freedom. There is
an inescapable parallel, noted by Aleksandr Blok (and more
recently by Vladimir Nabokov in his novel *The Gift*), between the
treatment of Puškin by Nicholas I and the demolishing of poets'
reputations by utilitarian critics (Baratynskij's by Belinskij, Puškin's
by Pisarev, Fet's by the whole of Russian criticism between the sixties
and the nineties.) Both the tsars and their liberal opponents
considered a dissenting and independent poet either a useless fool or
a dangerous criminal.

Within ten years after the October Revolution these two anti-
poetic traditions, which were dormant during the Russian cultural

renaissance of the early twentieth century, were brought back. Nicholas I could persecute and banish poets; Belinskij and Dobroljubov could expel them from literature for decades by discouraging their publishers and alienating prospective readers. Soviet literary authorities could do all of those things—and they did. In the reign of Nicholas I, only dissident poets suffered persecution. Those who were loyal to the regime and sincere in their support (Žukovskij, Tjutčev) were allowed to live and create in peace. But Soviet cultural policies brought total tragedy to every single one of the eighteen major poets who were active at the time of the Revolution, regardless of their attitude toward the revolution or their general political orientation (Annenskij died in 1909 and has suffered only in terms of having today a somewhat lesser reputation than he undoubtedly deserves).

Three of these poets were physically destroyed by the immediate consequences of the Revolution: Blok, who had accepted and hailed the Communist takeover in 1917, died of acute depression in 1921, disappointed and dejected, his last poem a grim warning against political control of literature; also in 1921, Nikolaj Gumilëv was shot for counter-revolutionary activities; Velimir Xlebnikov died in 1922 of malnutrition and privations suffered during the civil war period. Bal'mont, Gippius, Vjačeslav Ivanov, Georgij Ivanov, and Xodasevič lived out their lives in exile and poverty, their books banned in their country, their names unmentionable even in literary histories, their achievements concealed from new generations of readers. Brjusov, the only one of the Symbolists to accept Communism fully and genuinely, became a state functionary; a recent memoir by Majakovskij's mistress, Lili Brik, vividly describes the loneliness and bitterness Brjusov felt in his last years, despite the official accolades.[1] Andrej Belyj returned to the Soviet Union from a voluntary exile abroad, made desperate efforts to adapt to Soviet literary demands, but was utterly incapable of shaking off his uniqueness and originality. As a result, his work has been virtually banished from Soviet literature since his death in 1934 (he is occasionally mentioned by literary critics as a negative example). Esenin, Majakovskij, and Cvetaeva were driven to suicide. The

[1] L. Ju. Brik, "Čužie stixi," in *V. Majakovskij v vospominanijax sovremennikov* (Moscow, 1963), p. 353.

poets who remained in the Soviet Union and were not physically destroyed (Sologub, Kuzmin, Axmatova, Pasternak) could no longer write of the personal poetic universe that each one of them had discovered. In Marina Cvetaeva's phrase, it was now "the age of 'sing that we want you to—or else we'll abolish you.' " [2] Alternately neglected and vilified by the official press, they had to resort to various forms of so-called "internal emigration." Unable to write or to publish, they had to live by translating classical poetry of other literatures. Finally, two particularly harrowing cases are Kljuev and Mandel'štam, who perished in Stalin's forced labor camps. Nikolaj Zabolockij, the most original and brilliant poet to appear in Soviet times, shared the fate of the older poets: his, too, is a story of violent denunciations in the press, forced labor camps, and suppression of his best and most personal poems.

We are now living in a period when poetic creativity and true appreciation of poetry are being slowly and laboriously revived in the Soviet Union. Until recently, only four of major twentieth-century Russian poets had been recognized by the Soviet literary establishment, and, despite distortions and oversimplifications of their literary biographies, given their due: Brjusov, Blok, Majakovskij, and Esenin.[3] In each case, such acknowledgment had to do not with the quality and true value of each poet's work, but almost solely with his personal politics in the years immediately following the October Revolution. Only during the last ten years have some of the other of those twentieth-century poets been emerging from the obscurity to which they had been relegated in the later years of the Stalinist era, when poets were replaced by prize-winning nonenti-

---

[2] "Ici-Haut" (a cycle of poems dedicated to the memory of Maksimilian Vološin), *Vstreči,* IV (Paris, 1934).

[3] In some recent Soviet textbooks, this tendency has led to attempts to group these four poets (profoundly different from one another or even hostile to each other's work) into a separate school of poets who "outgrew decadence and were on the way to creating humanistic and democratic poetry" (N. A. Trifonov, ed. *Russkaja literatura XX veka* [Moscow, 1962]). Insofar as these terms are applicable to poetry, there are certainly more "humanistic" and "democratic" elements in Bal'mont's poetry and biography than in Brjusov's, but their respective political positions after 1917 cause Soviet literary historians to class Bal'mont as a "decadent" and Brjusov as a "democrat," all objective facts notwithstanding.

ties, appreciation of poetry by the demand for versified platitudes, and poetic craft by academic Victorianism. Xlebnikov, Axmatova, and Cvetaeva are being cautiously re-published (in limited editions and with many important poems missing); so is Pasternak, despite the international scandal which has made his name a household word throughout the world. Axmatova, the only surviving poet of that great age, has been allowed to travel abroad and receive literary honors in Italy and England. Partial re-establishment of contact with the pre-Stalin traditions is strikingly evident in the better work of such younger Soviet poets as Voznesenskij, Brodskij, and Novella Matveeva.

Yet the biased and prejudiced evaluation of early twentieth-century poetry (and culture in general) is still heavily felt in the contemporary Soviet press and criticism. Too many of the major poets are still proscribed, and their work is not available to those who could appreciate it. Gippius, Kuzmin, Kljuev, and Vjačeslav Ivanov might never have existed so far as the Soviet literary establishment is concerned. There are no sympathetic or full-scale Soviet studies of Mandel'štam or Cvetaeva or Pasternak. Since great poets belong not only to their country, but to the world, Western Slavicists, especially in America, have sought to fill in this important gap in Soviet scholarship and criticism—pending the day when Soviet scholars can again be guided by literary quality in their choice of subjects rather than by political expediency and party pressure.

Exile, neglect, persecution, and suicide have been the fate of Russian poets after the Revolution, but perhaps only Marina Cvetaeva has experienced *all* of these. Her personal and her literary biography exemplify the fate of Russian poets of her epoch. Cvetaeva began to write in the marvellous age when Russian poetry attained its maximal freedom and realized its potential to the fullest. She grew with that age and she contributed to it. She stayed in the Russia of Leninist dictatorship long enough to realize the situation of a creative poet subjected to intolerable political pressures. She attained her full poetic maturity during the years she spent as an exile abroad, suffering poverty, loneliness, and the active hostility of

fellow-exiles, who brought, along with other traditions of nineteenth-century Russian liberalism, the tradition of callousness and
hostility to independent individualists like Cvetaeva. The treatment
of poets in Stalin's U.S.S.R. that Cvetaeva encountered upon
returning there drove her in less than two years to take her own life.
Yet, through all of her ordeals she salvaged the poetic individuality
that enabled her to produce a body of poetry that is among the finest
in the twentieth century. It is this unique and unmistakable quality
of Cvetaeva (rather than the alleged "anti-bourgeois" satire her
Soviet commentators inevitably stress) which makes her such a
great favorite of the younger Soviet generation and such a potent
influence in the better Soviet poetry of the nineteen-sixties.

It would have been unwise to attempt a biography of Cvetaeva
without access to so much of the material that is not available in the
West, had she herself not told us so much about her life. The view
of the world reflected in the writings of Marina Cvetaeva is one of
the most personal ever recorded in literature. Except for her ethical-
philosophical essays, the autobiographical element played a major
role in everything Cvetaeva wrote. A considerable portion of her
prose works belongs to the autobiographical genre: personal memoirs, reminiscences, extracts from her diaries. Less personal prose
pieces, such as her memoirs about other writers (Belyj, Vološin,
Brjusov), about the historian Ilovajskij, and her critical studies (of
Pasternak, of Puškin and Pugačëv, or of the painter Natalija
Gončarova) often contain autobiographical digressions, at times
supported by precisely dated quotations from Cvetaeva's unpublished diaries.

The lyric poetry of Cvetaeva is collected into volumes which are
at the same time chronological journals of her emotional and
intellectual day-to-day life. This is why Cvetaeva found it necessary
to add explanatory notes whenever, for thematic reasons, she
dislodged a poem from its strict chronological sequence within such
collections as *Remeslo* (*Craft*) or *Lebedinyj stan* (*Swans' Encamp-
ment*). The collections of verse published by Cvetaeva between 1910
and 1928 (including the collection *Junošeskie stixi* [*Juvenilia*] still
unpublished in its entirety) constitute an uninterrupted lyrical diary

of her experiences and emotions between 1908 and 1925.[4] The biographical material in the lyrical poems of Cvetaeva appears at times in cryptic and veiled form, yet the comparison of many of these poems with some of the recently published Cvetaeva letters (especially those to G. Ivask and to A. Baxrax) and with some of her prose pieces (e.g., "Povest' o Sonečke" ["The Story of Sonečka"]) shows to what extent her poetry contains factual material. It has been said of Arthur Rimbaud that even in his most fantastic imaginings he invented nothing, using his poetic method instead to transform and distort his everyday experiences.[5] The method of Cvetaeva was often similar, and such longer poems as "Poèma konca" ("Poem of the End") are records of concrete personal experience which, quite apart from their great poetic worth, possess definite biographical significance. In the years to come, as more Cvetaeva correspondence is made public, we should be able to relate more of her poetry to the circumstances under which it was written.

Cvetaeva's dramatic works are less directly connected to her biography than are her prose and lyric poetry; still, her early plays all owe their origin to certain friendships and connections she had in the Moscow theatrical world prior to her emigration. The tragedies she wrote in the nineteen-twenties are not so obviously linked to her biography, although one could conceivably construct theories which would place the origin of her predilection for the myths of Ariadne and Phaedra in certain personal relationships which she had during that period.

In view of this wealth of factual material in Cvetaeva's own writings, the following biographical essay will be based primarily on her own testimony, drawing on other available sources to fill in gaps and to describe periods in her life for which she left no written record.

[4] In three of Cvetaeva's collections of verse (*Psixeja, Razluka,* and *Stixi k Bloku*) the poems are chosen and grouped not chronologically but thematically, and in these collections Cvetaeva omits her usual strict chronological annotations. But considerable portions of all three collections are included in their proper chronological sequence in *Versty I* and in *Remeslo.*

[5] Ernest Delahaye, *Rimbaud* (Paris, n.d.), pp. 37 and 41; Enid Starkie, *Arthur Rimbaud* (London, 1947), p. 217.

This study of Cvetaeva's life and art is based on my doctoral dissertation bearing the same title (University of California, Berkeley, 1964); those interested in a more detailed documentation of the biographical sections are referred to the original dissertation. I wish to express my gratitude to those who helped me in the course of my work on Cvetaeva. First of all, I am indebted to my dissertation director, Professor Gleb Struve. His encouragement, help, and advice took more forms than I could possibly enumerate or even remember; they were, to give a rather hackneyed adjective its original and full meaning, invaluable. While writing the book, I had the fortunate benefit of advice and suggestions by two other members of my dissertation committee, Professor Francis J. Whitfield and Dr. Dorothée Finkelstein, to both of whom I am deeply grateful.

I also owe a debt of gratitude to the following persons who had personally associated with Marina Cvetaeva or had been her friends, and who were kind enough to answer my inquiries, provide valuable information, or make unpublished Cvetaeva materials available to me: Professor George Ivask; Mmes Catherine Elène (E. I. Eleneva), Salomea Halpern, Aleksandra Žernakova-Nikolaeva, and Anna Kallin; Archbishop John of San Francisco, Professor Else Mahler, and Professor Marc Slonim. For advice or information on particular problems, I am grateful to Professor Roman Jakobson and to Mmes Anna Turgeneva, Vera Nabokova, and Nina Berberova. I shall always be indebted to Professor Tatiana Kosinski for encouraging me to undertake the work on Cvetaeva and for making available to me her Cvetaeva bibliography.

For research in remote libraries, inaccessible to me, I would like to thank my colleagues Dr. Margaret Dalton, Professor Kathryn B. Feuer (who also contributed much-appreciated editorial suggestions), Mr. Ralph Lindheim, and Professor Vladimir Markov. For joint and reciprocal exploration of California libraries which yielded some interesting Cvetaeva items, I thank Dr. Olga Sorokin and Dr. Alex M. Shane. I am indebted to Professor Kiril Taranovski for reading the sections on language and versification and for offering his criticism and advice.

I am responsible for the English renderings of the quotations from Cvetaeva's poetry. These aim at textual fidelity only and do not attempt to convey the artful sonorities of the Russian originals. English translation is left out when it cannot possibly convey the syntactic or onomatopoetic qualities that the example seeks to illustrate.

Berkeley, California
August, 1965   Simon Karlinsky

PART ONE: HER LIFE

I

"Her Mother and Poetry"

In the village of Drozdovo near the city of Šuja, *gubernija* of Vladimir, there lived in the middle of the nineteenth century a poor village priest named Vladimir Cvetaev. The name Cvetaev seems to have been fairly common among the provincial Russian clergy; when the bearers of that name left the clercial estate, they usually showed a bent for the learned professions and for research. Among the nineteenth-century Cvetaevs listed in various Russian encyclopedias, we find a professor of law, a translator, a bibliographer, and a lady paleontologist, and whenever antecedents are given for any of these, provincial clerical origin is the rule. Marina Cvetaeva has described her father's side of the family as an "uninterrupted and uninterruptible clan: a primeval one," and half-seriously suggested that its descent might be traced to the legendary epic hero Il'ja Muromec, supposedly a native of the region around Vladimir.

Father Vladimir was one of those impoverished village clerics, whose mode of life differed little from that of the surrounding peasants to whose spiritual needs he ministered. He plowed his own land, threshed grain, and mowed hay until the end of his days. At the same time, Father Vladimir enjoyed great esteem among the peasantry, and his moral authority and prestige were so great that his advice was often sought by the city folk of the neighboring towns. We do not know the first name of Father Vladimir's wife, but we do have a description of her in verse, written by a

15

granddaughter she never saw. Cvetaeva used simple and direct language to express her admiration for the stamina of the village *popad'ja,* who raised her four strapping sons in a dark hut furnished with one wooden candle (*lučina*) and a bag of hemp. The economic conditions under which she had to raise them are illustrated by the recollection of one of these sons that he never had shoes of his own until the age of twelve. All four of Father Vladimir's sons went to the traditional divinity school (*seminarija*), and two of them, following the trend of some other Cvetaevs we know of, as well as the general trend of nineteenth-century Russian life (exemplified by many sons of village clerics who became Populist writers and critics), broke out of the clerical estate by turning to the sciences and humanities.

The elder son, Ivan Vladimirovič (1847–1913), became interested in Latin and in classical philology while still at the divinity school in Šuja. He eventually found his way to the University of St. Petersburg, where he became the protégé of the famous philologist and lexicographer, I. I. Sreznevskij, and specialized in the study of Italic dialects and the history of ancient art. After 1877, I. V. Cvetaev settled in Moscow where he was appointed at the University first as a professor of Roman literature and later to the chair of the theory and history of the arts. His younger brother, Dmitrij (1851–?), also studied at the St. Petersburg University and became a popular and prolific historian.

At Moscow University, Professor I. V. Cvetaev embarked on a project that turned out to be his life's work: the organizing and building of an art museum suitable for housing the University's collection of ancient sculpture. His biographer, Prince B. A. Ščetinin,[1] describes the endeavor and the struggle to raise the funds for that project which began in the 1870's and culminated in 1912, one year before Professor Cvetaev's death, with the unveiling of the Alexander III Museum of Fine Arts in Moscow (now the Puškin Museum), in the presence of Nicholas II and the imperial family. The facade of the building still bears the memorial plaque honoring I. V. Cvetaev. The opening of the museum was witnessed by Professor Cvetaev's then recently married daughter Marina, who later described the occasion in a piece of impressionistic prose,

[1] Kn. B. A. Ščetinin, "Pamjati I. V. Cvetaeva," in *Istoričeskij Vestnik* CXXXIV (St. Petersburg, 1913).

"Otkrytie muzeja" ("Opening of a Museum"), which concludes with a subdued but unmistakable homage to her father.

Professor Cvetaev was married twice. In Moscow, he became close friends with the well-known reactionary historian, D. I. Ilovajskij (1832–1920). Ilovajskij's beautiful daughter, Varvara Dmitrievna, went to study voice in Naples and while there formed romantic attachments which her family judged unsuitable. Accordingly, upon her return to Moscow a marriage to Professor Ivan Cvetaev was arranged. In 1882 a daughter, Valerija, was born. In 1890, one year after the birth of her son Andrej, Varvara Dmitrievna died of tuberculosis, the illness that had killed most of Ilovajskij's children from his two marriages. One year after her death, Ivan Valdimirovič married the twenty-one-year-old Marija Aleksandrovna Mejn (Meyn), the half-Polish daughter of a wealthy Baltic German.

The second marriage of Professor Cvetaev followed the pattern of his first one in an uncanny manner. Again the bride was a musician —this time a concert pianist, a pupil of Anton Rubinstein, who after only one single concert appearance was not allowed by her father to appear publicly. Again the bride was in love with another man. "When my grandfather A. D. Mejn made her choose between the loved one and himself," wrote Marina Cvetaeva, who had access to some of her mother's early diaries, "she chose her father, and afterwards she chose what was the most difficult: a widower with two children, still in love with his late wife."

On September 26 (October 9), 1892, a daughter, Marina, was born to Marija Aleksandrovna and Ivan Vladmirovič Cvetaev.[2] Two

---

[2] There seems to be some disagreement on the exact year of Marina Cvetaeva's birth. The year 1892 is given in all sources prior to the nineteen-fifties, including Cvetaeva's own testimony in her letter to G. Ivask of April 3, 1934 (Letters to Ivask, p. 214). The introduction by F. Stepun to her prose selections (*Proza*, 1953) and the Great Soviet Encyclopedia of 1957 state the year of her birth as 1894. The biography appended to the Soviet edition of her selected poems (*Izbrannoe*, 1961), which was prepared with the assistance of Cvetaeva's daughter, Ariadna Èfron, reinstates the year 1892. The date 1894 seems to be a misunderstanding, based on Cvetaeva's frequently quoted statement that she wrote her first verse at the age of six and had her first publication at the age of sixteen. Since her first book, *Večernij al'bom*, appeared in 1910, this would indeed make it appear that she was born in 1894.

However, Cvetaeva's dating becomes a bit hazy for the period 1910–1912. Some passages in her memoirs give the impression that she was seventeen for at least two years. Two possibly embarrassing factors may be involved: her years later their second daughter, Anastasija (Asja), was born, and twelve years later in 1906, Marija Aleksandrovna followed the example of her predecessor and died of tuberculosis, "the hereditary illness" of the Ilovajskijs and the Cvetaevs.

Marina Cvetaeva's childhood plays a significant part in her works. Her first book of verse, *Večernij al'bom* (*Evening Album*) (1910), is largely devoted to the evocations of her then recent childhood; childhood themes appear in some of her later poetry, notably in the *poèma* "Na krasnom kone" ("On a Red Steed"), written in 1921. A number of her autobiographical prose pieces written during the nineteen-thirties are devoted entirely to her childhood reminiscences, many of them dealing with the period before the age of six. It is a childhood quite unlike the *paradis enfantins* dreamed of by Nerval or Proust. It was more like an infantine purgatory from which Cvetaeva was only too glad to escape by growing up.

It was not an entirely unhappy childhood, however. In the prose memoirs, we read of the leisurely life of Professor Cvetaev's family in their Moscow home at Number 7, Trëxprudnyj pereulok ("Street of Three Ponds"), with its dove-grey, dove-filled yard, the house of which the sixteen-year-old Marina was later to write:

> The marvellous house, our wonderful house in Trëxprudnyj,
> Which is now turning into verse.

---

unusually long stay at the gimnazija (she must have been eighteen when Maksimilian Vološin first visited her, yet she was still at the *gimnazija*, where she admittedly did nothing but write poetry; see "Živoe o živom," in *Proza*, p. 138). The second factor is her insistence that she and her husband were of the same age, whereas in fact he seemed to have been a year or two younger.

Before and after the period 1910–1912, the dates and her own age stated by Cvetaeva invariably point to the year 1892 as the real year of her birth. Two random examples: in describing how she met the mother of Valerij Brjusov at the age of six, Cvetaeva concludes that this must have been during the student disturbances of 1898–1899 ("Geroj truda," in *Proza*, p. 214). In the letter to A. Baxrax of July 25, 1923, Cvetaeva states her age as thirty (*Mosty*, V [Munich, 1960], 313). There are many other similar examples.

The clinching argument is provided by the calendar. In her correspondence and in two of her poems ("Krasnoju kist'ju," in *Izbrannoe*, p. 58, and "Meždu voskresen'em i subbotoj," quoted in Letters to Ivask, p. 216), Cvetaeva stresses the fact that she was born on a Saturday, which was also the feast of St. John the Divine. That feast (September 26, or October 9 according to the Gregorian Calendar) indeed fell on a Saturday in 1892. In 1894, it was on a Monday.

We read of their summers in the picturesque town of Tarusa on the river Oka. From Cvetaeva's reminiscences about her childhood, we become closely acquainted with the Cvetaev family and their retainers. We meet the governesses, at first the Baltic German Augusta Ivanovna from Riga (or Dorpat), from whom the little Marina got her first taste for German poets, later replaced by a Parisienne named Alphonsine Dijon, who may have brought *her* own literary tastes that would account for some of Cvetaeva's later odd preferences in French poetry. Marina had no traditional Russian nurse (*njanja*), but there was one for her younger sister Asja. This nurse was quite the opposite of Puškin's fairy-tale-reciting nurse, for in her case we find the six-year-old Marina ecstatically reciting Puškin to the uncomprehending and disapproving *njanja*.

The visits of her maternal grandfather, Aleksandr Danilovič Mejn, were particularly joyous occasions for little Marina, or Musen'ka, as she was then known. He brought her presents and bananas (an exotic treat in those days), recited German poetry, and above all he showed a partiality for her and an affection which she so desperately wanted and did not get from the members of her immediate family. The cheerful visits of Aleksandr Danilovič are contrasted with the visits of the dour, forbidding Professor Ilovajskij, the grandfather of Marina's half-sister Valerija and half-brother Andrej, who instead of presents brought anti-Semitic leaflets of his own manufacture and who otherwise showed little interest in the two younger girls who were not directly related to him.[3]

The siblings are clearly delineated through a number of scattered references in Cvetaeva's memoirs. Valerija Cvetaeva, ten years older than Marina, never forgave her stepmother for taking her mother's place in the household. The feud between the stepmother and the stepdaughter, while under reasonable control, was present throughout Marina's childhood; music, however, provided the common ground for an occasional armistice, when Marija Aleksandrovna would accompany, at the piano, Valerija's singing of traditional Russian *romansy*. It was through Valerija, significantly, that Marina had her first contact with Russian literature. In Valerija's room, the

[3] Cvetaeva's impressive memoir, "Dom u Starogo Pimena," is devoted largely to D. I. Ilovajskij and to the members of his family.

six-year-old Marina surreptitiously read Puškin's "The Gypsies,"
and still earlier, despite her stepmother's prohibition of unsuitable
reading, Valerija read to her half-sister passages from *Dead Souls,*
which Marina, the future Romantic poet, hoped would be about
corpses and ghosts.[4] With all that, Valerija seemed to have no
special love for her younger half-sister, and neither did the half-
brother Andrej, who in the Ilovajskij-Mejn division within the
household took his stepmother's side and was her particular
favorite.[5] Little Asja, who at the time of Marina's adolescence was
quite close to her, emerges in the childhood reminiscences as the
pampered baby of the family, spoiled and envious.[6]

✓   [4] Valerija Cvetaeva (1882–?) was a childhood friend of Ilovajskij's daughter
Nadja and through her of Vera Muromceva, who later became the wife of
Ivan Bunin. Her character seems to have been the very opposite of the
individualistic Marina, being that of an inverterate joiner. After her
graduation from the Ekaterininskij Institut, she attended a girls' college
("kursy Ger'e"), joined the Social Democratic Party, became a professional
dancer and later, refusing marriage proposals on ideological grounds, ended
as a village schoolteacher ("Čort," *Sovremennye Zapiski,* LIX [Paris, 1935],
210; Aleksandra Žernakova-Nikolaeva, "Cvetaevskij dom," *Russkaja Mysl'*
[Paris], March 23 and 26, 1963). Valerija's resentment of her stepmother
found its culmination in "a scene of biblical hatred" that she made to her
sister Asja at the funeral of their brother Andrej in 1933 (mentioned by
Marina in "Dom u Starogo Pimena," pp. 250–251, evidently on the basis of
Asja's description). According to the memoir of A. Žernakova-Nikolaeva, the
portrait of Valerija drawn by Marina is "not impartial." Mme Žernakova-
Nikolaeva remembers Valerija as a "friendly, pure, affectionate and very
religious person."

[5] Andrej Cvetaev (1890–1933) was musically gifted, but his stepmother,
who kept forcing music on her own daughters, did nothing about his musical
education. Soon after the death of his stepmother, he became a ward and sole
heir of his wealthy grandfather Ilovajskij. His father wanted him to study
philology, but he preferred law. He soon broke all ties with the academic
world of his father and the artistic and literary circles in which his younger
sisters moved, becoming involved in the elegant society of Moscow's financial
upper crust (Žernakova-Nikolaeva, *op. cit.;* "Mat' i muzyka," *Proza,* pp.
86–88). Two of Andrej's poems are quoted from memory in Mme Žernakova-
Nikolaeva's memoir. His last personal contact with Marina involved their
attempts to obtain the release of the ninety-year-old Ilovajskij, who had been
arrested by the Cheka in 1918. According to Mme Žernakova-Nikolaeva,
Andrej was put in charge of an industrial plant after the revolution. Like
most descendants of Ilovajskij, he died of tuberculosis.

[6] Anastasija (Asja) Cvetaeva (b. 1894), later Truxačëva, was the only
member of her family who could share Marina's literary interests. Following
the example of Marina in everything, she left the *gimnazija* before

Professor Cvetaev is described as a kindly and considerate man, whose main interests lay outside of his family, and who at home was absentminded to the verge of the faintly absurd: "my attentively uncomprehending father."[7] The family relationship that most strongly colored Marina Cvetaeva's subsequent attitude to her childhood and which resulted in many painful memories was the one with her mother.

A resolute young woman who grew up without a mother,[8] Marija Aleksandrovna was forced by her father to give up the two things she had most wanted: her concert career and the man she loved. She methodically decided to turn her two daughters into musicians, to make sure that they had the things she had missed, whether they wanted them or not. Little Asja played poorly and unwillingly, and the entire musical hope was placed on the uncomplaining Marina, who was willing to practice doggedly to please her mother. When the little Marina produced, at the age of six, a few childish and inept poems, her mother saw in this precocious literary bent something of

---

graduation, was married while still in her teens, and attempted to become a writer. The memoir of A. Žernakova-Nikolaeva describes her as "a second copy of Marina, but without her sister's talent, intelligence and depth." The principal literary production of Anastasija Cvetaeva is the novel *Dym, dym i dym* (*Smoke, Smoke and Smoke*) (Moscow, 1916). Boris Pasternak dedicated to her his poem "Vysokaja bolezn'" (B. Pasternak, *Stixi i poèmy 1912–1932* [Ann Arbor, 1961], pp. 264–272). In 1927, she visited Maksim Gor'kij in Sorrento and wrote a book on him which appeared in part in *Novyj Mir*, VIII–IX (1930), under the name of A. Mejn. On her return trip from Sorrento, she visited Cvetaeva in Paris for two weeks (September, 1927). She now lives in Moscow. Her memoirs about her and Marina's childhood, which *Novyj Mir* began serializing in January, 1966, present a far more happy and idyllic picture of this childhood than do Cvetaeva's own memoirs that deal with the same period. Later installments, not yet available at this writing, may contain valuable factual material for Cvetaeva's biography.

[7] "Mat' i muzyka," *Proza*, p. 8. Professor Cvetaev is seen at his most appealing in "Xlystovki" (*Vstreči*, VI [Paris, 1934], 243–248), and at his most absurd in "Moi služby," *Proza*, pp. 107–109.

[8] The maternal grandmother of Cvetaeva was a Polish gentlewoman, née Bernacka, who died young. She is mentioned in the poems "U pervoj babki" and "Babuške" (written in 1914, published for the first time in *Izbrannoe* in 1961). The contrast between her two grandmothers that Cvetaeva makes in the first of these poems gave Il'ja Èrenburg (in *Portrety russkix poètov* [Berlin, 1922], p. 150) the opportunity for a parallel contrast of the two main currents in Cvetaeva's poetry, the Russian-folkloristic and the European-Romantic.

a threat to the future musical career and reacted ruthlessly by ridiculing these poems in front of other children and by taking away Marina's supply of writing paper. Yet the bitterness of childhood memories came not from the forced piano practice, nor from her mother's prohibition and ridicule of her early attempts at versification, strange from a woman who liked and understood poetry, nor even from a generally prohibitive attitude to anything the little girl might enjoy. The worst part was the open and continuous preference which Marija Aleksandrovna accorded to her stepson and to her younger daughter at the expense of her first-born child. Between the slender, frisky Andrej and the ethereal, mincing Asja, the fat, clumsy, and plain Marina appears as the classical ugly duckling. As a grown-up woman, she rationalized her mother's coldness by describing a chance encounter her mother had with the man she had loved, an encounter about which she could have learned from her mother's diaries: ". . . having married (a widower with two children) to the misfortune of the children and of others, while loving and continuing to love the other one, whom she never afterwards sought to meet, and to whose question about her life, her happiness, etc., asked when she met him by chance at her husband's lecture, she replied:—My daughter is one year old, she is very husky and intelligent, I am entirely happy . . . (Lord, how at that moment she must have hated me, husky and intelligent, for not being his daughter!)"

The feeling of being unwanted came early. At the age of three, Cvetaeva "had a frenzied wish to be lost" in the city of Moscow. At a very early age she devised the daydream of being adopted by an imaginary, kindly devil.[9] The dream of escape was constant and took varied forms. When a group of Old-Believer nuns jokingly offered to adopt her during a summer visit to Tarusa, the child's reaction was unmistakable: "Within me there lights up a wild, burning, unrealizable hopeless hope: what if they could?" At the age of ten she dreamed of staying with an aunt in Switzerland, "where I would be alone without Asja and be the very favorite daughter and perhaps even the son Aleksandr." (An additional reason for Marija Aleksandrovna's disappointment at the time of Marina's birth was

[9] Described in "Čort," where she hopefully thinks of herself as "the devil's little orphan."

her great desire to have a son, whom she had already decided to name Aleksandr.)

The dogged piano practice and excelling in the discussion of German nursery rhymes did nothing to protect the little Marina from the overwhelming feeling of rejection, and the recurrent agonies of jealousy over the sight of Andrej and particularly Asja being rewarded for things that she could do better and which were taken for granted from her persisted throughout her childhood. In her first book of verse, Cvetaeva had many affectionate things to say about her mother; "Mat' i muzyka" is equally a grudging homage to her mother's culture, her love of the arts, and her individualism, described elsewhere as a "Tolstoyan against-the-current attitude" which Cvetaeva says she inherited and shared.[10] Yet, as a grown-up woman with a family of her own, Cvetaeva could write the series of memoirs which are a terrible indictment of what she felt her mother had done to her infancy, her childhood, her adolescence.

By the time she was six years old, Marina became proficient enough at the piano to enter the Moscow music school of Mme Zoograf-Plaksina, where she soon appeared in an open recital playing four-hand piano duets with the younger sister of the famous Symbolist poet Valerij Brjusov. Shortly thereafter she embarked on her first attempts at versification, which, as mentioned, were met with ridicule in her own family, but encouraged by Sergej Ilovajskij, Professor Ilovajskij's young son, who was soon to die of tuberculosis. Young Sergej was the first of the long line of Cvetaeva champions— a line that would eventually include Belyj, Pasternak and Rilke— who valued Marina's poems, urged her to go on writing and to ignore the official verdict of competent authorities that she had taken the wrong path. One of the earliest of her poems had to do with, of all things, a political meeting of university students about which the little girl had heard from one of her brother's tutors. But mostly these earliest poems were love lyrics (inept imitations of Puškin), which may in part explain her mother's negative attitude. As a child Marina Cvetaeva wrote poetry in German as well as in Russian.

[10] Reference to A. K. Tolstoj's poem "Protiv tečenija," in which he objects to the compulsion of nineteenth-century Russian intelligentsia to belong to an easily-labeled political faction, "progressive" or "reactionary."

In her memoir "Čort" ("The Devil"), Cvetaeva describes herself at the age of nine. By that time she was enrolled in one of the lower grades of the government-operated public school (*prigotovitel'nyj klass kazënnoj gimnazii*). It is Easter and she is convalescing from pneumonia. Her mother, in a particularly kindly mood, tries to engage her interest by explaining the mechanical principle by which a toy operates, but the little girl is interested only in rhymes for various Russian and German words that her mother had used. Marina's interest in poetry and her dislike of music notwithstanding (Marina never could make it clear to her mother that she did not dislike music as such, only the music which she herself had to produce, and that she had a great fondness for the music made by her mother), the plans for a musical career were followed through, with all the ensuing work and practice.

Her private adventures with Russian literature, which began with her first acquaintance with Puškin (described in brilliant detail in "Moj Puškin"), continued. Her brother Andrej was given a chrestomathy, "swollen with Bagrov-grandson and Bagrov-grandfather . . . and with 'Are you awake again, Nikolenka?' and with all those hunting hounds and borzois and with all the lyrical poets of Russia," which little Marina confiscated and read in its entirety, leaving to the end the didactic fables she disliked as being "prose disguised as poetry." The bookshelf of Valerija contained not only Gogol', but also some juvenile adventure literature by minor Russian writers. Particularly desirable reading, strictly prohibited by her mother, were the texts of Valerija's *romansy,* the anemic, often insipid lyrics of the worst period in Russian poetry, the eighteen-eighties.

In November of 1902, Marija Aleksandrovna was told by her doctor that she had tuberculosis. This began the first period of life abroad for Marina and Asja. At first, the entire family with the exception of Professor Cvetaev traveled to Nervi in Italy, where they joined several members of the Ilovajskij family, convalescing from the same illness. The condition of Marija Aleksandrovna progressively worsened, and Marina remembered visiting her mother at various sanatoriums on the Riviera, in the Black Forest, and in Yalta. The years 1903–1904 were spent by Marina in a private boarding school in Switzerland (Lausanne-Ouchy, 3, Boulevard de

Grancy, Pensionnat de Mlle Lacaze), where her most memorable experience was going to confession in a Catholic church and hearing the priest dismiss her fascination with the Devil as childish and trivial.

In February, 1905, we find Marina and Asja at another private boarding school, this time in Freiburg in the Black Forest. German literature was taught here by the unimaginative Fraülein Risky; piano was taught by Fraülein Annie, who assigned pieces by Weber and Beethoven and velocity exercises. There were ball games, hikes in the woods, and the sudden news of another death from tuberculosis—that of Ilovajskij's daughter, Nadja, whom Marina had particularly admired.

One unforgettable day, Marina and Asja were taken by one of the teachers to have tea with a real princess, Fürstin von Thurn und Taxis, who lived in a fairy-tale castle topped by an ivy-clad tower. Marina tried not to appear overawed and made a spirited case for the Russian side of the Russo-Japanese war which was then in the news. It was only when she read the letters of Rainer Maria Rilke, published after his death, that Cvetaeva realized that her hostess on that festive occasion was also a friend and correspondent of the poet she revered.

For many years afterwards, Cvetaeva fondly remembered the effigy of St. George on the Schwabentor in Freiburg. Her lifelong love affair with Germany and Germans can be traced to this stay in the Black Forest. In the essay "O Germanii" ("On Germany"), Cvetaeva shows that her affinity to German literature, music, and landscape was the exterior expression of the spiritual qualities which she felt were part of her innermost core and which were expressible and describable only in German: *Übermass* and *Schwärmerei*. Cvetaeva well realized that outside of their German context, the qualities these two words denote were undesirable and faintly ridiculous. Her admiration for the somewhat abstract Germany was expressed by Cvetaeva in her pro-German poetry written and read in public during the First World War and in "O Germanii" written after the war had ended. Recollections of Freiburg can usually be discerned whenever Cvetaeva evokes Germany.

By June, 1906, it had become clear that Marija Aleksandrovna was about to die. She preferred to die at home, and the entire family gathered for her return trip from Yalta to Moscow. She was judged too weak to travel, and the trip was interrupted at Tarusa. As her last show of strong will, Marija Aleksandrovna declined all help while entering the family's Tarusa house and insisted on playing the piano there for the last time. She died soon afterwards.

After his second wife's death, the household of Professor Cvetaev partially disintegrated. Valerija left home to pursue her varied career, Andrej became the ward of Professor Ilovajskij and went to live with his grandfather. The forced musical education of Marina was gradually discontinued, leaving only the occasional musical images used in her later poetry and prose. The two younger Cvetaev girls entered a *gimnazija*. The study at the *gimnazija* seems to have been one of Marina's least agreeable experiences, and in listing later three of the greatest joys of her life, all of them negative, she mentioned *not* having to go to the *gimnazija,* to awaken *not* in Moscow of 1919, and (a souvenir of her musical martyrdom) *not* to hear a metronome. She was constantly changing schools and taking entrance examinations. The reasons for these peregrinations are not clear, but if we keep in mind her total incapacity for any sort of mathematics, her aversion to all natural sciences, and the fact that at the age of eighteen she was still at the *gimnazija* (usual graduation age was sixteen or seventeen), we can only postulate lack of interest in her studies with the possible concomitant departures from schools or possibly even expulsions (this supposition is confirmed in the recent memoir of A. Žernakova-Nikolaeva).

To counter the boredom of her last years at the *gimnazija,* Marina wrote romantic poems, some of which were later included in her first two published collections of verse. Miss Anna Kallin, now of London, who was Asja Cvetaeva's school friend in 1908–1910 and to whom several poems of Cvetaeva's first collection are addressed or dedicated, recollects that in those years Marina had in part withdrawn into a poetic and fantastic world of her own making. The withdrawal into fantasy was a form of rebellion against the world of the adults; Marina's younger sister and Anna were among the select few allowed by the young poet to get a glimpse of her exalted private universe.

Her literary horizon must have broadened at that time. German literature, especially the Romantics, was an integral part of her cultural heritage, a constant feature of her education since earliest childhood. Her tastes in German literature, formed during her adolescence, were unexceptionable: Goethe, Heine, Hoelderlin, Wilhelm Hauff, later Rilke. A particularly strong impression was left by Friederich de Lamotte-Foucqué's German prose romance *Undine,* which Cvetaeva must have known also in the Russian version in verse by Žukovskij.[11] Her preferences in French literature were more peculiar. They were ultra-Romantic, heroic, and frankly adolescent, and, what is more significant, these preferences stayed with her long after adolescence. A particular favorite of hers was Edmond Rostand, whose *L'Aiglon,* much admired by the young Cvetaeva, was connected with her cult of Napoleon that had its origin in her early reading of Puškin's "To the Sea." Intense hero-worship was a habit Cvetaeva developed early and never quite cast off. The heroes of her youth were Napoleon I and his descendants; also Sarah Bernhardt and Marija Baškirceva. And even after the publication of her first book, the eighteen-year-old Cvetaeva admitted to Vološin that she had read Baudelaire, Rimbaud, and Claudel, but insisted that she did not care for them, that she loved only Napoleon "and Rostand, Rostand, Rostand."

In later years, Cvetaeva's literary enemies often accused her of lack of taste, usually on the basis of her professed admiration for some writer of whom they did not happen to approve. Her friends and allies, when writing of Cvetaeva's poetry, also occasionally found it necessary to offer apologies for her in this respect. Both the reproaches and the apologies seem to be beside the point. It makes no sense to criticize a poet's preferences in reading (not any more than it does to criticize a poet's faulty choice of friends or love affairs) when the alleged bad taste does not penetrate into the poet's own work, as it never does in Cvetaeva's case. Her early love for Baškirceva, Rostand, and Alexandre Dumas—père was as necessary for the formation of the unique poet that Cvetaeva is, as were Goethe, Puškin, Heine, and the Russian folklore.

After their mother's death, Marina and Asja attained a measure of personal and financial independence unusual for girls of their age. For example, in the summer of 1908 Marina managed to take a trip

[11] The German cultural ties of Cvetaeva are discussed by Gleb Struve in *Russkaja literatura v izgnanii* (New York, 1956), p. 149.

to Paris. She traveled all alone and settled, as might have been expected, on rue Bonaparte. The official reason for the sojourn was to study French literature with a certain Mlle James, but the real reason was to be in the city of Napoleon and to see Sarah Bernhardt, preferably in *L'Aiglon*. Mlle Bernhardt was not in Paris just then, but Marina was tremendously impressed with her Carmen-like teacher, Mlle James. While in Paris, Marina evidently attended some lectures on Old French literature at the Sorbonne. It is not likely that she was enrolled as a regular student (as is sometimes maintained), since after her return to Moscow we again find her attending a secondary school.[12]

When Marina Cvetaeva was fifteen, a new and important literary influence entered her life. Lev Kobylinskij, later known as a literary critic and minor Symbolist poet who published under the pseudonym of Èllis, was then a graduate student in history at Moscow University.[13] He was a great Baudelaire enthusiast, a propagandizer of new currents in Russian poetry and, during that period of his life, held advanced political views. Soon after his appearance in the Cvetaev household, Èllis gained complete sway over Marina and Asja.[14] He was the earliest competent judge of young Marina's

[12] The article on Cvetaeva in B. P. Koz'min, *Pisateli sovremennoj èpoxi* (Moscow, 1928), p. 262, which is apparently a somewhat garbled summary of a questionnaire Cvetaeva must have filled out, states: ". . . she finished seven 'classes' of the Brjuxonenko *gimnazija*. At the age of sixteen she attended a course of Old French literature at the Sorbonne." This entry seems to be the source of such later statements as, for example, that of Katia Granoff in *Anthologie de la poésie russe* (Paris, 1961), p. 486, where we read: "[Cvetaeva] après avoir terminé ses études secondaires, part étudier à la Sorbonne la littérature française ancienne." As noted, the trip to Paris took place before Cvetaeva ever reached the seventh "class." The *Dizionario universale della letteratura contemporanea* (n.p., 1959), I, 931, has Cvetaeva studying French literature at the Sorbonne in 1898 (when she was six).

[13] Lev Kobylinskij (1874–1947), better known under his pen name Èllis, was a close friend of Andrej Belyj, who devoted to him two chapters in his book of memoirs, *Načalo veka* (Moscow, 1933): "Student Kobylinskij," pp. 31–45, and "Èllis," pp. 45–54. He emigrated in 1913 to Switzerland and later became a Catholic monk. In 1948, his book in German on Puškin as a religious thinker was published posthumously. Cvetaeva describes him in "Plennyj dux" (p. 289) as "a disorganized poet, but a human being of genius."

[14] Andrej Belyj, *Meždu dvux revoljucij* (Leningrad, 1934), p. 370, states that under the influence of Èllis, Marina and Asja considered themselves to be Anarchists.

poetry, and for a while he became her literary mentor. At his lodgings at the Hotel Don, which the impractical and volatile Èllis shared with a more sedate fellow-student, Vladimir Nilender, the daughters of Professor Cvetaev heard the discussions of the latest literary theories and became acquainted with the poetry of Blok, Belyj, Kuzmin. They met young poets like Sergej Solov'ëv and other members of the circle of "Argonauts" which then centered around Andrej Belyj.

A romantic attachment developed between Marina and the twenty-four-year-old Nilender, and for a period of time she considered him her fiancé.[15] Under the impact of her new associates, not only the literary horizons but the appearance and habits of Marina began to change. At the age of seventeen, she bobbed her hair, started wearing high heels, and took up smoking. All this must have alarmed Professor Cvetaev, and in the summer of 1910 he packed Marina and Asja off to Germany. There they were boarded in a suburb of Dresden with the family of a pastor for the purpose of learning good habits in home economics. The training in home management was not a success, for at the end of the summer Marina was still unable to tell a beet from a carrot; her admiration for Germany and Germans, however, was only enhanced by her stay at the Saxon capital.

It is not clear whether Marina was in Moscow when the tremendous scandal involving Èllis and Professor Cvetaev broke. In 1909, the critic was accused of stealing a number of valuable etchings from a collection at the Rumjancev Museum to which he had allegedly gained free access through the negligence of his good friend, the museum's director, Professor I. V. Cvetaev. There was a series of official investigations, the matter was taken up by the Senate and became a *cause célèbre* in the press (the best known

---

[15] Vladimir Nilender was born in 1883. He was a philologist and literary critic, known mostly for his translations into Russian of Heraclitus and of the Orphic Hymns. Cvetaeva speaks of her relationship with him most directly in "Plennyj dux," p. 302, but she refers to him in a more cryptic way in "Živoe o živom," pp. 171–172, in "Geroj truda," p. 217, and in "Nezdešnij večer," p. 272. The particularly revealing reference to Nilender in "Živoe o živom" does not mention his name, but his identity is easily established if we compare Cvetaeva's description of his studies and interests with the descriptions of Nilender in the memoirs of Belyj and in Fëdor Stepun, *Byvšee i nesbyvšeesja* (New York, 1956), I, 270.

journalist of the day, Vlas Doroševič, devoted a thundering editorial to it). Although the charges against Èllis were subsequently dropped because of insufficient evidence and although Professor Cvetaev was cleared by the Senate investigation, he was nevertheless relieved of his duties at the Rumjancev Museum. He never quite recovered from the shock.[16]

The incident, which must have deeply inpressed Marina and was the possible cause for her trip to Dresden, is not mentioned anywhere in her memoirs. The outcome was that she was ordered to break off all contact with Nilender. Her dodge to overcome that prohibition spelled the beginning of Cvetaeva's literary career. Unable to communicate with Nilender, she simply gathered the poetry she had written at the ages of fifteen, sixteen, and seventeen (including a number of epistles to Nilender), and, a few months before her eighteenth birthday, while still studying in the last grade of the *gimnazija,* she had them privately printed at her own expense, in secret from her family. She called the book *Večernij al'bom (Evening Album).*

"I published it," Cvetaeva later wrote, "for reasons alien to literature, but related to poetry, as a substitute for a letter to a man with whom I was denied the possibility of communicating in any other way." After getting her book printed, Cvetaeva took all five hundred copies to one obscure bookstore, left them there and considered the affair closed. What occurred next was one of the minor miracles of literary history. The unadvertised book of a schoolgirl, which had not been sent anywhere for review, was nevertheless reviewed by four famous poets: Valerij Brjusov, Nikolaj Gumilëv, Marietta Šaginjan, and Maksimilian Vološin.

Nikolaj Gumilëv, the leader of the Acmeist movement in Russian

---

[16] *L'affaire* Èllis is described in detail in Ščetinin, *op. cit.,* pp. 229–230, and in Andrej Belyj, the special chapter, "Incident s Èllisom," pp. 368–397, in *Meždu dvux revoljucij.* The two versions are mutually contradictory. Prince Ščetinin, defending the honor of his late friend, asserts that the thefts did take place and that Professor Cvetaev was able to recover some of the etchings Èllis had sold to known collectors. Belyj, trying as always to settle his old accounts with the Moscow academic circles, shows Èllis as the innocent victim of a professorial conspiracy against modern art. He also brings up a lady with whom Professor Cvetaev was supposedly in love, but who had preferred Èllis.

poetry, wrote a short review that was sympathetic and showed enviable critical foresight. "Marina Cvetaeva," he wrote, "is inherently talented, inherently original (*vnutrenne talantliva, vnutrenne svoeobrazna*). It does not matter that her book is dedicated to 'the radiant memory of Marija Baškirceva,' the epigraph is taken from Rostand, the word 'mama' is almost never absent from the pages. All this only suggests the young age of the poetess, which is soon confirmed by her own lines of confession. There is much in this book that is new: the audacious (at times excessive) intimacy of tone, the new themes, such as childhood infatuation; the spontaneous, unthinking delight in the trivial details of [everyday] life. And, as one would have thought, all the principal laws of poetry have been instinctively guessed, so that this book is not only a charming book of a young girl's confessions, but also a book of excellent verse."

The review of Valerij Brjusov, one of the pillars of Russian Symbolism, then at the height of his renown, was more reserved. While admitting the talent and originality of the new poet, he took exception to the very things that charmed Gumilëv. The excessive intimacy of tone frightened him, the spontaneity of the book seemed to him to spill into slovenliness (*domašnost'*). Brjusov's review exhorted Cvetaeva to broaden her poetic horizon and not to waste her genuine and undoubted talent on "unnecessary, albeit elegant trifles." The demand for profundity at all costs is understandable for a poet of Brjusov's generation and would probably have been made, even if there had not been a disagreement in the form of an exchange of letters between him and the sixteen-year-old Cvetaeva on the subject of Rostand, which she describes in "Geroj truda" ("Hero of Labor") as having occurred long before the publication of her book and of his review. Cvetaeva's mocking reply in verse, in which she refuses "to sing that all is dark / that dreams hover over the world . . . / As is the fashion these days," showed a fine perception of the literary and philosophical issues involved in the trends of the period. The poetic rejoinder, printed in Cvetaeva's second collection in 1912, brought into the open her feud with Brjusov, which was to last until his death and which she described with considerable fairness in "Geroj truda." Èrenburg seems to

exaggerate when he compares her attack on Brjusov to Arthur
Rimbaud's *épatage* of the Parnassians.[17] Brjusov, for whom the
talented girl must have been an embarrassing adversary, continued
publishing hostile criticism of Cvetaeva's work and otherwise
hampering her literary career in the later years, acting always with a
discretion and decorum that were in keeping with his exalted
position in Russian literature of the time. There seemed to be no
way for him to understand that, as Cvetaeva's memoir on him
makes clear, her desperate attacks masked a great deal of awe and
admiration.

After the appearance of her book, the young poet returned to the
gimnazija and the secluded life imposed by her father. One day an
unannounced, corpulent visitor appeared at the house on Trëxprudnyj. It was the poet Maksimilian Vološin, who was greatly
impressed with the book and who became Cvetaeva's devoted
champion after its appearance. The first encounter with Vološin and
the subsequent literary impact which his friendship had on her are
lovingly described by Cvetaeva in her memoirs of him, "Živoe o
živom" ("The Living about the Living") (1933). Vološin replaced
Èllis as Marina's literary guide. It was Vološin, rather than Èllis,
who brought her to "Musaget," a combination of editorial offices (of
the newly-founded publishing house of the former members of the
"Argonaut" circle) and a literary café. At the literary discussions
there, the young girl met the poet Vjačeslav Ivanov, the literary
critic Geršenzon, the young philosopher Fëdor Stepun, and other
members of the Moscow literary community. Vološin also introduced her to Adelaida Gercyk, an essayist and poet who became a
close friend, and whose prose style was later to have a marked
impact on Cvetaeva's own prose writings. When the publishing
house of "Musaget" brought out an anthology of contemporary
Russian poetry early in 1911, the two latest poems of Marina
Cvetaeva appeared in it, along with those of some other promising
beginners (one such was Vladislav Xodasevič) together with the
work of the best known Russian poets of the day such as Blok,
Belyj, Gumilëv, Kuzmin, Vološin, and Vjačeslav Ivanov.

The final break with Nilender came shortly after the publication

---

[17] *Portrety russkix poètov*, p. 151.

of *Večernij al'bom*. The exact circumstances or reasons for the break are not stated by Cvetaeva, but in some of the poems in *Večernij al'bom* she blames herself for not being sufficiently brave and decisive in her dealing with Nilender. She spent the month of April all alone in the ruins of a Genovese fortress in Gurzuf, in the Crimea, reading George Sand and Dumas and trying to forget. At the end of the month she went to join Vološin and his mother in their famous Crimean retreat in Koktebel. The boarding house for poets and artists, which the Vološins owned and operated at this remote village on the wild Eastern coast of the Crimean peninsula, is a great favorite with writers of memoirs—innumerable reminiscences have been published about its colorful and amusing way of life. The memoirists have made the most of the excentric manners and way of dress of Vološin's mother, Elena Ottobal'dovna, nicknamed Pra, meaning "ancestress" (the dangling Russian prefix *pra-*, found in such words as *pramater', prababka*). During Marina Cvetaeva's first visit there, Koktebel had not acquired its subsequent celebrity. Another guest who stayed there in April of 1911 was the seventeen-year-old schoolboy named Sergej Èfron, whom Marina may have met earlier in Moscow.

Èfron was a member of a large and literary-minded Moscow family of Jewish origin, which published the famous Èfron-Brockhaus Encyclopedia. His older brother and sisters had many contacts among the writers and poets both in Moscow and St. Petersburg. Sergej himself wrote short stories, some of which he published in 1912 in a volume entitled *Detstvo* (*Childhood*). He was a particular favorite of Elena Ottobal'dovna. By the fall of 1911, Marina and Sergej Èfron became engaged. Soon after the engagement, Marina anonymously sent one of her farewell poems addressed to Nilender to a poetry contest organized by Brjusov, where it received one of the three prizes. Her marriage to Èfron took place early in 1912, and at approximately the same time her second collection of verse was published. *Vol'šebnyj fonar'* (*The Magic Lantern*), dedicated to Sergej Èfron, was brought out by the publisher Kožebatkin, whom Marina had met at the "Musaget" office. The cover design was to be by Anna (Asja) Turgeneva, but the plan did not materialize because Turgeneva married Andrej Belyj and left on her honeymoon. The critics for the most part overlooked the second collection.

A notable exception was Valerij Brjusov, whose hostility was understandable, since one of the poems in the new collection was a personal attack on him. In 1913, Cvetaeva published a third book—*Iz dvux knig* (*Selections from two Books*)—which consisted of selections from her first two books, with an added riposte to Brjusov's second review.

Marina's marriage came as a shock to her father. He considered her far too young, and the Jewish origins of the bridegroom clashed with the anti-Semitic family traditions of the Cvetaevs and Ilovajskijs. The wedding was celebrated quietly in great privacy, and it must have been embarrassing for Professor Cvetaev to have to answer the numerous inquiries from friends and associates who were not invited to his daughter's wedding.

After the wedding, the newlyweds went to Sicily. Their itinerary was planned to duplicate the wedding trip of Asja Turgeneva (on whom Marina had a girlish crush) and Belyj. The most memorable image of the stay in Sicily was a deaf-mute child who led Marina to a monument of August von Platen; after this, Platen entered the Pantheon of Cvetaeva's favorite poets. After a brief stop in Paris, the young couple returned to Moscow and established their residence with the bridegroom's family at their apartment on Borisoglebskij pereulok. Marina Cvetaeva's escape from the double prison of family and *gimnazija* had been achieved.

II 🖋

Marriage. Revolution.

(1912–1922)

Sergej Èfron figures prominently in Cvetaeva's lyric poetry, yet when she writes about him she is reluctant to supply concrete details and factual information. If one turns to the memoir literature about Cvetaeva, Èfron remains an equally shadowy figure. There is no doubt that he shared his wife's romantic outlook, that he had the exalted notions of honor and the old-fashioned courtesy that she admired in men. Whether we choose to believe the numerous accolades to his charm and basic humanity (including the enthusiastic testimony of Boris Pasternak and Il'ja Èrenburg, neither of whom knew him well) or to give credence to the more severe and hostile memoirs, it is clear that Marina Cvetaeva was a far stronger personality than her husband, a far more original human being, to say nothing of her immeasurable superiority to him as a writer. Thus, it is not very difficult to understand their subsequent separations and her later desperate quest for affection and understanding elsewhere. And yet, in spite of her later emotional involvements with other men, in spite of the recurrent periods of alienation and even estrangement and separation in their married life, there remained in Marina Cvetaeva a basic bond of loyalty to her husband. It was because of Sergej Èfron that she later left Russia (and thus preserved her creative freedom for almost two decades);

35

and it was to be with him, as far as we know, that she returned to
Stalin's U.S.S.R., where loneliness and death awaited her.

Their first two years together were apparently happy. Sergej
continued his secondary education, which had been interrupted by
his marriage. Marina, freed from the miseries of *gimnazija*, temporarily withdrew from literature as well. Late in 1912 (or early in
1913) a daughter was born to the young couple. They named her
Ariadna, but she was usually called Alja; frequently described and
addressed in her mother's prose and verse, she is one of the best-
known children in Russian poetry of the present century. At Alja's
christening, her godfather was Professor Cvetaev and her god-
mother was Maksimilian Vološin's mother, who out of respect for
the occasion for once wore a dress instead of her customary harem
trousers. Until her father's death, Marina and her husband occasionally participated in family reunions at Professor Cvetaev's, but
because of the presence of Valerija these were cheerless, unfriendly
occasions. Vacations were usually spent at the Vološins' in Koktebel.

Between the years 1913 and 1916, Cvetaeva wrote the poems that
make up her still unpublished collection, *Junošeskie stixi (Juvenilia)*. The poems from this collection which appeared in periodicals
show the steady growth of Cvetaeva's poetic craft. In them we
observe the theme that became almost obsessive with Cvetaeva in
her early twenties—the vision of her own death. In one mature and
precisely worded poem after another, the young wife and recent
mother writes of her own funeral and the imminence of her death,
addresses a passer-by at her future tomb, and speaks from her grave
to a remote descendant. There is no fear of death in these poems,
nor are they tragic. Ultimately, the tone is affirmative, almost
optimistic.

Her poetic reputation grew slowly. Occasionally she appeared in
public, reciting her poems. One such occasion is recorded in the
memoir of N. Elenev, who, returning to Russia shortly after the
outbreak of the First World War, encountered Marina and her
husband at a soirée organized by the well-known stage director
Tairov. Elenev describes Marina, elegant and self-assured, addressing an improvised greeting in verse to the aged actor Marius Petipa
(son of the famous *maître de ballet*), who at seventy was about to

appear in a Tairov-directed production of *Cyrano de Bergerac*.[1] The eulogy of Petipa, as described by Elenev, is quite in keeping with Cvetaeva's later often asserted admiration for courtly old men, which found its poetic expression in her poems addressed to Prince Volkonskij and in her two plays about the old age of Casanova.

The editors of the St. Petersburg literary journal *Severnye Zapiski*, S. I. Čackina and Ja. L. Saker, became interested in Cvetaeva's poetry sometime in 1915, and from that year until the journal was discontinued after the Revolution, in 1917, Cvetaeva became its regular contributor. Apart from a few of her poems that appeared in anthologies and miscellaneous collective publications, most of the poetry she published in the years preceding the Revolution, including portions of *Junošeskie stixi* and *Versty I,* is found in that journal In 1916, *Severnye Zapiski* serialized the novel *La Nouvelle espérance,* by Countess Anna de Noailles, in a Russian translation by Marina Cvetaeva (under the title *Novoe upovanie*). Since Cvetaeva refused at that time to accept any fees, the editors paid for her poems in presents and entertainment. The presents included two foxes (one stuffed and mounted, the other a furpiece), a bottle of perfume called "Jasmin de Corse" (possibly meant as a deliberate Napoleonic reference), and a three-volume edition of Afanas'ev's fairy tales. The gift of the Afanas'ev folklore collection seems to coincide with the first appearance in Cvetaeva's poetry of the manner and motifs connected with Russian folklore and popular poetry. The entertainment offered by Mme Čackina and Saker was also destined to enrich the scope of Cvetaeva's poetic themes. In Moscow, they took her to hear a Gypsy chorus. In St. Petersburg, they introduced her and her poetry to the leading poets and critics.

The year 1916 was particularly rich in emotional experiences and creative activity. The poems which later made up the collection *Versty I (Versts I)* constitute a lyrical diary which reflects in poetic form the personal and literary life of Cvetaeva from January to December, 1916. In January of that year, Marina parted from the three-year-old Alja for the first time and went to St. Petersburg at

---

[1] Nikolaj Elenev, "Kem byla Marina Cvetaeva," *Grani,* XXXIX (Frankfurt-Main, July–September, 1958), 141–159. M. M. Petipa was born in 1854 and was, therefore, sixty rather than seventy at the time.

the invitation of Mme Čackina. She recited her poetry to a brilliant gathering at a memorable literary soirée in the home of the noted naval architect Kannegiser, which she described in vivid detail many years later in the essay "Nezdešnij večer" ("An Otherworldly Evening"). Kannegiser's son, Leonid, who was to go down in history after the Revolution as the assassin of the dreaded G.P.U. chief, Urickij, was at that time a poet and translator of poetry, a close friend of the celebrated peasant poet Sergej Esenin, and Cvetaeva's fellow-contributor to *Severnye Zapiski*.[2] The absence of Anna Axmatova, then already the most popular poetess in Russia, was a disappointment for Marina, but there were present at the soirée two major poets with whom she was to establish lasting personal and literary ties: Mixail Kuzmin [3] and Osip Mandel'štam. Cvetaeva makes it clear in "Nezdešnij večer" that the understanding of poetry, the literary taste, and the genuine love of literature which she encountered at the Kannegiser home made that evening one of the most precious experiences of her life.

Cvetaeva had briefly met Osip Mandel'štam while both were staying at the Vološins' in Koktebel, in the summer of 1915. After seeing her again in St. Petersburg, he followed her to Moscow in February. Cvetaeva took Mandel'štam on tours of Moscow churches and cemeteries. Either at that time of even earlier he also became good friends with her husband. Throughout that spring the infatuated Mandel'štam kept returning to Moscow to be near Marina. When in summer she went to visit her sister Asja in the ancient town of Vladimir, in the vicinity of the ancestral home of

---

[2] Cvetaeva mentions Leonid Kannegiser in "Nezdešnij večer" and in "Vol'nyj proezd." There was evidently to be a chapter on him in her projected book of prose essays, *Zemnye primety*. A special volume devoted to his life and poetry was published in Paris in 1928 (*Leonid Kannegiser. Stat'i Georgija Adamoviča, M. A. Aldanova, Georgija Ivanova*). See also Georgij Ivanov, *Peterburgskie zimy* (New York, 1952), pp. 186–199.

[3] Mixail Kuzmin (1875–1936) is usually considered a forerunner and instigator of the Acmeist movement in Russian poetry. Cvetaeva was probably introduced to his poetry by Nilender at the age of fifteen. She described her impression of meeting him in person in one of the poems in her collection *Remeslo* ("Dva zareva!—net, zerkala," p. 37). "Nezdešnij večer," written in the year of Kuzmin's death, was meant as an act of homage to the memory of this remarkable and, at present, unfairly neglected poet. The title of Cvetaeva's essay refers to Kuzmin's book of verse, *Nezdešnie večera* (1921).

the Cvetaev family, Mandel'štam came along, but a short time later
he abruptly terminated his stay and left for the Crimea. Mandel'štam's short-lived infatuation with Marina Cvetaeva was later
described by her in her letters to the critic Aleksandr Baxrax (which
were not intended for publication);[4] it is confirmed in the recent
fragmentary memoirs of Anna Axmatova, who was Mandel'štam's
confidante during that period.[5] The mutual sentiments of Mandel'štam and Cvetaeva are reflected in their poems written in the
spring and summer of 1916. Not all admirers of Mandel'štam realize
that three of the most widely known and anthologized poems in his
collection *Tristia* were inspired by Marina Cvetaeva and dedicated
to her.[6] Cvetaeva's poems addressed to Mandel'štam originally
appeared in her collection *Versty I;* three of them were subsequently
published in a literary journal as a separate cycle under the title
"Provody" ("Seeing Off").[7] By the time both *Tristia* and *Versty I*
came to be published, some six years had elapsed since the time these
poems were written. The personal friendship between the two poets
was by then a thing of the past; the respective dedications did not
accompany the published poems (according to Cvetaeva, out of
consideration for the feelings of Mandel'štam's wife, "recent and
jealous"). In the later years, Cvetaeva continued to maintain her
high regard for Mandel'štam the poet, mentioning him with respect
and admiration in various letters and memoirs, even when he
himself, for reasons that are not entirely clear, took a strongly anti-
Cvetaeva position in some of his critical articles of the nineteen-
twenties, in which he had some harsh and unkind things to say
about her poetry. In 1929, when there was no longer any personal
contact between the two poets, Cvetaeva, irritated by the poet
Georgij Ivanov's spurious memoir of Mandel'štam (where the poem

[4] Letters to Baxrax, *Mosty,* V (Munich, 1960), 313.
[5] Anna Axmatova, "Mandel'štam," *Vozdušnye puti,* IV (1965), 27.
[6] "V raznogolosice devičeskogo xora," "Na rozval'njax uložennyx solomoj,"
and "Ne verja voskresen'ja čudu," in Osip Mandel'štam, *Sobranie sočinenij*
(New York, 1955), pp. 82–83, 86–87. See also Letters to Baxrax, *Mosty,* V,
316.
[7] *Russkaja mysl',* I–II (Berlin, 1923), 90–91. Two other poems, grouped in
Versty I with the three poems of "Provody" ("Ty zaprokidyvaeš' golovu," p.
12, and "Otkuda takaja nežnost'," p. 14), obviously belong to the same group
and are thus also addressed to Mandel'štam.

describing Mandel'štam's stay in Vladimir was said to have been inspired by a nonexistent lady doctor), wrote her own memoir "Istorija odnogo posvjaščenija" ("The History of a Dedication"), which contains a detailed account of her friendship with Mandel'štam and corrects Ivanov's distortions. This memoir had to wait until 1964 to be published.[8]

Other poems of Cvetaeva written in February and March of 1916 hint at still another emotional involvement with a young poet, described in rather Dostoevskian terms. Here we may have possible reference to Tixon Čurilin, a poet who in 1915, after several years in a mental institution, published a book of poems, *Vesna posle smerti* (*Springtime After Death*), which dealt with states of mind on the verge of insanity. Tixon Čurilin (1885–1944) is today a completely forgotten poet, even though his genuinely surrealistic, hallucinatory poems were once very highly regarded by poets as different from each other as Gumilëv and Majakovskij. Between 1915 and 1918 his poetry and prose frequently appeared in Russian Futurist publications. Having published two volumes of verse and a novel before the October Revolution, he subsequently withdrew from literary activities to devote himself to the theory and propaganda of Marxism. In her essay on the painter Natalija Gončarova, Cvetaeva mentions having met Čurilin in 1916 and calls him a poet of genius. A chapter entitled "Ljubov'" ("Love") from an autobiographical prose poem by Čurilin was published in the collection *Gjulistan 2* (1916) with the dedication "To Marina Cvetaeva. 5 March 1916."

The poems of Cvetaeva (including those we know to be addressed to Mandel'štam) written in February and March of 1916 abound in images of young male birds: cygnets, eaglets, doves, young ravens (Čurilin was associated for Cvetaeva with swans because of the sound correspondence between the Russian words for swan and cygnet—*lebed'*, *lebedënok*—and his home town of Lebedjan'). In a poem written on March 23, however, she says: "I solemnly assert: I have no further need of tame doves, swans, eaglets!" On April 27, in the throes of an emotional crisis the causes of which we can only guess at, she addressed her husband in a penitent poem in which she desperately pleads for help and

[8] *Oxford Slavonic Papers,* XI (Oxford, 1964), 111–136.

understanding, complains of being cheated by impostors, and compares herself to a sinking ship and to a homeless tramp. "At your palace, my lawful Tsar / I stand—a beggar," the poem concludes. We do not know what help Sergej Èfron had to offer, but literature, as usual with Cvetaeva, provided the never-failing retreat. The subsequent months see the beginning of several of Cvetaeva's major cycles of poems which spill from *Versty I* into her later collections: the cycle about her daughter Alja, the cycle dedicated to Anna Axmatova (these poems were a direct outcome of failing to meet Axmatova in St. Petersburg in January), and the beginning of the poems to Aleksandr Blok, whom Cvetaeva regarded with something close to worship. In the more personal poems of *Versty I,* however, the motifs of solitude, penitence, insomnia, and homelessness are sounded persistently until the end of the year.

At the time of the Liberal-Democratic Revolution of February, 1917, Marina Cvetaeva was in Moscow, awaiting the birth of her second child. On the second of March, she watched a parade of revolutionary troops, "the color of ashes and sand," faceless with their forest of banners, and described it in what is probably her first political poem: "Nad cerkovkoj—golubye oblaka . . ."[9] Two concepts basic to Cvetaeva's thinking help to explain why her reaction to the Revolution was that of "a lordly, a royal sadness." Her notion of rebellion was heroic and individualistic; her favorite heroes were the ones who raise themselves high above the crowd only to be ultimately vanquished by mediocrities: Joan of Arc, Napoleon, Byron, Puškin, the False Dmitrij, the Pugačëv of Puškin's *The Captain's Daughter.* There was nothing like this in the colorless politicians and dusty troops of the early days of the February Revolution. A few months later, however, when she briefly mistook Aleksandr Kerenskij for the Russian Bonaparte, she came close to accepting the February regime. Her basic humanity inevitably brought Cvetaeva to take the side of the underdog, which for her meant any individual threatened by a dehumanized collective—a crowd, a party, or a state. Listening as a child to a fairy tale about a cruel ogre, Cvetaeva immediately felt sympathy for the villain once

[9] *Lebedinyj stan,* p. 17. Originally published in *Trinadcat' poètov* (St. Petersburg, 1917).

he had been captured and punished; a year after the October Revolution, when she expected the White Army to take Moscow, Cvetaeva wrote a poem in which she wanted Sten'ka Razin (a seventeenth-century rebel who in this poem represented the Bolsheviks) to be spared. In a similar way, Nicholas II, whom she did not particularly admire before the Revolution, became an object of solicitude after his deposition and of veneration after he was assassinated. If we add to this Cvetaeva's insistence that any human life is more important and precious than ideology,[10] we can understand not only her political position, but also her rejection of the planned violence of any revolution.[11]

Her second daughter, Irina, was born on April 13, 1917. Sergej Èfron had entered an officers' training school sometime during the later stages of the war and continued his training after the Revolution. In October, we find Marina in the Crimea. It was there that she witnessed an aspect of the October Revolution that became for her an image, both symbolic and concrete, of what was happening to her country: the sacking of the wine cellars by the revolutionary troops and the ensuing orgy of drunken pillaging. On November 2, she started back for Moscow. She kept a diary during that trip, which she used later in her memoir "Oktjabr' v vagone" ("October Revolution in a Railroad Car") to describe the devastation and the desolation that she witnessed as the train passed through the cities of Orël and Xar'kov, the conversations which she had with peasants and revolutionary soldiers, her reaction on buying a local newspaper and learning that 9,000 persons had been killed. In an agony of apprehension about the possible fate of her husband and

[10] *Lebedinyj stan,* pp. 53–54. The subject and the central idea of this particular poem bear a close resemblance to the content of Chapter IX, 4 of *Doctor Zhivago,* the chapter that was attacked with particular indignation by Pasternak's Soviet critics. Similarly, Cvetaeva outraged a liberal émigré editor (see M. Višnjak, *Sovremennye Zapiski* [Indiana University Publications, 1957], p. 148) by likening the execution of a convicted political assassin in France to murders committed by the Cheka (Letters to G. Ivask, p. 212). Mark Višnjak completely misreads Cvetaeva's statement, which he quotes and criticizes, but his basic objection is clearly against her insistence on the value of life over and beyond ideology. To a mind dominated by politics, like Višnjak's, this spells anarchy.

[11] "I hate my century because it is a century of *organized* masses, which are no longer an elemental force . . ." (Letter of April 3, 1934, in Letters to G. Ivask, p. 214).

children, she made a diary entry addressed to Sergej Èfron: "If God leaves you among the living, I shall serve you like a dog." Her rejection of the October Revolution and of its results was total.

Moscow was still militarized when she arrived, with road blocks and patrols in the streets. Her husband had just graduated from his officers' school and, quite amazingly, had obtained from the newly victorious Communist authorities not only his graduation pay, but also permission to go to Southern Russia for the obvious purpose of joining one of the resistance groups that were being formed there. On the day she arrived, Marina again left Moscow to accompany Sergej Èfron and a fellow-officer to the Crimea, entrusting the children to the care of Èfron's relatives. In Crimea, the plans for the immediate future were made: Sergej was to join the White Army and Marina was to bring the children to the Crimea and live with the Vološins in Koktebel. On November 25, 1917, she went to Moscow to get the children, but by the time she arrived the Civil War was on.[12] The way back to the Crimea was cut off. Marina was separated from her husband for the next five years. In the most difficult time imaginable, she was trapped in Moscow with two small children and, for the first time in her life, was entirely on her own.

She was twenty-five years old, very near-sighted, and utterly impractical. She easily lost her way in the streets and even in buildings. Until then her life was lived on the emotional and the creative level, and the financial and material matters were looked after by others. It was her tremendous human vitality, rather than any practical accomplishments, that enabled Cvetaeva to survive through the cold and hungry years of the post-revolutionary period. The diaries she kept during the years 1917–1921 were reworked by Cvetaeva into the book *Zemnye primety* (*Terrestrial Indicia*) (pub- V + transl lished only in excerpts in various periodicals).[13] These excerpts give a unique description of life in Moscow in the first years after the

---

[12] This series of peregrinations of October–November, 1917 is described in "Oktjabr' v vagone," "Živoe o živom" (p. 195), and "Povest' o Sonečke" (p. 37). See also S. Èfron, "Oktjabr'," *Na Čuzoj Storone*, XI (Prague, 1925), 137–172, where he gives a version of his departure from Moscow that differs considerably from Cvetaeva's.

[13] See bibliography for listing of articles and essays that were originally a part of *Zemnye primety*.

October Revolution; Marina Cvetaeva as a person is outlined in them with all her ineptitude, her stamina and independence of spirit, and her occasional moments of unconscious heroism.

Several authors have left testimony on her miserable living conditions during those years: I. Èrenburg,[14] F. Stepun,[15] K. Bal'mont,[16] Prince Sergej Volkonskij. Most revealing perhaps is the anecdote told by the latter about the burglar who broke into Cvetaeva's apartment, was invited to stay for tea and, touched by her poverty, offered to lend her some money.[17] Cvetaeva herself describes that aspect of her life in the memoir "Čerdačnoe" ("Life in a Garret"). To save fuel, Marina and her two daughters lived in one room, which was formerly Sergej's den in the garret. All material possessions were gradually bartered for food. Soon, she had only one dress, which was also used for sleeping. Food consisted of frozen potatoes, which she boiled in a samovar that was badly clogged after an unfortunate attempt to use it for cooking porridge. To feed her children Marina often had to depend on the charity of friends and even on that of strangers who remembered and admired her poetry. One of the rooms in the apartment was rented to a pleasant young Communist official. He arranged for Cvetaeva a job as a filing clerk at the People's Commissariat of Nationalities, which she took in November, 1918, with considerable reluctance.

Cvetaeva's memoir "Moi služby" ("My Jobs") describes, with humor and bitterness, her ordeal by office work. "I enter, timid and incongruous, in a man's mouse-colored sweater, feeling like a mouse." She was depressed by the senseless task she was given (pasting clippings on sheets that were filed and forgotten), it was distasteful to her to work in the office that was concerned with recording the defeats of the White Army (which had all of her sympathy), and she keenly felt the absurdity of taking time from her intense creative work to engage in hours of mechanical drudgery. Yet, there was no other way of obtaining food under the

---

[14] I. G. Èrenburg, *Ljudi, gody, žizn'*, (Moscow, 1961), I–II 370. Both Èrenburg and F. Stepun (see note 15) point out that Cvetaeva's indigence during that period was exceptional even by the standard of the generally poor living conditions of the time.
[15] F. Stepun, *Byvšee i nesbyvšeesja*, I, 274.
[16] K. D. Bal'mont, *Gde moj dom* (Prague, 1924), pp. 172–182.
[17] Knjaz' Sergej Volkonskij, *Byt i bytie* (Berlin, 1924), p. xiii.

existing conditions. The one attempt at an excursion to the countryside for purposes of barter, which Marina made in September of 1918, ended in complete frustration. She was not a business-woman and certainly no match at bargaining with the crafty, hoarding peasants. She was subjected to humiliating treatment by the openly profiteering local Communist officials, lost some of the precious flour she obtained by packing it in a wicker basket, and was forced by the peasants to accept in payment dolls for her children V and an amber necklace, instead of the vitally needed grain and eggs.

Cvetaeva lasted at her first job for five and a half months, after which she had to leave, unable to produce a required report of insurmountable complexity. Her second attempt at working in a government office was such a nightmare of alien and incomprehensible activity that she herself quit, in tears, after a single unbearable day. The occasional public readings of her poetry brought a mere pittance. During the particularly hungry winter of 1919, unable to feed her two children, Marina was forced to place her younger daughter, Irina, in a state-operated orphanage (*Kuncevskij detskij dom*), where the child died of malnutrition on February 2, 1920. The terrible physical want was somewhat alleviated in 1921, one year before Cvetaeva's departure from Russia, through the efforts of P. S. Kogan, the prominent Marxist critic and Soviet government official, who arranged a steady food ration (*paëk*) for her. Shortly before her departure, two of her books were accepted for publication by the State Publishing House (earlier attempts in this direction were blocked by Valerij Brjusov, who had by then been put in charge of various official publishing projects).

In describing Cvetaeva's life in Moscow after the October Revolution, Prince Sergej Volkonskij carefully distinguishes between *byt* (in the sense of everyday material life) and *bytie* (the higher, subjective level of existence). This Cvetaeva-like distinction (with its typical dependence of semantics on variation around a word-root) has great validity, not only for her life during the period that Volkonskij has in mind, but later on as well. Those years of physical hardship were also the years of great creative development and evolution for Cvetaeva. Between 1917 and 1922 she wrote three books of verse: *Versty II* (1917–1921), *Lebedinyj stan* (also 1917–

1921) and *Remeslo* (*Craft*) (1921–1922). These were the years
during which Cvetaeva extended her range and, in addition to lyric
poetry, turned to larger epic forms (her first epic poem *Car'-devica*
[*Tsar-Maiden*] was written in 1920), to the theater, and eventually
to prose. The period was also rich in important literary contacts and
rewarding personal friendships.

Returning to Moscow from the Crimea in 1917, Cvetaeva heard a
young officer on the train recite a poem about the Revolution
written by a friend of his. In Moscow, Cvetaeva immediately looked
up the author of the poem, the young poet Pavel Antokol'skij, the
"Pavlik" of various memoirs and of "Povest' o Sonečke." This was
the beginning of a memorable friendship.[18] In addition to writing
poetry, Antokol'skij was also an actor at the experimental offshoot
of the Moscow Art Theater called the Third Studio (*Tret'ja
studija*), which was under the direction of Evgenij Vaxtangov.
Through Antokol'skij, Cvetaeva came into contact with a group of
young theatrical folk, the most important of whom for her were
Antokol'skij's closest friend "Jura" (Jurij Zavadskij, later a famous
Soviet stage director and in 1918 already something of a matinee
idol)[19] and the young, half-English actress Sof'ja Evgen'evna
Holliday ("Sonečka").[20] For a while, Marina was considerably

[18] Pavel Antokol'skij, the Soviet poet and essayist, was born on June 19,
1896. Therefore, Cvetaeva errs badly when, in speaking of meeting him in
November or December, 1917, she describes him as a schoolboy of seventeen.
Although he communicated with Cvetaeva during his trips to Germany and
France with the Vaxtangov Theater in the nineteen-twenties, Antokol'skij
never mentioned Cvetaeva in his numerous subsequent memoirs and critical
articles. The title of his book on poetry published in 1958, *Poèty i vremja,* is
obviously taken from Cvetaeva's essay "Poèt i vremja" (1932), which was
never published in the Soviet Union. With her growing new popularity and
rehabilitation, Antokol'skij finally admitted their old friendship in 1962.

[19] Jurij Zavadskij (b. 1894) is now a People's Artist of the U.S.S.R. He
achieved celebrity through his performance in Vaxtangov's production of
Gozzi's *Turandot* and in the late nineteen-twenties was one of the leading
actors at the Moscow Art Theater. His style in acting and directing, noted for
originality in the nineteen-twenties, gradually gave way to conformist
"Socialist Realism." Zavadskij joined the Communist Party in 1944 and was
awarded a Stalin prize in 1946.

[20] The group of young actors described by Cvetaeva in "Povest o Sonečke"
belonged for the most part to Vaxtangov's Third Studio. This allows
additional investigation of background material on most of them through the
available published material on Vaxtangov. Thus, a study of *Vaxtangov.*

smitten by Zavadskij's spectacular good looks and his acting talent; Sonečka Holliday, who became her closest friend in 1919, was equally taken up with him. The ensuing relationships with Antokol'skij, Zavadskij, and Sonečka were described by Cvetaeva nostalgically and with considerable frankness in "Povest' o Sonečke"; these relationships have left other memorable traces in Cvetaeva's work: in the poetic cycles "Komediant" ("The Comedian"), "Brat'ja" ("Brothers"), "Stixi o Sonečke" ("Poems about Sonečka"), and in the plays.

It was during this period that she first met Vladimir Majakovskij, Boris Pasternak, and Il'ja Èrenburg, all of whom were to play important roles in her literary biography. In January of 1918, Cvetaeva was present at the famous "encounter of two generations" at the residence of the poet Amari (or à Marie, real name: M. O. Cetlin), during which the poets of the older generation recognized and acclaimed Majakovskij's poetic genius, after the reading of his poem "Čelovek" ("Man"). Other literary ties were developed and consolidated. A warm friendship united her with the older Symbolist poet Konstantin Bal'mont.[21] Cvetaeva the poet felt equally close to the new Futurist poets like Majakovskij and Čurilin and to the

---

Zapiski. Pis'ma. Dokumenty (Leningrad, 1939) helps one identify Cvetaeva's "Jura S." as G. V. Serov (1894–1929), the actor son of the famous painter Valentin Serov; "Jura N." of "Povest' o Sonečke" is evidently Ju. S. Nikol'skij, the Soviet composer and conductor. There is less material, however, on Sonečka Holliday (Gollidèj), who was a member of the much less well documented Second Studio, directed by V. L. Mčedelov. Her most memorable performance was in a dramatized version of Dostoevskij's "White Nights" (see N. E. Èfros, *Moskovskij Xudožestvennyj Teatr* [Moscow-Petersburg, 1924], p. 414).

[21] Konstantin Bal'mont paid tribute to Cvetaeva the poet in his short essay "Marina Cvetaeva" (*Sovremennye Zapiski,* VII [1921], 92) and in the final chapter of his book *Gde moj dom* he described his friendship with her. Cvetaeva's literary homage to Bal'mont is paid in the poem "Bal'montu" (*Lebedinyj stan,* pp. 45–46), written in 1919, which is thematically related to the above-mentioned chapter of Bal'mont's book; in the essay "Bal'montu" (*Svoimi Putjami,* V [Prague, 1925], 13–15); in her speech at the ceremony commemorating the fiftieth anniversary of Bal'mont's literary activity, published only in Serbo-Croatian translation ("Reč o Baljmontu," *Ruski Arhiv,* XXXVIII–XXXIX [Belgrade, 1936], 58–67); and in several references in her critical prose, the most important of which is her comparison of Bal'mont and Brjusov in "Geroj truda" (part two, chapter four, pp. 255–264; see also passages on Bal'mont in chapter five of part two, pp. 267–268).

older Symbolists. At a festive gathering in honor of Bal'mont in May of 1921, Cvetaeva participated in the proceedings on terms of equality with two distinguished older poets: Vjačeslav Ivanov [22] and Fëdor Sologub. She later remembered "applauding furiously" when Sologub stated in his address: "True equality does not exist and thank God it doesn't." In 1920, under circumstances which we do not know, Cvetaeva saw or ~~met~~ on two occasions the poet she revered most of all: Aleksandr Blok. [23]

Sometime late in 1918, Cvetaeva was introduced to the elderly Aleksej Aleksandrovič Staxovič, who was originally an officer of the guards, later held the position of aide-de-camp at the Russian imperial court, still later became an actor at the Moscow Art Theater, and after the Revolution was a much admired teacher of deportment and etiquette at a dramatic school attended by Cvetaeva's new theatrical friends. [24] The single encounter with Staxovič (which took place when Cvetaeva was taken backstage by a mutual friend after one of his performances) impressed her in particular, because she saw in the courtly and understanding old gentleman the very personfication of the eighteenth century with which she was more and more identifying herself in her verse and in her plays at that time. The suicide of Staxovič in February of 1919 was felt by her as momentous and symbolic event, marking the disappearance

---

[22] Cvetaeva met Vjačeslav Ivanov in 1912, at the "Musaget" ("Plennyj dux," p. 299). She kept meeting him occasionally after that, although they had only "one real conversation in an entire lifetime" ("Geroj truda," p. 253). Ivanov dedicated his poem "Ispoved' zemle" ("Confession to Mother Earth") to Cvetaeva (orginally written in 1915, final text established in 1946; see V. Ivanov, *Svet večernij* [Oxford, 1962]). Cvetaeva's poem to V. Ivanov, written in 1920, is reproduced in *Svet večernij,* p. 201. The commentary to the Ivanov collection by Mme O. Deschartes states that Ivanov received the poem in the form of a newspaper clipping in 1920. This must be a mistake, because Cvetaeva's poem, "Vjačeslavu Ivanovu," appeared in the Paris newspaper *Poslednie Novosti* on July 3, 1928. The dating of Mme Deschartes is clearly based on the date of the writing and not on that of publication. It is not clear whether the two poets had any personal contact during the period of their emigration.

[23] Cvetaeva cryptically refers to her two encounters with Blok in "Geroj truda," p. 253, and "Moj Puškin," p. 62, and mentions her intention to write a memoir on Blok in "Plennyj dux," p. 313.

[24] On A. A. Staxovič, his connection with the Moscow Art Theater and his role in financing the Second Studio, see N. E. Êfros, *op. cit.,* pp. 411–412; on p. 429, a portrait of Staxovič is reproduced.

of cultural values which she associated with the eighteenth century, and which in her opinion had still survived in Russia before the Revolution. Cvetaeva made detailed diary entries of her thoughts on this subject, and she later reworked them into the memoir "Iz dnevnika" ("From the Diary"). The three poems she dedicated to the memory of Staxovič appear in the collection *Lebedinyj stan;* Cvetaeva was scheduled to recite one of them at a commemorative meeting held at the Moscow Art Theater, but her reading was vetoed at the last moment by one of the theater's directors, V. N. Nemirovič-Dančenko, as too outstpoken and dangerous in view of the presence of Communist officials in the audience.

Cvetaeva's friendship with Prince Sergej Volkonskij, author, lecturer, and former director of the imperial theaters, dates from 1921. Her reasons for admiring and seeking out the sixty-year-old Volkonskij were similar to the ones that attracted her to Staxovič. Again, here was a man of great culture and sophistication, trying to spread and preserve cultural values in a world that seemed to be steadily growing more impersonal and ignorant. Cvetaeva showed great solicitude for her older friends during those difficult years. At the height of the famine she shared her meager food supply with Bal'mont and even did household chores for him. While hating the drudgery of office work for pay, she did not mind performing secretarial duties for Volkonskij and personally copied his manuscripts. When she learned about the desperate material situation of Vološin in Koktebel, she arranged to be received by the powerful commissar Lunačarskij, in order to secure help from him for the starving writers in the Crimea. She started a collection herself among her literary friends in order to send a parcel to Vološin, and the philosopher N. A. Berdjaev earned her hostility by remarking: "You yourself have nothing, it is unwise to give others."

One of the most important relationships in the life of Cvetaeva at that time and one that looms large in her poetry was that with her older daughter. By the time she was six, little Alja was undoubtedly a literary and intellectual prodigy. Her verse appended to *Remeslo* and her prose quoted in "Geroj truda" and "Povest' o Sonečke" are certainly remarkable for so young a child, but they belong to an entirely different order of literary phenomena from her mother's writing; Cvetaeva must have spoiled the chances of her prose book,

Zemnye primety, to be published in 1923, by insisting on her daughter as co-author. Bal'mont and Vjačeslav Ivanov were charmed by the gifted girl, but one can also understand the squeamishness of Il'ja Èrenburg at the sight of a six-year-old reciting erotic poetry and discoursing on ethical problems. The personal relationship between mother and daughter was a mixture of an amazing equality and a studied, old-fashioned courtliness.

Little Alja was present at one of the more improbable events of her mother's literary life, and her diary description of it is used in the account given in "Geroj truda." In the winter of 1921, through the intercession of Brjusov's mistress Adalis (pen name of the poetess Adelina Èfron, apparently no relation), Cvetaeva was invited to take part in "An Evening of Poetesses" organized by Brjusov. She appeared on the stage, among eight frilly and overdressed versifying ladies, wearing a garment that resembled a priest's cassock ("a rephrasing of an overcoat that had seen better days"), with a leather belt, and grey felt boots. Following Brjusov's introductory lecture, in which he asserted that a woman can write only of love and passion, Cvetaeva mounted the podium to deliver ("feeling as if I were falling off a mountain") several of her poems from *Lebedinyj stan,* eulogizing the White Army. To an audience of Red Army men, Communists, and revolutionary students, Cvetaeva proclaimed her right to shout "Hurrah!" for the Tsar "the way street urchins shout in all the squares of the world." Developing an image borrowed from Griboedov's comedy, the last poem concluded: "The bonnet [tossed up] flies higher than the towers! But, passing the crown on the head of the idol, [it flies upward] to the stars!" After this assertion of total independence Cvetaeva was stopped by Brjusov, while the audience cheered.

"This was obvious insanity," Cvetaeva later wrote, "[but] I was guided by two, no three, four aims: 1) seven poems by a woman without the word 'love' and without the pronoun 'I', 2) proof that poetry makes no sense to an audience, 3) a dialogue with some one particular person, who *understood* (perhaps a student), 4) and the principal one: fulfilling, here in Moscow of 1921, an obligation of honor. And beyond any aims, aimlessly, stronger than aims, a simple and extreme feeling of: what if I do?"

By 1921 the Civil War was over. Sergej Èfron, who had fought it with the White forces, was evacuated with the remnants of the White Army and made his way to Prague, where he became a university student. In July, 1921, after many years of unknowing and uncertainty, Cvetaeva received the first communication from her husband since their separation in 1917.[25] Her emotions on that occasion are eloquently expressed in the cycle of poems "Blagaja vest'" ("Good Tidings") in *Remeslo*. Once again her love for Sergej Èfron became a major theme in her poetry. Very soon thereafter, Cvetaeva asked for official permission to leave the country in order to go to Berlin and later to join her husband in Czechoslovakia. The permission was granted, and in the spring of 1922 (evidently in May), after completing the manuscript of the long poem "Pereuločki" ("Sidestreets") with which *Remeslo* concludes and making arrangements with the State Publishing House (*Gosizdat*) for the publication of two of her books, Marina Cvetaeva, accompanied by her daughter, left Moscow and Russia.

[25] Èrenburg, *Ljudi, gody, žizn'* (Moscow, 1961), I–II, 372, claims that it was he who, in the spring of 1921, located Sergej Èfron and informed Cvetaeva of his whereabouts. Èrenburg's chronology is somewhat at variance with the chronology of the corresponding poems in *Remeslo*.

III 🍃
Exile

(1922–1929)

Marina Cvetaeva's first stop after she left Soviet Russia was Berlin. Because of the peculiar nature of the diplomatic and economic relations between the Weimar Republic and the new Soviet state (then just entering its period of the New Economic Policy), the German capital had for a time become a major center of Russian literature. There was a considerable number of Russian publishing houses with their headquarters in Berlin, and much of what they printed could still be sent to the Soviet Union. The atmosphere that Cvetaeva found was congenial. The émigré literature, as a phenomenon distinct from Soviet literature, did not as yet have a clearly separate existence, and the literary cafés of Berlin, as well as its Russian publishers, provided a meeting ground for writers who had aligned themselves with the Soviet regime, those who were opposed to it, and a number of undecided ones, the most active and prominent of the latter group being Il'ja Èrenburg. The literary journals published by Russians abroad were still read in the Soviet Union, and the books of émigré writers, including some extremely anti-Soviet ones, were being reviewed in the Soviet press. All these factors made it possible for the literary reputation of Cvetaeva to grow and expand in Russia precisely during the years immediately following her emigration.

When she left Moscow in 1922, her work was known only to her

fellow poets and to the segment of the reading public that followed
literary almanacs or heard her at public readings. Her latest book
had come out in 1913 and her literary standing up to 1922 can be
described as that of a minor poet. The year 1922 saw the publication,
both in Moscow and Berlin, of her 1916 collection of poems, *Versty
I* and of her epic poem, *Car'-devica*. A private publishing firm in
Moscow brought out her short play in verse, *Konec Kazanovy,* and
two other slim volumes appeared in Berlin, one containing the
poems dedicated to Aleksandr Blok (*Stixi k Bloku,* mostly
reprinted from *Versty I*) and the other, *Razluka,* consisting of a
section from the forthcoming collection *Remeslo* and the *poèma,*
"Na krasnom kone." *Russkaja Mysl',* one of the most respected pre-
revolutionary Russian literary journals, which was continued as an
émigré publication by P. B. Struve in Berlin and Prague, printed a
selection of Cvetaeva's poems from *Lebedinyj stan.* Another important émigré journal, *Sovremennye Zapiski,* which began publication in Paris in 1920, carried a group of Cvetaeva's poems in its very
first issue, probably through the efforts of Konstantin Bal'mont,
who became a regular contributor to that journal immediately after
his emigration. A year later (i.e., still before Cvetaeva herself
emigrated), *Sovremennye Zapiski* printed another and far larger
group of Cvetaeva's poems, accompanied by a short article by
Bal'mont, in which he claimed for Cvetaeva the place of the most
significant Russian woman poet of the period, on a par with Anna
Axmatova. Finally, Il'ja Èrenburg included her in two of his
popular anthologies, one of them entitled *The Poetry of Revolutionary Moscow.*[1] In less than a year after her departure from
Russia, Cvetaeva came to be regarded by many as one of the most
original and powerful post-revolutionary poets. The collection
Versty I, six years old at the time of its publication, was seen as a
revelation by such discerning poets as Adelaida Gercyk and Boris
Pasternak. Andrej Belyj was so impressed by the slim volume
Razluka that he evolved for himself a new poetic manner which, in
subtle homage to Cvetaeva, he tried out in a collection entitled *Posle*

---

[1] I. Èrenburg, ed. *Poèzija revoljucionnoj Moskvy* (Berlin, 1922). The other
anthology, *Portrety russkix poètov* (Berlin, 1922), in addition to her poetry,
contained an essay on Cvetaeva by Èrenburg.

Razluki (*After the Separation*). He ended *Posle Razluki* with a poem, "Marine Cvetaevoj," extolling her "invincible rhythms." [2] Critics, even hostile ones, spoke of Cvetaeva in a new tone of respect; only Valerij Brjusov, reviewing *Versty I* and *Stixi k Bloku,* persistently refused to recognize the originality of her new manner. The extent of the esteem and renown that Cvetaeva enjoyed after 1922 can be gauged by a perusal of the book on contemporary Russian literature by Lev Trockij, one of the leaders of the new Soviet state. Although he speaks of her without any special enthusiasm, Trockij inevitably includes her name after that of Anna Axmatova whenever he speaks of non-Communist women writers. [3]

In her personal, as well as in her literary biography, Cvetaeva's departure from Soviet Russia initiated a period of comparative affluence. She settled in Berlin in the Pragerpension—all establishments then patronized by Russian *literati* were located in the vicinity of Pragerplatz. Her closest friends at the time were Il'ja Èrenburg and his wife. As editor and literary critic, Èrenburg did much to spread Cvetaeva's literary reputation; on a more personal level, their friendship did not prove lasting. Cvetaeva's opposition to the Soviet regime was based on deeply reasoned ethical and moral grounds. Èrenburg, who by that time was close to justifying much of what he had denounced in his poetry written after the October Revolution, saw in Cvetaeva a romantic idealist unable to cope with reality. We know now that he used Cvetaeva as a model for the heroine of his novel *Žizn' i gibel' Nikolaja Kurbova* (*Life and Death of Nikolaj Kurbov*). [4] The comparison between the naive, misguided counterrevolutionary Katja of the novel and the strong and original personality of Marina Cvetaeva known to us through her letters of that period shows the lack of real mutual understand-

---

[2] A. Belyj, *Posle razluki* (Berlin, 1922), p. 123. The dependence of Belyj's style in this volume on that of Cvetaeva's *Razluka* has been asserted by V. Xodasevič, "Knigi i ljudi," *Vozroždenie* (Paris), May 31, 1934. A different version of Belyj's poem, "Marine Cvetaevoj," appeared in *Èpopeja,* No. 2 (Berlin, 1922), p. 11.

[3] L. Trockij, *Literatura i revoljucija* (Moscow, 1923). The inclusion of Cvetaeva in the humorous discussion of feminine religious poetry, p. 30, indicates that Trockij was not familiar with her work but mentions her simply because she was one of the best-known women poets at the time.

[4] Letters to Baxrax, *Mosty,* V, 317.

ing between the two writers and points to the possible causes of their estrangement that was soon to follow.[5]

At Èrenburg's table in Pragerdiele, Cvetaeva observed and participated in what she later called "a general exchange of fees and manuscripts." She often saw two of the most active publishers of the time, Solomon Kaplun and A. G. Višnjak. The latter, hearing of the diaries she had kept in Moscow, requested her to convert them into a book of memoirs. She was friendly with some other Russians who had left Moscow at approximately the same time: the painter N. D. Sinezubov, the very original and important prose writer Aleksej Remizov[6] and his wife, and a few others. The Berlin period was also the time of close contact with two great Russian writers: with Andrej Belyj in person and with Boris Pasternak through the impact of his poetry.

Belyj, the Symbolist poet and one of the most important Russian novelists of the twentieth century, who had met Cvetaeva briefly on several occasions in Moscow between 1910 and the time of her emigration, was then at a particularly desperate juncture of his life. Abandoned by his wife for a younger man, disappointed in the teachings of Rudolf Steiner (Belyj had devoted many years of his life and much of his creative energy to anthroposophy), and torn by doubts whether to return to Russia, he quite unexpectedly turned to Cvetaeva for understanding. ("You are the daughter of Professor Cvetaev. I am the son of Professor Bugaev.") Their Berlin

[5] Cvetaeva discusses her relations with Èrenburg in some detail in one of her letters to A. Baxrax (*Mosty,* V, 311). In conclusion she says: "I do not doubt for a second his basic nobility, his painful kindness and his essential suffering." Contemplating a visit to Berlin in July 1923, she found the idea of staying at the same hotel with the Èrenburgs distasteful (*ibid.,* p. 313). Cvetaeva and Èrenburg did not see each other during his numerous later visits to Paris. In a letter to Ivask in 1933 she wrote of Èrenburg: ". . . never, not for a second did I consider him a poet. Èrenburg is subjection to everyone, spinelessness. Besides, a cynic cannot be a poet" (Letters to Ivask, p. 209). Cvetaeva's subsequent relations with Èrenburg are disussed in Chapter V.

[6] During the nineteen-twenties, Cvetaeva regarded Aleksej Remizov as the most important of contemporary prose writers. Her admiration for him is expressed in a statement published in the journal *Svoimi Putjami,* No. 8 (1925): "Here, beyond the frontiers of the Russian state, not only the most alive of Russian writers, but a living treasury of Russian soul and Russian speech—this is so obvious that it is embarrassing to have to say it—I have in mind Aleksej Mixajlovič Remizov. . . . He has done more for the preservation of Russia, *sub specie aeternitatis,* than all the politicians combined."

friendship was subsequently described by her in "Plennyj dux." It was Belyj who, after reading *Razluka,* arranged for the Berlin publications of *Car'-devica* and *Versty I.*

Cvetaeva had also met Boris Pasternak before her departure from Moscow and had heard him recite. At that time she was unable to see the value of his poetry; her reading of his volume *Sestra moja žizn'* (*My Sister, Life*) shortly after her arrival in Berlin, however, came as an unforgettable experience. At the same time Pasternak, in Moscow, was reading *Versty I* and for his part discovering Cvetaeva. Their correspondence, which Pasternak started a little later, was a continuous inspiration and comfort to Cvetaeva. Her letters to him have been lost, but since she knew so little about his personal life, we can assume that their friendship developed primarily on the literary plane: "One more thing: I know nothing about P. and would like to know many things. Our correspondence is *ins Blaue!* I always fear the everyday life (*byt*) of others, for the most part it saddens me. I would like to know what Pasternak's wife is like . . . what he did in Berlin, why he is leaving, who his friends were" (Letters to Gul', p. 178).

Cvetaeva's enthusiasm for Pasternak's *Sestra moja žizn'* found its expression in the article "Svetovoj liven'" ("A Cloudburst of Light"), originally published in Andrej Belyj's journal *Èpopeja.* Her avowed intention in writing it was to vouch for Pasternak's quality to the Western World, "for the time being, pending the appearance of your 'Life' here. . . . And not because you need it; this is pure selfishness: it is a precious thing to participate in such a destiny!"

In July, 1922, Sergej Èfron came to Berlin for the long delayed reunion with his wife and daughter. Several weeks later they followed him to Czechoslovakia. They settled in a small village called Horní Mokropsy, not far from Prague, where President Masaryk's government supported a university for exiled Russians. Most of the students were White Army veterans. Cvetaeva described Horní Mikropsy in one of her letters to Baxrax: "A tiny mountain village, we live on its very edge, in a simple peasant hut. The *dramatis personae* of our life: a church-shaped well to which I run to fetch water, mostly at night or early in the morning; a chained dog; a squeaky garden gate. Directly beyond us is a forest. To the right, a high rocky crest. There are brooks all over the village. Two grocery stores, as in our provinces. A Catholic church with a flowery churchyard. A school. Two restaurants. Music every Sunday. The village is not rustic but *kleinbürgerlich* (*meščanskaja*). . . . And in every house one is sure to see a lighted window at night: a Russian student!"

The generous Czech authorities, in addition to offering a university scholarship to Sergej Èfron, provided Marina with a small stipend. The family lived in Horní Mokropsy for a little more than one year. Later Cvetaeva changed residences several times in Prague and in the suburbs or small villages near the city: Smíchov, Dolní Mokropsy, Jíloviště. In September, 1923, Alja was sent to a Russian boarding school in Moravská Třebová (in Moravia), and Sergej moved there too. Cvetaeva took an apartment in Prague, on top of a hill (the hill of "Poèma gory") with a large window and a view of the city.[7] The separation from Alja was not as painful as it would have been a few years earlier. The child, who had been a precocious intellectual and her mother's closest friend, suddenly became an ordinary little girl: "Alja, who from the age of two to nine was my 'echo in the mountains,' now plays with dolls and treats me with profound indifference. . . . O, God must indeed want to make me a major poet, otherwise He would not thus deprive me of everything!"[8]

In Prague, as in Horní Mokropsy, Cvetaeva took long walks into the hills, sometimes spending a day in the woods, alone or with some of the Russian students. Vladimir Nabokov recalls accompanying Cvetaeva on one such hike in the Russian version of his autobiography.[9] She usually stayed up writing until three or four in the morning, before retiring to her bed, a sack filled with hay and covered with a piece of striped cloth brought from Russia. She had many friends among the Russian scholars and intellectuals who had found refuge in Prague. When Andrej Belyj thought of coming to live in Prague in November, 1923, Cvetaeva was able to put her local connections at his service and to try and arrange a Czech government stipend for him (at the last moment Belyj preferred to return

---

[7] Praha-Smíchov, Švédská ulice. No. 1373.
[8] Letters to Baxrax, *Mosty*, VI, 325.
[9] Vladimir Nabokov, *Drugie berega* (New York, 1954), pp. 242–243.

to Russia). Among her new friends of the period were Mark Slonim, the literary editor of the Social-Revolutionary journal *Volja Rossii* (published in Prague on a Czech subsidy), who in his capacity as editor and critic did much to make the émigré community aware of the unique value of Cvetaeva's poetry, and Anna Tesková, a Czech journalist and translator of Cvetaeva's work, to whom the cycle "Derev'ja" ("Trees") is dedicated.[10] Anna Tesková was the president of the cultural section of the Prague Czech-Russian Society ("Česko-ruská jednota") where Cvetaeva occasionally appeared in poetry readings. Through Mme Tesková and her friends Cvetaeva came in contact with some members of the Czech literary community.

There were also two searing emotional involvements during this period. In June, 1923, Cvetaeva wrote to a young critic named Aleksandr Baxrax, who resided in Berlin, to thank him for his review of *Car'-devica.* This was not her usual practice. As a rule she disliked critics, but in the case of Baxrax she felt that he had described the essence of her folk epic instead of commenting on the external trappings of its *style russe,* as all the other critics had done. The correspondence that began soon reached a considerable level of intensity. Reading Cvetaeva's letters, which Baxrax published in the journal *Mosty* in 1960–1961, few readers will realize that she is writing to a man she had never met in person. She sensed in Baxrax an understanding that neither he nor any other man was capable of giving: "I want from you a miracle. A miracle of trust, a miracle of understanding, a miracle of unselfishness." The relationship with Baxrax is an example of a recurrent phenomenon in Cvetaeva's emotional life—the literary creator in her took over and, by embellishing and developing her initial impression of a person, produced a poetic creation, which Cvetaeva then proceeded to confuse with its model in real life. As a poet she would usually be stimulated to a new burst of activity after such encounters. To Cvetaeva the living woman they brought only misery. She realized that people were "horrified by the dimensions of emotions they arouse in me." This

---

[10] *Posle Rossii,* p. 30. The nine poem cycle is inscribed: "To my Czech friend, Anna Antonovna Tesková." A large number of Cvetaeva's unpublished letters to Anna Tesková is now in the possession of the Czechoslovak-Soviet Institute, Czechoslovak Academy of Sciences, Prague. Excerpts from this correspondence are quoted by Vadim Morkovin (see bibliography).

never stopped her from responding: "all my life, to this day, I was always the first to write, the first to offer my hand (and my hands) without fear of judgment . . . and afterwards, when they left (they always left), I not only did not stretch my hands after them, but did not even turn my head. . . ." These lines from "Moj Puškin," written in 1936, describe several relationships in Cvetaeva's life, relationships based on largely imaginary premises. Those with Baxrax and with the poet Štejger in the nineteen-thirties are the best documented ones because of the published correspondence. Only one man was able to live up to the impossibly high expectations Cvetaeva placed on her close male friends: Rainer Maria Rilke. The V "Bulletin of Illness" which Cvetaeva attached to one of her letters to Baxrax traces the suffering caused by the realization that Baxrax does not need her friendship and that he is altogether not the person she took him to be. It is the most harrowing reading in all her published work: "If you are he to whom I am writing, you must be tormented as much as I. 12 *bis* August, Monday: Pain has ceased being an event, it has become a state. I no longer believe you have ever existed, you are my pain."

In September, 1923, while still corresponding with Baxrax, Cvetaeva became involved with another man, a former White officer who lived in Prague. This was not an imaginary relationship, but a genuine love affair, probably the most intense and desperate one in Cvetaeva's life. The memoir of N. Elenev and certain poems in *Posle Rossii* which date from that period suggest that Cvetaeva, surrounded in her personal life by weaker and less original personalities than herself, saw in this man a human being of equal stature. The hopeless, doomed quality of the relationship is conveyed in the poem "Nočnye mesta" ("Nocturnal Places") written in October, 1923.[11] The affair lasted until January, 1924. Cvetaeva wrote no short poems between October 1923 and June 1924, concentrating instead on two long lyrical *poèmy,* "Poèma gory" and "Poèma konca," which give, in minute emotional detail, the account of her Prague love affair. Both poems deal with the end of the affair, again demonstrating the tragic fact of the particular value of losses and separations for Cvetaeva's poetic productivity.

Throughout her Czech period, Cvetaeva continued writing and

[11] *Posle Rossii,* pp. 122–123. Published sources on the love affair in question are N. Elenev, *op. cit.,* and Letters to Baxrax, *Mosty,* VI, 332–340.

publishing. In 1923 her collection *Remeslo* was brought out by A. G. Višnjak's publishing house in Berlin; the same year saw the publication of *Psixeja,* a selection of romantic poems from several of her other collections. Cvetaeva's plays "Metel'" ("The Snowstorm"), "Fortuna," "Priključenie" ("An Adventure"), "Feniks" ("Phoenix") all appeared in Russian émigré journals between 1922 and 1924. After 1922, she became a regular contributor to *Sovremennye Zapiski* in Paris and after 1924, to *Volja Rossii* in Prague; her poems and prose pieces also appeared in a number of other periodicals and miscellaneous collections. The fairy tale in verse *Mólodec* (*A Swain*) appeared as a separate volume in 1924. A book of prose memoirs of life in Soviet Russia, *Zemnye primety,* was rejected by A. G. Višnjak and turned down by several other Berlin publishers because of, oddly enough, its excessive preoccupation with politics and the violence of its anti-Communist passages.[12] Portions were subsequently published in periodicals. In the meantime, Cvetaeva continued to be an object of great interest to the critics in the Soviet Union. After two years abroad, it was still possible for her to plan to publish her forthcoming book of verse in Russia.[13] In 1924, two new poems by Cvetaeva appeared in the literary journal *Russkij Sovremennik,* published in Moscow and Leningrad with the close collaboration of Zamjatin and Maksim Gor'kij. The denunciation of the Soviet system in the memoir "Moi služby," published in *Sovremennye Zapiski* in 1925, brought down the wrath of official Soviet ideologues[14] and cut off any further possibility of Cvetaeva's work appearing in Soviet publications. After 1925, the reviews of new works by Cvetaeva in the Soviet press dwindle in number and after 1930, mention of her name becomes very rare indeed. In addition to publications in well-known émigré journals, Cvetaeva lent the prestige of her name to such literary publications of Russian students in Prague as *Svoimi Putjami,* where she published her memoir on Bal'mont. The title of that journal ("In One's Own Way") earned her particular approval, and when *Svoimi Putjami* was attacked by the Paris daily *Vozroždenie*

---

[12] Letters to R. Gul', p. 176.
[13] *Ibid.,* p. 186.
[14] E.g., D. Gorbov, "Mertvaja krasota i živučee bezobrazie," *Krasnaja Nov',* VII (Moscow, 1926), 244–245.

for the excessive independence of its political approach, Cvetaeva came out in print with a spirited defense of the right of the little journal to think for itself, without being bullied by larger émigré organizations and publications.[15] Cvetaeva was as intolerant of the political regimentation of literature that some émigré groups would occasionally attempt as she was of the Soviet regimentation.

The last year and a half of Cvetaeva's life in Czechoslovakia was spent in near-seculusion in the tiny village called Všenory. Her son was born there on February 1, 1925. Cvetaeva wished to name the boy Boris "in honor of my favorite contemporary, Boris Pasternak," but at Èfron's insistence the name finally selected was Georgij, the title of Cvetaeva's poetic cycle about St. George which was dedicated to her husband during the Civil War. By 1925, Russian émigré literature was a clearly defined phenomenon, with its own publishers and periodicals and a new center in Paris. In the fall of that year Cvetaeva began making plans for moving to Paris, at first only for a brief stay. By the time the final plans were formulated in October, the move was seen as permanent. Cvetaeva made her final public appearance in Prague on October 22, 1925, reading excerpts from "Geroj truda" at the Czech-Russian Society, and on October 31 she left for Paris with her son. Her husband, who had spent a part of 1925 in a tuberculosis sanatorium, remained temporarily in Prague. He joined her in Paris early in 1926.

The immediate object of Marina Cvetaeva's trip to Paris was to hold a poetry reading. The reading, initially scheduled for January, 1926, was postponed, and it finally took place in February. Cvetaeva appeared with two supporting artists, the soprano Cunelli and the violinist A. Mogilevskij. The event was treated by the Russian literary community of Paris as a gala occasion. The Russian daily press ran feature stories on Cvetaeva, and announcements of the reading are to be found in almost all Russian publications that came out in Paris during the two weeks preceding it.[16] Perhaps the most

---

[15] Marina Cvetaeva, "Vozroždenščina," in *Dni* (Berlin), October 16, 1925.

[16] E.g., Mix. Osorgin, "Poèt Marina Cvetaeva," *Poslednie Novosti* (Paris), January 21, 1926; D. —v. (Daniil Reznikov?), "Večer Mariny Cvetaevoj," *Dni* (Paris), February 6, 1926. In addition to the article in *Dni*, brief notices on the reading appeared in the February 6 issues of the newspapers *Poslednie Novosti* and *Vozroždenie*.

interesting report of the reading was to be found a few days later in
the Berlin daily newspaper *Rul'*:

Only recently considered among the lesser known names of contemporary poetry, Marina Cvetaeva has lately become not merely one of its
bigger names, but indubitably the biggest name. Her recital is a new
confirmation of her instantly grown popularity, her vogue. During my
four years in Paris I had no occasion to see such a multitude of people,
such a crowd which would come to listen to a contemporary poet. Long
before the recital began, not only were the large auditorium and the
balconies full to overflowing, but even the passages were so crowded that
it was impossible to move. The recital was a success and the audience
applauded generously after the performances of the singer Cunelli and
the violinist Mogilevskij, but the main attraction of the evening, Marina
Cvetaeva, had the greatest success of all. She recited both her old poems
from *Lebedinyj stan* . . . and her new poems. . . .[17]

Present at Cvetaeva's first public reading in Paris was the young
poet Irina Knorring. In a poem written on the day after the reading,
Irina Knorring described herself as wandering aimlessly about in
the rain, being stopped by a policeman, and barely escaping being
hit by passing automobiles, all because "that woman's voice yester-
day / Had taken too much out of me." [18] The great success of that
evening must have dispelled whatever doubts Marina Cvetaeva may
have had about staying in Paris permanently. After changing
several temporary addresses, she and her family finally settled
outside of Paris (in April, 1927,) in the suburb of Meudon (Seine-et-
Oise), where many exiled Russians lived, at 2, avenue Jeanne
d'Arc. The name of the street must have appealed to Cvetaeva, and
there were sound financial reasons for choosing the suburban
address; a contributing factor may have been her fear of big city

[17] *Rul'* (Berlin), February 12, 1926. The account, after reporting Cvetaeva's
success, ends by expressing the opinion that Cvetaeva has not yet found her
true poetic voice, and that her current successful poems represent a search for
a more genuine tone. It is signed with the initials M. G. and may have been
written by the noted Puškin scholar, Modest Gofman, who at that time
occasionally published in *Rul'*, under his full signature, hostile comments on
the more recent developments in Russian poetry.
[18] Irina Knorring, "Cvetaevoj," dated February 7, 1926, and published in
Poslednie Novosti (Paris), March 21, 1926. On the poetry of Irina Knorring
(1906–1943), see Gleb Struve, *Russkaja literatura v izgnanii*, p. 356, and note
93 on p. 332.

traffic: "I have a panic fear of automobiles. In a city square I am the most pitiable creature, like a sheep that has found itself in the middle of New York."[19] The forests around Meudon provided the appropriately poetic setting for her habitual long hikes and for mushroom and berry gathering trips. Cvetaeva's Meudon neighbor and friend of many years, Elena Izvol'skaja, who accompanied her on many of those excursions, wrote a sympathetic and informative account of Cvetaeva's first years in France. Mme Izvol'skaja originally met Cvetaeva in Paris at the apartment of one of the founders of the Eurasian movement, in which Sergej Èfron at that time participated. Here is her initial impression: "She was neither elegant nor pretty: thin, pale, almost emaciated; the oval of her face was narrow, severe, her cropped hair was still fair, but already strewn with gray. She was altogether not beautiful, but *icon-like*. Still, despite a certain severity, she quickly entered the atmosphere of our party and took part in the general conversation. . . . She responded to people, she sincerely wanted to communicate with them, but she did not know how, perhaps did not dare to. . . ."[20]

Mme Izvol'skaja's memoir also provides us with revealing glimpses of Cvetaeva coping with household chores, the inevitable *byt:*

She worked and wrote and gathered firewood and fed scraps to her family. She washed, laundered, sewed with her once thin fingers, now coarsened by work. I well remember those fingers, yellowed from smoking; they held a tea pot, a cooking pot, a frying pan, a kettle, an iron, they threaded a needle and started a fire. These very same fingers wielded a pen or a pencil over paper on the kitchen-table from which everything had been hastily removed. At this table Marina wrote—verse, prose, sketches for entire *poèmy,* sometimes she would trace two or three words and some particular rhyme and copy it many, many times. . . . Watching [her work] was like a naturalist observing the growth of a blade of grass, a leaf, a stem, the hatching of fledglings in forest nests, the metamorphosis of a chrysalis into a butterfly.[21]

[19] Letters to Baxrax, *Mosty,* V, 312.

[20] Elena Izvol'skaja, "Ten' na stenax. (O Cvetaevoj)," *Opyty,* III (New York, 1954), 153. Elena Izvol'skaja (Helene Iswolsky), the daughter of the Russian statesman and ambassador to France, A. P. Izvol'skij, is a translator of poetry and the author of books and articles on religious subjects; she is now resident in the United States.

[21] *Ibid.,* pp. 155–156.

Cvetaeva's growth as a poet between 1916 (*Versty I*) and 1925 (last poems in *Posle Rossii*) was rapid and bewildering to many of her readers. She herself compared the process to new bends of a river. Besides being affected, in a very personal and individual way, by the general post-revolutionary trends of Russian Futurism, she turned to the diction of folk laments and epics and, still later, to the archaic language of the Russian Bible and of Russian eighteenth-century poets. The evolution of Cvetaeva's work in the early nineteen-twenties has certain striking parallels in contemporary developments in music and painting, particularly in the work of Igor' Stravinskij, who during the same period was also drawing on the folk tales of Afanas'ev (*Histoire du soldat*), the popular Russian *zaplački,* and other traditional peasant motifs (*Svadebka,* usually called *Les Noces*). Like Cvetaeva, Stravinskij proceeded from a rococo view of the eighteenth century (cf. *Pulcinella,* 1919, and Cvetaeva's *Fortuna,* 1918) to the monumental Greek tragedy treated in eighteenth-century terms (cf. *Oedipus Rex,* 1927, and Cvetaeva's Theseus tragedies).

The appearance of "Poèma gory," "Poèma konca," and "Krysolov" enhanced the already strong admiration of Boris Pasternak for the poetry of Marina Cvetaeva. Several of his poems of the nineteen-twenties are dedicated to her, including his famous epic poem about the revolution of 1905, *Lejtenant Šmidt* (*Lieutenant Schmidt*). Apparently not daring to dedicate his revolutionary poem to an émigré poet openly, Pasternak resorted to the device of writing the dedication in form of an acrostic: read downward, the first letters of each line of the fifteen-line dedication spell "Marine Cvetaevoj" ("To Marina Cvetaeva"). This cryptic dedication, which accompanied *Lejtenant Šmidt* at the time of its original publication, was subsequently removed in the later editions of the poem; the fact that it was an acrostic remained generally unnoticed until it was revealed in the 1965 Soviet edition of Pasternak's poems.[22]

In one of his letters to Maksim Gor'kij in 1927, Pasternak emphasized his concern for the "huge talent of Marina Cvetaeva and for her unhappy, unbearably twisted fate." [23] Possibly in an

---

[22] Pasternak, *Proza 1915–1958,* p. 46. Pasternak, *Stixotvorenija i poèmy* (Moscow and Leningrad, 1965), p. 661.

[23] *Literaturnoe nasledstvo,* LXX (Moscow, 1963), 300.

effort to enlist the aid of Gor'kij, well known for his frequent
intercessions with Soviet authorities on behalf of poets, Pasternak
wrote in the same letter: "The role and the circumstances . . . of
Marina Cvetaeva are such, that if you would ask me what I intend
to *write* or do, I would reply: anything whatsoever that might help
her and uplift and restore to Russia this tremendous person, who
perhaps was not able to align her gift with destiny, or, more
correctly, vice versa." Gor'kij had no appreciation for Cvetaeva's role
or her poetry (although his negative reply, supported by quotations
from "Poèma konca" and *Posle Rossii,* shows a considerable familiarity with her work). He refused to take an interest in her fate and
saw her situation with a more realistic appreciation of the literary
and political factors involved than did Pasternak. He wrote: "M.
Cvetaeva, of course, ought to return to Russia, but this is hardly
possible." [24] Pasternak's hasty reply, for which he later offered
Gor'kij his apologies, is not reproduced in their published correspondence, but a note to one of Pasternak's letters makes it clear that
Pasternak's defense of Cvetaeva (and of her sister Anastasija) led to
a temporary break of his contact with Gor'kij.[25]

Maksim Gor'kij was not the only writer of the older generation to
reject Cvetaeva's new poetry. While the Soviet critics were turning
against Cvetaeva for political reasons, a considerable number of
émigré critics and writers came close to the view of Gor'kij and
began reacting against her on aesthetic and stylistic grounds.
Cvetaeva herself summed up this reaction in one of her letters to
Ivask in 1933, which is inevitably quoted in the recent Soviet articles
on her: "In the emigration they at first (hotheadedly!) publish me,
then, having come to their senses, withdraw me from circulation,
having realized that it is something that is not theirs: it is from over
there! The contents, it would seem, is 'ours' but the voice is
'theirs.' " [26] "Theirs" in the mid-twenties (bypassing the obvious
interpretations given by present-day Soviet commentators) meant to
a part of the émigré press a poetic voice belonging to the tradition of

---

[24] *Ibid.,* pp. 301–302.
[25] *Ibid.,* p. 307, and note 2 on p. 308, which states that Pasternak's still
unpublished letter, defending Cvetaeva from Gor'kij's criticism and dated
October 27, 1927, is in the Gor'kij Archive in Moscow.
[26] Letters to Ivask, p. 212.

Xlebnikov, Majakovskij, and Pasternak, whom many émigrés saw
merely as Soviet and were not prepared to acknowledge as the fine
Russian poets they were. A comparison of Cvetaeva's poetry of that
period to the work of those poets was made in print by Mirskij,
while most of the other émigré critics followed the example of
Bal'mont and continued comparing Cvetaeva with Anna Axmatova,
a mechanical juxtaposition based on sex, which adds nothing to the
understanding of either poet.

The rejection of Cvetaeva by the émigré criticism of the twenties
took several forms. There were older commentators, like P. B.
Struve, whose fixed concept of art could not encompass the new
trends which she represented.[27] Even more rigid was the dean of
émigré writers, Ivan Bunin, whose critical faculties were simply
unable to cope with any literary developments that arose after the
Symbolist period.[28] Of the surviving members of the Symbolist
generation, Zinaida Gippius, whose influence in Paris literary circles
was considerable, had no use for Cvetaeva's poetry.[29] The younger
Acmeists, like Nikolaj Ocup and Georgij Adamovič, who had
admired *Versty I* and *Stixi k Bloku,* showed themselves hostile to
Cvetaeva's poetry after *Remeslo.* As usually happens with a rapidly
developing artist of great originality, Cvetaeva kept losing a part of

---

[27] P. Struve, "Zametki pisatelja," *Vozroždenie* (Paris), May 6, 1926, where
Cvetaeva's prose and poetry are qualified as pointless, unnecessary, and
incomprehensible. ("Ni k čemu. Beznužno, ibo bespredmetno. Beznužno, ibo
nevnjatno . . . bessoderzatel'no, net 'suti' . . . Bolezn' èta načalas' davno,
edva li ne s Brjusova. . . .")

[28] Bunin's references to Cvetaeva, as to almost all other Russian poets after
the Symbolist generation, were invariably uncomplimentary. Typical of his
tone is the following reference to her found in his memoirs: "And how many
other pathological cases there were [among Russian writers]! Cvetaeva, with
her life-long flood of wild words and sounds in verse, who ended her life in a
noose after returning to Soviet Russia." (I. Bunin, *Vospominanija* [Paris,
1950], p. 43.) Cvetaeva dedicated her 1934 memoir "Dom u starogo Pimena"
to Bunin's wife, using the latter's maiden name, Vera Muromceva.

[29] The animosity of Zinaida Gippius to Cvetaeva's poetry is mentioned by
Ivask (*Lebedinyj stan,* p. 11) and by Ju. Terapiano, "Proza Mariny
Cvetaevoj," *Novoe Russkoe Slovo* (New York), March 7, 1954. M. V. Višnjak,
op. cit., p. 220, quotes the following passage from a letter Gippius wrote to
him in his capacity as one of the editors of *Sovremennye Zapiski* in 1926:
"The poems of Cvetaeva are of course a matter of the taste of the editorial
board, but having them *on the same page with mine,* such a conjunction is in
any case undoubtedly in bad taste. Don't you agree?"

her audience after each new "river bend." This phenomenon is best illustrated by the article on her poetry written in 1926 by the well-known émigré novelist and journalist, M. A. Osorgin. Osorgin calls Cvetaeva "the best Russian poet now writing" and has a few perceptive things to say about her stylistic affinity with the prose of Aleksej Remizov. Yet, his admiration extends only to her treatment of eighteenth-century subjects in "Fortuna," "Feniks," and certain poems in *Psixeja*. He describes her subsequent poetry as incoherent and dismisses Cvetaeva's *magnum opus* "Krysolov" ("The Pied Piper"), which at the time of his writing (January, 1926) was still being serialized in *Volja Rossii,* as a piece of "extremely melodious nonsense" ("ves'ma muzykal'naja nelepost' ").[30]

Not all the critics were hostile. In addition to the usually favorable Mark Slonim, Cvetaeva found a discerning and appreciative critic in Prince Dmitrij Svjatopolk-Mirskij, who wrote in English under the name D. S. Mirsky. Historian of Russian literature, lecturer at the School of Slavonic Studies at London University, and contributor to Russian, English, and French literary journals, Mirskij, like Boris Pasternak, did not at once appreciate Cvetaeva's difficult poetry. When preparing his anthology of Russian verse in 1923, he did not include Cvetaeva, describing her in his preface as "a talented, but hopelessly undisciplined Muscovite."[31] After reading *Mólodec* in 1924, Mirskij became an enthusiastic admirer of Cvetaeva and her active propagandizer both in Russian and in English. He met Cvetaeva's family and became a personal friend, usually paying Cvetaeva a visit every time he was in Paris.[32] On Mirskij's invitation, Cvetaeva traveled to London in March, 1926, for a two-week visit, during which she appeared in a reading of her poetry.[33]

[30] See note 16 above.

[31] Kn. D. Svjatopolk-Mirskij, *Russkaja lirika* (Paris, 1924), p. xii. The preface in which the statement occurs is dated August 8, 1923.

[32] Izvol'skaja, "Ten' na stenax," p. 156.

[33] The visit to London is mentioned in one of the letters to Ivask (Letters to Ivask, p. 218). The exact dates of the trip (March 10 to 25, 1926) can be established from an unpublished letter Cvetaeva wrote from London to Prince D. A. Šaxovskoj, which was kindly shown to the present writer by the recipient, now Archbishop John of San Francisco. According to Mrs. E. I. Eleneva, Cvetaeva stayed in London at the home of the civic leader and journalist Ariadna Tyrkova-Williams.

One of the contributing reasons for Cvetaeva's moving from Prague to Paris may have been Sergej Èfron's ambitions as writer and editor. Several of his articles and stories appeared in the mid-twenties in various journals, among them his troubled reappraisal of the White movement, "O dobrovol'čestve." [34] When asked by reporters to name the most significant new works of Russian prose (in one of the questionnaires which were customary in the Paris Russian newspapers at the end of each year), Cvetaeva loyally named her husband's stories, alongside prose works by Remizov and Pasternak.[35] Èfron, like Mirskij, was active in the Eurasian movement,[36] and both were keenly interested in the new literary developments in the Soviet Union. In 1926, Mirskij, Èfron, and the Eurasian critic and musicologist P. Suvčinskij started a literary journal. They called it *Versty* (the title of two of Cvetaeva's books), and it was clearly intended to be a showcase for the poetry of Marina Cvetaeva. Her name was featured on the cover of each issue, together with those of the other two regular contributors, Aleksej Remizov and the philosopher Lev Šestov (pseudonym of L. I. Švarcman). In addition to these three writers, *Versty* featured reprints of the most interesting new works of Soviet literature, critical articles by the three editor-publishers and by some better-known émigré philosophers, and some Eurasian material (reviews of travel and ethnological literature dealing with Central Asia and Siberia); in an appendix, every issue contained some signficant and neglected work of pre-Revolutionary Russian literature. The journal came out annually and altogether three issues appeared from 1927 to 1929. If not the best émigré journal, it was certainly the most original and imaginative in the whole history of the Russian émigré

[34] S. È., "O dobrovol'čestve," *Sovremennye Zapiski,* XXI (1924), 376–380. This piece was signed by the initials S. È.; the authorship of Èfron is confirmed, however, by one of the journal's editors, M. V. Višnjak, *op. cit.,* p. 145.

[35] See Cvetaeva's reply to the questionnaire in *Vozroždenie* (Paris), January 1, 1926, and March 4, 1926.

[36] On the Eurasian movement, see Gleb Struve, *Russkaja literatura v izgnanii,* pp. 40–49, and Otto Böss, *Die Lehre der Eurasier* (Wiesbaden, 1961). Marina Cvetaeva was not directly involved in the movement and came in touch with it through her husband and some of her friends. However, themes related to the preoccupations of the Eurasians can be discerned in her poetic cycles "Xanskij polon" in *Remeslo* and "Skifskie" in *Posle Rossii.*

press. Yet, because of its Eurasian tinge and the Soviet reprints, it was attacked by other émigré publications with what can only be described as fury. P. B. Struve, in the very last issue of *Russkaja Mysl'*, called *Versty* a "repellent superfluity" and characterized the Soviet contributions (by Pasternak, Esenin, Artem Veselyj, Babel', Tynjanov, and others) as "carrion."[37] Vladislav Xodasevič published in *Sovremennye Zapiski* a savage attack on the editors of *Versty* which later necessitated retractions and apologies.[38] Most of the fire was directed at the editorial policies, and there was no room in those articles for a fair appraisal of the major works by Cvetaeva ("Poèma gory," "Novogodnee," "S morja," and the tragedy "Tezej") which had appeared in *Versty*. Most commentators on *Versty* simply mentioned that she was a featured contributor. One notable exception was Bunin, for whom the mere presence of the names of Cvetaeva and Šestov on the same masthead was "nonsense and irresponsibility" and whose brief and high-handed comment on "Poèma gory" consists of a pun that verges on indecency.[39] Another exception was Zinaida Gippius, who, while attacking *Versty* on political grounds, used the opportunity to speak of Cvetaeva's poetry and person in a tone of utter contempt.[40]

Nevertheless, Cvetaeva exaggerated when she wrote to Ivask in the letter already quoted that in the late nineteen-twenties she was "withdrawn from circulation" in the émigré press. Those were, after all, the years when her work appeared regularly in the three most important journals of the emigration: *Sovremennye Zapiski, Versty,* and *Volja Rossii*. The latter published the whole series of Cvetaeva's *poèmy* which followed "Krysolov." There were occasional nonperiodical, miscellaneous collections, like *Kovčeg* in Prague, which in 1926 published "Poèma konca." Also in 1926, the young poet Prince D. A. Šaxovskoj brought out in Brussels two issues of an excellent, but short-lived literary journal called *Blagonamerennyj*. Poetry and prose by Marina Cvetaeva were featured in both issues of *Blagonamerennyj*. In the second one, she published

---

[37] P. Struve, "Otvratnaja nenužnost'," *Russkaja Mysl'* (no volume number) (Paris, 1927), p. 62.
[38] M. V. Višnjak, *op. cit.,* pp. 142–145.
[39] I. Bunin, "Versty," *Vozroždenie* (Paris), August 5, 1926.
[40] Anton Krajnij (pen name of Z. Gippius.) "O 'Verstax' i o pročem," *Poslednie Novosti* (Paris), August 14, 1926.

her searching examination of the relation between poetry and criticism, "Poèt o kritike" (the title can be variously understood as "A Poet on Criticism" or "A Poet about a Critic"; the first rendition is probably the correct one). In addition to investigating the problem in its general aspects, Cvetaeva's article contained a headlong attack on most practicing Russian critics, both Soviet and émigré. She objected in particular to the judging of new poetry on the basis of the styles and criteria of earlier epochs. It was from this angle that she defended Esenin and Majakovskij against Bunin, Pasternak against Gippius (which probably did not improve her relations with those two fellow émigré writers), and Remizov against the whole of émigré criticism. Cvetaeva criticized the Formalist school in the Soviet Union as overspecialized, but she also singled out the then famous master of the impressionistic form of criticism, Ajxenval'd (mostly in the form of comments on excerpts from his articles, quoted without credit, although there is one uncomplimentary reference to Ajxendal'd by name), for passing judgment on works he had not properly read or understood. Appended to "Poèt o kritike" under the title "Cvetnik" (contextual translation, "A Nosegay") was a section which consisted of excerpts from critical articles by one of the more popular of the younger émigré critics and Cvetaeva's erstwhile fellow contributor to *Severnye Zapiski,* Georgij Adamovič, interspersed with withering comments by Cvetaeva. The selection and the juxtaposition of quotations from Adamovič and the commentary showed him up as an inconsistent, irresponsible and superficial critic.

The article created a minor sensation in the Russian literary world abroad. It must have deeply hurt Julij Ajxenval'd. The dignified rebuttal of the elderly critic [41] (who in his own way had tried to be favorable to Cvetaeva in earlier articles published under the name Kameneckij) acknowledged his authorship of the passages quoted anonymously and expressed agreement with many of Cvetaeva's basic premises. His article makes touching reading: the tone of irony fails Ajxenval'd toward the end, leaving only dismay and bewilderment at being disliked by an admired poet. "Poèt o kritike" made an enemy of the previously friendly Mixail Osorgin, who attacked it

[41] Ju. Ajxenval'd, "Literaturnye zametki," *Rul'* (Berlin), May 5, 1926.

in a long article in *Poslednie Novosti*[42] and who thereafter usually wrote of Cvetaeva with hostility and scorn. There was no immediate rebuttal from Adamovič,[43] but his delayed reaction, expressed in numerous later statements and still developing to this day, is largely responsible for the insufficient and distorted idea of Cvetaeva's poetry that many literate Russians abroad now have. *Blagonamerennyj* also printed another Cvetaeva work which is connected with Georgij Adamovič: the poem "Starinnoe blagogoven'e," which Cvetaeva submitted to a contest organized by the journal *Zveno*. The jury of the contest, consisting of Adamovič, Z. Gippius, and Konstantin Močul'skij, selected twenty poems out of the two hundred submitted for publication in *Zveno*. Cvetaeva's poem was not among the twenty thus chosen.[44] In *Blagonamerennyj* it appeared with a note about its rejection in the contest.[45]

The literary tastes of Cvetaeva in her period of poetic maturity became more austere. While she retained a certain fond loyalty to the romantic idols of her youth, we find her, during her life abroad, turning more and more to world classics. She reread, with great attention, Homer, the Nibelungenlied, the Chanson de Roland, the Igor Tale,[46] Shakespeare, Racine; all these left traces in her poetry of the twenties. She felt close to certain of her Russian contemporaries, above all to Pasternak, Mandel'štam, and Majakovskij. Her relationship during the twenties with Vladislav Xodasevič, her only peer among Russian poets abroad, was a complex mixture of attraction and repulsion. The attitude of Xodasevič was equally mixed,[47] and only in the next decade did the two profoundly different poets, each progressively more isolated by new literary

---

[42] Mix. Osorgin, "Djadja i tëtja," *Poslednie Novosti* (Paris), April 29, 1926.

[43] Strong objections to Cvetaeva's treatment of Adamovič were expressed by Vladimir Pozner, "Sžigal'ščiki i sžigaemye," *Dni* (Berlin), May 6, 1926.

[44] G. Adamovič, *Odinočestvo i svoboda* (New York, 1955), pp. 154–157.

[45] In fairness to the jury, it may be stated that the poem, "Starinnoe blagogoven'e" ("Ancient Piety"), contains a grammatical *lapsus,* unique in Cvetaeva: "U nežnyx nog otdoxnoven'e / Perebiraja struny ljutni." The "dangling" participle *perebiraja* creates an ambiguous and almost comical impression.

[46] Koz'min, *op. cit.,* p. 262.

[47] An example of the ambivalent attitude of Xodasevič, the critic, to Cvetaeva's poetry in the nineteen-twenties is his review of *Posle Rossii* (*Vozroždenie* [Paris], June 19, 1928). Paraphrasing a verse from her "Xvala

trends, develop a deep mutual respect. There are numerous references to Goethe in Cvetaeva's later writings, and we learn from one of her letters to Ivask that she felt closer to Goethe than to either Tolstoj or Dostoevskij: "I love in this world not what is the most profound but what is highest, therefore Goethe's joy is more precious to me than Russian suffering and to Russian tossing about (*metanie*) I prefer *that* solitude." [48]

Cvetaeva had little contact with contemporary foreign writers, either in person or through their writings. The two exceptions were Marcel Proust, whom she hugely admired, and Rainer Maria Rilke. As far as we know, Cvetaeva and Rilke never met personally.[49] Their relationship started in all probability when Rilke sent Cvetaeva copies of his *Duineser Elegien* and *Sonnette an Orpheus* at the request of Boris Pasternak.[50] Cvetaeva had admired Rilke's poetry earlier, and he must have been familiar with hers from Èrenburg's anthology of 1922, which we know he had in his

---

bogatym" ("Eulogy of the Rich"), he asserts that he loves Cvetaeva's poetry. Then, after selecting a few poems that he approves of, Xodasevič condemns the rest of the volume as unformed, raw poetic material and takes issue with the whole of Cvetaeva's style and poetics. A comparison of the poems that Xodasevič considers as finished with the ones he condemns as sketchy and unpolished shows that he had no fixed standard or basis for his distinction. The far more complimentary references to Cvetaeva in his articles of the nineteen-thirties may be due to his greater familiarity with her poetry. Cvetaeva's guarded attitude to Xodasevič in the nineteen-twenties was partly due to a misunderstanding: she considered his poem "Živ Bog! umën a ne zaumen" (1923) as a direct attack on herself and Pasternak, whereas it was obviously aimed against the metalogical language of Kručenyx and Xlebnikov (see Letters to Baxrax, *Mosty*, V, 316).

[48] Letters to Ivask, p. 217.

[49] In "Tvoja smert' " there is a cryptic reference to a meeting, either real or imaginary, or perhaps only planned, at a certain Auberge des Trois Rois somewhere in the Savoy (*Volja Rossii*, V–VI [1927], 24). E. Izvol'skaja ("Ten' na stenax," p. 157) and E. I. Eleneva (in a letter to the present writer), who were close to Cvetaeva at the time of her correspondence with Rilke, both assert that the two poets never met in person. In a letter to Ivask, Cvetaeva wrote that she met Rilke "in writing, half a year before his death" (Letters to Ivask, p. 222).

[50] Rainer Maria Rilke, *Briefe aus Muzot* (Leipzig, 1936), p. 355. In a public lecture at the University of California on April 30, 1962, Professor Günther Wytrzens stated that the "poetess" mentioned in Rilke's letter to Pasternak is Cvetaeva, and that Pasternak served as an intermediary in originating the Cvetaeva-Rilke correspondence. If this is so, their initial contact was not earlier than December, 1925 or January, 1926.

possession.[51] Their correspondence has not been published, and Cvetaeva may have taken Rilke's letters to the Soviet Union at the time of her return. What we do have is their poetry addressed to each other and the marked trace that Rilke left in some of Cvetaeva's theoretical writings on literature and art. Rilke had less than a year to live at the time the correspondence began. On June 9, 1926, Rilke sent Cvetaeva the long and very beautiful "Elegie an Marina Zwetajewa-Efron," and several weeks later he sent her a copy of his volume of French poems, *Vergers,* with the following inscription:

> Marina: voici galets et coquillages
> ramassés récemment à la française plage
> de mon étrange coeur . . . (J'aimerais que tu connusses
> toutes les étendues de son divers paysage
> depuis sa côte bleue jusqu'à ses plaines russes).

We know of no poem by Cvetaeva addressed to Rilke while he was still alive (one strongly suspects there must have been some), but after he died she wrote two works that described the impact of his death on her: the long lament in verse, "Novogodnee" ("New Year's Greetings"), and a prose essay, "Tvoja smert'" ("Your Death"). In 1929, she published in *Volja Rossii* a selection of Rilke's letters in her own translation into Russian with an introductory essay. Among her theoretical statements on Rilke's poetry, the most important one is to be found in "Poèt i vremja," although all her references to him are interesting and revealing. The whole brief relationship evolved on the lofty poetic level best understood and appreciated by Cvetaeva. Rilke was one of the very few objects of her admiration and affection not to disappoint her. In a candid statement to Ivask in 1935, Cvetaeva wrote that she had met in her life only two people who equalled her in human and poetic strength: Rilke and Pasternak.

Because of the intolerant attitude of the Russian émigré literary community (or perhaps, "establishment") to anyone connected with the journal *Versty,* the social contacts of the Èfrons came to be restricted mainly to people sympathetic to Eurasianism. In the late

[51] *Ibid.,* p. 365, letter to Leonid Pasternak.

nineteen-twenties, Cvetaeva's friends were Mirskij, Salomea Halpern (née Princess Andronikova, friend of Axmatova and Mandel'štam, the heroine of the latter's famous poem "Solominka"),
Mme Izol'skaja, Suvčinskij and his wife Vera, and the composer
Sergej Prokof'ev. The financial situation of Cvetaeva's family, although not quite as desperate as it became in the nineteen-thirties,
was far from comfortable. In addition to his infrequent editorial and
literary activities, Sergej Èfron found occasional employment appearing as an extra in French film productions, which necessitated
humiliating pleadings by Marina with their more affluent friends to
lend him presentable clothing for those appearances. Their modest
Czech pension continued until about 1931. What apparently enabled
the family to survive were the voluntary contributions from their
regularly employed friends, Mrs. Halpern and Mirskij being particularly generous.

In 1928, Cvetaeva published a collection of poems she had written
in Berlin and in Prague between 1922 and 1925. Called *Posle Rossii*
(*After Russia*), it represents a successful synthesis of several of her
previous styles and is the most mature and perfect of her collections.
It was noticed by very few critics. There was nothing like the wave
of acclaim and interest occasioned by the publication of *Versty I* and
Remeslo only six years earlier. Mark Slonim was the only émigré
critic to give the collection his unreserved praise.[52] Xodasevič chided
Cvetaeva for constantly changing her style.[53] The Soviet press did
not review the book at all. The sales must have been disastrous:
despite the small printing, one could still see copies of *Posle Rossii*
gathering dust in the back rooms of Russian bookstores in Paris and
New York as late as the nineteen-fifties. To augment her small
income, Cvetaeva appeared once or twice a year in public readings
of her work in Paris. These later readings were not anywhere as
successful or popular as her first Paris appearance in 1926. The
proceeds from Cvetaeva's lectures and her friends' generosity
enabled her to spend her summers on the Breton coast, usually at St.
Gilles-sur-Vie, where Bal'mont also spent his summers, or at Dives-
sur-Mer, which she jokingly rendered into Russian as "Morskoe

---

[52] Review of *Posle Rossii* in *Dni* (Berlin), June 17, 1928.
[53] See the Xodasevič review mentioned in note 47 above. Later, A. Bem
reproached the émigré critics for having overlooked and underestimated *Posle
Rossii* (A. Bem, "V zaščitu čitatelja," *Rul'* [Berlin], August 16, 1931).

divo." The summer months were her most productive ones, and most of her long poems of the period were written on such vacations.

There were also poetic disciples in her life, most notably Nikolaj Gronskij. He was eighteen at the time his friendship with Cvetaeva began. His father was a well-known politician and political scientist, his mother a sculptress. Gronskij was a hiking and mountain-climbing enthusiast, and in 1928 he accompanied Cvetaeva on her hikes in the woods around Meudon: "the military friendship in the royal forest," as Cvetaeva later wrote.[54] In the summer of that year, while Cvetaeva was at the seacoast, there was a lively correspondence between her and Gronskij. Soon thereafter, Gronskij, like most other heroes of her intense friendships, drifted away from her—to his studies of law and Russian literature, to mountain climbing, to religion. But during his brief span in Cvetaeva's orbit, the young student became a poet. His earliest poetry, written during their friendship, is filled with stylistic reminiscences from *Posle Rossii*. Two of these early poems are addressed to "M.C.," including the admirable "Iz glubiny morej podnjavšeesja imja" ("The Name That Arose from the Depth of the Seas") (the imagery of the entire poem is built on the etymology of the name Marina).[55] In later poems of Gronskij one encounters epigraphs from *Posle Rossii* and in the long *poèma* about mountain climbing, "Belladonna," which Cvetaeva considered his finest work, the influence of her poetry blends in an original and organic way with the influences of the odic manner of Lomonosov and the mystical poems of Blok. Early death prevented Gronskij from becoming the significant poet he might have been. (Nikolaj Gronskij was killed in a subway accident in 1934, at the age of twenty-five.) His two poems to Cvetaeva are a fulfillment of the challenge and the hope one finds in her poetry in *Posle Rossii* that was addressed originally to Baxrax and found no response in him.

The paradoxical literary and ideological situation in which Cvetaeva found herself in the late nineteen-twenties is exemplified

[54] Letters to Ivask, p. 222. The passages in Cvetaeva's letters to Ivask which give the account of her friendship with Gronskij (pp. 222–228) have unfortunately been heavily censored by the editor.

[55] N. P. Gronskij, *Stixi i poèmy*, (Paris, ca. 1935), p. 16. This poem is reprinted both in a defective version quoted by Cvetaeva from memory and in full in Cvetaeva's letters to Ivask, p. 223.

in a series of events that took place in the fall of 1928. In April of that year, she completed a long and violently anti-Communist poem, "Krasnyj byčok" ("The Red Bull-Calf"), which appeared in *Volja Rossii* at the end of 1928.[56] In the summer and in the fall, she worked on her epic poem "Perekóp" (based on the wartime diaries of her husband), in which she glorified the heroism of the White Army. At the same time, Cvetaeva's poetry was regularly and prominently featured in the largest of Paris émigré daily newspapers, *Poslednie Novosti*, edited by the historian and political figure P. N. Miljukov. After reprinting several poems from *Versty I*[57] as well as a few unpublished poems (possibly from *Versty II*)[58] during the summer months, *Poslednie Novosti* began in October what looked like a serialization of Cvetaeva's Civil War collection *Lebedinyj stan*, for which she had until then been unable to find an émigré publisher.[59] At the end of October, Vladimir Majakovskij, the staunchest supporter of the Soviet regime among the major Russian poets, came to Paris. Cvetaeva saw him and presented him with a copy of *Posle Rossii* with the inscription: "To one as fleetfooted as myself. Paris, October, 1928."[60] She attended his public readings and was particularly impressed by the one held at the Café Voltaire on November 7. A few weeks later, the official newspaper

---

[56] *Volja Rossii*, XII (1928), 35–38.

[57] Poems from *Versty I* appeared in *Poslednie Novosti* on July 12, 22, and 26, and on October 18, 1928.

[58] Six previously unpublished poems (including the poem to Vjačeslav Ivanov), all of which could chronologically belong to Cvetaeva's unpublished collection *Versty II* (1917–1921), appeared on June 28, July 3, and October 4, 1928.

[59] Under the general heading "Iz knigi 'Lebedinyj stan,'" *Poslednie Novosti* printed the poems "Ja ètu knigu poručaju vetru" on October 25, "Ob ušedšix, otošedšix" on November 1, and "Noč'.—Nord-Ost.—Rev soldat.—Rev voln . . ." on November 8. Cvetaeva's letter to Majakovskij (see note 62 below) makes it clear that the printing of further poems was discontinued because of her association with him. The last of the poems appeared on the morning after her public statement at the Café Voltaire. Èrenburg's statement in his memoirs that émigré publishers were anxious to publish *Lebedinyj stan* but were not allowed to do so by the penitent Cvetaeva is pure invention, aimed at placating the current Soviet sensibilities and prejudices.

[60] V. Katanjan, *Majakovskij: Literaturnaja xronika* (Moscow, 1961), p. 488. This inscription is a paraphrased line from Majakovskij's poem "Gorod" ("City"). The volume thus inscribed is in the possession of Elsa Triolet (the wife of Louis Aragon) in Paris.

of the Eurasian movement published a statement of Cvetaeva's
addressed to Majakovskij ("Majakovskomu"):

On the twenty-eighth of April, 1922, on the eve of my departure from
Russia, in the early hours of the morning I met Majakovskij on the
completely empty Kuzneckij [Most Boulevard].
  "Well, Majakovskij, what message do you have for Europe?"
  "That truth is over here."
On the seventh of November, late at night, leaving Café Voltaire, to the
question:
  "What can you say about Russia after Majakovskij's recital?" I replied
without hesitation:
  "That strength is over there." [61]

Strength to Cvetaeva clearly meant the strength of the new poetry
then being written in the Soviet Union by Majakovskij, Pasternak,
Sel'vinskij, Tixonov, the strength that she so badly missed in the
work of both the older and the younger Russian poets resident
abroad. Yet a part of the émigré press in Paris took her declaration
for an endorsement of the entire Soviet system. No further poems
from *Lebedinyj stan* appeared in *Poslednie Novosti,* and for the
next two years Cvetaeva was barred from that newspaper. It is
ironic to read Cvetaeva's indignant letter to Majakovskij about the
incident, when one realizes to whom she is complaining of
Miljukov's refusal to continue the publication of *Lebedinyj stan*.[62]
But the full irony and pathos of Cvetaeva's position can be
appreciated only in the light of Majakovskij's attitude to her. The
most egocentric of Russian poets, Majakovskij habitually evaluated
his contemporaries through the double prism of loyalty to the Soviet
regime and official adherence to his own Futurist group. Despite
cordial personal relations and Cvetaeva's long-standing championing of his poetry, his public pronouncements on Cvetaeva were
invariably hostile.[63] Less than a year after their Paris encounter, we

[61] *Evrazija* (Paris), November 28, 1928. Reprinted in full in Katanjan, *op.
cit.,* p. 375.
  [62] Letter of Cvetaeva to Majakovskij of December 3, 1928, quoted by
Katanjan, p. 375. The letter is now in the Central State Archive of Literature
(CGALI) in Moscow.
  [63] In his 1918 book review, "Bratskaja mogila," Majakovskij chides Cvetaeva
for mentioning "God's servant Nicholas" (i.e., the Tsar) in one of her poems.
In his article "Podoždem obvinjat' poètov" (originally in *Krasnaja Nov'*, No.

find him speaking of her poetry with cold scorn. Polemicizing at the Congress of the Russian Association of Proletarian Writers with the Marxist critic Gorbačëv, who saw positive value in Cvetaeva's artistic achievements, Majakovskij replied by lumping Cvetaeva together with Gumilëv and summed up his attitude to her poetry with the statement: "And I consider that a work directed against us has no right to exist and it is our task to show it up as maximally repulsive and not make use of it to teach anything to anyone." [64] This did not prevent Majakovskij from making propagandistic use of Cvetaeva's anti-Miljukov letter during his anniversary exhibit in 1930.

The incident with Majakovskij points to the problem with which Cvetaeva was increasingly faced with the advent of the nineteen-thirties. The romantic conservative in politics finally had to face the fact that she was a revolutionary in poetry. The realization came when there was a trend toward conservatism in Russian literature— the forced conservatism of Socialist Realism in the Soviet Union and the self-imposed conservatism of the Russian literary community in Paris (the realism or mysticism of older writers or the ostentatious drabness and modesty of form championed by Adamovič and some of his followers). The White officers glorified in "Perekóp" were unable to understand the poem, just as the hero of Cvetaeva's love affair in Prague preferred Gumilëv to "Poèma konca." Cvetaeva's true audience, she came to realize gradually, was in Russia, the audience that despite the mounting ideological pressure could appreciate the rhythm of Pasternak and the imagery of Zabolockij and would respond to her poetry the way the émigrés, with a few significant exceptions, could not. "I went abroad in 1922 and my reader remained in Russia where my poems no longer penetrate," she wrote to Ivask in 1933. Even more pointedly in the same letter: "And thus, I am here without readers; in Russia, without books."

---

4 [Moscow-Leningrad, 1926]), he qualifies Cvetaeva's poetry as "Gypsy lyrics" and suggests that booksellers in the Soviet Union discourage young Communist Youth girls from buying her books, advising them instead to buy Sel'vinskij ("at least he's a man") or, still better, Aseev. (Vladimir Majakovskij, *Polnoe sobranie sočinenij* [Moscow, 1959], XII, 10 and 79.

[64] *Ibid.*, p. 391.

IV 🖋

Last Decade In Paris

(1929–1939)

Marina Cvetaeva's last decade in Paris presents a tragic, ever darkening picture that has its parallels in the ominous turn of European history in the years 1929–1939. Gradually, imperceptibly, Cvetaeva found herself more and more isolated as a human being, more and more neglected as a poet, more and more subjected to intolerable emotional and material burdens. There is no immediate and observable change in her position as one of the leading figures in Russian literature abroad at any given point during the decade. Her ultimate alienation from the literary community in Paris represents the cumulative effect of varied and dramatic developments, most of which were beyond her control.

At the beginning of the decade, we find Cvetaeva involved in numerous literary activities. In 1929, on a commission from the journal *Volja Rossii,* she wrote a long, book-length study of the life and art of the painter Natalija Gončarova. She frequently participated in the meetings and discussions at the literary association of "Kočev'e," which was conducted by Mark Slonim. On May 25, 1929, she gave a joint literary recital with Prince Sergej Volkonskij, at which she read her *poèma* "Perekóp." There were also attempts to establish contact with the French literary community. When Natalija Gončarova, who did a series of illustrations for Cvetaeva's epic poem *Mólodec,* expressed a wish to arrange for a translation of the poem into French with a view to its possible publication with the illustrations, Cvetaeva attempted the translation herself. Dissatisfied with the result, she decided to write a new French poem, "Gars," based on *Mólodec*. A recital of this French poem at one of the Paris literary salons ended in a complete fiasco, and Cvetaeva made no further attempts in this direction. Brice Parrain considered publishing "Gars" in *Nouvelle Revue Française* but gave up the idea. Nothing of consequence came from her participation in the Franco-Russian literary discussions which were organized by the French literary publication *Cahiers de la quinzaine* in 1929–1930.[1]

In April, 1930, Vladimir Majakovskij committed suicide. Two months later, the Russian cultural community in Paris found itself bitterly divided over an obituary of the Soviet poet, rude and contemptuous in tone, written by A. Levinson, the émigré critic of literature and ballet, and published in the French newspaper *Les Nouvelles littéraires*.[2] The protest against Levinson's treatment of Majakovskij, signed by many well-known French and Russian writers and painters,[3] was answered on July 12 by a "counter-protest" which read in part: "Quelles que puissent être les nuances possibles quant à l'appréciation du talent poètique de Maiakovsky, nous, les écrivains russes, mieux informés que les étrangers de la situation actuelle de notre littérature, nous affirmons que Maiakovsky n'a jamais été un grand poète russe, mais uniquement un compositeur de vers attaché au parti communiste et au gouvernement de l'U.R.S.S." This document bore the signatures of, among others, Adamovič, Aldanov, Berberova, Bunin, Gippius, Xodasevič, Kuprin, Merežkovskij, Močul'skij, Vladimir Nabokov (as "Wladimir Syrine"), Terapiano, Tèffi, and Vejdle (Wladimir Weidlé).[4]

[1] See the following volumes of *Cahiers de la quinzaine* (Paris): "Recontres," Series 20, special unnumbered issue (1930), pp. 10, 87, 147 and 212; "Paul Valéry" Series 21, No. 2 (1931), p. 76; "Marcel Proust" Series 20, No. 5 (1930), pp. 50–51.

[2] André Levinson, "La poésie chez les Soviets: le suicide de Maiakovsky," *Les Nouvelles littéraires* (Paris), May 31, 1930.

[3] Letter of protest, *ibid.*, June 14, 1930. The protesting writers included André Malraux, Blaise Cendrars, Èrenburg, Vladimir Pozner, Il'ja Zdanevič; among the painters one finds Picasso, Fernand Léger (twice), Natalija Gončarova, Larionov, Tereškovič, and Jurij Annenkov. See also Katanjan, *op. cit.*, p. 447.

[4] "Autour de Maiakovsky," *Les Nouvelles littéraires* (Paris), July 12, 1930. The passions generated by Levinson's article reached a high point in a physical attack on Levinson by Louis Aragon (*Poslednie Novosti* [Paris], July 12, 1930).

Cvetaeva, as might have been expected, did not attach her signature to either of the two declarations. Instead, she expressed her attitude to Majakovskij and his suicide in a magnificent cycle of seven poems, "Majakovskomu" ("To Majakovskij"),[5] in which, among the laments and eulogies, she vented her contempt for both the Soviet and émigré press for viewing the death of a great Russian poet solely from the political and propagandistic angle. The disparaging reference to the followers of Miljukov in the first poem of the cycle must have particularly irked some of Cvetaeva's fellow émigrés. The sixth poem of the cycle, which is probably the high point of Cvetaeva's political poetry, depicts an imaginary conversation in the Kingdom of Heaven between the two suicide poets, Esenin and Majakovskij. The unity of poetry over and beyond politics is symbolized in Majakovskij's affectionate inquiry about other Russian poets of diverse political orientation whose lives ended tragically in the nineteen-twenties: "L'san Aleksanyč" (Blok), "Fëdor Kuz'mič" (Sologub), and "Gumilëv, Nikolaj." The Majakovskij cycle represents a major change of tone in Cvetaeva's lyric poetry. It marks the appearance of a new, harsher, and deliberately coarser diction and ushers in the trend toward general invective, both of which become important in her poetry of the nineteen-thirties. A combination of compassion and irony is vividly conveyed in the last line of the brief seventh poem of the cycle, which is a paraphrase of the well-known formula from the requiem mass: "Rest, O Lord, the soul of Thy late enemy."[6] In May, 1931, Cvetaeva recited this cycle during a public lecture that also included her Mandel'štam memoir; the audience found her imitation of Majakovskij's own delivery most impressive (she describes the recital in an unpublished letter to Salomea Halpern, dated May 31, 1931).

In May, 1932, Cvetaeva's family moved to cheaper lodgings in the suburb of Clamart (101, rue Condorcet). Sergej Èfron was periodically ill and had to be treated at various sanatoriums. Some of the

[5] Written in August, 1930, published in *Volja Rossii*, XI–XII (1930), 964–971.

[6] "Upokoj, Gospodi, dušu usopšego vraga Tvoego." The substitution of *vraga* (enemy) for the traditional *raba* (servant) is especially startling and explosive because the euphony of the Church Slavic diction makes it almost imperceptible at first reading.

friends who contributed to Cvetaeva's financial support in the late nineteen-twenties were forced to stop their assistance because of the generally worsening economic situation. In 1932, Cvetaeva's main literary outlet, *Volja Rossii,* lost its Czech government subsidy and stopped publication. In her published letters to G. P. Fedotov and in her letters to Ivask, we see Cvetaeva living in utter indigence and often on the brink of physical starvation. The oft-quoted phrase in her letter to Ivask of April 4, 1933 ("My daughter earns five francs a day by knitting bonnets and on these the four of us . . . live, i.e., are slowly starving to death") is the best known reflection of her living conditions of the period, but there are others. "Because of my total poverty, I go nowhere and see no one, " Cvetaeva wrote to Fedotov on December 20, 1932. In an unpublished letter to Salomea Halpern, dated March 18, 1932, we read: "Hunger and cold are in our home." When the newspaper *Vozroždenie* wished to obtain an interview, Cvetaeva preferred to meet the interviewer, Nadežda Gorodeckaja, in one of the Paris railroad stations rather than risk a published description of her living conditions.[7] The most telling incident of all perhaps is mentioned in her letter to Fedotov and his wife in which she explains that she could not visit them as promised because the soles of her only shoes fell apart as she was starting. The payment of rent was a constant source of anguish and in March, 1933, Cvetaeva's belongings were about to be confiscated for nonpayment. No wonder that while discussing Dostoevskij (to whose work she was rather indifferent) in a letter to Ivask Cvetaeva wrote that of all Dostoevskij's heroines she felt closest to Katerina Ivanovna Marmeladova "with her shawl, her children, her French dialect. That is myself—whether at home, in everyday life, with my children, in Soviet Russia, in emigration, myself in that all-too-real puddle of soapy dishwater which has been my life since 1917 and from which I judge and threaten (*sužu i grožu*)."

With the closing of *Volja Rossii,* the problem of publishing her work became an acute one for Cvetaeva. During the nineteen-twenties, in addition to publishing separate books, Cvetaeva was a highly valued contributor to journals like *Versty, Blagonamerennyj,*

[7] N. Gorodeckaja, "V gostjax u M. I. Cvetaevoj," *Vozroždenie* (Paris), March 7, 1931.

and *Volja Rossii*. The editors of these journals were sensitive men who realized the importance of her work and treated it with due respect. In the thirties, Cvetaeva's work appeared mainly in *Sovremennye Zapiski*. This was the most respectable and durable of the Russian literary journals abroad, but the treatment of Marina Cvetaeva by this undoubtedly fine publication constitutes a black page in its history. After Cvetaeva's letters to Ivask containing eloquent denunciations of the editors of *Sovremennye Zapiski,* with specific reference to Vadim Rudnev, were published in 1957, another editor, Mark Višnjak, stated in his history of the journal, published in 1958, that Cvetaeva's complaints and even curses addressed to *Sovremennye Zapiski* had no factual basis.[8] However, the publication of Cvetaeva's letters to G. P. Fedotov (himself a prominent contributor to *Sovremennye Zapiski*) three years later revealed an even more depressing picture of Cvetaeva's constant fight against Rudnev's editorial mutilation of her work, which must have been intolerable to a writer of her experience and reputation. We owe to *Sovremennye Zapiski* the publication of an important body of work by Cvetaeva that would otherwise have remained unpublished, but we must also remember that her most significant theoretical pronouncement on art, "Iskusstvo pri svete sovesti" ("Art in the Light of Conscience"), was cut by Rudnev to one half of its original length,[9] that her poem in memory of N. Gronskij was arbitrarily mutilated by the editors,[10] and that the journal rejected some of her important work of the nineteen-thirties.[11]

In the late nineteen-twenties, there arose in Paris a whole new

[8] M. Višnjak, *op. cit.,* p. 417.

[9] Letters to Ivask, p. 214.

[10] *Izbrannoe*, note on p. 294. The Soviet editors of *Izbrannoe*, on the other hand, while reinstating the "anticlerical" stanza deleted in *Sovremennye Zapiski*, left out the first and the last sections of this poem, publishing only its middle part.

[11] E.g., her cycle of poems in memory of Vološin (see Letters to Fedotov, p. 167). The remarkable "Oda pešemu xodu" ("Ode to Walking"), published for the first time in *Izbrannoe*, pp. 187–191, was rejected by *Sovremennye Zapiski* in 1934 as allegedly "incomprehensible to the average reader" (Letters to Ivask, p. 217). "Živoe o živom," as published in *Sovremennye Zapiski* and reprinted in *Proza*, lacks several delightful pages devoted to Pra (Vološin's mother) which are found in the manuscript of this memoir at Basel University Library.

generation of Russian poets and prose writers which has recently
been dubbed the Unnoticed Generation.[12] The writings of these
younger men and women sounded what is now referred to as the
Paris Note[13]—metaphysical anguish, despair, existential boredom,
which went hand in hand with distrust of technical brilliance and a
lack of concern for the verbal aspect of literary art. The Paris Note
suited the talents of certain minor younger poets (Anatolij Štejger,
Terapiano, Lidija Červinskaja), but adherence to it also had a
disastrous effect on the most gifted poet of that generation, Boris
Poplavskij, by causing him to renounce in his later poems the
remarkable visual imagery and verbal melodiousness which constituted the main strength of his poetry. The phenomenon was a very
odd case of the lesser poets and critics revolting against and rejecting
the poetry of their major contemporaries—Pasternak, Xodasevič,
and Marina Cvetaeva (Mandel'štam was all but forgotten in Paris
in the thirties). Cvetaeva's peripheral role, as far as those younger
writers were concerned, can be gauged by examining their main
literary organ, the journal Čisla. In the eight thick volumes of Čisla
published between 1930 and 1934, we find only one poem and one
brief piece of literary criticism by Cvetaeva.[14] Another new Paris
literary journal, Vstreči, edited by G. Adamovič and M. Kantor,
turned out to be surprisingly hospitable to Cvetaeva,[15] but it was
discontinued after only six months of publication on a monthly
basis. Despite Cvetaeva's lack of influence on the younger poets
connected with Čisla, she was still enough of a member of the
Russian literary community in Paris to be invited to participate in a
public poetry reading organized by Čisla in March, 1933, in which
she appeared in the second half of the program, alongside such older

[12] In the book by V. S. Varšavskij (Nezamečennoe pokolenie [New York,
1956]) which discusses the work of these writers.

[13] For discussion of the "Paris Note," see G. Adamovič, "Poèzija v
èmigracii," Opyty, IV (1955), 45–61, and the articles by Vladimir Markov and
N. Berberova in Mosty, I (Munich, 1958), 174–178, 179–180. V. Nabokov
ridicules the same phenomenon in Speak, Memory (New York, n.d.), pp.
213–214.

[14] "Dva Lesnyx Carja," Čisla, X (1934), 212–216; "Nereida," Čisla, II–III
(1930), 5–7. There was no critical discussion of Cvetaeva's work on the pages
of Čisla.

[15] Vstreči published Cvetaeva's memoirs, "Otkrytie muzeja" and "Xlystovki," and a portion of her cycle of poems "Ici-haut." (See bibliography.)

poets as Bal'mont, Gippius, and Merežkovskij.[16] The journal *Novyj Grad*, which specialized in philosophical and religious problems, commissioned Cvetaeva to write a comparative study of the poetry of Pasternak and Majakovskij, which it printed in two installments in 1933. In her letters to G. P. Fedotov, who was one of the editors of *Novyj Grad*, Cvetaeva repeatedly expresses her gratitude for his "humane editing" of her text, pointing out that she had not been so decently treated by an editor since *Volja Rossii* closed.

After the departure of Svjatopolk-Mirskij for the Soviet Union in 1932 (where he was to perish in the purges of the late thirties), the only émigré critic to devote separate articles to Cvetaeva's poetry was the poet Jurij (George) Ivask, then resident in Tallinn, Estonia.[17] The occasional references to Cvetaeva in Soviet criticism in the nineteen-thirties, while hostile for political reasons, make it clear that the authors realized the quality of her poetic achievement.[18] In Paris, however, despite the occasional complimentary tone of Adamovič, the only critic to give Cvetaeva her due in the thirties was Vladislav Xodasevič.[19] Otherwise, the general attitude of the Russian literary community in Paris during the thirties was that an extremely talented poet had somehow wrecked her talent by following wrong influences,[20] by being undesirably brilliant, or by becoming obscure and incomprehensible. Outside of Paris, the

[16] The first part of the program was devoted to the younger poets: Ladinskij, Poplavskij, Knut, Červinskaja. *Poslednie Novosti* (Paris), March 16, 1933; *Čisla*, IX (1933), 193.

[17] Jurij Ivask, "Cvetaeva," in *Nov'*, VI (Tallinn, 1934), 61–66; Jurij Ivask, "Popytka nametit' temu," *Meč* (Warsaw), March 8, 1936.

[18] E.g., K. Zelinskij, *Kritičeskie pis'ma*, II (Moscow, 1934), 147.

[19] Reviewing regularly in the newspaper *Vozroždenie* the works of Cvetaeva which appeared in *Sovremennye Zapiski*, Xodasevič, despite an occasional reservation, wrote of her poetry in the nineteen-thirties with far greater enthusiasm and admiration than he did in the twenties (e.g., V. Xodasevič, "Knigi i ljudi," *Vozroždenie* [Paris], April 6, 1933). He had nothing but glowing praise for her prose of the thirties.

[20] This theory was most recently reasserted by Georgij Adamovič in his book *Odinočestvo i svoboda* (New York, 1955), p. 223, where we read: "She attempted to acquire Pasternak's traits and ruined her once charming talent." Adamovič goes on to list the stylistic traits of Cvetaeva which he ascribes to Pasternak's influence. The idea is untenable chronologically, since the traits in question appear in *Lebedinyj stan*, "Na krasnom kone," and *Remeslo*, all of which were written before Cvetaeva became familiar with Pasternak's poetry in 1922.

legend of Cvetaeva's decline was not necessarily shared by the émigré critics. The literary scholar and critic A. L. Bem, who resided in Prague, wrote of Cvetaeva with respect and admiration in his periodic surveys of current literature that were published in the early nineteen-thirties in the Berlin newspaper *Rul'* and the Warsaw newspaper *Molva*. The Russian poets and critics who resided in the Far East (Arsenij Nesmelov, Natalija Reznikova) likewise did not cease to consider Cvetaeva one of the major twentieth-century Russian poets.

In 1933, Jurij Ivask was contemplating writing a book on Marina Cvetaeva.[21] He wrote to her, and for the next four years, led on by Ivask's skillful questioning, Cvetaeva kept writing to him about her past, her literary tastes, her current activities. Cvetaeva's letters to Ivask, now in the Houghton Library, Harvard University, are a basic, enormously rich source for studying her life, her work, and her *Weltanschauung*. They also contain valuable and helpful commentary on some of Cvetaeva's more difficult poems, most notably "Pereuločki" and "Tezej."

Despite the material and physical hardship (in one of her letters to Ivask, Cvetaeva speaks of suffering from boils which resulted from chronic malnutrition and which were treated with injections at a charity clinic for unemployed Russians), despite critical misunderstanding and neglect, Cvetaeva steadily went on writing. A new tragic note in her poetry is sounded most powerfully in two of her best known short poems of the thirties, "Rolandov rog" ("Roland's Horn") and "Toska po rodine! Davno . . ." ("Homesickness"), her two supreme declarations of loneliness and independence.[22] The themes of homelessness and homesickness for Russia become important, and there is an occasional touch of interest in and sympathy for the current life in the U.S.S.R.[23]

In Cvetaeva's work of the nineteen-thirties, there occurs an important shift in genres. There are no more works for the theater and no more *poèmy* after the nineteen-twenties. On the other hand,

[21] Jurij Ivask, "Cvetaeva," footnote on p. 61. According to the author, now Professor George Ivask of the University of Washington, the book was never finished and the manuscript has been lost.

[22] *Izbrannoe*, p. 199 and pp. 206–207.

[23] *Ibid.*, "Stixi k synu" ("Verses to My Son"), pp. 192–196; "Čeljuskincy" ("The Celjuskin Expedition"), pp. 208–209.

there is a marked increase of prose in her output, and her prose works grow not only in quantity, but in quality as well. Cvetaeva's intense meditations on the relationship between the ethical and the aesthetic in art led to plans for a book on the subject. A portion of this planned book was published in *Sovremennye Zapiski* under the title "Iskusstvo pri svete sovesti" (as we have seen, in a mutilated and abridged form), and another essay on related topics, "Poèt i vremja" ("The Poet and Time"), possibly a part of the same projected book, appeared in one of the last issues of *Volja Rossii*.[24] A third related essay, "Poets with History and Poets without History," in which she discusses the later poetry of Pasternak and compares it with the work of Axmatova, Blok, and Mandel'štam, found no publisher in Paris and we know it only from a Serbo-Croatian translation which appeared in the Belgrade journal devoted to Russian culture, *Ruski Arhiv*.[25]

Another group of Cvetaeva's prose works is ushered in by her memoir about Maksimilian Vološin, published in *Sovremennye Zapiski* as "Živoe o živom." Natalija Reznikova, a poet and novelist who lived in the Far East, wrote of this memoir: "Marina Cvetaeva in her memoirs of Maksimilian Vološin . . . scales the heights of artistic prose. It would seem that Cvetaeva has overcome all the feminine weaknesses and has retained only that which is most beautiful in a woman—tenderness, sensitivity, loyalty to the past and nobility." [26] As the news of Vološin's death led to "Živoe o živom" in 1933, so the news of Andrej Belyj's death brought about "Plennyj dux" in 1934, and the death of Mixail Kuzmin inspired "Nezdešnij večer" in 1936. At the end of 1934, Nikolaj Gronskij was accidentally killed by a subway train and his poems were published posthumously. Cvetaeva was not personally close to him during the last years of his life, but she felt close to him as a poet and considered him the most important of the younger Russian poets in Paris. Gronskij's father, who was on the editorial board of Milju-kov's newspaper *Poslednie Novosti*, requested Cvetaeva to write an

---

[24] *Volja Rossii*, I–III (1932), 3–22.

[25] "Pesnici sa istorijom i pesnici bez istorije," *Ruski Arhiv*, XXVI–XXVII (Belgrade, 1934), 104–142.

[26] N. R. (Natalija Reznikova), "Knižnye novinki," *Rubež*, No. 26 (Harbin, 1933), p. 24.

essay on his son's poetry, which he hoped to publish in that newspaper.[27] Cvetaeva's relations with *Poslednie Novosti* had improved since the Majakovskij incident of 1928 to the point where the newspaper again began to publish her work—the memoirs "Bašnja v pljušče" and "Skazka materi," the latter of which to her horror appeared with forty editorial corrections and deletions. Cvetaeva's essay on Gronskij was found too long by *Poslednie Novosti,* and she was requested to rework it into two shorter articles. After she had complied with the request, the editors delayed publication for three months and finally refused to publish the essay at all.[28] In the meantime, *Poslednie Novosti* chose to run an article on Gronskij by G. Adamovič who was their regular literary critic. Adamovič had not heard of Nikolaj Gronskij or his poetry prior to his death, and he produced a glib and superficial review, which was bound to irritate Cvetaeva.[29] In describing the incident to Ivask, she had every reason to exclaim: "I am being *viciously* mocked here, they play with my *pride,* my *need,* my *lack of rights* (There is no defense)." Cvetaeva had her say on Gronskij's poetry at a public lecture and in a brief half-page review of his posthumous collection in *Sovremennye Zapiski.* Her long essay about his death and about his poem "Belladonna" is another of Cvetaeva's works from the thirties that we know only from a Serbo-Croatian translation.[30]

That loyalty to the past of which Natalija Reznikova wrote did not mean for Marina Cvetaeva only celebrating the memory of dead writer-friends like Vološin and Gronskij in prose and poetry. It also meant trying to defend Mandel'štam against grotesque and distorted presentation in memoirs of his former friends. It meant keeping up friendly relations with old friends who were still alive, such as Prince Sergej Volkonskij and Bal'mont, both of whom she kept seeing in the thirties. At that time Bal'mont was in his sixties, unjustly forgotten, lonely, and subject to periodic mental breakdowns which necessitated hospitalization. Cvetaeva helped organize

[27] Letters to Ivask, pp. 223–224.

[28] *Ibid.,* p. 224.

[29] G. Adamovič, "N. P. Gronskij," *Poslednie Novosti* (Paris), December 9, 1934.

[30] "Pesnik Alpinist" ("Poet-Mountain Climber"), *Ruski Arhiv,* XXXII–XXXIII (Belgrade, 1935), 62–88.

the commemoration of the fiftieth anniversary of Bal'mont's literary activity at which she recited a valedictory speech in honor of the aged poet, written for the occasion.[31] The same loyalty to the past caused Cvetaeva to reexamine her own childhood and adolescence in a series of memoirs which appeared in the thirties in *Sovremennye Zapiski* and *Vstreči*. Her personal memoirs, as well as those about writers, often served Cvetaeva as topics for her one or two annual public readings.

In January, 1933, Cvetaeva changed residence, moving to 10, rue Lazare Carnot, Clamart; early in 1935 she again moved, this time to the suburb of Vanves (33, rue Jean Baptiste Potin). She continued sharing residence with Sergej Èfron, and they remained on cordial terms. But they had been drifting more and more apart since the nineteen-twenties, and by 1935 each of them led a separate existence and each knew very little about the activities of the other. While recovering from his illness and regaining his ability to work, Èfron underwent a political evolution which eventually led him to join the Union of Returnees, a pro-Soviet organization among the Russian émigrés in Paris, the official purpose of which was to facilitate the return of exiled Russians to the Soviet Union. Soon he became a full-time official of the Union. Cvetaeva's daughter Alja, who was studying to become an artist, shared her father's convictions.[32]

Cvetaeva's unpublished letters to her friend Salomea Halpern give us important insights into her and her husband's states of mind during those years. In her letter of October 2, 1933, we read: "Sergej is here, there is still no passport [apparently, Èfron had applied for a Soviet passport and was refused], which makes me profoundly happy, for the letters of those who have returned (I myself saw them off and waved goodbye!) are most eloquent [. . .]. Besides, I am definitely not going, this would mean separation, which, for all our bickering, would be hard after twenty years of togetherness

[31] The celebration took place on April 24, 1936. Cvetaeva's Bal'mont speech was published only in a Serbo-Croatian translation ("Reč o Baljmontu," *Ruski Arhiv*, XXXVIII–XXXIX [Belgrade, 1936], 58–67).

[32] According to F. Kubka (*Hlasy od Východu*, p. 23), in the mid-thirties, Ariadna Èfron took a job with a French Communist newspaper. Kubka also states that Sergej Èfron's connection with the Union of Returnees dates from 1932.

(*sovmestnost'*). And the reason I am not going is that I had already left once. (Salomea, did you happen to see the film *Je suis un évadé* [the American film *I Am a Fugitive from the Chain Gang*, starring Paul Muni], where a convict voluntarily returns to forced labor—well, then!)." A year and a half later, the situation is similar: "S. Ja. [Sergej Jakovlevič] is torn between his country and his family. I *firmly* refuse to go, and ending a twenty-year togetherness, even when one has 'new ideas' is hard. So he is torn asunder" (April 6, 1934). Cvetaeva did not realize at the time that her husband, to alleviate his sense of guilt for participating in the Civil War on the White side and for failing to return to Soviet Russia after his conversion, had entered the services of Soviet intelligence agencies and was engaging on their behalf in activities directed against other émigré Russians.

In June, 1935, there was held in Paris a Communist-sponsored "Congress of Writers in Defense of Culture," in which Boris Pasternak participated as one of the Soviet delegates. This gave Cvetaeva and Pasternak a chance to meet in person after many years of correspondence, and it is typical of both poets that during the debates of the congress they retired to the corridor, where Cvetaeva recited her new poems to Pasternak.[33] In his autobiography, Pasternak tells of visiting Cvetaeva's home during the congress, of meeting her family, and of being asked by Cvetaeva whether she should return to the Soviet Union. "Members of Cvetaeva's family were urging her to return to Russia. They were motivated in part by homesickness and by sympathies for Communism and the Soviet Union and in part by the realization that life in Paris was not right for Cvetaeva and that she was wasted there without any responsive readers. Cvetaeva asked me what I thought about it. I had no definite opinion on the subject. I did not know what to advise her and was all too afraid that in our country she and her remarkable family would experience difficulty and insecurity. The total tragedy of the family exceeded by far my fears." [34]

Early in the summer of 1936, Cvetaeva received a book of verse from Anatolij Štejger, one of the most typical of the Russian poets

[33] Èrenburg, "Ljudi, gody, žizn'," *Novyj Mir,* IV (1962), 48.
[34] Pasternak, *Proza 1915–1958,* pp. 46–47.

of the Unnoticed Generation. Cvetaeva had met him briefly at one of
her public lectures, and she was on friendly terms with his sister, the
poet Alla Golovina. She replied with a letter which reached Štejger
in a tubercular sanatorium in Switzerland. The correspondence that
ensued gave rise to a relationship between the two poets that has
been described, with fairness and sensitivity, by Štejger's friend
Kirill Vil'čkovskij.[35] Štejger's poetry, aphoristic and fragile, did not
particularly impress or interest Cvetaeva. She did, however, see him
primarily as a poet, a romantic wanderer who lay desperately ill in a
sanatorium and who pleaded urgently for her help and understanding. His descent from a historical figure she admired may have
contributed to his attraction[36] as did his belonging to a hostile
literary camp (Štejger was a close friend of Cvetaeva's literary
adversary Adamovič and an admirer of the poetry of Poplavskij
which Cvetaeva disliked). In one of her earlier letters to Štejger,
Cvetaeva wrote: "For years now—eight years, I believe[37]—I have
been living in absolute indifference, that is loving very much this
one or that one or a third one, doing for them everything I can,
because someone has to do things, but without any personal joy—or
pain: when they leave for Russia I see them off, when they come to
visit me I offer them food. You with your letter broke through my
icy crust, under which I at once fell, head and all. You."

The relationship with Štejger is in many ways similar to the one
with Baxrax. In both cases Cvetaeva's main motivation was the need
to be needed. In August and September of 1936, Štejger was
recovering from an operation in a Berne hospital, while Cvetaeva
lived in the Savoy (St. Pierre-de-Rumilly, Haute Savoie, Chateau
d'Arcine), not far from the Swiss border. She wrote to him every
few days and at the same time composed a cycle of poems about him
which were later published under the misleading general title "Stixi

---

[35] Kirill Vil'čkovskij, "Perepiska Mariny Cvetaevoj s Anatoliem Štejgerom,"
Opyty, V (New York, 1955), 40–45.
[36] Nikolaus Friedrich von Steiger (1729–1799), leader of the conservative
Swiss emigration at the time of the French Revolution. Cvetaeva showed a
lack of understanding for Štejger's personality and for the nature of his talent
when she proposed that he should write a *poèma* about his militant ancestor
(Letters to Štejger, *Opyty,* V [New York, 1955], 48–49).
[37] I.e., since the "military friendship" with Nikolaj Gronskij in 1928.

sirote" ("Verses to an Orphan").[38] In the last poem of the cycle, the theme of mutual need is sounded by Cvetaeva in a frankly joyous key:

Наконец-то встретила	At last I met
Надобного — мне:	The very one I need:
У кого-то смертная	The one who has a mortal
Надоба — во мне.	Need of me.

Štejger's need of Cvetaeva did not prove lasting. As his poetry makes amply clear, his own strong emotional involvements were with other males. He was of solitary, independent character (Vil'čkovskij speaks of Štejger's "catlike independence"), and Cvetaeva's affection and possessiveness ended by frightening him. When he recovered sufficiently from his illness, he made Cvetaeva's mistake clear to her. For several months in the summer of 1936 her correspondence with Štejger was the central fact of Cvetaeva's existence. There remain from it twenty-seven emotional and witty letters (of which only a portion has been published so far),[39] and a cycle of six poems was added to Cvetaeva's poetic canon. When her poems to Štejger were published, Cvetaeva provided them with a bitterly ironic epigraph from a popular Russian ditty: "There walked along the street a little baby / He turned blue and was shivering / Along the same road there walked an old lady / She took pity on the orphan. . . ."[40] After the end of their correspondence, Cvetaeva was still concerned about Štejger's welfare (in her letters to Ivask the following winter she urged him to meet Štejger and to try to help him), though she spoke of him with frank

[38] Originally published in *Sovremennye Zapiski,* LXVI, (1938) 188–191, and reprinted in *Izbrannoe,* pp. 221–226, in both cases without any reference to Štejger.

[39] Of Cvetaeva's twenty-seven letters to Štejger, to which Vil'čkovskij had access when he wrote his article, only seventeen were released for publication by Štejger's family. Ten of these appeared in *Opyty,* V (1955), 45–67, two in *Opyty,* VII (1956), 8–18, and one in *Opyty,* VIII (1957), 21–26. Copies of the four remaining letters are in the possession of Professor Ivask. Several editorial deletions were made in the letters by Štejger's family before they were released for publication.

[40] Cvetaeva was fourteen years older than Štejger (1907–1944). The ironic epigraph accompanied the cycle at the time of its publication in *Sovremennye Zapiski.* It has not been reprinted in *Izbrannoe,* although without it the title of the cycle loses its *raison d'être.*

disappointment. Once again she returned to her familiar emotional vacuum and to her literary work.

Puškin had always been for Cvetaeva the central phenomenon of Russian literature, and his life and work had provided themes for several of her poems written in July, 1931, and for numerous digressions in "Natalija Gončarova." In 1937, with the commemoration of the centenary of Puškin's death, he assumed a major importance in Cvetaeva's work, inspiring the memoir "Moj Puškin" (possibly the last echo of Cvetaeva's quarrel with Valerij Brjusov, since the title of the memoir is identical with that of Brjusov's volume of Puškin essays published posthumously in 1929); the critical essay "Puškin i Pugačëv" ("Puškin and Pugačëv"), one of Cvetaeva's finest, which examines Puškin's treatment of the eighteenth-century rebel in a work of fiction (*Captain's Daughter*) and in an historical study (*History of Pugačëv's Rebellion*); and a cycle of poems, some of which, however, were written several years earlier.[41]

Early in 1937, Cvetaeva's daughter, Ariadna Èfron, voluntarily returned to Russia; she settled in Moscow and obtained work as an illustrator. One of her daughter's first letters from Moscow brought Cvetaeva the news that her old friend Sonečka Holliday, with whom she had not corresponded since she left Russia, had died of cancer a few years earlier. The news of Sonečka's death brought back the memories of their deep mutual affection in the cold and starving Moscow of 1918–1919, of the friendships with Antokol'skij and with a heroic young actor identified as Volodja A. (Vladimir Alekseev?), and of Cvetaeva's infatuation with Jurij Zavadskij. Using her own diaries of the period and those of her daughter, Cvetaeva spent the summer of 1937 at the seacoast, writing a lengthy memoir about that time of meager rations and intense emotions. "Povest' o Sonečke" ("The Story of Sonečka") brings to life not only Sonečka herself but the whole of Cvetaeva's disorganized postrevolutionary existence, with its particular mixture of privation and creativity. The figure of Volodja A., who gives up a successful acting career in Moscow and makes his way to the Crimea to join

[41] *Sovremennye Zapiski*, LXIII, 172–176, and LXIV, 173–174. As the dating in *Izbrannoe* indicates, some of "Stixi k Puškinu" printed in these two volumes were written as early as 1931.

the White forces there, losing his life in the process, is particularly revealing. Appearing in a work written at a time when Cvetaeva herself must have been seriously planning to return to the Soviet Union, the figure of this actor, with his halo of unselfishness and heroism, testifies to Cvetaeva's total lack of opportunism and her utter inability (and unwillingness) to betray her own past.

Among the editors of *Sovremennye Zapiski,* in which her work continued to appear, the one who was on best terms with Cvetaeva was I. I. Bunakov-Fondaminskij (1880–1942) of whom Vladimir Nabokov wrote that he was "a saintly and heroic soul who did more for Russian émigré literature than any other man and who died in a German prison."[42] It was Bunakov-Fondaminskij who organized the publishing venture "Russkie poèty" in which a volume of Cvetaeva's poems was scheduled to appear (but never did because of Cvetaeva's departure from Paris and the beginning of the Second World War). He was evidently also responsible for the prominent position given to Cvetaeva's work in the new journal, *Russkie Zapiski,* which he helped edit and which was an offshoot of *Sovremennye Zapiski.* However, with the fourth volume of *Russkie Zapiski,* Bunakov-Fondaminskij's editorial job was taken over by P. N. Miljukov, with the result that the promised continuation of "Povest' o Sonečke" scheduled for that fourth volume never appeared and no further work by Marina Cvetaeva was published in *Russkie Zapiski.*[43] It is ironical indeed that Miljukov, one of the acknowledged leaders of the White emigration, thus prevented the émigrés from reading the section of the memoir that glorified the pro-White Volodja, the same Miljukov who a decade earlier had discontinued the publication of *Lebedinyj stan* because of Cvetaeva's sympathy for Majakovskij. This time, however, he might have had an additional reason for his ban on Cvetaeva. By the end of 1937, Marina Cvetaeva's personal situation in Paris and her relations with

[42] *Speak, Memory,* p. 216. In the Russian version of this book, Nabokov called Bunakov-Fondaminskij "the most humane of human beings" (*Drugie berega,* p. 242).

[43] The first part of "Povest' o Sonečke" appeared in *Russkie Zapiski,* III (1938), 36–103. The complete manuscript of this work was deposited by Cvetaeva before her departure for the Soviet Union in the library of Basel University, Switzerland. A copy of the manuscript of the second part has been made available to me through the courtesy of Professor Else Mahler.

other Russian émigrés took a turn which was truly appalling and which was due to the political activities and involvements of Sergej Èfron.

In September, 1937, a bullet-riddled corpse of an unknown man was found on a road near Lausanne. The dead man turned out to be Ignatij Reis (Ignace Reiss), an important official of the G.P.U. who had been sent to France and Holland on an intelligence assignment; he subsequently became disillusioned with Stalin's policies and decided to remain abroad. An investigation by French and Swiss authorities of the circumstances of the murder revealed a large international network of Soviet espionage and terror in France, in which the Paris Union of Returnees was deeply involved. At the trial of Renate Steiner, a Swiss girl who was an accessory to the murder of Reis, the accused testified that she was recruited for espionage activities at the Union of Returnees by Sergej Èfron. Other investigations disclosed that Èfron had helped plan the murder of Andrej Sedov, the son of Trockij.[44] Very soon after the discovery of Reis's body, Sergej Èfron disappeared from Paris, making his way according to some accounts first to Spain and eventually to the Soviet Union.

We have several contradictory versions of how Marina Cvetaeva learned of the accusations against her husband. According to E. N. Fedotova (the widow of G. P. Fedotov), "I. I. Fondaminskij . . . immediately rushed off to see Marina Ivanovna. He told us later that M. I. sobbed violently and was ready to swear to him that Èfron could not be involved in the bloody affair." In the account of Elena Izvol'skaja, Cvetaeva was picked up by the French police for interrogation on the very night of Èfron's disappearance and

---

[44] The most detailed account of the murders of Reis and Sedov and Sergej Èfron's role in each is to be found in N. Vakar, "Agenty Ežova za-granicej," *Poslednie Novosti* (Paris), July 19, 1938. There was a special brochure on the Reis case published in French (Victor Serge, Maurice Wullens, Alfred Rosmer, *L'Assassinat politique et l'U.R.S.S.* [Paris, 1938]), and numerous stories on various ramifications of the case are to be found in Russian émigré newspapers throughout 1938 (e.g., V. Zenzinov's articles on the Reis case in *Meč* [Warsaw], May 29 and June 5, 1938). Almost all reports mention Èfron, but only the New York Russian-language newspaper *Novoe Russkoe Slovo* made any specific reference to Cvetaeva in connection with the case (A. Sedyx, "Kakuju rol' igrala Lidija Grozovskaja v ubijstve Reisa i poxiščenii gen. E. K. Millera," issue of February 9, 1938).

countered their questioning by reciting the French version of *Mólodec.* Whatever the sequence of events was, Mme Izvol'skaja is evidently right when she says that Cvetaeva knew nothing of her husband's activities and that her "loyalty, absolute confidence in Serëža remained unshaken." [45]

Cvetaeva remained in France until the summer of 1939. It is during those last eighteen months that the subsequent remark of Vladimir Markov, "Cvetaeva is on the conscience of Paris" [46] (meaning Russian Paris), is applicable in its full literary and human sense. It was the time when many Russians in Paris were badly demoralized by the Reis case and by the spectacular trial of the famous singer Plevickaja for her complicity in the Soviet abduction of the émigré leader General Miller. Rumors about Èfron's activities circulated in the Russian colony long before the Reis case began to be mentioned in the press early in 1938. Almost all accounts of Cvetaeva's last year in Paris indicate persecution by fellow Russians. The activities of her husband of which she did not know and which she did not understand were repeatedly denounced in the émigré press. She refused to believe these accounts and had to suffer the predictable and dreary consequences of guilt-by-association. Her Russian neighbors forced her to leave her home in Vanves, and she had to move to a cheap hotel at 13, Boulevard Pasteur. On October 31, 1937, she attended a requiem mass for Prince Sergej Volkonskij. She gave no public readings (her last one took place in March, 1937) and her last appearance in print in Paris was in *Sovremennye Zapiski* early in 1938 ("Stixi sirote"). From then on she was to all intents and purposes ostracized by the literary community in Paris. In her last conversation with Mme Fedotova sometime in 1938, Cvetaeva stated that she would have to go to Russia because no one would publish her in Paris. At the end of that year, Jurij Ivask, who was visiting Paris, asked one of the more popular of younger Russian writers

---

[45] According to Zinaida Šaxovskaja (Zinaida Schakovskoy, "Tombeau de poètes," *L'Age nouveau,* LXII [Paris, 1951], 12–16), Cvetaeva's reply to the questions of the French police was: "La bonne foi d'Èfron a pu être surprise . . . ma foi en lui reste intacte" (p. 14).

[46] Vladimir Markov, "Zametki na poljax," *Opyty,* VI (1956), 62. As Z. Šaxovskaja rather dramatically expressed the same idea, "Marina Tzvetaéva resta seule face à l'émigration qui ne pardonne et n'oublie rien" (*op. cit.,* p. 14).

why he never saw Cvetaeva and the reply was: "Oh, there is no need to and it isn't done." [47] Ivask met Cvetaeva during the visit, and she told him that she was planning to leave for the Soviet Union, where she had no hopes of publishing and expected to live by doing literary translations.

In the spring of 1938, there was a great deal of Russian literary activity in Paris. A newly organized Russian theater presented new plays by Aldanov, Berberova, Vladimir Nabokov. In April, a Russian writers' ball was held, attended by all the well-known literary figures in Paris.[48] In May, there was an "Evening of Contemporary Poetry" with readings by all Russian poets of any repute.[49] The name of Marina Cvetaeva is conspicuously absent from the announcements of all those events. She was on the seacoast at Dives-sur-Mer, revising and correcting the manuscripts of her unpublished earlier poems. There is no sufficient, reliable material at the present time to evaluate fully Cvetaeva's mood and motives during that period. The paramount factor in her final decision was undoubtedly her concern for the future of her son. Memoirs describe young Georgij Èfron as a husky, unruly boy, not particularly imaginative, and certainly not as close to his mother intellectually as his older sister had once been. According to the recollections of Professor Ivask, the fourteen-year-old Georgij, or Mur as he was usually called, kept pleading with his mother to leave for the U.S.S.R. where he could have a future and complaining of his inability to get along with French boys because of his political views. In a conversation reported by Mme Fedotova, Cvetaeva's concern for her son's situation is likewise emphasized. E. Izvol'skaja ("Ten' na stenax," p. 154) also advances the supposition that Cvetaeva returned to Russia because of her son. It is in this light that we can understand Pasternak's perceptive statement that Cvetaeva hid from the everyday world behind her creative work all her life, until "it appeared to her that this was an impermissible luxury and for the sake of her son she had to sacrifice temporarily her absorbing passion and look around herself soberly." [50]

[47] Jurij Ivask, "O čitateljax Cvetaevoj," *Novoe Russkoe Slovo,* June 30, 1957.
[48] *Poslednie Novosti* (Paris), April 2, 1938.
[49] *Ibid.,* May 10, 1938.
[50] Pasternak, *Proza 1915–1958,* p. 38.

The intrusion of politics and violence into her life made Cvetaeva, the poet, also take a closer look at the world in which she was living. The Spanish Civil War, the invasion of Czechoslovakia, the menacing stance of Hitler's Germany outraged and repelled her. In September, 1938 and in March, 1939, politics again entered her poetry as strongly as during the Russian Civil War. Cvetaeva expressed her indignation at Hitler's takeover of Czechoslovakia in two cycles of poems [51] written with fire and passion, technical brilliance and precision, and a great human solicitude. These cycles show that Cvetaeva's stature as a poet remained undiminished at the time of her worst trials. The note of despair expressed in the poem beginning "O slëzy na glazax!" (dated March 15–May 11, 1939) is stronger than anything comparable in her previous poetry. The poem paraphrases the famous Schiller-Dostoevskij formula ("Pora —pora—pora / Tvorcu vernut' bilet" ["It is time—it is time—it is time / To return the entrance ticket to the Creator"] and ends with the following apostrophe to God:

> На Твой безумный мир
> Ответ один — отказ.

> To Thy insane world
> [There is only] one answer: a refusal.

During her stay at Dives-sur-Mer in the spring of 1938, Cvetaeva prepared clean and legible manuscripts of her works connected with the White Army—the collection *Lebedinyj stan* and the *poèma* "Perekóp," for which she provided a new set of annotations. Shortly before her final departure for the Soviet Union she deposited these manuscripts in the library of Basel University with a note indicating her hope that those works might be eventually published and requesting that in such case the old, pre-Revolutionary Russian orthography be used.[52]

In the Houghton Library, Harvard, there is a letter written by Marina Cvetaeva to M. and Mme Bogenhardt (apparently friends of Sergej Èfron), dated July 7, 1939. In this letter she bids her final

---

[51] *Izbrannoe*, pp. 227–242. The first of the two cycles ("Sentjabr' ") has not yet been published in its entirety.

[52] *Lebedinyj stan*, p. 4 (Introduction by Gleb Struve).

farewell and expresses her great regret at having to leave Paris. It is clear from the letter that she was looking forward to the reunion with her husband. The departure was sad. After her decision became known, Cvetaeva met in the street Štejger's sister, Alla Golovina. To questions about her departure, Cvetaeva replied with a brief improvised poem in which she compared her departure with that of Mary, Queen of Scots: "Dano mne proščan'e Marii Stjuart ("Mary Stuart's farewell is my lot"). One of the last public appearances of Cvetaeva in Paris was described by Jurij Terapiano in words that read like a *mea culpa* of the Paris writers of his generation: "Now, when one thinks of Cvetaeva's fate, of her death, one is perplexed: how could we allow her to reach such depths of despair, how could we allow her to leave amidst general indifference? A few days before Cvetaeva's departure, Prince Širinskij-Šixmatov (who was later tortured to death in a Nazi concentration camp) gave a literary soirée. Among those present were Cvetaeva and her son—aloof, remote from everyone; she talked to almost no one and almost no one talked to her—she's leaving—let her leave! Who in the world cares?"[53]

Very shortly afterwards, Marina Cvetaeva and her son Georgij left Paris for the Soviet Union.[54] Within days after her departure, strong rumors began circulating among the Russians in Paris that Sergej Èfron had already been executed by shooting in Moscow.[55] The rumors reached the poet Zinaida Šaxovskaja in Brussels where she was then living. She sent a telegram to friends in Warsaw, asking them to intercept Marina Cvetaeva at the railroad station there and to warn her. The telegram came too late, but, as Mme Šaxovskaja so aptly put it: "d'ailleurs, vers quoi aurait-elle pu retourner?"[56]

[53] Ju. Terapiano, "Proza Mariny Cvetaevoj," *Novoe Russkoe Slovo*, March 7, 1954.

[54] By piecing together the information provided by F. Kubka (*op. cit.*, p. 24), E. N. Fedotova, and Z. Šaxovskaja, one can deduce that Cvetaeva traveled by ship from Le Havre to a Polish port (Gdynia?), and from there went by train to Moscow via Warsaw. Kubka's statement that she left from Le Havre in June, 1939, is disproved by the letter to the Bogenhardts, written in Paris in July, 1939.

[55] Gleb Struve, *Russkaja literatura v izgnanii*, p. 154.

[56] Zinaida Schakovskoy, *op. cit.*, p. 16. The author is the sister of Prince D. A. Šaxovskoj. She published poetry in Russian in Paris in the thirties and later

became known for her book of travel impressions of the Soviet Union, *Ma Russie déguisée en U.R.S.S.* (American edition, *The Privilege Was Mine* [New York, 1959]). Her account of Cvetaeva's last years in Paris, for all its noble and just indignation, is marred by unfortunate factual inaccuracies. Thus, Mme Šaxovskaja states that Èfron personally assassinated Reis and describes Cvetaeva's living conditions in the suburb of Issy-les-Moulineaux at a time when Cvetaeva actually lived in Vanves. There are other errors of fact in her article, and they make us disregard such interesting testimony as, for example, "Elle parle de ses rencontres avec Rainer Maria Rilke" (p. 13).

V

Elabuga And After

(1939–1941 and on to 1965)

Ах, Марина, давно уже время,
Да и труд не такой уж ахти,
Твой заброшенный прах в реквиеме
Из Елабуги перенести.

Ah, Marina, it is high time
And no great trouble to boot
To bring back your neglected remains
From Elabuga in a requiem.

BORIS PASTERNAK, 1942

Marina Cvetaeva's departure from Paris in the summer of 1939 was not reported in the Russian émigré press. Nor is there any record in the Soviet newspapers of her arrival in Moscow. No detailed, reliable material on her life between the time of her departure from Paris and her death has been published so far. No original literary works by Cvetaeva from that period are known to us; as yet, we know of no letters, no detailed or informative memoirs about her life in Moscow by other writers she must have met upon her return.

The memoirs of Èrenburg sum up the cricumstances surrounding Cvetaeva's return in three brief sentences: "S. Ja. Èfron was dead. Alja was far away. In Moscow, as well, Marina found herself alone."[1] To interpret Èrenburg's Aesopian language, this means that Èfron had already been executed at the time of her arrival, that Ariadna (Alja) Èfron, like the majority of émigré returnees to Stalin's Russia, was serving a sentence in a labor camp, and that the majority of Soviet writers and poets thought it best to shun Cvetaeva because of her émigré past.

Works of imaginative literature, and especially poetry, should not normally be used as materials for biography. In view of the paucity of other sources, however, it would seem permissible to draw on two remarkable poems which deal with Marina Cvetaeva's return to Russia. One is by Anna Axmatova, published in New York in 1963, but dated March, 1940.[2] It is an extremely beautiful and moving poem, amply repaying Cvetaeva's 1916 cycle in warmth and compassion. In the middle of the poem, the echo of Cvetaeva's voice is made to exclaim: "Today I have returned home, / Admire, O my native fields / What has happened to me for this. / Abyss has swallowed my loved ones / And my parents' home has been pillaged." The rest of the poem amounts to an eloquent summary of the tragedy of twentieth-century Russian literature: "Tonight, Marina, you and I / Are walking through the midnight capital / And behind us there are millions of such as we / And there is no procession more silent / All around ring the funeral bells / And the savage Muscovite moaning / Of the snowstorm which obliterates our traces."

The other poem, entitled "Marina," is by Pavel Antokol'skij.[3] Antokol'skij describes meeting the aged and grey-haired Cvetaeva[4] on an unidentified seacoast, and it is not clear whether the meeting was real or an imaginary one. Antokol'skij invites the heroine of the poem to look into the future out of her remote past and in this way to find the husband, the daughter, and the sister for whom she is so desparately searching. In terms of concrete information, the mentioning of a "sister" in Antokol'skij's poem may possibly indicate that Cvetaeva was prevented from seeing her sister Anastasija at the

---

[1] *Ljudi, gody, žizn'*, I–II, 378.

[2] *Vozdušnye Puti*, III (New York, 1963), 10.

[3] "Marina," in *Den' poèzii* (Moscow, 1962), p. 42.

[4] Those who saw Cvetaeva before her departure from Paris (e.g., Izvol'skaja, "Poèt obrečennosti," p. 159) mention the physical effect that the ordeal of her last year there had on her.

time of her arrival. The ninth stanza of the eleven-stanza poem is apparently an act of homage to the memory of Georgij Èfron.

V. Orlov's introduction to the 1961 Soviet edition of Cvetaeva's selected poems, which devotes twelve pages to her biography, has a single idyllic but obviously inadequate sentence about her life in Moscow after her return: "Cvetaeva settled in Moscow, occupied herself with translations, was preparing a collection of verse."[5] Èrenburg supplements this with a brief account of Cvetaeva's short and unsuccessful visit to him in search of help in August, 1941, less than one month before her death.[6] Boris Pasternak's autobiography has nothing to say about that period and does not even mention whether he met her after her return. Axmatova's poem indicates that the meeting for which Cvetaeva had hoped during her trip to St. Petersburg in 1916 had finally taken place in Moscow in 1940. Antokol'skij's poem likewise implies a reunion. These are the meager facts.[7]

Only one poem by Cvetaeva appeared in the Soviet Union during those two years (in fact, the only one to be printed there between 1924 and 1956), but it was a reprint of an old poem, written and published in Prague in the early nineteen-twenties.[8] The ban on

[5] *Izbrannoe*, p. 15.

[6] Èrenburg's account would indicate that Cvetaeva lived in Moscow from the time of her return until her evacuation sometime in August, 1941.

[7] The extremely well informed unsigned article on Cvetaeva in the (London) *Times Literary Supplement* (May 4, 1962, p. 312) speaks of an "ugly persecution" of Cvetaeva by some Soviet writers at the beginning of the German invasion of the Soviet Union (end of June, 1941). According to the article, Cvetaeva was "savagely attacked as 'parasite' and 'sponger' by some of her actively patriotic colleagues in the Writers' Union." No sources for this assertion are quoted, and no confirmation of the incident has been found in the Soviet press of the period. The recent memoirs of the writer Lidija Tolstaja-Libedinskaja (serialized in the early months of 1965 in the provincial journal *Sibirskie ogni* and reprinted in abridged form by M. Korjakov in his column "Listki iz bloknota," *NRS*, July 4, 1965) tell us that in her Moscow days Cvetaeva associated with the creator of "trans-sense" poetry, Aleksej Kručenyx, and the painter Lev Bruni—artists who like herself were tainted with the suspect and dangerous label of "modernism." A remarkable and courageous woman, Tolstaja-Libedinskaja met Cvetaeva on two occasions only (once at a picnic and once at the railroad station when Cvetaeva was leaving Moscow for Elabuga). For all their warmth and admiration, her memoirs tell us little of Cvetaeva that is of factual interest.

[8] "Starinnaja pesnja" ("An Ancient Song"), in the journal *30 Dnej* in 1941; originally, one of the set of three poems published in *Studenčeskie Gody*

original and independent poetry being a hard fact of Soviet life under Stalin, Cvetaeva was reduced to working as a literary translator, translating poets to whom she did not feel particularly close and who wrote in languages she did not know. Two of her translations were published during her lifetime: a brief poem by the Yiddish poet Perec and "The Ballad of Robin Hood" from a collection of old English ballads. The French-style final stress of the proper names (required by the meter) in Cvetaeva's translation of the latter poem testifies to her lack of familiarity with English. In 1947 an edition of epic poems by the nineteenth-century Georgian poet Važa Pšavela (real name, Luka Razikišvili) was brought out in Leningrad which contained Cvetaeva's translations of three of his long epics. More recently Cvetaeva's translations of contemporary Polish poets were made public; there is no telling what other translations by Cvetaeva may eventually emerge from the Soviet literary archives.

Elabuga is a town in the Tatar Autonomous Soviet Socialist Republic, located at the confluence of the rivers Tojma and Kama. In the eighteen-thirties it was the residence of the "cavalrymaiden" (*kavalerist-devica*) Nadežda Durova (1783–1866), the onetime transvestite heroine of the Napoleonic wars, whose memoirs were published by Puškin. Frequently idealized as a frail, sentimental girl in turn-of-the-century biographical novels by such juvenile favorites as Lidija Čarskaja (and in a popular Soviet musical comedy of the nineteen-forties), the real Durova was a gruff, pipe-smoking virago, whose rock-throwing fights with Elabuga street urchins became a local legend. Durova's money-mad younger brother, who was at one time the mayor of Elabuga, is the subject of several not particularly edifying anecdotes in Puškin's collection "Table Talk," including the unpleasant little episode involving an obese peasant woman who was sentenced to flogging and then seduced by Mayor Durov immediately after her punishment. Elabuga's further claim to distinction is as the birthplace of Ivan Šiškin, whose sentimental and mediocre painting of bear cubs in a pine forest is much admired by

---

(Prague, 1924), No. 1 (12). (Publication information on this poem is quoted from *Lebedinyj stan*, introductory note by the editor, Gleb Struve, p. 6.) The poem is reprinted in Ju. P. Ivask, ed. *Na Zapade* (New York, 1953), pp. 85–86.

Russians of middlebrow tastes. This was where Marina Cvetaeva found herself after being evacuated from Moscow in August of 1941.

She arrived on the 21st and, after a lengthy search, found a room that she rented for herself and her son. The room was small and separated by a flimsy partition from the quarters of the owners of the house, a local Elabuga couple named Bredel'ščikov, to whom her name meant nothing and who were puzzled by her conversations with her son in French. Georgij Èfron was given part-time work at ∨ a nearby airfield that was being built. Marina Cvetaeva also looked for work; the only job she was offered was that of a kitchen maid in a public mess hall. Several days after reaching Elabuga, she traveled to the town of Čistopol' to visit the poet Nikolaj Aseev, one-time Futurist, a disciple and protégé of Majakovskij, and formerly a close friend of Boris Pasternak, but after the nineteen-thirties a cautious and sycophantic conformist to the official line. Aseev, who was living with a group of other evacuated writers, never made public what happened during that visit. Apart from assuming that Cvetaeva's visit to Aseev was as uncomfortable for both sides as her visit to Èrenburg had been a few weeks earlier, speculations would be pointless. In Aseev's archive there may yet be a document that would tell us about Cvetaeva's mood during her last days. What we do know is that she returned from her trip to Čistopol' in a state of acute mental depression and utter hopelessness.[9]

On August 31, 1941, Marina Cvetaeva hanged herself in Elabuga. ∨ Her suicide note was addressed to Nikolaj Aseev; in it she asked him to look after her son (to no avail, as it turned out). She was forty-eight years old. Her death was not reported in the Soviet press. There was no drawn-out funeral procession of her friends through the streets of Moscow, as she had predicted in the famous poem from *Versty I,* written at Easter of 1916. The unknown young passerby, addressed in a poem of 1913, will never be able to follow the invitation to pause briefly at a tombstone, a bunch of lupine and wild poppies in his hand, to read her epitaph; for Marina Cvetaeva, one of Russia's great poets of the twentieth century, was buried in

[9] The description of Cvetaeva's last days and of her burial is based on a reliable document received from the Soviet Union which cannot, at the moment, be further identified.

Elabuga with strangers in a common unmarked grave. The Bredel'ščikovs, unaware that their tenant was someone exceptional, did not bother to attend her funeral. In 1960, Cvetaeva's sister Anastasija, who was apparently in a labor camp at the time of her suicide, traveled to Elabuga to locate her sister's grave. No one there was able to tell her the exact location of the burial; an approximate spot was finally selected and on it Anastasija Cvetaeva arranged to have a wooden cross placed with the inscription: "On this side of the cemetery is buried Marina Ivanovna Cvetaeva. Born 26 September, 1892, old style, in Moscow; died 31 August 1941, new style, in Elabuga." The contrast of the two calendars in the dating subtly yet overwhelmingly points to the contrast between the two epochs—the old one into which Cvetaeva was born and in which she was able to develop into the poet she was and the new one in which there was no room for her or her poetry. For all its simplicity, the inscription respects Cvetaeva's oft-expressed preference for the Julian calendar; one wishes that her preference for the old orthography had likewise been respected.

Other Russian writers learned of Cvetaeva's death by word of mouth, and a year after she died Boris Pasternak devoted two poems to her memory. It was several years before her death became known in the outside world, and fifteen years had to elapse before the fact of her suicide could be mentioned in print in the Soviet Union.[10] Cvetaeva's son, after selling her few belongings in Elabuga, somehow made his way to Tashkent, where, early in 1942, he was enrolled at the Literary Institute. Later in the same year, he volunteered for military service and was soon thereafter reported missing in action.

At the time of Cvetaeva's death, it might have seemed to some that both her person and her poetry were universally forgotten. But, as Cvetaeva had written of Heine's, poetry is "life and therefore inextinguishable." Her personal legend was only beginning. There were still many articulate people in the world in whose lives she had left indelible traces. In the Soviet Union they were forced to remain silent. When Russian literary journals resumed publication in Paris after the end of the Second World War, Aleksandr Baxrax wrote an

[10] By Il'ja Èrenburg in his essay on Cvetaeva in *Literaturnaja Moskva*. See note 30 below.

article which is the only obituary anywhere on Cvetaeva's death. In this article, along with a few unfair comments about her poetry (commonplaces of Paris criticism in the nineteen-thirties), Baxrax drew a sympathetic and sensitive portrait of her personality: ". . . a unique person and a major Russian poet is gone, leaving in the memory of people who knew her an image which cannot be erased. One continues seeing before one's eyes the beak-nosed profile, the high forehead enveloped in clouds of cigarette smoke and the hand weighed down with silver rings and bracelets, myopically rummaging in a chaos of papers finely covered by the characteristic ornamental handwriting." [11]

By and large, the nineteen-forties were the period during which Cvetaeva's work was not published and she was not written about. In 1946, her old (1934) poem in praise of the Čeljuskin expedition somehow found its way into *Sovetskij Patriot,* a propagandistic publication put out by the Soviet embassy in Paris.[12] Among the few meager references to Cvetaeva in the nineteen-forties which one finds in Russian publications abroad, two set the pattern for subsequent arguments about the value of her achievement. In 1942, Cvetaeva's friend and admirer G. P. Fedotov wrote in New York: "Without being guilty of partiality, one can call Marina Cvetaeva the foremost Russian poet of our epoch." [13] In his history of Russian literature, published in Paris in 1946, I. Txorževskij wrote: "Marina Cvetaeva is entirely engrossed in trying to astound the reader with her talent . . . giving him nothing in return. Cvetaeva has nothing at all to say. Her art resembles a gaping, empty stone quarry." [14] As far as Soviet literature, criticism, and news media in the nineteen-forties are concerned, it is as if Marina Cvetaeva had never existed.

The situation changes in the nineteen-fifties, due to the literary "thaw" in the Soviet Union on the one hand and to the increase in Russian-language literary publications in the United States on the other. In 1953, the Chekhov Publishing House in New York, largely

[11] A. Baxrax, "Zvukovoj liven'," *Russkij Sbornik,* I (Paris, 1946), 183–186.

[12] *Sovetskij Patriot* (Paris), July 19, 1946.

[13] G. P. Fedotov, "O parižskoj poèzii," in *Kovčeg* (New York, 1942), p. 190.

[14] I. Txorževskij, *Russkaja literatura* (Paris, 1950), p. 506. Originally published in 1946.

through the efforts of E. I. Eleneva and Fëdor Stepun, brought out a selection of Cvetaeva's prose writings in book form. In the same year, there appeared the anthology of émigré poetry edited by Professor Ivask which contained thirteen poems by Cvetaeva, including the three-poem cycle "Čuzoj" ("The Stranger"), apparently a set of afterthoughts about the death of Majakovskij, which was published for the first time.[15] Also in 1953, the New York *Novyj Žurnal* published for the first time the last poem from Cvetaeva's cycle in memory of Maksimilian Vološin, the cycle that had been rejected by *Sovremennye Zapiski* in the thirties and that had appeared in part in *Vstreči*.[16]

The appearance of the collection *Proza* was treated by the émigré press in Paris and New York as an important literary event. The reviews of the volume in émigré publications begin a new period of Cvetaeva criticism in which we discern three major critical outlooks on the place of Marina Cvetaeva in Russian literature. Those who acclaim the value of her poetry and recognize her important position in Russian literature of this century are now in the majority. They include not only longtime admirers like Slonim [17] and Ivask,[18] but such writers as Vladimir Vejdle [19] and Vladimir Nabokov [20] who used to write of Cvetaeva's work with disdain but who over the

[15] *Na Zapade*, pp. 74–90.

[16] "Maksimilianu Vološinu," *Novyj Žurnal*, XXXIII (1953), 129–130.

[17] Mark (or Marc) Slonim's more recent statements on Cvetaeva are to be found in his English-language publications, e.g., *An Outline of Russian Literature* (New York and London, 1958), pp. 214–215, where we read: "future generations will undoubtedly discover her work with astonishment and gratitude."

[18] Jurij Ivask, "Blagorodnaja Cvetaeva," in *Lebedinyj stan*, pp. 7–15; "O čitateljax Cvetaevoj" (a defense of Cvetaeva's poetry against the critical attacks of Georgij Adamovič), *Novoe Russkoe Slovo* (New York), June 30, 1957; the introduction and annotations to Cvetaeva's letters to him (Letters to Ivask, pp. 73–75).

[19] There is a striking difference in tone between Vejdle's critical evaluation of Cvetaeva in 1929 ("Sovremennye Zapiski XXXVII," in *Vozroždenie* [Paris], January 10, 1929) and in 1955 ("Proza Cvetaevoj," *Opyty*, IV [New York], 73–75).

[20] In 1929, Nabokov accused Cvetaeva of amusing herself with unintelligible rhyme-weaving (*razvlekajuščujusja temnym rifmopletstvom*) and stated that her tragedy "Tezej" can only cause "astonishment and a severe headache" (V. Sirin, "Sovremennye Zapiski XXXVII," *Rul'* [Berlin], January 30, 1929). In the nineteen-fifties he called her a "poet of genius" (Vladimir Nabokov, *Speak, Memory,* p. 216).

years grew to appreciate it. In the second group belong the poets and critics who were instrumental in the formulation of the prevailing attitude to Cvetaeva in Paris of the nineteen-thirties: Adamovič, N. Ocup, Terapiano. These writers recognize the great talent of Cvetaeva, but their recognition is usually accompanied by reservations of such magnitude as to minimize or negate the actual value of her work. In the case of Ocup[21] and Terapiano,[22] the negation is connected with their inability to visualize the paramount role in Russian poetry of the present century of a whole poetic tradition descending from Russian Futurism. The numerous attempts of Georgij Adamovič in his writings of the nineteen-fifties to prove to himself and to the world that Cvetaeva cannot possibly be as good as others maintain have assumed the proportions of an obsession.[23]

[21] N. Ocup, "Gumanizm v S.S.S.R.," *Grani*, XXXIV–XXXV (Frankfurt-Main, 1957), 264–265. Reprinted in his book *Literaturnye očerki* (Paris, 1961), pp. 221–224. See also his book *Sovremenniki* (Paris, 1961), pp. 134 and 147.

[22] Ju. Terapiano, "Proza Mariny Cvetaevoj," *Novoe Russkoe Slovo* (New York), March 7, 1954; "Po povodu 'Myslej o russkom futurizme' V. Markova," *ibid.*, February 6, 1955; "Sovremennik No. 6," *Russkaja Mysl'* (Paris), December 15, 1962.

[23] In reviewing Adamovič's book *Odinočestvo i svoboda*, Vladimir Markov has pointed out the slighting references to Cvetaeva made in it "sometimes for no reason, unjustly, or even without relation to the surrounding context" (V. Markov, "Zametki na poljax," *Opyty*, VI, 1956). Other examples of Adamovič's obsessive preoccupation with Cvetaeva in his critical writings: "Iz zapisnoj knižki," *Novosel'e*, XXIX–XLI (New York, 1949), 146 (proving that Majakovskij and Cvetaeva are unreadable poets); "Sumerki Bloka," *Novoe Russkoe Slovo* (New York), August 17, 1952 (Cvetaeva's "hysterical babbling"); "Neskol'ko slov o Marine Cvetaevoj," *ibid.*, June 9, 1957 (a long article, polemicizing with Cvetaeva's admirers and reiterating the accusations of unintelligibility, graphomania, and hysteria); "Temy," *Vozdušnye Puti*, I (New York, 1960), 47 (allegation of Cvetaeva's lack of taste in poetry, illustrated with two lines from a poem by Fet which Cvetaeva admired and Adamovič doesn't). The ostensibly favorable statement on Cvetaeva in his article "Poèzija v èmigracii" (*Opyty*, IV [1955], 49) is equally typical of this critic's practice. There we read: "That there were in Cvetaeva's poems some lines straight from Paradise—who has ever denied it? 'Like some sort of cherub . . . ,' without any exaggeration. [This refers to a statement of Puškin's Salieri about Mozart and has deeper implications than Adamovič may have intended.] But she had nothing to offer. Cvetaeva was undoubtedly very intelligent, but too demonstratively intelligent, too much in her own way —which is perhaps a sign of weakness—and with constant 'quirks.'" The passage ends with the following bit of hypocrisy: "No, we did not care for any of it at all! There was in her apparently something else as well, something very sorrowful: unfortunately it remained unknown to us."

Finally, a very small group of émigré critics write of Cvetaeva with undisguised hostility. The lowest point among them was reached by Professor Boris Širjaev in his review of *Proza,* in which the violence of the attack is matched only by the author's total lack of familiarity with Cvetaeva's work and his ignorance of the most elementary facts of her biography.[24]

Of extreme importance in Cvetaeva publication and criticism abroad in the fifties are the activities of Gleb Struve. His section on Cvetaeva in his 1955 book on émigré literature[25] is the first (and so far only) fair, thorough, and scholarly examination of her émigré period.[26] His publication in 1957 of the complete *Lebedinyj stan* is of course the most significant single Cvetaeva publication since *Posle Rossii* in 1928. Between 1956 and 1961, five sets of letters by Cvetaeva have appeared in Russian-language publications abroad: her letters to Ivask, to Gul', to Fedotov, to Štejger, and to Baxrax, opening

[24] B. Širjaev, "Izlom i vyvix," *Vozroždenie,* XXXII (Paris, 1954), 143–146. The author considers Cvetaeva a "coeval and collaborator" (*"sverstnica i soratnica"*) of the Futurist poetess Habeas (pseudonym of a Mme Komarova, with whom Cvetaeva had nothing to do whatsoever) and states that they were both members of a literary gang (*banda*) led by Valerij Brjusov. Later in the article, Cvetaeva is somehow grouped with Sologub, Gippius, and Annenskij, and these four "twisted and mutilated" poets are opposed to Puškin-like poets, who are represented for Širjaev by Gumilëv and Vološin.

[25] *Russkaja literatura v izgnanii,* part I, chapter vi, section 5, pp. 146–157. Professor Struve writes in this section, *inter alia:* "That Cvetaeva will enter the history of Russian poetry as a major and genuine poet, cannot be doubted" p. 154). Interesting material on Cvetaeva is also to be found in Professor Struve's publications on Boris Pasternak, e.g., Pasternak's statement about the impact on him of Cvetaeva's "Poèma konca," *Grani,* LIII (1963), 78–79. The Michigan Press edition of Pasternak's poetry, edited by Professor Struve and B. A. Filippov, includes the two Pasternak poems addressed to Cvetaeva: "M.C." (Vol. I, p. 225) and the two-part memorial poem (Vol. III, pp. 39–40).

[26] Among the recent less complete treatments of Cvetaeva in works on modern Russian literature, one might mention Ettore Lo Gatto, *Storia della letteratura russa contemporanea* (Milan, 1958), the section "Marina Cvetaeva," pp. 344–347. The section on Cvetaeva in Renato Poggioli's prize-winning *Poets of Russia* (Cambridge, 1960), pp. 312–315, contains factual errors and is woefully inadequate as a survey of Cvetaeva's work, for Professor Poggioli does not know any of her poetry written later than 1921 (there is no reference to any poem later than *Remeslo*), is unaware of any of the dramatic and prose works, and knows the larger *poèmy,* including "Krysolov," only from the cursory reference to them in Pasternak's autobiography (Professor Poggioli believed the longer poems mentioned by Pasternak had never been published).

entire new vistas. Other Cvetaeva correspondence as well as a few
unpublished works are known to be in the possession of private
persons and in Western university libraries and will, it is hoped, be
published in the not too remote future.[27]

We know from Pasternak's autobiography that Cvetaeva's poems
were clandestinely circulated in Moscow in manuscript copies in the
nineteen-twenties.[28] The practice went on in the period after the
Second World War.[29] The real revival of Cvetaeva publication and
criticism in the Soviet Union, however, begins with Èrenburg's
article "Poèzija Mariny Cvetaevoj," published at the height of the
literary "thaw" of 1956.[30] Èrenburg's article was accompanied by a
selection of Cvetaeva's poems from various periods. In the same
year, poems by Cvetaeva appeared in the annual collection *Den'*
poèzii, and a year later a few more poems were included in an
Anthology of Russian Soviet Poetry.[31] The last two publications
limited their selection almost exclusively to the anti-German poems
from Cvetaeva's 1938–1939 cycles on Czechoslovakia. Despite the
somewhat slanted selection, these poems were very popular and
brought into the open a veritable cult of Cvetaeva among the
younger Soviet generation. The thaw of 1956 was followed by a

[27] Manuscripts of unpublished works by Cvetaeva abroad include the *poèma*
"Perekòp" and the complete "Povest' o Sonečke" at the Basel University
Library. Unpublished letters by Cvetaeva to various persons are known to be
at the Houghton Library, Harvard, and in the personal collections of
Professor Marc Slonim (including drafts of Cvetaeva's letters to Rilke),
Professor George Ivask, Archbishop John of San Francisco, E. I. Eleneva
(Catherine Elène), Washington, D.C., Salomea Andronikova-Halpern, Lon-
don, and Ol'ga Kolbasina (Černova), Paris. In January, 1964, several letters
addressed to the writer Nina Berberova were donated to the Beinecke Rare
Book and Manuscript library, Yale University (*The Yale University Library*
Gazette, Vol. XXXVIII, No. 3, p. 85). Mme Berberova also has several letters
of Cvetaeva addressed to Vladislav Xodasevič.

[28] *Proza 1915–1958,* p. 46.

[29] *Sovetskaja potaennaja muza* (Munich, 1961), pp. 19–24. Members of the
Yale Russian Seminar of 1963, conducted by Professor Frederick C.
Barghoorn, found Leningrad students reciting Cvetaeva at parties, writing
poems that imitate her style, and offering their American friends hand-typed
copies of poems by Cvetaeva and Gumilëv as presents (*The Yale Russian*
Seminar [New Haven, 1963], pp. 12–13).

[30] I. Èrenburg, "Poèzija Mariny Cvetaevoj," *Literaturnaja Moskva,* II
(Moscow, 1956), 709–714.

[31] Eleven poems appeared in *Den' poèzii* (Moscow, 1956), and four poems
appeared in *Antologija russkoj sovetskoj poèzii,* I (Moscow, 1957). This
information is taken from the editor's note in *Izbrannoe,* p. 289.

temporary freeze and further Cvetaeva publications had to be discontinued for the next few years. In the meantime, Boris Pasternak's "Avtobiografičeskij ocerk" ("Autobiographical Essay"; American edition entitled *I Remember*), which could not be published in the Soviet Union but appeared in book form in many Western countries, did for Cvetaeva what she had once attempted to do for Pasternak: in its affectionate and enthusiastic passages on Cvetaeva, it vouched before the West for the quality of her as yet untranslated work. The publication of Èrenburg's memoirs both inside and outside the Soviet Union generated further interest in Cvetaeva's work and personality, and between them Èrenburg and Pasternak succeeded in bringing her to the attention of a great number of people who were not aware that she had ever existed.

The one-volume Soviet edition of Cvetaeva's selected poems which Èrenburg had announced in his 1956 article finally appeared in 1961. The poems were selected and edited by V. Orlov, a Soviet specialist on Blok (who also provided the introductory biographical and critical essay), with the assistance of Cvetaeva's daughter, Ariadna Èfron, who evidently had been released from labor camp sometime in the early nineteen-fifties.[32] The choice of poems, necessarily slanted and selective, represented a cross-section of Cvetaeva's work from all periods, and the volume also contained twenty-one poems which had never been published before. Orlov's essay was a fine piece of writing in its own way, but it distorted Cvetaeva's biography and the meaning of her work by the usual Soviet method of omission of significant fact and change of emphasis. Like all Soviet commentators who attempt the rehabilitation of an ideologically suspect writer, Orlov was placed in the position of a defense attorney at a trial, with the task of minimizing the objectionable actions of his client and the problem of finding mitigating circumstances. He accordingly followed the example of Èrenburg in emphasizing Sergej Èfron's pro-Soviet activities in Paris, while carefully refraining from an explanation of the precise nature of those activities. He also stressed Cvetaeva's admiration for Blok and Majakovskij and omitted all reference to her admiration for Axmatova, Mandel'štam and Pasternak, replacing them instead

[32] See the poem "Poželanie," dedicated to A.S.È., in P. Vostokov, *Stixi* (Paris, 1961), p. 43.

with Esenin (who was far less significant in Cvetaeva's literary and personal biography). An example of out-and-out falsification is the statement that Cvetaeva was noticed and encouraged by Valerij Brjusov. Brjusov, who was actually Cvetaeva's enemy, but who is favorably regarded in current Soviet criticism for extra-literary reasons, thus replaced the still proscribed Gumilëv and Vološin, who actually did the approving and the encouraging. There are several instances in the essay where quotations from Cvetaeva are placed outside their original context in such a way as to say the very opposite of what they originally meant. Despite all this and despite Orlov's pious nonsense about Cvetaeva's "alienation from the people" and "betrayal of the spirit of her epoch," the critical part of the essay is a definite contribution to Cvetaeva scholarship.

The appearance of Cvetaeva's selected poems coincided with the Soviet publication of selected poems by Pasternak. The reaction of the orthodox Soviet-conditioned mind to these two events is reflected with a sort of charming naiveté in the Moscow diary of Mexti Gussejn, the Azerbaijani writer who was a delegate at the Party Congress held at the time: "Collections of poetry by Boris Pasternak and Marina Cvetaeva have been published in large editions.[33] Some were, possibly, puzzled by this circumstance ('Why were they published?'), while others reacted with an ecstatic sigh ('They've published them! At last!')." Mexti Gussejn was perplexed by all the talk he heard in Moscow about Cvetaeva being a genius: ". . . all this talk about her being a genius was started by the philistines (*obyvateli*)," he finally decided. "It was they who created this myth about Cvetaeva's genius. . . ." Being a writer himself, Mexti Gussejn knows that great literature contains Communist ideas and follows Party directions. As proof he cites the fact that "*Doctor Zhivago* has been forgotten even by the bourgeois traffickers in literature (*del'cy ot literatury*), while *The Rout* and *The Young Guard* [by A. Fadeev] are alive and shall live forever."[34]

[33] *Izbrannoe* was published in 25,000 copies, a large portion of which was exported abroad. According to an article in the (London) *Times Literary Supplement* (May 4, 1962), the copies made available in Moscow were sold out in a day or two and subsequently brought high prices on the black market.

[34] Mexti Gussejn, "Stranicy dnevnika," *Znamja* (Moscow, 1962), III, 110.

Another important development in making the work of Cvetaeva available to the Soviet reader was the appearance of the collection *Tarusskie stranicy* (*Pages from Tarusa*), devoted to the artistic and literary heritage of the little town of Tarusa, the summer residence of the Cvetaev family during Marina's childhood and the present residence of her daughter. The volume contained forty-one poems by Cvetaeva, most of them never before published in Russia (including several early poems from *Vol'šebnyj fonar'*, a fine selection of poems from *Posle Rossii*, and excerpts from the *poèma* "Lestnica"); the prose memoir "Kirillovny" (originally published in *Vstreči* as "Xlystovki" ["Women of the Flagellant Sect"]; the title was possibly changed because of its religious connotations), the first original prose work by Cvetaeva to be published in the Soviet Union; an unfamiliar early portrait of Marina Cvetaeva; and a short appreciation of her work written by the eminent Soviet novelist and playwright Vsevolod Ivanov.[35]

At the present time, Marina Cvetaeva is a recognized phenomenon in Soviet literary history and criticism. The article on her in the Great Soviet Encyclopedia of 1957, although short and full of factual errors, is a far cry from the abusive article on her in the encyclopedia of 1934. However, the fact that her work is printed in limited quantities and discussed in print within certain prescribed limits has brought forth considerable opposition on the part of the guardians of Soviet orthodoxy. During the last few years, when a certain amount of literary controversy has become possible in the Soviet Union, there has been a clear division of Soviet literary opinion into two camps on the subject of Cvetaeva. It takes courage to champion Cvetaeva too openly, as Èrenburg and Vsevolod Ivanov have learned after the official critical attacks on their articles. A considerable number of Soviet critics have been brought up on the notion that only ideology matters and that literary value and artistic achievement are a mere adjunct; to such critics her poetry is an alien and worthless thing.[36] As is the case with their counterparts among

---

[35] *Tarusskie stranicy* (Kaluga, 1961). The article "Poèzija Mariny Cvetaevoj" by Vsevolod Ivanov is on p. 251; other Cvetaeva material is on pp. 252–261. An English translation (with Cvetaeva's poems mostly mistranslated), *Pages from Tarusa*, ed. Andrew Field, appeared in 1964.

[36] E.g., G. Čeremnin, "N'ju Jorkskij sbornik materialov po istorii russkoj literatury," *Voprosy Literatury*, 1957, VIII, 248; V. Buznik, "Liričeskaja poèzija našego vremeni," *Russkaja Literatura* (Moscow, 1959), I, 95.

the émigrés, the most virulent Soviet critics of Cvetaeva are usually
the ones least familiar with her work. There is a peculiar resemblance between the denunciations of a Širjaev abroad and such
Soviet criticism as the statements of Elena Serebrovskaja, a young
critic who can be best described as a neo-Stalinist literary hatchet
woman and who has repeatedly written of Cvetaeva with contempt,
complaining of her supposed thematic poverty, and proclaiming,
against all factual evidence, that Cvetaeva's talent was stunted by
her emigration. How blind the critics of this ilk can be to originality
and to literary values in general has been demonstrated by Dmitrij
Moldavskij who, in his denunciation of the collection *Tarusskie
stranicy,* managed to find some of Cvetaeva's most mature and
perfect poems from *Posle Rossii* "weak and derivative." [37] An
obscure but orthodox Soviet poet who described Cvetaeva as the
darling of apolitical aesthetes in one of his poems [38] probably did
not realize how closely he was echoing, although from the opposite
position, the sonnet which the former leader of the Ego-Futurists,
Igor Severjanin, included in one of his émigré-period collections and
which proclaimed Cvetaeva "the little idol of homeless atheists." [39]
And one of the principal poet-laureates of the Stalinist period,
Aleksej Surkov, who to this day retains his position as the party
watchdog over literature, has persistently warned the younger Soviet
poets against excessive enthusiasm for Cvetaeva's poetry. But,
significantly, the tone of Surkov's statements on Cvetaeva has been
mellowing during the past decade. His invective of the nineteen-
fifties is now replaced by pleading that Cvetaeva, Mandel'štam,
Xlebnikov, and Pasternak are not suitable examples for poets of the
Communist future because "we are looking forward while they are
facing the past." [40] Coming from a man who helped push Russian
poetry into the neo-Victorian limbo of the nineteen-thirties by

[37] D. Moldavskij's review of *Tarusskie stranicy* in *Zvezda,* IV (Leningrad,
1962), 212–216.
[38] Genrix Rudjakov, "V gostjax u èstetov," *Oktjabr',* I (Moscow, 1963),
124–125.
[39] The sonnet "Cvetaeva," in I. Severjanin (Lotarev), *Medal'ony* (Belgrade,
1934), p. 96. Unlike the poem of Rudjakov, the sonnet, for all its satire,
betrays a careful study of Cvetaeva's poetry. Ironically enough, the attack
occurred at the time when Cvetaeva became an admirer of Severjanin's later
poetry (as can be seen from enthusiastic passages about it in her letters to
Salomea Halpern).
[40] *Komsomol'skaja pravda* (Moscow), May 9, 1963.

reviving the most hackneyed traditions of the eighteen-sixties and eighties, this statement on the alleged backwardness of Xlebnikov and Cvetaeva is at least paradoxical.

In 1925, Cvetaeva wrote that she would return to Russia "not as a permitted 'relic of the past' but as a desired, eagerly-awaited guest." A poem by the noted Soviet translator and poet Samuil Maršak, addressed to Cvetaeva and published in 1963, ends with the assurance that Cvetaeva has now returned to her country, "down to every last line."[41] But in fact, as far as the whole of her work is concerned, that day has not yet come. True, a part of her literary production is gradually returning to the Russian people, where it belongs. Every year sees a re-publication of several Cvetaeva poems, long available abroad, but unknown in the Soviet Union. Almost inevitably, such publications are accompanied by clichés about Cvetaeva's "anti-bourgeois" or "anti-Western" ideology, sometimes supported by excerpts from her correspondence quoted out of context. As could have been predicted, the first two cantos of "Krysolov," in which the German bourgeoisie is satirized, found their way into print in the Soviet Union.[42] But inconceivable changes will have to take place in Soviet mentality and practice before the Russian readers are allowed to read "Perekóp," the third canto of "Krysolov" (in which the rat plague is depicted as a Communist revolution) or any of the memoirs dealing with Cvetaeva's life in 1917–1922. A recent publication of excerpts from her memoir "Moj Puškin" (in *Den' poèzii,* 1962) shows that the problem of the Soviet censor with Cvetaeva is by no means limited to political matters. By now the Soviet *Weltanschauung* has evolved into a rigid system of beliefs and taboos which Cvetaeva's free and individualistic thinking shocks and offends at every turn. The mutilations, transpositions of passages, and changes in emphasis through omission that were inflicted on five pages of Cvetaeva's prose make the editorial corrections of Vadim Rudnev, of which she once so bitterly complained, look very gentle indeed. A larger and more significant excerpt from "Moj Puškin" has appeared since then in the provin-

[41] S. Maršak, *Izbrannaja lirika* (Moscow, 1963), p. 144.
[42] The prediction made in my dissertation in the spring of 1964 that the first two cantos of *Krysolov* would soon be published in the Soviet Union has now been realized (see *Novyj Mir,* III [Moscow, 1965], 158–166).

cial Soviet literary journal *Don*. This time, Cvetaeva's daughter, Ariadna Èfron, was in charge of preparing and introducing the text, and the omissions are not quite so drastic. Still, even here we can find deletions of the reference to the modernistic painter Gončarova (not yet "rehabilitated") and to Soviet revisions of Puškin (even though this is asserted by a negative character who is Cvetaeva's opponent).[43] In the fall of 1965, a large selection of her poetry, including the folklore-based *poèmy,* her two Greek tragedies, and "Lestnica," was scheduled to appear in the prestigious series (*Biblioteka Poèta, Bol'šaja serija*) that is usually reserved for the major classics of Russian poetry.[44]

[43] Cf. "Moj Puškin" in *Proza*, pp. 28 and 52, and in *Don*, III (Rostov, 1965), 182 and 190.

[44] This collection (Marina Cvetaeva, *Izbrannye proizvedenija* [*Selected Works*] [Moscow-Leningrad, 1965]) became available only after the present volume had been typeset. A vastly expanded version of the 1961 Soviet edition of Cvetaeva, it offers the largest sampling of the poet's work ever to be collected in a single volume. Fifty-five poems are published in it for the first time, including a large group of previously unknown poems from the unpublished collection *Junošeskie stixi* and complete versions of the two cycles about the fall of Czechoslovakia in 1938–1939. Some of the known poems appear in versions revised by Cvetaeva during the last two years of her life, and some of the previously untitled poems now bear new titles. In addition to the previously published "Poèma konca" and "Poèma gory," five other *poèmy* and three plays, all of them previously unavailable in the Soviet Union, have also been included (see the bibliography for listing). A hitherto unknown short and humorous anti-gastronomic *poèma,* "Avtobus" ("The Bus"), written by Cvetaeva between 1934 and 1938, makes its first appearance in print in this collection.

The introductory essay by V. Orlov is a greatly expanded and amplified version of his introduction to the 1961 edition (*Izbrannoe*). It contains some new biographical material and corrects many of the distortions and omissions it contained in 1961. Thus, it is no longer necessary to present Brjusov as a champion of Cvetaeva—Gumilëv and Vološin, unmentionable in 1961, can now be given the credit due to them for their early recognition of Cvetaeva's talent. This time, the introduction and the annotation give a fuller account of Cvetaeva's literary relations with Pasternak and Mandel'štam. The dedications on the poems addressed to Anna Axmatova, omitted in the previous edition, have now been restored and the commentary reveals that Axmatova and Cvetaeva carried on a correspondence during the nineteen-thirties. The annotations contain much valuable information drawn from Cvetaeva's letters in various Soviet archives.

But omissions and distortions are still very much a feature of Cvetaeva publications in the Soviet Union. Some of the most significant poems from *Posle Rossii* have been omitted in this collection because of their religious subject matter (for example, the poem "Bog" ["God"]) or because of their

Although the Soviet Cvetaeva revival was led by Èrenburg, with
support, at times unexpected, from such older Soviet writers as
Vsevolod Ivanov and Aleksandr Tvardovskij, it is among the
younger poets who came to prominence after 1956 that she is most
popular. In reviewing *Izbrannoe,* Aleksandr Tvardovskij pointed
out that the younger Soviet poets of the fifties began to be influenced
by Cvetaeva even before the publication of that volume. The
influence is often superficial, and in the work of such a member of
the younger generation as Evgenij Vinokurov the traces of reading
Cvetaeva appear in vulgarized and watered-down form.[45]

On December 26, 1962, both the older and the younger generations of Soviet writers joined hands in a commemorative meeting
marking Cvetaeva's seventieth birthday (which actually occurred
three months earlier), held at the Moscow Writers' Club (*Dom
literatorov*).[46] Il'ja Èrenburg was the chairman, and among the

idealistic philosophy and otherworldly orientation ("Sivilla—mladencu"),
or, possibly, because of their generally pessimistic mood (the poem about
Lethe). None of Cvetaeva's political poetry of the Civil War period or the
nineteen-twenties is included; the 1930 cycle on the death of Majakovskij
(mentioned in Orlov's introduction as "a controversial work which sounds
some false notes") has been likewise left out. There are also cases of outright
censorship of Cvetaeva's texts. The problem of what to do about the satirical
anti-Communist passages in the purportedly complete version of "Krysolov"
has been solved in this edition very simply by leaving out all such passages.
According to the annotations, this poem "is printed with a few insignificant
cuts"; in fact, the whole middle section of Canto 3 (134 lines) has been
deleted and a total of 24 lines of verse, containing ironic references to the
Bolsheviks or the Red Army and satirical parallels between the rat plague and
the Communist takeover of power, have been carefully removed throughout
Canto 4. In the *poèma* "Lestnica" (called "Poèma lestnicy" in this edition), a
passage that contains a humorous juxtaposition of Karl Marx and the devil
was replaced by a dotted line. The desire of the annotators (Ariadna Èfron and
A. Saakjanc) to render Cvetaeva more "respectable" from the orthodox
Soviet point of view has led to a certain amount of factual misrepresentation
and deliberate distortion of Cvetaeva's views and attitudes in the otherwise
quite valuable appended commentary.

Even with all these strictures, however, the new edition is a remarkable
and most welcome milestone in the publication of Cvetaeva's work in her
native country.

[45] Cf. especially "Poèma o dviženii," in Evgenij Vinokurov, *Lirika*
(Moscow, 1962), pp. 262–264, with Cvetaeva's "Poloterskaja," *Posle Rossii*, pp.
140–143.

[46] The information on the commemorative meeting is quoted from a
photostat of the official invitation. See also Theodore Shabad, "Russians Pay

speakers we find Pavel Antokol'skij (who on this occasion broke the silence of decades about his early friendship with Cvetaeva), the Soviet Rilke specialist, M. Vaksmaxer, the editor of *Izbrannoe,* V. Orlov, and the younger Soviet poets, Bella Axmadulina, Viktor Bokov, Evgenij Vinokurov, and David Samojlov. Celebrated Soviet actors and actresses recited Cvetaeva's poetry and prose and a special exhibit of materials and documents pertaining to Cvetaeva's life and work was opened in the lobby of the club. The attendance of the meeting was by invitation only, and it was not announced in the press. Only one hundred and forty persons received an invitation, but according to eyewitness accounts, several hundred other persons stood outside in the snow for hours, hoping somehow to gain admission to the meeting.

Clearly, there is a large number of people in the Soviet Union who realize that the work of Cvetaeva is an important part of the Russian national cultural heritage. Their efforts to make as much as possible of it available to all Russians are at present met with formidable opposition. It is impossible to predict when the works of Cvetaeva that were published only abroad will be reprinted in the Soviet Union or when the large body of her unpublished poetry and letters that is known to be in Soviet archives [47] and in the possession of Ariadna Èfron in Tarusa will be made public. Because of Cvetaeva's explosive individuality, we have to reckon with a certain amount of editorial suppression and distortion in any Soviet publication of her work in the forseeable future. Neither her gradually approaching status as a national classic, nor the popularity and prestige of her name among the younger generation can at the present time protect Cvetaeva from such suppression and distortion.

Tribute to a Disputed Poet. Tsvetayeva is Memorialized Despite Dim View of Her Held by the Party," *New York Times,* Western edition, December 29, 1962.

[47] The recently published directory of personal literary archives in the state collections of the U.S.S.R. lists twelve Cvetaeva items pertaining to the years 1913–1921 at the Central State Archive of Literature and Art, Moscow; six items (1922–1956) at the Gorky Institute of World Literature, U.S.S.R. Academy of Sciences, Moscow; and one item at the State Museum of Literature dating from 1912 to 1915 (which sounds like the manuscript of *Junošeskie stixi*). See *Ličnye arxivnye fondy v gosudarstvennyx xraniliščax SSSR* (Moscow, 1963), II, 281.

Knowing that certain works of Dostoevskij have still not been
reprinted since *his* post-Stalinist rehabilitation, we are not too
surprised to learn that when private persons, responding to the great
demand for unfamiliar Cvetaeva, attempted a clandestine publication of her romantic play "Priključenie" ("An Adventure"), as well
as of some poetry by Gumilëv, they were charged by the Soviet
authorities with black-marketeering and the sale of "pornography"
(and jailed). [48] With all that, it is still only a matter of time—years,
decades or centuries—before the realization of Boris Pasternak's
prediction: "I believe that the greatest reevaluation and the greatest
recognition of all await Cvetaeva."

[48] *Večernjaja Moskva,* May 14, 1964, quoted by Maurice Friedberg in
Problems of Communism (Washington, November–December, 1964), p. 30.

PART TWO: HER ART

VI ✍

Technical Aspects: Language, Versification, Poetic Devices

Before going on to a survey of Marina Cvetaeva's work, we will attempt to indicate some of the more striking and original of her literary usages: peculiarities of her vocabulary and syntax, her contributions to Russian versification, and her exploitation of the connection between the phonetic and the semantic aspects of language (paronomasia). No exhaustive, or even adequate, treatment of these aspects of her work is envisaged—this is the task of future literary scholars, linguists, and statisticians who should find in Cvetaeva's prose and poetry a fertile field for research in numerous and various directions. It is hoped that some of the avenues such research may take will be suggested on the following pages.

Marina Cvetaeva's stylistic traits are closely connected with the subject matter and the emotional content of her work. "The choice of words," she wrote in the nineteen-twenties, "is first of all the choice and purging of emotions. Not all emotions are equally valid, believe me; here, too, work is required!" (Letter to Baxrax, September 5 and 6, 1923.)

During the early stages of her work, her choice of words and of emotions was largely conditioned by nineteenth-century sensibility and poetic traditions. After about 1916, Cvetaeva's style took a tortuous and independent path, which led her to the language-conscious area of the Russian literary tradition, mapped out in the

nineteenth century by Gogol' and Leskov and continued in the
twentieth by Remizov, Rozanov and, in their own way, by the
Futurists. In the poetry of the Symbolist generation, language aimed
at indirect suggestion, and individual words were merged and
dissolved in the evocative flow of the whole. The Acmeists and their
predecessor Kuzmin returned to the word its simple, direct connota-
tion. Futurists—Majakovskij and Xlebnikov—gave the individual
word a new autonomy, using it openly and pointedly as the basic
unit of their poetic structure. The use of the word by the Symbolists
and its use by Futurists are comparable to the uses of form in
Impressionistic painting as opposed to Cubism. In the latter, the
forms do not merge into the whole of the canvas, are not suggested
by subtle color effects, but come to the foreground, sharply outlined,
forcefully stated, and clearly defined. In the mature Cvetaeva, words
are not used to connote or to imply or to suggest; they are selected
equally on the basis of their shape, sound, and meaning, each of
these qualities being equally necessary for the total poetic impression. If, in her use of language, Cvetaeva sometimes came close to the
practice of her Futurist contemporaries, it has to be understood that
she arrived at her stylistic usage along largely independent paths,
and that the content, the emotional and human orientation of her
poetry are often diametrically opposed to those of any Russian poet
associated with Futurism.

Vocabulary and Syntax

Writing of her post-Revolutionary stylistic evolution, Cvetaeva
ascribed it to the sense of the epoch in which she was living: "There
exists not a single major contemporary poet whose voice did not
break and grow after the Revolution." Cvetaeva's own poetic voice
began evolving long before the Revolution; the nature of its
development can be understood by tracing the evolution of her
poetic voice between ca. 1908 and the late nineteen-thirties: ". . .
one could isolate [in Cvetaeva's work] at least *seven* poets, not to
speak of prose writers, kinds of prose, from the driest thought to the
most vivid depiction. That is why I am so difficult—as a whole, to

encompass and to comprehend," Cvetaeva wrote in one of her letters to Ivask.

In her first two books of verse, we meet what can be stylistically termed the romantic Cvetaeva. Her romantic style owes less to major romantics like Žukovskij or Lermontov than to their followers of the second half of the nineteenth century (Fet, Polonskij, possibly even Apuxtin). At the same time, the young poet obviously had read some of the Symbolists, and the favorites of her adolescence have also left their traces (the theater of Rostand, the juvenile romances of Lidija Čarskaja [L. Čurilova, 1875–?]). The resulting style is not free from affectation; there is a certain self-conscious elegance and artificiality about its ladylike tone, a flavor of the upper-class Moscow salon, and more than an echo of the kindergarten and the nursery. This late-Victorian, romantic diction of Cvetaeva's earliest poetry is subsequently developed and perfected in her later poetry whenever the subject matter calls for it. We find it in her plays with eighteenth-century background, in her cycle of poems "Komediant," in certain romantic poems from *Versty II* that were included in *Psixeja,* and in the courtly, aristocratic tone of the poems addressed to A. A. Staxovič in *Lebedinyj stan.* It is not found in its typical form in her poetry after the nineteen-twenties, although its remnants were merged in the mature and unified style used in *Posle Rossii* and later. In Cvetaeva's prose of the thirties, one finds this cultivated romantic manner put to satirical uses in the speeches of the unidentified professor's wife in "Živoe o živom."

Very soon after establishing and mastering this style in her first books, Cvetaeva arrived at a much simpler and more direct vocabulary and diction. Some poems of *Junošeskie stixi* and especially of *Versty I* have that magical simplicity, which we associate with the very earliest poems of Mandel'štam and the last poems written by Boris Pasternak, and which is so very difficult for a poet to achieve or for a critic to define. As early as 1913, the poem "Ideš' na menja proxožij"[1] shows us this simple diction of Cvetaeva, her own voice at its purest and most personal. The vocabulary of this style had an odd neutrality, the individual words do not yet

---

[1] *Izbrannoe,* pp. 28–29.

boldly step forward as they do in her later poetry, the tone and syntax are direct and seemingly inevitable. It was this style, apparent in such poems of *Versty I* as the group addressed to Mandel'štam, that captivated Boris Pasternak, who discerned in its seeming simplicity the pure extract of poetic creativity.[2] Pasternak leaves no doubt about the extreme technical difficulty of this apparently artless manner.

Already in *Versty I,* however, this basic style becomes complicated by two new strains, which enter Cvetaeva's poetry in certain poems of this particularly pivotal book and eventually become organically fused in her mature style. These can very schematically be described as her use of archaism and of colloquial or vulgar diction. Cvetaeva was not a linguist and her use of these two strata of language was intuitive, creative, and at times indiscriminate. By the term "archaism," we can describe her use of Church Slavic and Old Russian vocabulary and of the remnants of the chancery language of Muscovite Russia, as well as her later deliberate imitation of the vocabulary and grammar of the Russian eighteenth-century poets. Cvetaeva's colloquial diction likewise includes a number of linguistic phenomena of various origins—imitation of uneducated and peasant speech, regional expressions, use of deliberately coarse language in such cycles as "Xanskij polon" and "Majakovskomu," and a number of other evocations of Russian speech of the kinds that differ or deviate from the accepted literary and poetic usage. Some future student of Cvetaeva, who is a professional linguist, should have a field day identifying and delimiting these various strata of language in her work and discovering her specific use of each of them.

The use of archaisms in *Versty I* appears most obviously in the poems addressed to Blok, where she incorporated quotations from traditional Church Slavic prayers and subtly attuned her own diction to their tone and archaic grammar.[3] Such instances were probably modeled on the example of Blok himself, quoting passages from Russian Orthodox prayers in his poems: "Ty v polja otošla bez vozvrata / Da svjatitsja imja tvoe. . . ." Similar use of archaisms based on religious usage and quotations of prayers was made by

[2] Boris Pasternak, *Proza 1915–1958,* p. 46.
[3] E.g., *Versty I,* p. 68.

Majakovskij in his poem "Čelovek" (1918), and still later by Cvetaeva in the set of poems in *Stixi k Bloku* which are addressed to the woman Blok supposedly loved shortly before his death.[4] In Cvetaeva's later poetic practice, especially in *Posle Rossii* and in the Greek tragedies, we find a whole array of systematically used archaic lexical and grammatical forms: nominal declension of adjectives, short-form participles, vocative case, occasional masculine dative endings in -*ovi* and -*evi,* the archaic feminine genitive singular, and the metathesized Church Slavic forms of the *tort* and *tolt* groups regularly replacing their pleophonic Russian equivalents (i.e., *grad* and *zlato* used instead of *gorod* and *zoloto*). Leafing casually through *Posle Rossii,* one notes *dnes', stogny, drevesa, esm'* (several times), *očesami, otč i zrjač* (in another poem of the same collection, the latter appears as *zrjašč* in the same meaning), *xoščem, slovesa sii* (in reference to words of a telegram), *s onogo sošed, dušu živu.* The demonstrative particle *se,* the use of which was ridiculed by Puškin as obsolete in his "Ode to Count Xvostov" (although he himself occasionally resorted to it), it used quite matter-of-factly by Cvetaeva and is undoubtedly derived from the practice of eighteenth-century poets. The mature Cvetaeva quite regularly uses the two archaic pronoun-adjectives that are typical of the usage of the Muscovite scribes: *sej* (the use of which earned her the approval of Aleksej Remizov),[5] and *onyj.* The use of the latter is beautifully illustrated in the poem in *Versty I* which Cvetaeva built on free variations on the standard phrase *vo vremja ono:*

В оны но́чи ты мне была как мать,
Я в ночи́ тебя могла позвать,
Свет горячечный, свет бессоный,
Свет очей моих в ночи оны.[6]

In the nights of yore you were unto me as a mother,
In the night I could call upon you,
Feverish light, sleepless light,
Light of my eyes in the nights of yore.

---

[4] *Stixi k Bloku,* pp. 41–47.
[5] Natal'ja Kodrjanskaja, *Aleksej Remizov* (Paris, 1959), p. 145.
[6] *Versty I,* p. 60.

The archaism, very sparingly used, recurs throughout the poem, giving it its particular style and quality. Most of Cvetaeva's archaisms are easily comprehensible to a person versed in classical Russian poetry, although an occasional one may require a footnote, like the Church Slavic *koemuždy* (to each) in "Poèma gory." The archaisms diminish in quantity in the thirties, but we still find them whenever the context seems appropriate in both Cvetaeva's poetry and prose.

The use of untutored speech and vulgarisms was also initially tried out in *Versty I,* the collection that in general marks a watershed in her work. Such use is connected with Cvetaeva's stylistic masks or *personae* employed in this collection: the homeless vagabond, the sorceress, the "tavern queen" (*kabackaja carica*). The diction at times delicately suggests a folk song, and the colloquial flavor may be achieved by such economic means as the replacement of *kak* by *čto* ("jabloni, čto angely, bely") [7] or by the repetition of prepositions before modifiers, which is typical of Slavic folk poetry ("po staroj po doroge po kalužskoj").[8] At times, Cvetaeva's use of colloquial diction is restrained, as in her poem to Anna Axmatova in *Remeslo* and at others it is almost imperceptible, remaining as it were on the very border of literary usage:

> За девками доглядывать, не скис
> Ли в жбане квас, оладьи не остыли ль,
> Да перстни пересчитывать, анис
> Всыпая в узкогорлые бутыли.[9]

> To keep an eye on the maidservants, [to see]
> If the quass in the jug went sour, the fritters grown cold,
> And to keep counting [all the] rings, while pouring aniseed
> Into narrow-necked bottles.

Here, folk poetry is suggested only by the colloquial phrase "dogljadyvat' za devkami" and by the conjunction "da"; this suggestion of the colloquial and the connotations of the objects mentioned in the poem ("kvas v žbane," "olad'i," "perstni") suffice

[7] *Ibid.,* p. 31.
[8] *Ibid.,* p. 44.
[9] *Ibid,* p. 31.

to evoke traditional Old Russia, despite the clearly literary diction of the fourth line, with its adverbial participle and compound adjective. The heterogeneous stylistic elements do not clash but blend organically, giving the poem a stylistic unity. In such instances, her style, despite a completely different initial point of departure, approaches the style of such pre-Revolutionary peasant poets as Nikolaj Kljuev. In its most extreme manifestations, the colloquial language of Cvetaeva comes uncannily close to the best in genuine Russian folk poetry. This applies primarily to her epic poems based on folklore material: *Car'-devica, Mólodec,* "Pereuločki." At other times, the colloquial or vulgar speech may be used either for a single colorful effect (the sudden quoted shout of a coachman to his horses in one of the poems to Blok: "Èj idoly, čtob vy sdoxli!") [10] or to give a particular tone and coloring to an entire poem. The four poems in the cycle "Xanskij polon," which draw a parallel by implication between the unsettled conditions and the savagery during the Mongol occupation of medieval Russia and the life during the Civil War, achieve their effect by a subtle juxtaposition of medieval allusions, including references to the Igor Tale (cryptic mentionings of Končak, Gzak, Deva-Obida, the times of Bus ["*vremjačko Busovo*"]), and of deliberately harsh colloquialisms and regional vocabulary:

> Корою нажрусь, —
> Не диковинка нонь!
> — Ох, Родина-Русь,
> Зачарованный конь! [11]

> I'll gorge myself with [tree] bark, —
> It's not rare these days!
> — Oh, Motherland-Russia,
> Enchanted steed!

Here again, the coarse verb *nažrat'sja*, the colloquial adverb *non'*, and the romantically poetic *začarovannyj kon'* are blended into an organic whole, despite the stylistic heterogeneity of the components.

Psychologically and semantically, the use of colloquial and

---

[10] *Ibid.,* p. 72. "May you croak, you bastards!" would be an approximate English equivalent, but it does not convey the specific coachman-like color of these words.

[11] *Remeslo,* p. 70.

folkloristic diction and vocabulary is usually related by Cvetaeva to definite historical, local, or social situations described or evoked. Such situations are the fairy-tale ancient Russia of *Car'-devica* and "Pereuločki," the lower-class milieus suggested in some of the poems in *Versty I,* and the soliloquies of semi-fictionalized uneducated women in her prose works: the former seamstress whose son has become a prominent Communist in "Vol'nyj proezd," Zavadskij's nurse in "Povest' o Sonečke," and the wonderful *hypothetical* cook of Xodasevič or some other poet, in "Živoe o živom," with her lower-class dialect: "Ja ix i čaem napoila—i sama pila i im nalila, obidy ne bylo." [12] The Russian lower-class dialect is so firmly connected with servants in Cvetaeva's mind that we find Phaedra's Athenian maidservants speaking in a sort of Nekrasov-like stylization of a Russian peasant song:

> А глаза какие — сказу нет!
> Пуще рученек жаль глазынек.
> Две руки ломать да скручивать —
> Пуще глазынек жаль рученек.
> Знай выламывать, знай стискивать!
> Шепотком начнешь: "Ай при́ смерти?"
> Говорком — ладони на́ уши.
> Не своя уж, не она уже. [13]

> And what eyes — undescribable!
> [We] pity those dear eyes more than [her] little hands.
> [But when she] wrings and twists those two hands —
> [We] pity those dear hands more than her dear eyes.
> The way she wrings them, the way she presses them!
> You begin in a whisper. [She:] "Is he dying?"
> In a normal tone — she covers her ears.
> She is no longer her own, no longer herself.

In the cycle "Majakovskomu," Cvetaeva shows herself equally adept at the diction of a big-city hoodlum, in imitation of Majakovskij's own (and Esenin's) poetic use of such diction, aptly described by

---

[12] *Proza,* p. 186. Here and later, English translations are dispensed with when they cannot possibly convey the stylistic, syntactic, or onomatopoetic points illustrated by the quoted examples.

[13] "Tezej" ("Fedra"), *Sovremennye Zapiski,* XXXVI (1928), 135.

Remizov as "the brilliant, 'how-would-you-like-a-punch-in-the-face-style' popular diction of Majakovskij" (*blestjaščij—mordu nabju—raëk Majakovskogo*).[14] All these varieties of popular speech are used by Cvetaeva with great freedom, and when the occasion calls for it, are sometimes introduced into her personal lyrical poetry when no particular historical or social references are implied. "I myself am the people and I never knew any other." Cvetaeva wrote,[15] and this can be illustrated by one of the poems from "Stixi sirote" in which the growing emotional tension is allowed to reach a new height by the introduction of the untutored, peasant vocabulary in the last line: "I net takoj jamy, i net takoj bezdny—/Ljubimyj! želannyj! žalennyj! boleznyj!"[16] The reversal of the vowels that turns the romantic-poetic word *želannyj* into the regional *žalennyj* (from the verb *žalet'* in the sense of *ljubit'*) is a typical Cvetaeva device, and the following *boleznyj* reinforces the accomplished linquistic switch.

If the regional and the colloquial are exploited by Cvetaeva for their evocative possibilities, the archaic has the function of rendering the speech more pronouncedly literary and poetic. In discussing her use of archaisms, Gleb Struve has mentioned Trediakovskij and the Russian Archaists of the early nineteenth century, particularly Kjuxel'beker.[17] Cvetaeva herself confirms the justice of this comparison in her commentary on two quotations from the writings of Admiral Šiškov, the leader of the Archaists, which were sent to her by Ivask. The quotations in question read: "1) To be able to mix the high Slavonic style with the colloquial one so artfully that the solemnity of one would become pleasingly entwined with the simplicity of the other; 2) To be able to place in high style low words and thoughts . . . without lowering the style and preserving its entire seriousness."[18] These quotations read remarkably like a description of Cvetaeva's mature style made a century *en avance* and we are not surprised at her pleasure in receiving them and seeing in

---

[14] Kodrjanskaja, *op. cit.,* p. 144.

[15] Letters to Ivask, p. 227.

[16] *Izbrannoe*, p. 224.

[17] Gleb Struve, *Russkaja literatura v izgnanii,* pp. 150–152. Writing of Cvetaeva in 1923, Professor Struve connected her with the eighteenth-century poet Deržavin (*Rul'* [Berlin], June 24, 1923).

[18] Letters to Ivask, p. 232, note 2. The passages are from Šiškov's "Disquisition on the Old and New Style of the Russian Language" (1803).

them an epigraph to her language.[19] One might add that while for Šiškov and Kjuxel'beker the archaic usage meant a direct link to the odic poetry of the eighteenth century and a preservation of traditions of the ecclesiastic literature, for Cvetaeva, in the twentieth century, such usage had added romantic implications—conveying a sense of poetic exclusiveness and individuality and providing the means for an essentially romantic idealization of the past.

The syntactic aspect of Cvetaeva's poetry and prose is what gives them their most distinctive quality. It is also the aspect of her writing that makes her work most difficult, at times inaccessible, for the reader who does not wish to make the necessary effort of imagination or who lacks the patience to read Cvetaeva with the attention she requires. When hostile critics write of Cvetaeva's trans-sense language (*zaum'*), of her incomprehensibility, of her "poor command of Russian," they are most likely thinking of the difficulty of her syntax. The difficulty is not noticeable in her early work, and the new syntax dates approximately from *Lebedinyj stan* (1917–1921) and "Na krasnom kone" (1920). Basically, Cvetaeva's syntactic originality is expressed in her revolt against the standard literary well-constructed sentence, with subject, verb, direct and indirect objects and all the usual complements in accordance with nineteenth-century literary and grammatical usage. Cvetaeva's rejection of a part of current syntactic practice was not a pioneering event in twentieth-century Russian literature. As early as 1907, in *Posolon'* (*The Sun Circle*), Aleksej Remizov abandoned the literary usages that he felt were based on imported Latin and German norms, and by study of pre-Petrine literature sought to re-establish native Russian syntactical relationships. Remizov's prose reflects some aspects of current speech used daily by Russians, especially the uneducated classes, and utilizes a large area of syntactic usage not employed by the literary language of the nineteenth century. In addition to Remizov's example in such books as *Posolon'*, there were the somewhat earlier similar experiments in the ornamental prose of Andrej Belyj. The use of syntax based on the native ear rather than on the literary norm was later developed still further by many of the younger prose writers who appeared after the Revolution. Cve-

[19] *Ibid.*, p. 209.

taeva's syntactic contribution is essentially within this general trend.

In terms of conventional grammar, this contribution can be described as a maximal exploitation of grammatical and syntactic ellipses. The part of speech most likely to be subjected to ellipsis is the verb, and critics have occasionally mentioned the phenomenon of Cvetaeva's "verblessness" (*bezglagol'nost'*). Here, the ancestor of Cvetaeva in the history of Russian poetry is Fet, one of whose several verbless poems, "Šopot, robkoe dyxan'e," was much mocked and parodied by the "progressive" nineteenth-century critics. Like Fet, Cvetaeva sometimes builds entire stanzas on long chains of nouns with modifiers:

> Но вот, как чорт из черных чащ —
> Плащ — чернокнижник, вихорь — плащ,
> Плащ — вороном над стаей пестрой
> Великосветских мотыльков.
> Плащ цвета времени и снов —
> Плащ Кавалера Калиостро.[20]

> But now, like a devil out of black thickets —
> A necromancer cloak, a whirlwind cloak,
> A cloak like a raven over a motley swarm
> Of socially prominent butterflies.
> A cloak the color of time and dreams —
> The cloak of Cavaliere Cagliostro.

The few participles that may occur in such verbless poems are used strictly as adjectives. Other poems may consist of a series of prepositional clauses:

> По холмам — круглым и смуглым,
> Под лучем — сильным и пыльным,
> Сапожком — робким и кротким —
> За плащем — рдяным и рваным.[21]

> Over the hills — rounded and dusky,
> Under a ray — strong and dusty,
> With little boot[s] — timid and meek —
> After the cloak — crimson and tattered.

[20] *Psixeja*, p. 80.
[21] *Remeslo*, p. 14.

(This pattern is retained throughout the three stanzas of this poem.) Or of verbless questions and answers:

> Ятаган? Огонь?
> Поскромнее, — куда так громко!
>
> Боль, знакомая, как глазам — ладонь,
> Как губам —
> Имя собственного ребенка.[22]

> (*Love*)

> A dagger? Fire?
> [No,] more modestly, — why so loud?
>
> A pain, as familiar as your hand to your eyes,
> As the name of your own child
> To your lips.

In addition to entire verbless poems, we find passages and individual lines in which the verb is avoided. This may happen in the first lines of a poem, where the setting is stated:

> Ночь. — Норд-Ост. — Рев солдат. — Рев волн.[23]

> Night. — A northeaster. — Roar of the soldiers. — Roar of the waves.

Чешский лесок —	A Czech woods —
Самый лесной.	As woodsy as they come.
Год — девятьсот	Year — nineteen
Тридцать восьмой.[24]	Thirty eight.

The standard Russian omission of the verb "to be" in the present tense is of course a major source of verbal ellipsis, and Cvetaeva uses it very often for construction of lengthy passages, especially with the complement in the dative functioning as a predicate:

Зверю — берлога,	For a beast — its lair,
Страннику — дорога,	For a wanderer — the road,
Мертвому — дроги,	For the dead — the hearse;
Каждому — своё.[25]	To each his own.

---

[22] *Posle Rossii*, p. 139.
[23] *Lebedinyj stan*, p. 24.
[24] *Izbrannoe*, p. 228.
[25] *Versty I*, p. 69.

Verbal forms, when used, often appear in non-verbal functions and there is a preference for the infinite verbal forms—the infinitive and the various participles—and sometimes for the imperative. The following two examples show the nominal uses of the infinitive and the imperative in Cvetaeva's poetry:

Женщине — лукавить,	For a woman — to dissemble,
Царю — править,	For the tsar — to rule,
Мне — славить	For me — to glorify
Имя твоё.[26]	Your name.

Все древности, кроме: *дай* и *мой*,
Все ревности, кроме той, земной[27]

All the antiquities, except "give me" and "it's mine;"
All the jealousies, except that earthly kind

The same absence of verbs is a hallmark of Cvetaeva's prose style. A description of the street in which Natalija Gončarova lived begins with a short paragraph of six sentences which contains only one verb: "Ne ulička, a uščel'e. Na otstojanie ruki ot steny: bok gory. Ne doma, a gory, starye, starye gory. (Molodyx gor net, poka moloda ne gora, gora—tak stara.) Gory i nory. V gore i nore živet." [28] The same phenomenon is observable in Cvetaeva's critical and philosophical prose. Here are several verbless sentences, culled from a few pages of "Poèt o kritike": "Provinivšijsja sud'ja! Spešnyj peresmotr vsex del." "Itak, xronologija—ključ k ponimaniju. Dva primera: sud i ljubov'." "Gospoda, spravedlivosti, a net—xot' zdravogo smysla." [29] Most examples quoted up to now demonstrate the avoidance or absence of verbs, but the very last sentence cited shows a true verbal ellipsis: a verb has been omitted and can be reconstructed by implication. In this particular case, the implied verb is not entirely clear (it may be either *prošu* or *dajte*). In many cases of Cvetaeva's true verbal ellipses, the omitted verb is easier to supply. In the following excerpt from the description of the first

---

[26] *Ibid.*
[27] *Posle Rossii,* p. 9.
[28] "Natalija Gončarova," *Volja Rossii,* V–VI (1929), 37.
[29] "Poèt o kritike," *passim.*

appearance of the werewolf hero of *Mólodec,* we have attempted to supply the missing verbs in parentheses after each verse:

На круг поклон,	(отвесил)
Кошель на стол,	(положил)
Из кошеля — казна ручьем, дождем.[30]	(посыпалась, потекла)

A bow all around,	(he made)
His purse on the table,	(he placed)
From the purse, money in a stream, like rain.	(poured, flowed)

Another example of genuine verbal ellipsis is the typical Russian omission of the verbs "to speak," "to say" when describing quoted speech:

> А уж мать с мосточку-то:
> Как любились-сватались?[31]

> And the mother from the bridge:
> How was your loving, your matchmaking?

The group of verbs which are most frequently omitted are the verbs of motion. In this connection we note that Cvetaeva's major means of doing without verbs is her maximal exploitation of the expressive possibilities of two oblique cases, the instrumental and the dative. The instrumental is used by Cvetaeva with a frequency that seems to exceed its average occurrence in Russian. In many of her poems one is struck by its preponderance. It occurs as instrumental of manner or even of place:

> Потусторонним
> Залом царей.
> А неприклонный
> Мраморный сей?[32]

> [We pass through] an otherworldly
> Hall of Tsars.
> And [who is] this inflexible
> Marble one?

---

[30] *Mólodec,* p. 10.
[31] *Ibid.,* p. 23.
[32] *Izbrannoe,* p. 181.

Here the instrumental case makes possible the ellipsis of a verb of motion (something like *proxodim*); the entire stanza is made additionally difficult by the ellipsis of the interrogative pronoun "kto" in the second sentence.

There is also a definite preference for prepositions and verbs that govern the instrumental. In the following short poem from the 1939 cycle of poems on Czechoslovakia, the verbs of motion are omitted, while the sense of motion is conveyed by a series of prepositional clauses, with prepositions that govern the instrumental and the dative:

Не бесы — за иноком,
Не горе — за гением,
Не горной лавины ком,
Не вал наводнения,

Не красный пожар лесной,
Не заяц — по зарослям,
Не ветлы — под бурею, —
За фюрером — фурии![33]

Not the demons — after a monk,
Not sorrow — after a genius,
Not the mass of a mountain avalanche,
Not the flood's tidal wave,

Not the red forest fire,
Not a hare [rushing] through the scrub,
Not the tempest-driven willows, —
The furies are after the Führer!

In the fourth section of "Poèma konca," the question "Čem paxnet?" ("Of what does it smell?") in the second stanza is immediately answered by a set of nouns in the instrumental, as is required by the government of the verb. In the subsequent stanzas of this section, there regularly occur separate disjointed instrumental clauses, which the reader has to understand as additional answers to the question of the second stanza. Since they are inserted in an alien context, their instrumental case provides the only clue to the

[33] *Ibid.*, p. 240.

reference of these clauses.[34] A similar syntactic procedure is used in one of the Hamlet poems in *Posle Rossii:*

Гамлетом — перетянутым — нáтуго
В нимбе разуверенья и знания,
Бледный — до последнего атома . . .
(Год тысяча который — издания?)[35]

As Hamlet — straightlaced — tightly
In a nimbus of disillusionment and knowledge,
Pale — down to the last atom . . .
(Edition of the year one thousand and what?)

Five more quatrains follow before the instrumental case in the first line of the poem is finally explained by the verb supplied in the last line: "Gamletom—peretjanutym—vstanete . . ." ("You shall arise—as straightlaced—Hamlet . . .")

Cvetaeva's partiality to the instrumental often leads to anacolutha, either with or without ellipsis of the verb. The first two stanzas of "Pëtr i Puškin" have to be classified as an anacoluthon, despite the period at the end of the second stanza. The verb is neither supplied nor implied, the reason for the energetic-sounding instrumental case is never made clear, and the grammatical construction (illustrated by the first stanza of the poem) is changed after the third stanza:

Не флотом, не потом, не задом
В заплатах, не шведом у ног,
Не ростом — из всякого ряду,
Не сносом — всего, чему срок, (и т.д.)[36]

Not by his fleet, not by his sweat, nor by his rear end
Full of patches, not by the Swede at [our] feet,
Not by his height — above any norm,
Not by the demolition of everything whose time had come, (etc.)

The following example of the instrumental can also be described as anacolutha:

[34] *Ibid.,* pp. 262–264.
[35] *Posle Rossii,* p. 59.
[36] *Izbrannoe,* p. 183.

Каким наитием,	By what inspiration,
Какими истинами,	By what [revealed] truths,
О чем шумите вы,	Of what do you rustle
Разливы лиственные?	O leafy cascades?
Какой неистовой	By the mysteries
Сивиллы таинствами —	Of which frenzied sibyl —
О чем шумите вы,	Why do you rustle?
О чем беспамятствуете?[37]	Why do you wax ecstatic?

Here, although the verb "šumet'" may at times take the instrumental, the introduction of the preposition "o" perceptibly shifts the grammatical structure.

The dative case likewise enables Cvetaeva to omit verbs. It is frequently used in the idiomatic Russian predicative statements of the type "komu čto," and it may also be used to avoid the verbs in quoted speech: "—Možet byt', tol'ko segodnja priexala i potomu zapazdyvaet? A ty točno znaeš' (deti drug drugu), čto imenno segodnja pervyj urok?" [38] In the following passage from "Krysolov" there is an ellipsis of the verb "snitsja." The context of the passage, which is a long discussion of dreams, enables the dative case of the indirect object to supplant the function of the verb that governs it:

Суд видит весы,
Весы же — аптекарь,
Наставнику — трость,
Плод дел его швейных —
Швецу. Псу же — кость?
Ошибилсь: ошейник![39]

The court dreams of scales,
The apothecary — also of scales,
The preceptor [dreams] of a cane,
The tailor — of the fruit of his sewing
Labors. And the dog — of a bone?
You are mistaken: of a dog collar!

The consequences of the failure to realize that in Cvetaeva the grammatical case of a noun may elliptically represent the omitted verb which is the reason for that case were vividly illustrated

[37] *Posle Rossii*, pp. 37–38.
[38] "Tvoja smert'," *Volja Rossii*, V–VI (1927), 9.
[39] "Krysolov," second canto, *Volija Rossii*, V 1925), 42.

recently by the sadly unsuccessful attempt of the talented American poet Denise Levertov to translate Cvetaeva's poem "Pis'mo" ("A Letter") from *Posle Rossii*. Failing to realize the elementary fact of Russian grammar that the verb *ždat'* ("to wait," "to expect") almost inevitably puts a direct masculine or neuter object in the genitive case, Miss Levertov (or her Russian consultant) not only misunderstood the first two lines of the poem, but also all the unattached genitive clauses later on in the poem, which are governed by that verb and which, to make sense in English, needed some form of "wait" or "expect" to precede them. Thus, the line "Ne ščast'ja—stara!" which in its Russian context can only mean "[I am] no [longer expecting] happiness—[I am] too old [for it]!" was rendered by Miss Levertov, unaware of the ellipses involved, as "It's not happiness, old girl!" [40]

The verb is the part of speech that is most frequently subject to ellipsis. In one of her letters to Štejger in 1936, Cvetaeva wrote: ". . . it is not for nothing that I dislike verbs (a terrible coarseness!), but to do without them one needs verse or personal presence." But other parts of speech may also be omitted although implied. This occasionally happens to nouns and pronouns. At the beginning of *Mólodec* there occurs a repeated varied refrain in which the subject noun is regularly replaced by a possessive adjective:

Бегут русы,	The blond ones flow,
Бегут круты,	The tightly braided ones flow,
Шелком скрученныя —	Intertwined with silk —
Эх!	Hey!
Моя — круче,	Mine is braided tighter,
Твоя — круче,	Yours is braided tighter,
У Маруси — круче всех!	Marusja's is tightest braided of all!
Ходи шибче,	Ripple faster,
Ходи выше,	Ripple higher,
Медом сыщенная —	You honey-fed one —
Эх!	Hey!
Моя — выше,	Mine is higher,
Твоя — выше,	Yours is higher,
У Маруси — выше всех! [41]	Marusja's is highest of all!

[40] *Pages from Tarusa*, pp. 288–289. Reprinted in *Tri-Quarterly* (Spring, 1965), p. 65.
[41] *Mólodec*, pp. 9–10

It takes a certain effort on the part of the reader's imagination to reconstruct the missing subject on the basis of clues provided by the number and the gender of the modifiers (the two quoted stanzas will yield *kosy,* "braided tresses," and *grud',* "breast," respectively).

A special study could be made of Cvetaeva's syntactic use derived from colloquial Russian and from poetic folklore. In this area, she comes very close to the prose of Remizov, making wide use of idiomatic syntactic structures, the comprehension of which requires familiarity with the oral folk tradition. The very beginning of *Car'-devica* provides an example of the syntactic parallelism and comparison by antithesis typical of Russian folk poetry:

Как у молодой змеи — да старый уж,
Как у молодой жены — да старый муж,
Морда тыквой, живот шаром, дышит — терем дрожит,
От усов-то перегаром на сто верст округ разит.[42]

Once upon a time a young viper had an old grass snake;
Once upon a time a young wife had an old husband;
Mug like a pumpkin, belly like a globe, he breathes —
    the palace **tower** quakes;
His whiskers reek of liquor a hundred versts around.

In her prose and poetry that is not connected to folklore, the syntax is often complicated by unexpected parenthetical incursions and what may be called a scrambled syntax. In one of Cvetaeva's best known poems, "Popytka revnosti," the image of the oar is introduced before the comparison to which it refers is actually stated:

Как живется вам с другою, —
Проще ведь? — Удар весла! —
Линией береговою
Скоро ль память отошла

Обо мне, пловучем острове. . .[43]

---

[42] *Car'-devica,* p. 9.
[43] *Posle Rossii,* p. 134.

How does it feel to live with another?
Isn't it simpler? A stroke of the oar!
Like a coastline
Did the memory soon recede

Of me, a floating island . . .

Here we have not only the syntactic ellipsis of the connection between the terms of comparison, but the reversal of the expected logical sequence of the comparison. Two more typical passages may be quoted to sum up Cvetaeva's personalized use of syntax. The first one, in prose, is a passage from "Tvoja smert'," in which the author and her daughter select and purchase a box of stationery intended as a present for the girl's French teacher:

Korobki, s legkim kartonnym gromom, gromozdjatsja. Odno—vidno, drugoe—skudno, tret'e—nudno, četvertoe—dorogo, pjatoe—dorogo, šestoe—dorogo. I, kak vsegda, s vozglasom: 'Ah, il y a encore une que j'oublie'—poslednjaja—ta samaja. (Kak by proverka točnosti našego vkusa, legkij iskus ego prikazčikom) . . .
Golubaja. Polotnjanaja. S golubymi že cvetočkami na kryške, do togo prostymi, čto ne smešnymi. Bez zubcov i jakoby anglijskoj šeroxovatosti kraev. . . . Mnogo. Sxodno.[44]

This passage well illustrates the avoidance of verbs, the utilization of the expressive possibilities of the instrumental case, the brief clauses and separate words used to convey something like the stream of consciousness. The one-word sentences are almost a trademark of Cvetaeva, and they are the reason for at least one foreign commentator's use of the term "telegraphic style" in connection with Cvetaeva.[45] The following excerpt from the poem "Škola stixa," written in the nineteen-thirties, shows many of the traits discussed on the previous pages (e.g., avoidance of verbs by means of the instrumental and the dative), and also illustrates the parenthetical self-interruption and the free use of syntactic inversion that recalls Cvetaeva's eighteenth-century predecessor Trediakovskij:

[44] "Tvoja smert'," p. 8.
[45] Theodore Shabad, *op. cit.* in Chapter V, note 45.

Глыбами лбу
Лавры похвал.
Петь не могу.
Будешь! Пропал
(На толокно
Переводи!)
Как молоко
Звук из груди.[46]

The laurels of praise
Are like rocks to [my] forehead.
I cannot sing.
You must! The sound has vanished
(Put me on [a diet
Of] lactogenic cereal!)
Like milk
From [my] breast.

Paronomasia

Many Russian writers have manifested an interest in the possible connection between the phonetic and the semantic sides of language.[47] The linguistic phenomenon involved is essentially what is known in classical poetics and rhetoric as *paronomasia,* defined as exploitation of accidental sound similarities of etymologically unrelated (or, occasionally, related) words to produce striking verbal effects. In such Russian writers of the twentieth century as Remizov, Majakovskij, and especially Marina Cvetaeva, this exploitation aims at considerably more than mere effect. In Cvetaeva's later work,

[46] *Sovremennye Zapiski,* XLVI (1931), 160. The last two lines quoted have been amusingly mistranslated into German as: "Strömt denn gleich Milch / Klang aus der Brust." The translator saw a verbal ellipsis where there is none and did not connect the verb *propal* with the lines he quoted. (See Juri Semenow, "Einleitung," in *Neue russische Lyrik. Herausgegeben von Johannes v. Günther* [Frankfurt-Main, 1960], p. 19.)

[47] Maksim Gor'kij reports Lev Tolstoj's interest in the connection between the sound and the meaning in such combinations as *podoždem* (let us wait) and *pod doždem* (under the rain), or in *stolkovat'sja* (to agree), *stol* (a table), and *kovat'sja* (to be forged or welded). (M. Gor'kij, *Sobranie sočinenij,* XIV [Moscow, 1951], 263–264.

paronomasia is no longer a trope, but an integral part of her thinking, an awareness of an important aspect of language which led her to develop a personal system of verbal devices and allusions that constitute an important contribution to a widespread trend in modern Russian literature which Remizov has called "verbalism." [48] In later Cvetaeva, we can perceive a belief in a sort of mystical bond between the shape and the sound of a word and the object which this word is used to designate. "Every object should have its own word," Cvetaeva wrote in 1934, and added: "a single word only." [49]

The awareness of the connection between the phonetic and the semantic is manifested in Cvetaeva's poetry quite early. In *Večernij al'bom*, we find the poem "Mukà i mùka," [50] the point of which depends on the semantic difference produced by the shift of stress in an otherwise identical sequence of phonemes, which results in two unrelated meanings (flour and torment). Russian folksongs often achieve a subtle effect by exploiting a movable stress, but without the shift in the meaning of the word. Cvetaeva occasionally used this device ("Zaterjannym tak dalekó-dalëko"), [51] but in her later practice she is far more interested in the startling contrast in meaning that such displacement of the stress can achieve:

По голубы́м и голу́бым лестницам[52]

Over pale blue and endearing staircases

Восхи́щенной и восхищённой[53]

As one ravished and delighted

Я про́воды вверяю провода́м
И в телеграфный столб упершись плачу.[54]

---

[48] Aleksej Remizov, *Pljašuščij Demon* (Paris, 1949), p. 49.
[49] Letters to Ivask, p. 218.
[50] *Večernij al'bom*, p. 101.
[51] *Psixeja*, p. 14.
[52] *Versty I*, p. 19. (The change in stress is not indicated in the edition used, but the metrical pattern makes it necessary. The same poem also uses the combination "ne vetrom vetrennym," where the subtle semantic shift is not dependent on change of stress.)
[53] *Izbrannoe*, p. 113. Originally in *Sovremennye Zapiski*, VII (1921), 103, without the indispensable stress marks and with catastrophic results in terms of comprehension.
[54] *Posle Rossii*, p. 67.

> I entrust the farewells to the wires
> And stopped by the telegraph pole, I weep.

The last quoted example is from the cycle "Provodá" ("Telegraph Wires"), which describes a forced separation of two lovers. In the second poem of the cycle, the heroine, after comparing her sufferings to those of Phaedra and Ariadne, realizes that she cannot even perform for her lost lover the warm Russian rite of preparing him for the trip, seeing him off to the station, and bidding him farewell (*próvody*). She is reduced instead to delegate her farewells to telegraph wires (*provodá*), which will follow his train or carry to him her farewell telegram. The telegraph pole which supports these wires and makes the farewell message possible is at the same time an evocation of the "dumb rock of Fate" mentioned in the German epigraph to the entire cycle (". . . wenn nicht der alte stumme Fels, das Schicksal, ihr entgegenstände"). It is thus both something that stops the heroine from following her lover and something that makes later contact with him (the wires that run after him) possible.

The verbal elegance of this example and its profundity within the context of the poem show that we have here something of greater artistic significance than mere verbal play. The poetic thinking of Cvetaeva, like that of her contemporaries, the Russian Futurists, was word-conscious to a far greater degree than that of the poets of preceding generations. In this connection, one should mention a major Russian poet in whose work Cvetaeva was apparently not interested: Velimir Xlebnikov. Cvetaeva mentioned Xlebnikov only once, in "Poèma konca," in a passage that makes one suspect she had confused him with Aleksej Kručenyx.[55] Cvetaeva never spoke of Xlebnikov in her critical writings, and her lack of interest in literary theory makes it fairly certain that she never bothered to look at any of Xlebnikov's theoretical writings. Yet, Cvetaeva would have found much to agree with in Xlebnikov's theory of active and inactive vowels that he originally stated in his article "Učitel' i učenik,"[56] and according to which the reason for the semantic difference between the Russian words *byk* (bull) and *bok* (side) is

---

[55] *Izbrannoe*, p. 280.
[56] For discussion and illustration of Xlebnikov's theory of active and inactive vowels, see N. Gumilëv, *Pis'ma o russkoj poèzii*, pp. 175–176.

their respective active and inactive vowels. Cvetaeva had no systematic theory or unified practice in this respect, but her interest in poetic
exploitation of the phonetic-semantic relationship remains a constant feature throughout her career. The instances of movable stress
quoted above demonstrate only one aspect of such exploitation.

As early as Cvetaeva's second collection of verse, *Volšebnyj fonar'*,
we find a poem entitled "Staruxa" ("Old Woman").[57] The poem
does not deal with an old woman, but only with a description of the
sound of the word *staruxa,* which is compared to a sound made by an
empty seashell placed at one's ear. The semantic aspect of the word
is only hinted at in the second stanza when the breath of time is
said to be heard in the sound of this word. Usually, however,
Cvetaeva is equally interested in the phonetic and the semantic. The
following examples should make clear the extent and nature of this
interest.

A poem in *Posle Rossii* begins with the words: "Minuta:
minuščaja: mineš' "[58] ("A minute: passing one: you shall pass"); a
letter to Aleksandr Baxrax written at approximately the same time
(summer 1923) elucidates this statement more simply: "Minuta: to
čto minet"[59] ("A minute is something that shall pass"). After
mentioning in "Mat' i muzyka" that as a child she always associated
the words *pedal'* (pedal on a piano) and *pedel'* (a beadle), Cvetaeva
continues: "No nazvav pedelja, ne mogu ne upomjanut' ego
slovesnoj rodni: pudelja, belogo učenogo Kapi iz *Sans famille,*
kotoryj rvet pedelja za pantalony— . . . i ix obščej, pedelja i pedali,
slovesnoj rodni, dvojurodnoj sestry p a d a l i, toj padali, kotoroj
paxnet—odnu sekundu—i každyj raz—i bezumno sil'no—v buzine,
u samogo podstupa k našej tarusskoj dače. . . ."[60] ("But having
brought up the beadle [*pedel'*, masc.], I cannot help mentioning his
verbal relative, the poodle [*pudel'*, masc.], the white and trained
Capi from *Sans Famille* who tears the beadle's trousers— . . . and
the mutual verbal relative of both beadle and poodle, their female
cousin c a r r i o n [*padal'*, fem.], that very same carrion [the odor of
which] you can smell, for one second only—and every time—and

[57] *Volšebnyj fonar'*, p. 136.
[58] *Posle Rossii*, p. 109.
[59] Letters to Baxrax, *Mosty*, V, 314.
[60] *Proza*, pp. 85–86.

overwhelmingly—by the elder trees, just as you approach our summer cottage in Tarusa. . . .") Here the phonetic similarity of the words starts a train of free association which brings on one set of childhood recollections after another.

The next two examples are given without translation, because in them Cvetaeva's fusion of the phonetic and the semantic makes any attempt to convey her thought in any words but her own tantamount to distortion of this thought. In the first example, an assertion that Valerij Brjusov was essentially an ancient Roman is supported by a series of associations between three Russian nouns which Cvetaeva believes are equally representative of qualities typical both of Brjusov and of Rome: *volja, vol,* and *volk (will, ox,* and *wolf).* "Tri slova javljajut nam Brjusova: volja, vol, volk. Triedinstvo ne tol'ko zvukovoe—smyslovoe: i volja—Rim, i vol—Rim, i volk—Rim. Triždy rimljaninom byl Valerij Brjusov: volej i volom v poèzii, volkom (homo homini lupus est) v žizni." [61] Another example of such a phonetic-semantic train of associations is found in "Svetovoj liven'" (in the section entitled "Pasternak i byt"): "Byt. Tjažkoe slovo. Počti kak: byk. Vynošu ego tol'ko, kogda za nim sleduet: kočevnikov. Byt, èto dub, i pod dubom (v krug) skam'ja, i na skam'e ded, kotoryj včera byl vnuk, i vnuk, kotoryj zavtra budet ded. Bytovoj dub i dubovyj byt." [62] In this example, the mutual dependence of semantics and phonetics is so close that it is difficult to say which of the two brings forth the suggestion for the other. In the same article, we find the interesting and convincing association between the noun *dožd'* (rain) and the Church Slavic imperative *dažd'* (give!),[63] which would undoubtedly have met with Xlebnikov's approval.

Words for Cvetaeva often contain their meaning within their sound pattern, and such meaning can be revealed by finding the proper phonetic associations: "Èstrada. Èstrada mesto javnoe. Javlennost' že i v samom zvuke. 'Zdravstvuj! Radujtes'!" ("The stage [or the podium]. The stage [or the podium] is an open place. The openness is within the sound itself [which suggests]: 'All hail! Re-

---

[61] *Ibid.,* p. 214. Cf. Brjusov's famous line: "Vpered, mečta, moj vernyj vol!" ("Forward, imagination, my faithful ox!")

[62] *Ibid.,* p. 359.

[63] *Ibid.,* p. 365.

joice ye!' ") [64] Occasionally, the standard meaning of a word differs too widely from what Cvetaeva feels to be the implications of its phonetic pattern: "Panegirik—durackoe slovo, vrode ponomarja, ili drobnogo cerkovnogo 'din'-din' ', čto-to židkoe, bessmyslennoe i veselen'koe. Po smyslu: vosxvalenie." ("Panegyric is an idiotic word, something like a bellringer or a fractured 'ding-dong' of churchbells, something puny, mindless and mirthful. The meaning [turns out to be]: words of praise.") [65] Equally inadequate from the point of view of Cvetaeva's phonetic sensitivity is another foreign loan word, *ègoizm,* and she refuses to use such phonetically inadequate words on the grounds that they do not deserve to be sounded or heard ("ne zasluživaet daže sobstvennogo zvučanija i moego ušnogo slyšan'ja). [66]

On the other hand, the phenomenon of the homonym may reveal for Cvetaeva hidden relationships between things, as did the near-homonyms with stress differences discussed at the beginning of this section. Striking use of homonyms is made in the very first stanza of "Poèma gory":

Вздрогнешь — и горы с плеч,
И душа — горе́.
Дай мне о го́ре спеть:
О моей горе́![67]

A shiver goes through you — and the load is off your shoulders,
And the soul [flies] upwards.
Let me sing of sorrow:
Of my hill!

Equally striking is the play on the word *zvezda* in "S morja," where it is used alternately to mean Red Army insignia, the Star of Bethlehem, and a starfish. [68] The *pointe* in the last line of the poem in memory of Nikolaj Gronskij is based on two homonymously-sounding phrases, in which the change in meaning is provided by the different place of word boundaries: "Sovsem ušel. So vsem ušel" ("He left altogether. He left, taking everything"). [69] The association

[64] *Ibid.,* p. 240.
[65] Letters to Gul', p. 185.
[66] Letters to Ivask, p. 218.
[67] *Izbrannoe,* p. 247.
[68] "S morja," in *Versty,* III (1928), 12.
[69] *Izbrannoe,* p. 211.

in one poem of many phonetically similar words often results in alliterations or alliterative effects; such is the case in the amassing of the sound *m* in the poem "Minuta," to which we have already alluded in this section: "Minuta: merjaščaja! Malost' / Obmerivajuščaja . . . ," "O mel'! O meloč'!," "majatnikov majata," and so forth.[70] Such alliterations very rarely aim at a musical effect in the poetry of Cvetaeva, as they do, for example, in the poetry of Bal'mont; their function is almost always conditioned by the interplay between the phonetic and the semantic, and any musical effect, although contributing to the total impression, usually arises as a by-product.

A very important area of Cvetaeva's art in which her phonetic sensitivity and verbal inventiveness find an outlet is her use of newly coined expressions and neologisms of various kinds. This is another aspect of Cvetaeva that has brought forth the charge of *zaum'* and incomprehensibility. Such accusations are clearly based on misunderstanding or inattentive reading. At no point did Cvetaeva attempt to invent any new, hitherto nonexistent words or try to create a new language as is implied by the term *zaum'*, which refers to such attempts and practices in the work of Aleksej Kručenyx and some of his followers (and, to a much lesser extent, to Xlebnikov). Cvetaeva's neologisms, on the contrary, are always based on existing lexical material, and their aim is to convey a definite meaning to the reader, rather than to evoke in the reader a vague and undefinable association. A possible exception to this may be Cvetaeva's imitations of magical spells and incantations in some poems of *Remeslo* and especially in "Pereuločki"; yet, even in the most extreme of these, such as the weird feminine patronymics in "Pereuločki" (Ajurajuški Raevna, Sin'-Ladanovna, Vys'-Jastrebovna, Zyb'-Radugovna),[71] the derivation and the referents are clear ("Ring-Around-the-Rosy, Daughter of Paradise," "Azure, Daughter of Incense," "Height, Daughter of Hawk," and "Ripples, Daughter of Rainbow," respectively, although there is no American Indian flavor in the Russian originals), and the realization of this enhances the poetic value of these coinages. But the greater part of Cvetaeva's neologisms are based on simple procedures. "Verbal creativity,"

[70] *Posle Rossii*, pp. 109–110.
[71] "Pereuločki," *Remeslo*, pp. 147–160, *passim*.

wrote Cvetaeva, "like any other creativity means only walking in step with the popular and natural ear. Only following the ear. Et tout le reste n'est que littérature." [72]

The most time-honored method of producing new words used by Cvetaeva is the Russian quasi-Homeric compound adjective. Here we see another point of contact between Cvetaeva and Vasilij Trediakovskij, who revived the use of such adjectives in his often ridiculed *Tilemaxida* (there are also examples of such adjectives in pre-Petrine Russian literature) and who, because of his stubborn and violent wrestling with the spirit of the Russian language may be considered an eighteenth-century precursor of Futurism. We find an epigraph from Trediakovskij's theoretical writings in *Posle Rossii*,[73] and Cvetaeva's study of his poetry has perhaps manifested itself in the series of the compound adjectives in the poem dealing with the river Lethe: *slepotekuščij* (blindly-flowing), *slepoletejskij* (blindly-Lethean), *srebrotekuščij* (silvery-flowing), *srebrosedoj* (silvery-grey-haired), *srebro-suxoj* (silvery-dry).[74] In another poem in *Posle Rossii*, which has to do with Helen of Troy and thus also refers to Greek antiquity, the Trediakovskian-Homeric archaic flavor is conveyed by the periodic recurrence of words with the prefix *obez-*, some of them belonging to standard Russian usage, but most of them coined for use in this particular poem: (Cvetaeva's orthography preserved) *obezkrovleno* (deprived of either blood or roof), *obeznadeženo* (deprived of hope), *obezznoeno* (deprived of heat), *obezžemčuženo* (deprived of pearls), *obezdomlennyx* (made homeless), *obessynovlenost'* (destruction of sons), *obezmužennyj* (deprived of men or of husbands).[75] In this instance, the suggestion that may have come from the poetry of Vasilij Trediakovskij could just as easily have come from a source almost two centuries later: the poetry of Vladimir Majakovskij.

The compound neologisms we find in "Krysolov" are quite indubitably Cvetaeva's own: *bredovar* (boiler of ravings), *toskomer* (sadness-meter), or the startling series of compound nouns using *oko*

---

[72] *Proza*, p. 395. The quotation from Verlaine's "L'art poètique" should of course read: "Et tout le reste est littérature."
[73] *Posle Rossii*, p. 5.
[74] *Ibid.*, p. 22.
[75] *Ibid.*, p. 133.

(Church Slavic word for "eye") as their first component and verbal stems as the second: *okoём* (an existing word, meaning "horizon," which serves as the model for the rest), *okoim* (eyetaker), *okoder* (eyepuller), *okoryv* (eyewrencher), *okolom* (eyecrusher).[76] None of these present any difficulties in comprehension and neither do the occasional Cvetaeva neologisms based on fusion or contraction. Taking the English loan word *sportsmen* and fusing it with the pejorative slang expression *mednyj lob* (from the French *le front d'airain*), Cvetaeva coined a new term of opprobrium, which she used in one of the poems she addressed to her son in 1932:

Не быть тебе нулем	You shall not be a zero,
Из молодых — да вредным!	Young, but already vicious!
Ни медным королем	Nor a copper king,
Ни попросту — спортсмедным	Nor simply a brazen-faced
Лбом[77]	Sports-brat

The variation on the popular locution *iz molodyx da rannij* (young but already precocious) in the second line of the quoted example could also be described as a frequent and typical Cvetaeva device, although in this particular case the variation is not Cvetaeva's own, since it occurs in popular usage.

Finally, we have a group of neologisms in Cvetaeva's poetry that are derived from nursery talk (not baby talk used by infants, but an imitation of it, used by mothers and nurses when addressing babies). These find their rightful place in Cvetaeva's lullabies, which are often situated in the remote historical past. The following example is from "Xanskij polon" in *Remeslo*:

> — Спи, неустан,
> Спи, недослух,
> Чтоб тебя сам
> Хан карнаух!
>
> Хвать — да и в стан!
> Каши не даст!
> Чтоб тебя сам
> Гзак-загребаст![78]

[76] "Krysolov," *passim.*
[77] *Izbrannoe*, p. 194.
[78] *Remeslo*, p. 73.

Sleep, you tireless thing,
Sleep, you disobedient thing,
Or else the clip-eared
Khan himself [will get you]!

[He'll] snatch [you] — and off to his camp!
Won't give [you any] porridge!
May the grabby-handed
Gzak himself [get you]!

(The verbal expletive *xvat'* and the nominal forms derived from verbal stems like *vsxlip* or *šip* are widely used by Cvetaeva, in contradistinction to her usual avoidance of active verbal forms. The use of such verbal derivations in poetry was sanctioned by Puškin himself in his annotations to *Evgenij Onegin*.) [79]

The lullaby from the cycle "Skifskie" in *Posle Rossii* contains a set of varied refrains, which make wide use of nursery-type neologisms:

Дыши да не дунь,
Гляди да не глянь.
Волынь-криволунь,
Хвалынь-колывань. [80]

Breathe, but don't blow;
Look, but don't glance.
Volhynia — crooked moon,
Caspian sea [obs.] — Tallinn [obs.].

The self-contradicting imperative forms in the first two lines of this example (not meant as any kind of literal instructions) are echoed by the obsolete geographical designations in the second part of the quatrain. The proper nouns are not capitalized and have endings that contain a vague suggestion of verbs in the imperative form—not however as strongly and startlingly as in Xlebnikov's celebrated neologisms which derive verbal imperative forms from

[79] A. S. Puškin, *Polnoe sobranie sočinenij v desjati tomax* (Moscow-Leningrad, 1949), V, 195.
[80] *Posle Rossii*, p. 54.

such proper names as Genghis Khan and Mozart. The use of all these words can be described as decorative. The infant addressed in the lullaby cannot understand the implications, and the mother's preoccupations or daydreams merely seep into her song, with phonetics clearly predominant over semantics. These lullabies are one of the two areas in Cvetaeva's poetry where she approaches something like *zaum'*. The other such occurrence is in her poems based on imitations of magical spells and incantations. These are the *poèma* "Pereluočki" and the poems of the section "Sugroby" ("Snow Drifts") which precede it in *Remeslo*. Yet, while genuine magical spells are often deliberately obscure, those in Cvetaeva's poetry usually have easily recognizable meanings and their strange effect is achieved by the formation of uncommon and unexpected derivations from usual and familiar verbal stems:

Цельный день грызет, докучня,
Леденцовы зерна.
Дребезга, дрызга, разлучня,
Бойня, живодерня.[81]

(*dialectally and colloquially; a snowstorm is described*)
All the live-long day that bore keeps munching
Grains of hard candy.
The rattler, the splasher, the homewrecker,
The butchery, the slaughterhouse.

It has been demonstrated, it is hoped, that Marina Cvetaeva's verbal inventiveness and her exploitation of phonetic relationships inherent in the language have led her into new and original literary paths. Her exploration of this area of literary art follows the traditions of Trediakovskij and Gogol' (in whose work one can find examples of neologisms and of genuine *zaum'* that go beyond anything comparable in Cvetaeva's practice).[82] Far from obscuring her meaning, these devices have enabled her to find fresh and valid ways of expression in poetry and prose.

[81] *Remeslo*, p. 140.
[82] See Andrej Belyj, *Masterstvo Gogolja* (Moscow and Leningrad, 1934), p. 203.

Versification

The technical aspects of Marina Cvetaeva's poetry will one day serve as the subject of an extensive and detailed separate study. Her mastery of Russian verse is quite exceptional, the range of her techniques is wide and complex. For sheer brilliance and virtuosity, Cvetaeva's verse has few equals in the whole history of Russian poetry, but her virtuosity is at all times a vehicle of poetic expression and never (some critical opinion to the contrary) an end in itself.

The very first published book of Marina Cvetaeva (*Večernij al'bom*) opens with a dedication in the form of a strict Petrarchan sonnet.[83] The rest of the collection shows that although the sixteen and seventeen-year-old Cvetaeva was only a promising, at times immature, poet, she was already a skillful and imaginative versifier. *Večernij al'bom* uses only the five canonic meters of Russian versification: the iamb, the trochee, the dactyl, the amphibrach, and the anapest, without any mixing of the binary and ternary meters that result from the omission of unstressed syllables in the ternary meters (*dol'niki* or *pauzniki*), and which at the time of publication of *Večernij al'bom* (1910) had gained wide acceptance in Russian poetic practice. Any metrical monotony that might have resulted is easily overcome by young Cvetaeva's amazing strophic inventiveness. In this respect, we have to place her early poetry alongside that of such Russian poets as Žukovskij and Fet, who are particularly noted for variety and originality in inventing new types of stanzas. In addition to the traditional quatrains, we find in *Večernij al'bom* stanzas of five, six, seven, eight, and even twelve lines, with imaginative and at times complex rhyming schemes.

The rhymes Cvetaeva uses in her first collection are the traditional nineteenth-century ones, without any disregard of the unstressed syllables. The rhyming is competent, although not particularly striking or unexpected.

Between 1912 and 1916, Cvetaeva's versification underwent an evolution that parallels the development of Russian verse between, roughly, 1890 and 1910. First of all, this means an introduction of

---

[83] *Večernij al'bom*, p. 3.

metrical pauses, i.e., the omission of unstressed syllables in ternary meters. Verse of this type is usually described as accentual verse, *dol'niki* or *pauzniki*.

The idea of *dol'niki* and of metrical pauses presupposes a free selection for the location of the metrical pause and a certain amount of free and irregular mixing of all the three ternary meters. In fact, this type of verse inevitably has one or more ternary meters as a basic unit. This was the way of the historical development of the Russian *dol'nik* from the few scattered nineteenth-century examples in the work of Lermontov, Tjutčev, and Fet to the *dol'nik* as it was used by its principal twentieth-century practitioners: Gippius, Blok, Axmatova, Kuzmin, and Mandel'štam. Most of Cvetaeva's poems after *Versty I* do not mix the ternary meters; the alternation of bisyllabic and trisyllabic units in her verse follows a certain rigid pattern; at times bisyllabic units outnumber the trisyllabic ones, so that there is a doubt whether we have a ternary meter with pauses or a binary meter with added unstressed syllables. All this proves that Professor George Ivask had a strong point when he applied to Cvetaeva's mixed meters the ancient Greek term *logaoedic*, i.e., regular lines made up of more than one meter.[84] As Cvetaeva's subsequent metrical practice shows, much of her verse can be better explained as definite sequences of ternary and binary meters than in terms of pauses and *dol'niki*.[85]

The usual Russian *dol'niki*, with irregularly placed pauses and the free mixing of the ternary meters enter the poetry of Marina Cvetaeva in 1916, in her collection *Versty I.* The book was written during the period when Cvetaeva was particularly friendly with Mandel'štam and Kuzmin and contains cycles of poems dedicated to Blok and to Axmatova. It is perhaps to the impact of these poets, and to the fact that in certain poems of the collection Cvetaeva deliberately tries to evoke the styles of Blok and of Axmatova, that

[84] Jurij Ivask, "Cvetaeva," p. 63, where we read: "Usually in ternary meters the pauses wander all over the verse (both in the hexameter and in *pauzniki*). In Cvetaeva, however, there is a tendency toward strict regularity in the distribution of pauses (in the collection *Posle Rossii* about 40% of all the poems are written in 'regular' *pauzniki,* in logaoedic verse)."

[85] For a more detailed discussion of Cvetaeva's metrics, the reader is referred to my dissertation on Cvetaeva; I now consider some of the points I made on her versification subject to revision.

we owe the poems which mix the three ternary and binary meters at unpredictable points. If we can credit Cvetaeva's *dol'niki* to the practice of the contemporary Symbolist and Acmeist poets, we must not forget the German poetic practice as a possible source of suggestion for both *dol'niki* and the *logaoedic* meters of *Junošeskie stixi*. Cvetaeva was familiar with German poetry since childhood, and many poems of Goethe and Heine would be considered as *dol'niki* in terms of Russian versification.[86]

Versty I is Cvetaeva's most venturesome book in terms of verse techniques. In addition to *dol'niki* and to various new uses of the standard meters, we find in this collection strict *logaoedic* mixtures, free unrhymed verse, and verse forms based on imitation of popular Russian poetry: the *raëšnik* in the poem beginning "Prodaju! Prodaju!" (an unscannable mixture of meters in lines of varying length with assonance rhymes, of the type used by hawkers and carnival barkers, possibly suggested in this instance by Annenskij's imitation of *raëšnik* in his poem "Šariki detskie" ["Children's Balloons"]) ;[87] and the pentasyllabic popular verse of the type used in the nineteenth century by A. Kol'cov ("Čto dremučij les / Prizadumalsja") and A. K. Tolstoj in their imitations of folk poetry. In *Versty I* we see the appearance (in three poems) of one of Cvetaeva's favorite *logaoedic* mixtures, a ternary trimeter made up of two anapests followed by an amphibrach, which becomes a regular feature of her later poetic practice.[88]

A prominent feature of Cvetaeva's versification beginning with *Versty I* is her predilection for additional and irregularly placed stressed syllables, resulting in combinations not always explicable in terms of traditional Russian metrics. It was this aspect of Cvetaeva's versification that Vladislav Xodasevič had in mind when he wrote of her impact on the versification of Andrej Belyj in terms of Belyj's

[86] See the comparison of Russian and German versification in V. Žirmunskij, *Vvedenie v metriku* (Leningrad, 1925), pp. 80–83.

[87] I. Annenskij, *Stixotvorenija i tragedii* (Leningrad, 1959), p. 141.

[88] The poems in *Versty I* written in this meter are those beginning: "Sobiraja ljubimyx v put'" (p. 11), "Ty proxodiš'" (p. 67), and "Ne otstat' tebe! Ja ostrožnik . . . " (p. 84). Some notable examples of Cvetaeva's later use of this meter are the poem to Chevalier de Grieux (*Psixeja*, p. 78), "Xvala bogatym" ("Eulogy of the Rich") (*Posle Rossii*, pp. 44–45), one of the poems to her son written in 1932 (*Izbrannoe*, pp. 193–194), and finally, one of the poems about Czechoslovakia of 1939 ("Vzjali," *Izbrannoe*, p. 23

use of the spondee and the molossus (a succession of three stressed syllables).[89] A particularly charming example of Cvetaeva's use of additional stressed syllables occurs in the often-reprinted poem which originally appeared in *Versty I*:

> В огромном городе моем — ночь.
> Из дома сонного иду — прочь,
> И люди думают: жена, дочь.
> А я запомнила одно: ночь.[90]

> In my huge city it is night.
> From the sleepy house I walk — away.
> And people think: a wife, a daughter.
> But I remembered one [thing only]: the night.

Here, the stressed monosyllabic word placed at the end of a line turns what would otherwise have been the usual Russian iambic tetrameter into something quite unique. Repeated for four quatrains, each of which has only one set of rhymes, the metrical pattern creates a hypnotic effect quite in keeping with the sense of unreality that is the subject of the poem.

Verses containing predominantly or exclusively stressed monosyllabic words are also found in the work of Cvetaeva's contemporary Futurist poets, Majakovskij and especially Nikolaj Aseev (1889–1963). The same tendency had led Cvetaeva to write her "Vozvraščenie voždja" ("Return of the Chief") in what can be described as either spondees or a monomacer (one stressed syllable) dimeter:

> Конь — хром,   The horse is lame;
> Меч — ржав.   The sword is rusty.
> Кто — сей?   Who is this?
> Вождь толп.[91]   A leader of crowds.

The ultimate possibility of this trend is realized in the two monomacer "quatrains" we find in "Krysolov." Here is one

---

[89] V. Xodasevič, "Knigi i ljudi," *Vozroždenie*, May 31, 1934.

[90] *Versty I*, p. 92; reprinted in *Psixeja*, pp. 21–22 and *Izbrannoe*, p. 53. The recurring pyrrhic in the third foot is typical in its regularity.

[91] *Remeslo*, p. 58.

describing a landscape in India as imagined by the hypnotized
rats:

Смол	Hum
Гул.	Of resins.
Вол.	An ox.
Мул.[92]	A mule.

Throughout her career as a poet, Cvetaeva continued to use the
classical Russian meters. About one half of her verse in the nineteen-
twenties and thirties is written in one of the standard meters,
although in her later practice these meters are used with greater
rhythmic freedom than they were in her first book. This is
manifested in the somewhat freer distribution of pyrrhics in the
binary meters and in the introduction of additional suprametrical
stresses in the amphibrach and the anapest, especially at the
beginning of the line. The *dol'niki* become quite rare in her work
after the nineteen-twenties, and instead we find a highly individual
system of meters, which Cvetaeva began evolving in *Versty I* and
which reach their highest development in *Remeslo* and the two
classical tragedies. The *dol'niki* of the Russian twentieth-century
poetry and the metrical system of Majakovskij (which, as Boris
Tomaševskij has shown,[93] is an extension of *dol'niki*) all tend
toward various free combinations of binary and ternary meters,
usually superimposed on a basically ternary pattern. Cvetaeva's
metrics after *Remeslo* go a step further and accomplish a mutual
contamination or fusion of binary and ternary meters. A comparable
phenomenon in music was the simultaneous use of the major and
the minor modes by composers like Maurice Ravel, and the metrical
shimmer in some poems in *Posle Rossii* produced by the uncertain
wavering between binary and ternary metrical patterns and the
concomitant metrical harshness of such combinations is not unlike
the effect of some of Ravel's harmonies.

[92] Fourth canto of "Krysolov," *Volja Rossii,* VII–VIII (1925), 51. The
passage is spoken by the Pied Piper's flute, which here apparently descends
into its lowest register. Cf. the experimental "sonnet," "Poxorony" ("Funeral") by V. Xodasevič, written entirely in monosyllabic lines (*Sobranie stixov*
[Munich, 1961], p. 198.
[93] B. V. Tomaševskij, *Stilistika i stixosloženie* (Leningrad, 1959), pp.
480–493.

The basic unit of such metrical fusion in Cvetaeva is what old-fashioned treatises on metrics call the choriamb: a tetrasyllabic unit in which the first and the fourth syllables are stressed and the second and third are unstressed. Regarded in terms of binary meters, this sequence is rare in Russian metrics.[94] It occurred in the infrequent cases of substitution of the opposite meter in iambic and trochaic lines and never had any independent existence on its own. But considered in terms of ternary meters, the same unit is seen as the very common dactylic dimeter, very usual in all dactylic lines with masculine ending and frequently occurring in *dol'niki* ("Imja tvoe —ptica v ruke" in the first line of one of Cvetaeva's poems to Blok). Cvetaeva makes frequent use of this unit as a basic line in her poetry of the nineteen-twenties and thirties:

Помни закон:	Remember the law:
Здесь не владей!	Own nothing here!
Чтобы потом —	So that later,
В Граде Друзей:	In the City of Friends:
В этом пустом,	In that empty,
В этом крутом	In that steep
Небе мужском	Masculine heaven
— Сплошь золотом —[95]	— Totally golden —

If this were the only way Cvetaeva used this combination, we could not recognize its binary possibilities and, despite its frequency,

---

[94] See B. O. Unbegaun, *Russian Versification* (Oxford, 1956), pp. 89–92. The clash of trochee and iambic occurs in the traditional Russian iambic tetrameter in the infrequent cases when a trochee is used to replace the first foot:

> Boj barabannyj, kliki, skrežet;
> (Puškin)
> Sem' — osenit' sebja krestom.
> (Blok)

The dactylic implications of the choriambic combination are not felt against the background of the preceding and following iambic lines in such incidental passages.

[95] *Posle Rossii*, p. 11. Discussing a metrically similar chorus in Annenskij's tragedy *Thamyris, the Cythara Player*, Vsevolod Setchkarev describes the metrical pattern as follows: "The choriamb prevails and mixes with dactylo-iambs." (*Studies in the Life and Works of Innokentij Annenskij* [The Hague, 1963], p. 196).

would simply note that Cvetaeva was fond of dactylic dimeter with masculine ending. But the point is that in much of Cvetaeva's poetry of the nineteen-twenties and in the two Greek tragedies the choriambic combination of stressed-unstressed-unstressed-stressed syllables becomes a part of a regular and systematically applied pattern. Occurring repeatedly in some fixed section of an otherwise usual iambic or trochaic line of verse, this combination jars the ear accustomed to traditional Russian versification and to the accentual verse of Symbolists and Acmeists in two ways: the "clash" of two adjacent stressed syllables, incidental, rare, and almost always unexpected in Russian verse, here becomes normal, recurring in certain predictable and expected positions; and the dactylic rhythm of the first three syllables of the choriamb brings a constant suggestion of the ternary into what are basically binary meters. The following examples illustrate an almost consistently choriambic meter (from "Na krasnom kone"); an iambic trimeter in which the second foot is systematically replaced by a trochee; and the particularly frequently used iambic trimeter with a trochee in the first foot:

> Что это вдруг — рухнуло? — Нет,
> Это не мир — рухнул!
> То две руки — конному — вслед
> Девочка — без — куклы.[96]

> What is it that suddenly collapsed? No,
> It is not the world that collapsed!
> It is the girl without [her] doll
> [Stretching] two hands after the horseman.

Любовь: зноб до кости!	Love: chills to the bone!
Любовь: зной до бела!	Love: burns till white heat!
Вода — любит концы.	Water loves ends.
Река — любит тела.[97]	The river loves bodies.

[96] "Na krasnom kone," *Psixeja*, p. 89. Note the careful distribution of the dividing dashes between words, indicating the desired pattern of stresses (these dashes usually precede the syllables where strong stress is wanted). The typographical pattern of the passage brings out the choriambic design and precludes a metrical interpretation in terms of dactyl only.

[97] *Posle Rossii*, p. 123.

Леты подводный свет.
Красного солнца риф.
Застолбенел ланцет,
Певчее горло вскрыв.[98]

Lethe's subaqueous light.
The red sun's reef.
The lancet grew numb
After cutting the singing throat open.

The above discussion of Cvetaeva's choriamb-based meters is meant only as a *description* of a part of her metrical practice in the later period of her literary career. A full explanation of this practice would require the kind of taxonomic and statistical approach that has been applied in the last five years to the versification of Majakovskij by such mathematically-minded Soviet linguists as A. N. Kolmogorov and A. M. Kondratov. A completely new approach to metrics was tried when M. L. Gasparov used electronic computers for investigation of Russian *dol'niki*.[99] Cvetaeva was one of the poets thus investigated; Gasparov's conclusion that her three-stress *dol'nik* was predominantly anapestic (as contrasted to Esenin's "isolating tendency" and Gumilëv's "isosyllabic tendency") seems to indicate that her verse of the nineteen-twenties has not been used in the investigation (neither *Posle Rossii* nor the *poèmy* of the nineteen-twenties were available in the Soviet Union at that time.) Nevertheless, the beginning is a promising one, and future studies along the same lines should reveal the exact character of Cvetaeva's metrical contributions.

It is in connection with her choriambic meters that Cvetaeva makes one of her most audacious demands on the rules of Russian prosody. An additional stressed syllable is sometimes placed *before* the choriambic sequence. For such cases Cvetaeva introduced the dividing dash after the first syllable of polysyllabic words at the beginning of the line to assure the two initial stressed syllables

---

[98] *Ibid.*, p. 29.
[99] M. L. Gasparov, "Statstičeskoe obsledovanie russkogo trexudarnogo dol'nika," *Teorija verojatnostej i ee primenenija,* VIII: 1 (Moscow, 1963), 102–108. I am indebted to Professor K. Taranovski for pointing out this study to me.

required by this meter. In doing so, she of course violated the very basis of Russian prosody by requiring more than one stress per word:

Му—жайся же сердце!	Take courage then, O heart!
Му—жайся и чай!	Take courage and hope!
Не—бесный разверзся	The heavenly vault is riven!
Свод! В трепете стай[100]	Aquiver with swarms

When using this device in her tragedy "Tezej" and in *Posle Rossii*, Cvetaeva was careful to make her wishes clear in footnotes: "Between the first and the second syllable there is a break, i.e., there is equal stress on the first and the second syllables. I have not placed a dash in all such cases. M.C." [101] and "The first syllable is emphasized and broken off. This is not indicated everywhere." [102] In the poem in *Posle Rossii* to which the last footnote refers, the dividing dashes appear only in the second stanza:

Не — поздно еще!	It is not late still!
В рас—светные щели	Through the slits at sunrise
(Не поздно!) — еще	(It is not late!) — still
Нам птицы не пели.[103]	No birds sang for us.

(Note the additional use of parentheses and the exclamation mark to suggest the desired intonation.) In the remainder of the poem, the dashes are absent, although a parallel metrical pattern is obviously implied. The dividing dash within a word, calling for additional stress, also occurs in such poems where it is not a part of basic metrical pattern:

У меня к тебе наклон лба,
Дозирающего вер—ховья.[104]

My forehead is inclined toward you,
Discerning the sources.

---

[100] "Tezej," in *Versty*, II (Paris, 1927), 42.
[101] *Ibid.*, p. 41.
[102] *Posle Rossii*, p. 18.
[103] *Ibid.*, p. 18.
[104] *Ibid.*, p. 105.

In certain poems of *Posle Rossii* and in *Mólodec,* words may be provided with more syllables than they would normally have, as imitation of either a slow drawling diction, or, as in the following example, of shouting:

> Выше, выше — и сли—лись
> В Ариаднино: ве—ер—нись
> Обернись![105]

> Higher, higher, — and they merged
> Into Ariadne's: re — ee — turn,
> Turn around!

Cvetaeva knew that she was introducing something quite new in Russian prosody with her demand for hyperprosodic stresses. She points out the similarity of her practice with that of Russian composers of vocal music in whose prosody additional stresses are often produced, not only by placing a normally unstressed syllable on the strong time in a bar, but also by assigning a longer duration to the unstressed syllable than to the stressed one, which, due to absence of vowel length in the language, has the effect of additional stress. It was the separation of words by internal dashes in printed music that suggested the device to Cvetaeva: "Later, when I was forced by the rhythmic structure to break words, to tear the words apart by means of the dividing dash unfamiliar in verse, and everyone scolded me for this while a few praised (in both cases for 'modernity'), I was not able to say anything except 'it has to be.' Suddenly I saw once with my eyes those song texts of my infancy, shot through with completely legal dashes—and I felt myself washed clean by all of Music from my charge of 'modernity': washed clean, supported, confirmed and legalized. . . ." [106] In this connection, Cvetaeva quotes the accusation of Bal'mont that she demands from versification what only music can give.[107]

Cvetaeva was not interested in theoretical aspects of metrics and prosody. She had undergone a complex evolution as a poet and was the author of *Remeslo* and of *Car'-devica,* before she learned the

---

[105] *Ibid.,* p. 65.
[106] "Mat' i muzyka," *Proza,* p. 82.
[107] *Ibid.*

meaning of the terms "dactyl" and "trochee."[108] She was not interested in issuing literary manifestos, although she must have realized that at least two of her innovations, the syncretism of the binary meters with the dactyl in the choriamb-based poems and the introduction of the artificial, hyperprosodic stresses, constituted revolutionary developments in the history of Russian versification. It is strange, however, to what extent her innovations have been overlooked in the literature on Russian versification as well as in the works on Cvetaeva. In reviewing "Tezej," Nikolaj Kul'man wrote: "An unpleasant affectation is evident in division of words. . . . This is supposed, if you please, to indicate equal stress of the first and the second syllables."[109] Kul'man (1871–1940), a distinguished literary scholar, was so annoyed by the unfamiliar dashes that he completely failed to see them as a metrical device. Similarly, Jurij Terapiano, himself a practicing poet, should have known better than to say that Cvetaeva divided words by dashes "in order to increase the expressivity."[110] Finally, Aleksandr Baxrax, with a rather amazing lack of tact, chose to devote a passage in his obituary of Cvetaeva to attacking her versification. Without bothering to analyze or explain this versification, Baxrax wrote: "Some of her devices can fatigue the most unprejudiced reader. The frequent necessity of footnotes indicating the places of stress in the verse makes reading bothersome, smacking of didacticism."[111] These are all the comments I could find on Cvetaeva's metrical system and they are truly amazing: the commentators clearly begrudge the poet her attempt to fix on paper the rhythmic and metrical structure of her work. The dividing dashes occur in a very small percentage of Cvetaeva's work, but where they do appear, they are indispensable, and without them the lilt and pulsation of Ariadne's magnificent

---

[108] Letters to Baxrax, *Mosty*, V, 305.

[109] N. Kul'man, "Versty N⁰ 2," *Vozroždenie* (Paris), February 10, 1927.

[110] Ju. Terapiano, "Proza Mariny Cvetaevoj," *Novoe Russkoe Slovo*, March 7, 1954. The example of dividing dashes quoted in Terapiano's article is untypical of Cvetaeva and seems to have been invented *ad hoc* by Terapiano.

[111] A. Baxrax, "Zvukovoj liven'," p. 184. To these three commentators I cannot unfortunately add Andrej Belyj's metrical analysis of *Razluka*, mentioned in "Plennyj dux" (*Proza*, p. 318), which I have been unable to locate and Ivask's analysis mentioned in one of Cvetaeva's letters to him (p. 209), which has apparently been lost.

speeches in "Tezej" would completely elude us. In the same way, Cvetaeva's occasional stress marks over certain vowels are essential for the comprehension of the rhythm, as is shown by the comparison between certain poems printed in *Sovremennye Zapiski* in the nineteen-thirties without stress marks and the same poems reprinted in the Soviet edition of Cvetaeva with the stress marks restored.

To sum up Marina Cvetaeva's metrical practice of the nineteen-twenties and thirties, we can state that more than one half of her verse of that period was written in the five conventional Russian meters, with definite predominance of iambics over the other meters, while the rest of her verse falls into either her own syncretic binary-dactylic meters (with the choriamb as both the basic unit and the catalytic agent of fusion) or *logaoedic* mixtures of varying meters arranged into definite rigid patterns.

Other Aspects

Metrics is only one aspect of Cvetaeva's originality in versification. Particular features of her versification will be discussed in this work during the examination of individual collections and *poèmy*, but some of the salient and typical traits of her verse should be pointed out now. In the period of her poetic maturity, Cvetaeva tends to use the twentieth-century rhyming system (the rhyming element being the last stressed vowel in the line, supported by the identity or similarity of either the preceding or the following consonant). Typical Cvetaeva rhymes are quoted in Boris Unbegaun's *Russian Versification* (pp. 144–146).

Structurally, the two most important devices of the mature Cvetaeva are her use of enjambment and her use of parallel constructions. Enjambment in the later works of Cvetaeva may be said to cease being a literary device. It becomes instead an internal part of her poetic thinking. A long study could be devoted to the uses to which she puts it and the effects she extracts from it. Its role in the structure of her verse is analogous to the role of the choriamb in her metrics: a constant source of tension and of a potential clash between lines and stanzas, just as the choriamb creates tension between the feet of verse. In many of her later poems, the enjambment appears after the last line of the final stanza, as if the rhythmic drive had caused the last word to overflow the boundaries of the poem.

A very special kind of enjambment used by Cvetaeva consists of transmitting a word from one line to the next, which necessitates rhyming *the first half* of the transmitted word:

Впытываются — и сти-   They peer — and [smash] a clen-
снутым кулаком — в пески![112] chèd fist into the sands!

A related device is used in "Čitateli gazet" ("Newspaper Readers"), in which transmitting of a word from the *middle* of one line to the beginning of the next one vividly illustrates the lurchings of a subway train filled with newspaper readers:

Кача — ''живет с сестрой'' —
ются — ''убил отца!'' —
Качаются — тщетой
накачиваются.[113]

They are sway —   "seduced his sister" —
ing —   "murdered his father!" —
They are swaying — drivel
Is pumped into them.

Equally typical and constant are the parallel structures: the anaphora, refrains of various sorts, periodic repetitions of passages, verbatim or with significant minor alterations, and finally, parallel syntactic and grammatical structures. All these are closely connected to Cvetaeva's sense of verbal stems and her flair for verbal inventiveness discussed earlier. Typical parallel constructions make their appearance as early as *Večernij al'bom,* e.g., in the poem "Rouge et bleue," [114] in which the two heroines are successively shown as little children, as young girls, and as grown-up women in frustrating situations appropriate to each age. The three long

---

[112] *Posle Rossii,* p. 15. See the discussion of Cvetaeva's enjambment in K. Taranovski, "Some Problems of Enjambment in Slavic and Western European Verse," *International Journal of Slavic Linguistics and Poetics,* VII (The Hague, 1963), 80–87, where this example is used as illustration.
[113] *Izbrannoe,* p. 215.
[114] *Večernij al'bom,* pp. 186–187.

stanzas describing this are three variations on a basic established structural and syntactic pattern. In Cvetaeva's later poetry, these parallelisms take varied and subtle forms, contributing to the "well-built," craftsmanlike quality of her verse. The typical example of anaphora can be found in the well-known "Popytka revnosti" ("An Attempt at Jealousy"),[115] where the words "Kak živetsja vam" ("What is your life like?") appear in the first lines of the first, the third, and the fourth stanzas, and keep recurring throughout the poem in the first, third, or fourth lines of all the succeeding stanzas. In the same poem, the refrain and the variation on an earlier structure can be seen when the lines,

> С пошлиной бессмертной пошлости
> Как справляетесь, бедняк?

> How do you deal with the import tax
> Of the immortal triviality, you poor man?

in the fourth stanza are repeated in the eighth stanza as

> С язвою бессмертной совести
> Как справляетесь, бедняк?

> How do you deal with the festering wound
> Of immortal [pangs of] conscience, you poor man?

In some poems in *Posle Rossii* and in the fourth section of "Poèma konca," the verse structure is so saturated by several simultaneously moving parallel devices that one is tempted to call such passages contrapuntal or even fugal.

As already mentioned, alliteration as such does not particularly interest Cvetaeva, and the rich "sound instrumentation" of some of her poetry is due to the verbal invention and concentration and to her constant effort to render the inner meaning by the amassing of phonetically similar words. Cvetaeva's typically Futuristic sense (as the term is applicable to Xlebnikov and Majakovskij) of the psychological value of phonetics is the basis of the alliterative effects that permeate much of her verse:

---

[115] *Posle Rossii*, pp. 135–136; frequently reprinted.

Не для льстивых этих риз, лживых ряс
Голосистою на свет родилась![116]

It was not for the sake of these flattering chasubles, these false cassocks
That I was born into the world with a singing voice!

of her frequent internal rhymes:

И за то что в учетах, в скуках
В позолотах, в зевотах, в ватах[117]

And because among the inventories, the boredom,
Among the gilded [furniture], the yawns, the cotton [waddings]

of her hypnotic reiterations of the same word:

Чужой человек,	Stranger man,
Дорогой человек,	Precious man,
Ночлег-человек	For-one-night man,
Навек-человек![118]	Forever man!

or of such breath-taking onomatopoetic effects as the imitation of
the drowsy splashing of the river Lethe:

Ивовый сребролетейский плеск
Плачущий. . . В слепотекущий склеп
Памятей — перетомилась — спрячь
В ивовый сребролетейский плач.[119]

Willowy, silvery-Lethean splashes,
Weeping . . . Hide it in the blindly-flowing tomb
Of memories (— you are exhausted —),
In willowy, silvery-Lethean weeping.

It is the expressive and the psychological effect of such phonetic
combinations that Cvetaeva exploits, rather than their musical
sound as Maksim Gor'kij had thought.[120]
   Much as Cvetaeva objected to being classified with any of the

---

[116] *Izbrannoe*, p. 140.
[117] *Posle Rossii*, p. 44.
[118] *Remeslo*, p. 128.
[119] *Posle Rossii*, p. 22.
[120] *Literaturnoe nasledstvo*, LXX, 301. In one of his letters to Pasternak,
Gor'kij wrote of Cvetaeva: "Phonetics is not yet music, but she thinks: it's
already music."

Futurists,[121] an examination of her favorite tropes and figures of speech shows her unmistakable affinity to Majakovskij, Xlebnikov, and Pasternak in this area, as in many others. This aspect of Cvetaeva's verse, like her metrics, strophics, and structural patterns, deserves a detailed study. Her two most usual tropes are also the favorite ones of Majakovskij and Pasternak: the hyperbole and the developed, "realized" metaphor. Like Majakovskij and, to a lesser degree, Pasternak,[122] Cvetaeva often thinks of herself and her world in sweeping, cosmic terms. She presents the Kremlin to her three-year-old daughter and hands the city of Moscow to Anna Axmatova in homage. Axmatova's son shall inherit the Arctic and the Antarctic, and Blok is addressed in terms suitable for speaking to the Creator. A Communist friend (possibly Majakovskij) is told: "You and I are not at two [opposite] ends of the earth—we are on two [different] constellations!" [123] When Cvetaeva is unhappy, all of Racine and all of Shakespeare would be unable to express it.[124]

Closely related to Cvetaeva's use of the hyperbole is her use of developed ("realized") metaphors which at times serve as the basic image of entire poems. Here one might cite the poem "Zanaves" ("The Curtain"),[125] entirely built on the metaphor of the author as the curtain, protecting a suffering young man (shown as an actor on the stage) from practical life (shown as the audience). The metaphor is partially explained in the fourth line of the poem ("Scena—ty, zanaves—ja" ["You are the stage, I am the curtain"]) and made entirely clear only in the last line of the eight-quatrain poem ("Zala —žizn', zanaves—ja" ["Life is the theater, I am the curtain"]). A very similar procedure is employed in the poem originally dedicated to Jurij Zavadskij, in which he is represented as the sun,[126] or in the poem where the poet's gift of song is shown as a fluttering, singing bird.[127] Neither the hyperbole nor the extended developed metaphors

---

[121] Letters to Ivask, pp. 209–210.

[122] On hyperbole in Pasternak, see I. N. Bušman, "O rannej lirike Pasternaka," *Sbornik statej posvjaščennyx tvorčestvu B. L. Pasternaka* (Munich, 1962), pp. 220–221.

[123] "Čuzoj" ("A Stranger") *Na Zapade,* ed. Ju. Ivask, p. 82.

[124] *Posle Rossii,* p. 66.

[125] *Ibid.,* pp. 97–98.

[126] *Izbrannoe,* p. 98.

[127] *Ibid.,* p. 111.

are mere devices: both are manifestations of Cvetaeva's *Übermass* and imaginative sweep.

In a poet as genuine and sincere as Cvetaeva, it is not easy to separate the manner from the matter. Her elaborate versification, her difficult syntax, her unexpected imagery, and the rich sonority of her verse all combine and contribute to the unique quality of her poetic vision of the world. Yet, her accomplishment would not have been possible without her secure grasp of the tools of her craft, attained by single-minded and determined hard work. Cvetaeva disapproved of formal analysis of verse structure, feeling it as a dissection of living tissue.[128] But such analysis shows that Cvetaeva's arrival at poetic mastery was not merely intuitive. This is confirmed by her own lines in *Posle Rossii* in which she proudly asserted: "I know that Venus is the work of hands; I am a craftsman and I know my craft." [129]

[128] "Poèt o kritike," p. 121.
[129] *Posle Rossii*, p. 10.

VII ✍

Lyric Poetry

The earliest published poetry of Marina Cvetaeva is to be found in her first two collections of verse, *Večernij al'bom* and *Vol'šebynj fonar'*. Very little is know about the verse Cvetaeva wrote as a child, antedating the earliest poems included in *Večernij al'bom*. We know, however, that Cvetaeva had the manuscripts of her earliest work in Paris, because on December 29, 1932, she gave a poetry reading, the program of which included some of her *infantilia,* such as "revolutionary poems written as a child,"[1] which have not been published or described in any biographical literature on Cvetaeva. The whereabouts of the manuscripts of this earliest poetry are not known. We can form an idea of these poems only from a few brief fragments that had found their way into Cvetaeva's memoirs of her childhood and from the childishly melodramatic little poem quoted in her memoir of Mandel'štam.[2]

Evening Album (Večernij al'bom),
Magic Lantern (Vol'šebnyj fonar'),
From Two Books (Iz dvux knig): 1908–1912

The first two volumes of Cvetaeva's work can best be considered as a unit, not only thematically and stylistically, but chronologically

---

[1] *Poslednie Novosti,* December 29, 1932. The program of the reading included "childhood poems about children, childhood revolutionary poems, poems written at school and in early youth."

[2] "Istorija odnogo posvjaščenija," p. 116.

as well. The dated poems in *Volšebnyj fonar'* mostly bear the date
of 1911, but this collection contains undated poems about the
summer holiday of the Cvetaev family in Tarusa in 1908,[3] as well as
a set of poems in which Cvetaeva speaks of her mother as recently
dead or even still alive.[4] The general theme and style of these poems
would lead one to conclude that they were written concurrently and
in some cases possibly earlier than the poems in *Verčernij al'bom*.
On the other hand, a considerable portion of *Volšebnyj fonar'* was
undoubtedly written after the appearance of the first collection. In
terms of poetic technique and versification, everything that can be
said about *Večernij al'bom* is fully applicable to the second
collection.

In the evolution of Cvetaeva's poetic personality, the first two
collections have a place that is analogous to the place of Puškin's
verse written at the Lycée of Carskoe Selo within his work as a
whole. The early Cvetaeva is a poet of a definite historical and even
philosophical orientation in the sense that the young Puškin of the
Lycée period was a Karamzinian poet. In her poetic culture, the
young Cvetaeva was rooted in the traditions of the second half of
the nineteenth century, while at the same time being clearly aware
of the magnificent flowering of new Russian poetry in the midst of
which she was living. Her emotional and intellectual outlook,
however, can best be explained in terms of the idealistic and
romantic revival among certain lesser French writers at the end of
the nineteenth century. This revival is best exemplified in the
Faustian drama *Axel* by Villiers de l'Isle Adam; we also find it in
the novel *Les Pléiades* by Gobineau and, in vulgarized and diluted
form, in the plays of Edmond Rostand, whose *L'Aiglon* and *La
Princesse lointaine* were essential for the intellectual formation of
Cvetaeva at the time of *Večernij al'bom*.

These romantic and idealistic views lead the poet to expect from
life more than it can possibly give; a concomitant tendency is to

---

[3] The two poems from *Volšebnyj fonar'* (pp. 42 and 43), which appeared
undated at the time of the original publication, were dated 1909 when
reprinted in *Tarusskie stranicy* in 1961, possibly on the basis of manuscripts in
the possession of Ariadna Èfron.

[4] *Volšebnyj fonar'*, pp. 9, 10, 12, 20, 26.

admire everything that is exceptional and heroic and to reject the average, the everyday, the prosaic. The most perfect expression of this attitude in Cvetaeva is found in the poem she wrote in Tarusa on her seventeenth birthday. The poem is called "Molitva" ("A Prayer") and its first two stanzas read:

Христос и Бог! Я жажду чуда
Теперь, сейчас, в начале дня!
О, дай мне умереть, покуда
Вся жизнь как книга для меня.

Ты мудрый, Ты не скажешь строго:
— "Терпи, еще не кончен срок."
Ты сам мне подал — слишком много!
Я жажду сразу всех дорог![5]

Christ and God! I yearn for a miracle,
Right now, immediately, at break of day!
O let me die, while still
All life is like a book to me.

Thou art wise, Thou wouldst not sternly say:
"Endure, the time is not yet come."
Thou Thyself gavest me too much!
I yearn for all the roads at once.

A heroic, miraculous early death is preferable to disappointment and frustration inevitable on attaining maturity. The fascination of an early death of an exceptional, gifted person is very strong for Cvetaeva at seventeen. It is this fascination that makes the biography of Napoleon's son, the Duke of Reichstadt, and its poetic treatment in Rostand's play the central myth of Cvetaeva's youth. The pathos of the young duke's inherited exceptional destiny, the doomed nature of his attempts to realize this destiny, and the heroism and matchless loyalty to the Bonapartist cause displayed by the heroine of *L'Aiglon,* the Countess Camerata—all these make Cvetaeva overlook the shoddy theatrical effects that fill Rostand's

[5] *Večernij al'bom,* p. 168; *Iz dvux knig,* p. 50.

play and the frequent clumsiness of its jangling alexandrine couplets.

The Bonapartism of Cvetaeva is manifested in her first two books not only thematically, but also in the epigraphs from Napoleon and his son, as well as from Rostand. When writing her poems about the Duke of Reichstadt and the Countess Camerata, Cvetaeva consulted sources other than *L'Aiglon,* among them the memoirs of Count Prokesch-Osten.[6] The series of L'Aiglon poems in *Večernij al'bom* ("V Pariže," "V Šenbrunne," "Kamerata," "Rasstavanie") is continued in *Volšebnyj fonar'* (the poems "Gercog Rejxštadtskij" and "Bonapartisty"); this group of poems reaches its slightly absurb climax in "Rasstavanie" ("Separation"), where the fate of Napoleon's son is compared to that of Christ and the site of his exile, the palace of Schönbrunn, is likened to Golgotha. While the life of the Duke of Reichstadt is "the most beautiful of legends"[7] for the young Cvetaeva, she is also attracted to other figures who by accident of birth or effort of will have succeeded in turning their tragic fate and untimely death into popular legends. There is little discrimination in Cvetaeva's choice of admired personalities at this stage: Louis XVII of France, Marija Baškirceva (to whose "radiant memory" *Večernij al'bom* is dedicated), and Cvetaeva's cousin Sergej Ilovajskij are found side by side with such literary characters as Princess Nina Džavaxa, the heroine of Čarskaja's lachrymose juvenile romance. In the second collection, there is a poem in praise of Marceline Desbordes-Valmore, to whose poetry Cvetaeva was introduced by Vološin.[8] A poem addressed to Maksim Gor'kij's first wife laments the death of Gor'kij's little daughter, Katja, who was Anastasija Cvetaeva's playmate when Gor'kij's family lived next door to the Cvetaevs in the Crimea some years earlier (*Večernij al'bom,* pp. 144–45).

Like Cvetaeva's later poetry, her first two books strongly reflect her current reading, which during that period was the typical juvenile literature read by a young person of her class. It is essentially minor literature, and the most significant writer of the ones mentioned in these poems is probably Mark Twain, whose

---

[6] *Večernij al'bom,* epigraph on p. 163.
[7] *Ibid.,* "Kamerata."
[8] "V zerkale knigi M. D.-V.," *Volšebnyj fonar',* p. 102.

books are the subject of the delightful poem "Knigi v krasnom pereplete" ("Books in Red Bindings"),[9] which concludes with these lines:

О золотые времена,
Где взор смелей и сердце чище!
О золотые имена:
Гекк Финн, Том Сойер, Принц и Нищий!

Ah, those golden times
When the gaze [was] bolder and the heart purer!
Ah, those golden names:
Huck Finn, Tom Sawyer, the Prince and the Pauper!

The poem "Sara v Versal'skom monastyre" ("Sara at the Versailles Nunnery"),[10] which, at first glance, we are tempted to connect with Villiers de l'Isle Adam's *Axel,* turns out on closer study to describe the childhood of Sarah Bernhardt, another admired heroine of the young Cvetaeva and the stage incarnation of *La Princesse lointaine* and of *L'Aiglon.* Although Cvetaeva was not introduced to *Axel* by Vološin until after the appearance of her first collection (and, of course, she admired it tremendously),[11] the mention of the heroine of this ultra-romantic drama is not irrelevant to Cvetaeva's early poetry. Like Sara, Marina Cvetaeva felt and understood the value and the attraction of the external world, which she nonetheless ultimately rejected as a matter of principle.

While the romantic solitude and heroism of literary and historical figures provide the early poetry of Cvetaeva with its outlook and give it direction, the hero-worshipping poet of the first two books is also a child, and the substance of her poetry is drawn from minor, everyday trifles and the daily life of her family and friends. The atmosphere of the nursery is strong in both books—in the abundance of diminutives, in certain recurring catchwords (*skazka, mama, detočka*), in the frequent fairy-tale imagery. The childhood that Cvetaeva was to depict in such somber colors in her prose of the nineteen-thirties is seen here as a magical region one should enjoy because one may be expelled from it at any time. In some of the

---

[9] *Večernij al'bom,* pp. 55–56.
[10] *Ibid.,* pp. 59–60.
[11] *Proza,* p. 147 ("Živoe o živom").

later poems in *Volšebnyj fonar'*, the nineteen-year-old poet is desperately fighting the impending eviction into the prosaic adult world. Cvetaeva's temporary solution of the problem is implicit in two poems of the second collection, which bear related titles. The poem "Iz skazki v žizn'" ("From a Fairy Tale into Life") is a farewell lament for Asja Turgeneva, newly married to the famous and adult Andrej Belyj. The poem "Iz skazki v skazku" ("From One Fairy Tale into Another") is addressed by Cvetaeva to Sergej Èfron at the time of their marriage. In it, she asserts her intention to remain a little girl for the rest of her days and promises to teach her husband how to remain a child. Two of the finer poems in *Volšebnyj fonar'*, "Podrastajuščej" ("To a Growing Girl") and "V pjatnadcat' let" ("At the Age of Fifteen") are dirges for departed childhood. There are poems about the childhood of Sergej Èfron and even of Maksimilian Vološin ("Žar-Ptica" ["The Firebird"] in *Volšebnyj fonar'*). Vladimir Nilender, however, after the break with him described in *Večernij al'bom* in a group of poems dating from January, 1910, is no longer admitted into the enchanted world of childhood and is described as "a wise philologist with a pile of books," a wise man "who finds his repose in Heraclitus and whose glance is lighted up by the shade of Orpheus." The numerous diminutive forms of first names scattered in the two books (which so annoyed Brjusov) are helpful for biographical study but must be confusing to the uninitiated reader: Asja may mean either Cvetaeva's sister or Anna Turgeneva; "Volodja" for the most part does not refer to Nilender, but to some hard-to-identify childhood friend; there are two boys named Serëža, Sergej Ilovajskij (in *Večernij al'bom*) and Sergej Èfron (in *Volšebnyj fonar'*). The various young girls to whom certain poems of the first collection are dedicated are apparently casual school acquaintances, not mentioned in any way in Cvetaeva's later autobiographical prose; one exception among these is Anna Kallin (also mentioned as "Anja Lanina"), whom Cvetaeva was to meet again during her visit to London.

The poem "Mama v sadu" ("Mama in the Garden") (*Večernij al'bom*, pp. 65–66) is dedicated to another of Asja Cvetaeva's classmates, a girl named Galja D'jakonova, who was later to become famous, first as the wife of the French poet Paul Eluard, and later as the fabled Gala Dali, depicted as the center of many an apocalyptic vision by her second husband, the painter Salvador Dali.

The books faithfully reflect Cvetaeva's travels to France and to the Black Forest, the details of her schooling and everyday life, her relations with her relatives and friends. This is the "Acmeist" side of the early Cvetaeva. Her preoccupation with everyday detail (which bored Brjusov but delighted Gumilëv) may at first glance appear incongruous in a poet of her idealistic outlook. But she justifies this preoccupation with great passion in the poem "Literaturnym prokuroram" ("To Literary Prosecutors"), which concludes the second collection, as her only way to preserve her evanescent youth from oblivion. The collection *Iz dvux knig,* published early in 1913, contains forty-one poems from the first two collections and is preceded by a sort of manifesto in which Cvetaeva again defends her right to concentrate her attention on her own private little world. The manifesto, quoted here in its entirety, is not so much the poetic credo of Cvetaeva at the beginning of her literary career, as a reply to the Symbolist criticism of her early work and an expression of a certain solidarity with Kuzmin's manifesto about "beautiful clarity."

All this did happen. My verse is a diary, my poetry is a poetry of proper names.

We shall all pass. In fifty years we shall all be in the ground. There will be new faces under the eternal sky. And I feel like shouting to everyone still alive:

Write, write more! Record each instant, each gesture, each sigh! But not only the gesture—the shape of the hand that made it; not only the sigh, but the cut of the lips from which it flew, the light one.

Do not disdain the "external"! The color of your eyes is as important as their expression; the upholstery of a divan no less so than the words that were said on it. Be more precise in your notations! Nothing is unimportant! Speak of your room: is it high or low, and how many windows are there in it, and what sort of window curtains and is there a rug and what sort of flowers are there on this rug?

The color of your eyes and of your lampshade, the paper knife and the pattern on the wallpaper, the precious stone in your favorite ring—all this shall be the body of your poor, poor soul abandoned in the huge world.[12]

The poems included in *Iz dvux knig* were selected to illustrate this declaration. This little volume is Cvetaeva's last tribute to the

[12] *Iz dvux knig,* p. 3.

themes of romantic exaltation and of childhood. Had Cvetaeva written nothing else or continued repeating the manner of her first two collections (and the title of a planned collection—*Marija Baškirceva*—which is announced on the back cover of *Iz dvux knig* points to such a possibility), she would have remained in the history of Russian poetry as a very special, very minor poet of the post-Symbolist period. The connection of the early Cvetaeva to her Russian contemporaries is less tenuous than she herself and some critics have later maintained. The contemporary poets who had undoubtedly left an imprint on the first two collections are Kuzmin, from whom Cvetaeva took her manner of light badinage and whom she resembles in her absence of all Symbolist-mystical leanings; Bal'mont, who like young Cvetaeva was unabashedly interested in his own self and cultivated in his verse the same festive, dressed-up attitude to life's phenomena; and Blok, the impact of whose poetry can be clearly observed in the poem "Privet iz bašni" ("Greeting from a Tower"), which begins:

Скоро вечер: от тьмы не укрыться,
Чья-то тень замелькает в окне . . .
Уезжай, уезжай же мой рыцарь
На своем золотистом коне!

В неизвестном, в сияющем свете
Помяни незнакомку добром!
Уж играет изменчивый ветер
Золотым и зеленым пером.[13]

Evening is nigh; there's no hiding from darkness;
A shadow will flicker in the window . . .
Ride off, then, ride off, O my knight
On your golden-hued steed!

In the unfamiliar, radiant world
Speak kindly of the lady you do not know!
The changeable wind is already toying
With [your] gold and green plume.

Not only does the imagery of this poem suggest Blok, but the assonance rhymes (večer-veter), unique in the practice of the early

[13] *Volšebnyj fonar'*, p. 91.

Cvetaeva, also point to his poetry. An echo of Bal'mont's poem
"Ona otdalas' bez upreka . . ." ("She surrendered herself without
reproach . . .") is discernible in Cvetaeva's "Na skalax" ("On the
Rocks") in *Večernij al'bom:*

> Забыто, что в платьицах дыры,
> Что новый костюмчик измят.
> Как скалы заманчиво-сыры!
> Как радостно пиньи шумят![14]

> They forget that the [girls'] frocks are torn,
> That the [boy's] new suit is crumpled.
> How enticingly damp are the cliffs!
> How joyously the [Italian] pines rustle!

In general, one can agree with the opinion of the literary historian
N. Kadmin, writing of Cvetaeva's first two collections: "M.
Cvetaeva has delineated for herself a little world of childhood
impressions and dreams; within these limits the poetess is fresh,
naive, sincere; these are her first timid steps; the future will show
the poetic personality of this gifted poetess." [15] But of course the
early Cvetaeva was neither naive nor timid. For all the comparative
immaturity of her first two collections, they may well contribute a
dozen poems or so to any future comprehensive selection of
Cvetaeva's poetry, while such gems as "Molitva" or "V raju" ("In
Paradise") [16] are both first-rate poetry and first-rate Cvetaeva. But
without abandoning the manner of her early period, Cvetaeva could
not become a truly major poet, and we can only be grateful that the
promised collection *Marija Baškirceva* never materialized.

Juvenilia (Junošeskie stixi): 1913–1916

The early period ends with Cvetaeva's marriage. The next stage
in her poetic development is represented by the poems written

---

[14] *Večernij al'bom*, p. 41. Cf. Bal'mont's "Kak skazočno svetjat soz-
vezd'ja/Kak zvezdy bessmertno gorjat."
[15] N. Kadmin (N. Ja. Abramovič), *Istorija russkoj poèzii*, (Moscow, 1915),
311.
[16] *Volšebnyj fonar'*, p. 75. Quoted by Cvetaeva in "Geroj truda" (*Proza*, p.
224).

between 1913 and 1915 and gathered in the collection *Junošeskie stixi,* which has never been published in its entirety. We know this period only from a dozen-odd poems published in *Severnye Zapiski* and later in *Volja Rossii,* poems which show a considerable evolution of the poet's technique and outlook. The main trend is toward maturity and a simplicity that borders on austerity when compared to the romantic style of the first two collections. The literary references are now Puškin and Byron rather than Rostand and Baškirceva. The preoccupation with the subject of death, manifest in Cvetaeva's early poetry, is now even more marked, but the basic attitude to death is quite different; the desire for an early and glorious end is replaced by a calm acceptance of death as an inevitable fact. The militant Bonapartism of the first two collections gives way to a definite pacifist strain in the poem "Ja znaju pravdu" ("I Know the Truth") [17] and in the pro-German poem quoted in "Nezdešnij večer." [18] The technical and stylistic maturity of *Junošeskie stixi* has already been discussed. The hero-worshipping of the early Cvetaeva is continued during this period; her Napoleonic sympathies did not prevent her from becoming interested in the Russian generals of the war of 1812 who fought against Napoleon— the earliest example of Cvetaeva's later tendency to multiple points of view.[19] One of the lesser known poems from that period may illustrate Cvetaeva's new detachment:

Солнцем жилки налиты — не кровью
На руке коричневой уже.
Я одна с моей большой любовью
К собственной моей душе.

Жду кузнечика, считаю до ста,
Стебелек срываю и жую.
— Странно чувствовать так сильно и так просто
Мимолетность жизни и свою.[20]

---

[17] *Severnye Zapiski,* VII–VIII (1916), 5.

[18] *Proza,* p. 277.

[19] "Generalam dvenadcatogo goda" ("To the Generals of 1812"), *Izbrannoe,* pp. 32–34. Originally, in a slightly different version, in *Severnye Zapiski,* I (1915), 94–95.

[20] *Severnye Zapiski,* V–VI (1915), 104.

Sunlight, not blood, flows
In my arm, already browned.
I am alone with my great love
For my own soul.

I await the grasshopper, I count to a hundred,
I pluck and chew a stem.
It is odd to feel so strongly and so simply
The evanescence of life and my own.

The love theme is conspicuously absent from the known poems of this period (unless we choose to read the poem about the two extinguished suns allegorically),[21] but the theme of maternity makes its impressive first appearance in the poem "Alja" in which Cvetaeva predicts a stormy and romantic future for her oldest daughter.[22]

Versts I (Versty I): 1916

The collection *Versty I* is the book in which the poet Cvetaeva rises to her full stature. She went on maturing and developing in her later poetry, but *Versty I* is the first book in which her magnitude as a poet becomes apparent. It was of this collection that Pasternak wrote that the work of many Symbolist poets (Pasternak's exceptions are Annenskij, Blok, and Belyj) "floundered helplessly in a universe of labored abstractions and lifeless archaisms, [while] Cvetaeva easily soared over the difficulties of true creativity, playfully solving its problems with an incomparable technical brilliance."[23] Pasternak goes on to speak of the form of Cvetaeva's verse in *Versty I* as "lyrically powerful," "most intimately experienced, not weak-chested, tightly wound and concentrated, not running out of breath on separate lines, encompassing in its extended periods whole sequences of stanzas without a break of rhythm."[24]

[21] *Severnye Zapiski*, VII–VIII (1916), 5.
[22] *Volja Rossii*, II (1925), 44.
[23] Boris Pasternak, *Proza 1915–1958*, p. 46.
[24] *Ibid*.

As has already been indicated, *Versty I* adds up to a lyrical diary
of Cvetaeva's personal and literary life during the year 1916. For all
its technical and thematic variety, the collection has a central
unifying leitmotif: the city of Moscow. Cvetaeva wrote of the
Moscow Kremlin in one of the poems in *Večernij al'bom,* using an
exalted, almost melodramatic diction.[25] In *Versty I* she is conscious
of Moscow as her home, as her rightful dwelling place, almost as her
personal property. It was possibly the contact with the important St.
Petersburg poets during her February trip that made her so
conscious of her native city. Moscow enters as an important
component in all the main cycles of the book: Cvetaeva shows the
city to Mandel'štam, contemplates Blok with the Kremlin as her
vantage point, bequeaths it to her daughter Alja, and offers it to
Anna Axmatova in homage. It may be paradoxical that in the
collection in which Cvetaeva's originality becomes so powerfully
manifest, we can also discern more clearly than in any other the
influence of several contemporary Russian poets. This is most true
in the cycles addressed to Blok and to Axmatova, where Cvetaeva at
times tries to speak to these poets in approximations of their own
voice. Here, for example, is a brief poem from the Axmatova
cycle:

На базаре кричал народ,
Пар вылетал из булочной.
Я запомнила алый рот
Узколицей певицы уличной.

В темном — с цветиками — платке,
— Милости удостоиться —
Ты, потупленная, в толпе
Богомолок у Сергий-Троицы.

Помолись за меня, краса,
Грустная и бесовская,
Как поставят тебя леса
Богородицей хлыстовскою.[26]

---

[25] "V Kremle," *Večernij al'bom,* pp. 141–143.
[26] *Versty I,* p. 86.

At the market place people were shouting.
[Clouds of] steam floated out of a bakery.
I retain in memory the crimson mouth
Of the gaunt-faced street songstress.

In a dark, tiny-flowered kerchief
(— The grace be granted —)
You, [standing,] eyes downcast
In a crowd of praying women in St. Sergius-Trinity [Monastery],

Pray for me, [my] beauty,
Melancholy and diabolical,
When the [dissenter sects of the] forests
Elect you Our Lady of the Flagellants.

Here we have a very clever imitation of certain stylistic mannerisms of Axmatova, including the typical irrelevant "ja zapomnila," the final *concetto* involving religion and hinting at some undisclosed, probably tragic relationship between the observer and the observed, the free *dol'nik* meter, and the elegant Axmatova-like assonance rhymes, at times so tenuous that they verge on consonances. In addition to Blok and Axmatova, one can sense in *Versty I* a faint but distinct echo of Tixon Čurilin—in the loose construction of certain free-verse poems, in sudden vivid and insistent rhymes in the generally rhymeless structure of such poems. Čurilin's hallucinatory imagery, however, is quite alien to Cvetaeva and so is the "magic classicism" of Osip Mandel'štam, who is felt in *Versty I* as a human presence, rather than as a literary influence.

To express the personal drama which is the subject of much of *Versty I*,[27] Cvetaeva makes a wide use of stylistic masks or *personae*. The idealistic Romanticism of the early collections is now largely dormant, coming occasionally to the surface in such a poem as "Iskatelnica priključenij" ("An Adventuress"), in which the mask happens to be that of the heroine of Madame de Staël's novel *Corinne*.[28] But for the most part, Cvetaeva speaks through the

[27] See Chapter II
[28] *Versty* I, pp. 97–98.

persona of a Moscow woman of the lower classes, sinful, proud, passionate, occasionally a criminal, occasionally dabbling in magic. This enables Cvetaeva to make use of a wide range of colloquial diction, which becomes a prominent feature of her poetry from this point on. Stylistically and technically, this is the most daringly experimental of Cvetaeva's collections, yet for all the variety of its versification and for all its stylistic range, *Versty I* possesses a unity and produces a more definite total effect than the first two published collections. In keeping with her new preoccupation with Moscow (of which she was later to write: "Yes, it was I who in 1916 was the first to speak thus about Moscow. . . . And I am happy and proud of this, for that was the Moscow of the last hour and last time"),[29] Cvetaeva shows a new interest in Russian history, as for example in a long poem about one of her favorite rebels, the False Dmitrij and his Polish wife.[30]

Versts II (Versty II), The Swans' Encampment (Lebedinyj stan): 1917–1921

The body of lyric poetry which Cvetaeva wrote between 1917 and 1921 is varied and extensive. We know that the majority of poems written during these years was meant to be included in two collections, *Lebedinyj stan* and *Versty II,* neither of which was published during the poet's lifetime. The first of these collections finally appeared in 1957. Although some of the poems of *Lebedinyj stan* were known earlier from publication in periodicals, they acquire a new significance and interest when seen in the context of the collection as a whole, as originally conceived by the poet. The poetry of *Lebedinyj stan* is primarily political, which in relation to Cvetaeva's earlier work represents an entirely new departure. Specifically, the volume is a record of Cvetaeva's reactions to the events of the February and October revolutions and of the ensuing Civil War. The poems are full of topical political and military references; the arrest of Nicholas II, the brief government of Kerenskij, the White army leader Lavr Kornilov, and the individual military defeats and triumphs of the White army are described and

[29] *Letters to Ivask,* p. 231.
[30] *Versty I,* pp. 32–35.

meditated upon in separate poems. The personal preoccupations of
the poet which are the subject of certain poems (the death of
Staxovič, the friendship with Bal'mont, the impact of the last poems
of Blok) are all treated against the strongly suggested background
of the Civil War and the hungry epoch of early Communism.
Historical themes are also selected for their pertinence to the current
situation—the occupation of Moscow by the False Dmitrij, the death
of André Chénier during the French Revolution, the attack on the
reign of Peter the Great as the supposed cause of the Revolution,
and the sudden and unexpected championing of Peter's sister Sof'ja,
whose role is regarded by most historians as negative and sinister. A
most striking historical reference in *Lebedinyj stan* is the recurrent
one to the period of the nomadic invasions of Kievan Russia:

> Рыжим татарином рыщет вольность,
> С прахом равняя алтарь и трон.[31]

> Like a red-haired Tatar, license is rampant,
> Levelling the altar and the throne to dust.

This likening of the Civil War situation to the destruction of
cultural values and the general chaotic conditions during the
medieval Mongol invasions, which is continued and developed by
Cvetaeva in *Remeslo,* enables her to draw on the imagery and
themes of the famous medieval Russian epic, the *Igor Tale,* which
she does with great effect in several of the poems of *Lebedinyj
stan.*

There is no doubt that all of Cvetaeva's sympathy was on the side
of the doomed White effort. Her concept of loyalty to the past is
eloquently expressed in the poem which begins "Nadobno smelo
priznat'sja, Lira," and in which she proclaims her fidelity to
"greatness, guilt and misfortune" ("Vernost' velič'ju—vine—bede, /
Vernost' velikoj vine venčannoj!"); the poem concludes:

> Ветренный век мы застали, Лира!
> Ветер в клоки изодрал мундиры,
> Треплет последний лоскут шатра . . .
> Новыя толпы — иные флаги!
> Мы ж остаемся верны присяге,
> Ибо дурные вожди — ветра.[32]

---

[31] *Lebedinyj stan,* p. 29.
[32] *Ibid.,* pp. 36–37.

It's a volatile age that we live in, O Lyre!
The wind has ripped the [dress] uniforms to tatters,
[And] is flapping the last shred of the tent . . .
New throngs — other flags!
But we shall remain faithful to our allegiance,
For winds are bad leaders.

The poems of *Lebedinyj stan* have their counterpart in certain of
Cvetaeva's prose memoirs dealing with the same period: "Oktjabr' v
vagone," "Moi služby," "Iz dnevnika." Her view of the October
Revolution as an unprecedented unleashing of savagery and destruction of culture was not unique. At the time, it was shared not
only by such uncompromising opponents of the Soviet regime as
Zinaida Gippius and Fëdor Sologub, but even by such later
supporters as Èrenburg and A. N. Tolstoj. The Soviet feeling of
outrage at the publication of *Lebedinyj stan* in 1957 is a measure of
the current Soviet intolerance to anything that contributes to a
historically balanced view of the Civil War period. The poetry of
Lebedinyj stan, subdued and simple in comparison to Cvetaeva's
preceding and following collections, reveals its fine texture and great
verbal subtlety only on repeated and attentive reading. Such poems
of the collection as "Nad cerkovkoj," "Nadobno smelo priznat'sja,"
or the second poem of the cycle "Don" are masterpieces of Russian
poetry, and should be read as such regardless of the reader's attitude
to the issues and results of the Russian Civil War. Deržavin's
"Felica," Puškin's "Klevetnikam Rossii," and Majakovskij's "Stixi o
Sovetskom pasporte" are, after all, masterful poems even for the
reader who may disapprove of the idealization of Catherine the
Great, sympathize with the Polish uprising of 1830, and not consider
the Soviet Union of the nineteen-twenties the finest place in the
world.

Since there is no available manuscript of the collection *Versty II,*
we cannot for the time being determine which of Cvetaeva's poems
written between 1917 and 1921 and not included in *Lebedinyj stan*
were a part of that collection. The most likely possibilities are the
poems included in the collection *Psixeja* in the sections "Ioann,"
"Mariula," "Brat'ja," and, except for a few poems included in *Versty*

I, in the section "Plašč." To these one should add the cycles "Komediant" and "Stixi k Sonečke," published in periodicals during Cvetaeva's stay abroad, as well as a large group of poems (not counting those included in *Psixeja*) which appear in the collection *Izbrannoe* on pages 62–124, and a few separate poems dating from the period in question which appeared in various periodical publications. Considered as a whole, these poems add up to a definite and defined unit. They are as unconcerned with the current history as the poems included in *Lebedinyj stan* are passionately involved with it. *Versty II* can be described as Cretaeva's second wave of Romanticism. The escape from the unbearable present into the past is as apparent in these poems as it is in the plays which she was writing in the same years. The period chosen is also the same as in the plays: the late eighteenth century and the beginning of the nineteenth. The world of the theater, very important during this period of Cvetaeva's life, provides both the source of inspiration ("Stixi k Sonečke," "Brat'ja") and the subject matter ("Komediant"). The romantic and deliberately elegant diction, stemming from the early collections, is given a free rein for the last time, but Cvetaeva returns to it as an infinitely more accomplished and self-controlled poet:

> Вы столь забывчивы, сколь незабвенны.
> — Ах, Вы похожи на улыбку Вашу!
> Сказать еще? — Златого утра краше!
> Сказать еще? — Одни во всей вселенной!
> Самой любви младой военнопленый!
> Рукой Челлини ваянная чаша.[33]

> You are as forgetful as you are unforgettable.
> — Ah, but you resemble your [own] smile!
> Shall I say more? — Fairer than golden morning!
> Shall I say more? — Only you in the entire universe!
> Love's own young prisoner-of-war!
> A chalice sculpted by Cellini's hand.

The literary references, always revealing in Cvetaeva, are now predominantly eighteenth-century ones: Manon Lescaut, Cagliostro,

---

[33] "Komediant," *Sovremennye Zapiski*, XIX (1924).

Casanova, and other adventurers whose memoirs Cvetaeva was using for her verse plays of the period. There is also a certain interest in England, not at all usual for Cvetaeva—references to Dickens, a poem about the death of Byron (with the epigraph from Batjuškov: "Ja bereg pokidal tumannyj Al'biona"), and the London setting in the poem "Ljubvi starinnye tumany" ("The Ancient Mists of Love").[34] At the same time, the line of colloquial, folkloristic poetry initiated in *Versty I* is continued in the sets of poems "Babuška," "Dve pesni," and "Sten'ka Razin."[35] Cvetaeva's preoccupation with this seventeenth-century rebel was shared at the time by the Futurist poets Kamenskij and Xlebnikov. The cycle "Stixi k Sonečke" makes use of the urban folklore genre of sentimental *žestokij romans,* which here serves Cvetaeva as a stylistic mask rather than as an object of parody. In the second poem of this cycle we find a striking and on the whole successful fusion of *žestokij romans*[36] with a kind of surrealistic nursery rhyme called *nebylica*:

> Пел в лесочке птенчик,
> Под окном — шарманщик:
> — Обманщик, изменщик,
> Изменщик, обманщик!
>
> Подпевали хором
> Черти из боченка:
> — Всю тебя, девчонка,
> За копейку продал![37]

> A nestling sang in the woods,
> An organ-grinder — under the window:
> — [He's a] deceiver, a betrayer,
> A betrayer, a deceiver!

[34] "Ja pomnju noč' na sklone nojabrja . . . ," *Izbrannoe,* p. 95; "Ja bereg pokidal . . . ," *Izbrannoe,* pp. 96–97; "Ljubvi starinnye tumany," *Vozrož-denie,* II, (Moscow, 1923) 21–22 (reprinted in *Poslednie Novosti* [Paris], October 4, 1928, where it was broken into four numbered sections).

[35] *Izbrannoe,* pp. 99–103, 115–118, and 69–72.

[36] For a discussion and examples of *žestokij romans,* see Vladimir Markov, *The Longer Poems of Velimir Khlebnikov* (Berkeley and Los Angeles, 1962), pp. 43–45.

[37] "Stixi k Sonečke," *Russkie Zapiski,* III (Paris, 1938), 167.

> Devils in a barrell
> Chimed in in chorus:
> — He's sold you out, girlie,
> All of you, for a penny.

Cvetaeva's versatility is seen in a new theme that is added to her poetic canon during this period, that of Gypsy life and lore, treated in the poems included in the section "Mariula" in *Psixeja*. The subject and its treatment are the final flowering of the purely romantic vein in Cvetaeva's lyric poetry. In general, the poems of the *Versty II* period are best considered in conjunction with the verse plays of the same period; the invaluable biographical commentary on many of them is found in "Povest' o Sonečke."

Craft (Remeslo): 1921–1922

Remeslo, which Cvetaeva began in April of 1921 with a cycle of poems "Učenik" ("The Disciple") addressed to Prince Sergej Volkonskij, is a collection that again represents a radical new departure. The romantic manner is suddenly abandoned for good. The impact of Russian Futurism, mildly felt in *Versty I* and very strongly in the *poèma* "Na krasnom kone" written in 1920, now becomes organically blended with a newly evolved style that may be described as classical and odic. The choriambic meters, tried out in *Versty I,* are now extremely important and so is the new persistent use of archaisms. The poems are grouped into cycles according to their subject matter, but at the same time *Remeslo* repeats the precedent of *Versty I* in being an uninterrupted poetic diary of a single year: April 1921 to April 1922. The archaic, biblical diction is most apparent in the cycles "Učenik" and "Otrok," the last apparently dedicated to the publisher A. G. Višnjak ("Gelikonu"). Literature as such plays a smaller role in this collection than in the others, although there are several poems addressed to individual poets: Axmatova (a poem in the colloquial diction of a peasant lament [*zaplačka*], offering Axmatova sympathy for her personal losses after the Revolution), Kuzmin, Majakovskij ("Arxangeltjaželostup / Zdorovo, v vekax Vladimir!"),[38] and Èrenburg (the cycle "Sugroby").

Remeslo does not have a unifying theme or leitmotif, as did *Versty I* and *Lebedinyj stan*. Its essential unity is due to the great energy and expressiveness of its verse. The combination of a passionate tone with the wide use of syntactic ellipsis in this collection has led some hostile critics to speak of obscurity and hysteria—the two charges that have been repeatedly made against Cvetaeva's poetry from *Remeslo* onward. Thematically, much of *Remeslo* is a continuation of *Lebedinyj stan*. The Civil War is still a major preoccupation in the cycles "Georgij" (which, together with Kuzmin's cantata on the same subject, possibly served Pasternak as a source of inspiration for his poem about Saint George the dragon-slayer in *Doctor Zhivago*) and "Blagaja vest'," both of which were inspired by Sergej Èfron's military service with the White forces. The cycle "Xanskij polon" ("Captured by the Khan") develops with verve and energy the comparison, already made in *Lebedinyj stan,* between the Civil War and the epoch of the *Igor Tale*. The cycle "1922 god" ("Year 1922") celebrates and laments the White defeat in two impressive drinking songs and in the poem "Posmertynj marš" ("The Posthumous March"), in which Death is the implied, never-mentioned heroine, and the debacle is visually symbolized by the initial stanza:

И марш вперед уже,	And now it's "forward, march!"
Трубят в поход.	The bugle is sounded.
О, как встает она,	Oh, how [large] she looms,
О, как встает . . .[39]	Oh, how she looms . . .

This stanza serves as a refrain and loses several words on each repetition until it is finally reduced to its first two words: "I marš."

In *Remeslo,* the manner derived from folklore is less a stylistic mask than an integral part of the poet's style. It is widely used in the section "Sugroby" ("Snowdrifts") and in two anti-revolutionary poems which begin "Pereselencami / V kakoj N'ju Jork?" and

---

[38] *Remeslo,* p. 95 ("Axmatovoj"), p. 37 ("Dva zareva," dedicated to Kuzmin), and p. 65 ("Majakovskomu").

[39] *Ibid.,* pp. 111–112.

"Maslenica široka!," in the latter of which the Revolution is shown symbolically as a drunken village celebration that gets out of hand. These two poems may be read as a comment on and a possible polemic with Blok's "Dvenadcat'" ("The Twelve") and Belyj's "Xristos Voskres" ("Christ is Arisen"). While the attitude of Blok and Belyj to the Revolution in these poems is at times ambiguous and open to varying interpretations, Cvetaeva's attitude to the coming world revolution (confidently predicted by many at that time) is definite and specific:

— Во имя Господа!	"In the name of the Lord!
Во имя Разума! —	In the name of Reason!"
Ведь и короста мы,	What a fester we are;
Ведь и проказа мы!	What a leprosy we are!
Волчьими искрами	With a wolfish sparkle
Сквозь вьюжный мех —	Through snowstorms' fur,
Звезда российская:	The Star of Russia
Противу всех!	Against the world!
Отцеубийцами —	[Whither,] parricides,
В какую дичь?	Into what wilderness?
Не ошибиться бы,	Careful you're not mistaken,
Вселенский бич![40]	[You] scourge of the universe!

The new classicist strain is most noticeable in the cycle about the destructive power of erotic love, "Xvala Afrodite" ("Eulogy of Aphrodite"), which introduces some of the principal themes of *Posle Rossii*. Such "classical" poems form one pole of *Remeslo*, while at the opposite pole we find the veritable explosion of magic chants and incantations in the cycle "Sugroby" and in the *poèma* "Pereuločki" which closes the collection and which is discussed separately in the next chapter. The incantatory poems explore to the full Cvetaeva's gift for verbal creativity and colloquial diction.

Poems to Blok (Stixi k Bloku): 1916–1921

The slim volume *Stixi k Bloku* which Cvetaeva published in Berlin in 1922 contains a set of poems from *Versty I* addressed to

[40] *Ibid.*, pp. 122–123.

Blok in 1916; a new group of poems written after the poet's death in 1921, i.e. at the time of *Remeslo:* and an additional section, "Podruga," addressed to Blok's last love. Two poems under the heading "Vifleem" ("Bethlehem") in *Remeslo* were printed with a dedication to "Blok's son Saša" and with an explanatory note that these two poems were accidentally not included in *Stixi k Bloku* as originally intended.[41] The dedication caused a certain amount of consternation at the time *Remeslo* was published, since Blok was not known to have had a son named Saša (i.e., Aleksandr). The explanation of the dedication and of the section "Podruga" in *Stixi k Bloku* is to be sought in the claim of Nadežda Nolle, the wife of the well-known Marxist critic and Soviet government official, P. S. Kogan, that her son, born shortly before Blok's death, was fathered by the poet. Although not mentioned in Blok's biographies, this supposed fatherhood was widely known in Moscow and was accepted as a fact by Cvetaeva, who was on friendly terms with the Kogans.[42]

Of the seven new poems about Blok in *Stixi k Bloku,* the fifth one is the most remarkable. It deals with a possible new incarnation of the poet:

> Без зова, без слова, —
> Так кровельщик падает с крыш.
> А может-быть снова
> Пришел, — в колыбели лежишь?
>
> Горишь и не меркнешь,
> Светильник немногих недель . . .
> Какая из смертных
> Качает твою колыбель?[43]

> Without a call, without a word, —
> Thus a roofer falls from the roofs.
> But perhaps you've come back
> [And] are being lulled in a cradle?

---

[41] *Ibid.,* p. 87.

[42] Blok's son is described by Cvetaeva in her letter to Roman Gul' of April 11, 1924 (Letters to Gul', p. 187). In "Plennyj dux" Cvetaeva spoke of the Kogans as "Blok's last friends" and indicated her intention to speak of them in great detail should she ever write a memoir on Blok (*Proza*, pp. 310, 313). See also Blok's heavily censored letters to N. A. Nolle-Kogan, *Sobranie sočinenij* (Moscow, 1963), VIII, 532–533 and 534–535.

[43] *Stixi k Bloku,* pp. 33–35; reprinted in *Izbrannoe,* pp. 46–47.

You burn without dimming,
A luminary a few weeks old . . .
Which of the mortal women
Is rocking your cradle?

After building up the possibility of reincarnation, Cvetaeva, in the final stanzas of the poem, rejects all possibility of afterlife and reincarnation. This is one of the earliest examples of a structure observable in several of her poems in the subsequent two decades, where a position that is strongly asserted and carefully developed in the early part of the poem is negated at the end (cf. such later poems as "Popytka revnosti," "Toska po rodine. . . ," or the fifth poem in the cycle "Provoda" in *Posle Rossii*). The poems in "Podruga" and the two poems to Blok's son in *Remeslo* treat the birth of the boy in terms of the Nativity and address his mother in liturgical language, using quotations from prayers traditionally addressed to the Virgin. It is ironic that Valerij Brjusov, an avowed Communist by the time *Stixi k Bloku* was published, was the one to accuse Cvetaeva of sacrilege.[44] The 1916 poem describing Blok's future death ("Dumali —čelovek! I umeret' zastavili!") acquired an uncanny prophetic ring when republished in 1921.

After Russia (*Posle Rossii*): 1922–1925

Remeslo and *Stixi k Bloku* contain the last lyric poetry Cvetaeva wrote before leaving Russia. She was to publish only one more collection, *Posle Rossii* (published in 1928), which contained the poems she wrote during her stay in Berlin and Prague. The title of the collection *Remeslo* originally referred to an epigraph from a poem by Karolina Pavlova in which poetry is called "my misfortune, my wealth, my sacred craft," and which Cvetaeva decided to remove at the time of publication "not wishing, according to my custom, to facilitate anything for the reader, respecting the reader."[45] But if we were to select the verse collection by Cvetaeva

[44] V. Brjusov, "Sredi stixov," *Pečat' i Revoljucija*, I (1923), 74–75.
[45] Letters to Baxrax, *Mosty*, V, 305.

in which her poetic craft reaches its highest peak, and her human and poetic stature its most awesome dimensions and sweep, we would have to choose *Posle Rossii* and wonder if this is not perhaps the collection which most deserves the accolade in the epigraph from Pavlova and the title derived from it. This collection of poems, written by Marina Cvetaeva at the peak of her poetic power, was either overlooked or underrated by the émigré critics, with writers as different as Adamovič [46] and Xodasevič [47] for once agreeing on the supposed weaknesses of this book. The fact that Majakovskij left with Elsa Triolet the copy of *Posle Rossii* presented to him by Cvetaeva does not speak for the fairness and impartiality of *his* poetic judgment either. On the other hand, one cannot help agreeing with Alfred Bem, who wrote in 1931 with considerable critical acumen that "Marina Cvetaeva, finding herself abroad, was unjustly deprived of the position that was reserved for her when she was in her native land. And her book *Posle Rossii* is, in my opinion, objectively far more significant than we now realize." [48]

In the poems of *Posle Rossii,* Cvetaeva accomplishes a synthesis of the ripe romanticism of *Versty II,* the colloquial diction of *Versty I,* and the new kind of twentieth-century classicism which had appeared in *Remeslo* rather incidentally in the cycles "Otrok" and "Xvala Afrodite." The new classical-archaist diction in conjunction with choriambic meters and additional supra-metrical stresses results in a certain elegant, ponderous heaviness, that is not unlike the elegance of the Ingres-derived, heavy-limbed goddesses Picasso was painting at the same time:

> Леты слепотекущий всхлип.
> Долг твой тебе отпущен: слит
> С Летою, — еле-еле жив
> В лепете сребротекущих ив.

---

[46] G. Adamovič, "Posle Rossii," *Poslednie Novosti* (Paris), June 21, 1928.

[47] V. Xodasevič, "Posle Rossii," *Vozroždenie* (Paris), June 19, 1928.

[48] A. Bem, "Pis'ma o literature. V zaščitu čitatelja," *Rul'* (Berlin), July 16, 1931. Bem's high opinion of this collection was shared by the writer of humorous and topical verse, Don Aminado (pseudonym of A. P. Špoljanskij), who in his autobiography called *Posle Rossii* the most remarkable of Cvetaeva's books (Don Aminado, *Poezd na tret'em puti* [New York, 1954], p. 346 and *passim*).

Ивовый сребролетейский плеск
Плачущий . . . В слепотекущий склеп
Памятей — перетомилась — спрячь
В ивовый сребролетейский плач.[49]

The blindly-flowing sob of Lethe.
Your debt is forgiven you: merged
With Lethe; — barely, barely alive
In the murmuring of silvery-flowing willows.

Willowy, silvery-Lethean splashes,
Weeping . . . Hide it in the blindly-flowing tomb
Of memories (— you are exhausted —),
In willowy, silvery-Lethean weeping.

The provenance of Cvetaeva's new classicism is indicated by the
three major epigraphs which we find in *Posle Rossii*. The three
writers drawn upon are Trediakovskij, Montaigne, and Goethe.
Goethe is also mentioned in several of the poems in *Posle Rossii*,
and it is to his work that we can best compare Cvetaeva's new
universalism and the occasional almost Olympian detachment.
Except for the almost total absence of political poetry, Cvetaeva's
basic interests remain the same as before, but her poetic horizon has
become both wider and higher. While remaining her rebellious and
passionate self, the poet can view and express her experience from a
new perspective and with a new perception, for which the style
derived from the study of Goethe and of the Russian poets of the
eighteenth century is admirably suited. And, while using her
personal experiences and literature as points of departure as she
always did, Cvetaeva attempts and achieves in *Posle Rossii* something she had never tried before—she writes philosophical poetry.
The meditations on the nature of time in "Minuta," of space in
"Zaočnost'," and of human speech and communication in "Emče
organa" (reprinted in *Izbrannoe* under the title "Molv'") take their
place next to the best poems in the Russian tradition of philosophical poetry which is associated with the names of Baratynskij and
Tjutčev. The point of view in these poems is Cvetaeva's intensely

---

[49] *Posle Rossii*, p. 22.

personal one, but the conclusions she reaches have a general and universal significance.

On the basis of the published letters and memoirs of Cvetaeva, we can read parts of *Posle Rossii* as poetic commentary on the vicissitudes of her emotional biography. Thus, the first section of the book often concerns the little-documented, disappointing relationship between Cvetaeva and the handsome young publisher A. G. Višnjak. The three-poem cycle "Čas duši" ("Hour of the Soul") and the seven poems that follow are amply commented upon in the published letters of Cvetaeva to A. Baxrax, while the cycle "Dvoe" ("The Two") apparently refers to Cvetaeva's correspondence with Boris Pasternak.

One aspect of the universality of *Posle Rossii* is Cvetaeva's use of traditional myths as subject matter in the poems derived from literary sources. The poet of *Posle Rossii* has traveled a long way from the naive, romantic myth of the Duke of Reichstadt. The glorification of contemporary poets that was practiced in *Versty I* and *Remeslo* is temporarily abandoned. Instead, the heroes and heroines of Cvetaeva's poems come from the *Iliad* ("Axill na valu," "Tak—tol'ko Elena," the first two poems of the cycle "Dvoe"), from Greek mythology (Ariadne and Phaedra, about each of whom Cvetaeva was to write a tragedy during the same decade; Orpheus and Eurydice), and from Shakespeare (the three poems about Hamlet, in which the Shakespearean tragedy is radically revised by Cvetaeva, with Hamlet as the dry, unemotional villain and the Queen and Ophelia as his victims).

A significant portion of *Posle Rossii* is devoted to the poems with pointedly realistic settings—a possible result of the impact on Cvetaeva of the imagery of Pasternak's *Sestra moja žizn'*. The origin of this trend, however, is traceable to Cvetaeva's interest in the Moscow poor and its underworld, expressed in certain poems of *Versty I* and *Lebedinyj stan*. In *Posle Rossii,* the frequent settings of the industrial suburbs of Prague, its railroad yards, its barrack-like housing projects provide the poet with an appropriately drab contrast to the powerful and colorful world of poetry and mythology. Several striking symbols, associated with such settings, reappear throughout the whole volume: railroad tracks, trains, telegraph wires. Railroad imagery in particular is put to a variety of uses, both concrete and symbolic, and it is also connected to the theme of homesickness for Russia, which despite the title of the collection finds its expression in only two of the poems. The theme of a poet's loneliness, which is deliberately sought in order to survive in a world where love is either slavery or pain, is very important in *Posle Rossii* and is eloquently expressed in several poems ("No tesna vdvoem," "Pomni zakon," the cycle "Poèty"). The cycle "Derev'ja" ("Trees") may be considered as an interesting attempt to revive the classical sylvan idyll (also attempted in twentieth-century Russian poetry in an entirely different way by Velimir Xlebnikov): unable to deal with other people, the poet humanizes the trees of the forest and finds both peace of mind and quasi-human dramatic events among them.

In terms of language and versification, the poetry of *Posle Rossii* is a staggering accomplishment—a synthesis of meaning, word, and verbal music which the Russian Futurist poetry strove for and so rarely achieved to such a degree. The fusion of sense and language expressed in unique sequences of internal rhymes is so organic that for once it seems irrelevant to discuss sound instrumentation, the clashing consonants, or the alliterative vowels. The following examples (which one could go on quoting for pages) should illustrate this fusion and synthesis:

Мой неженка! Сединой отцов:
Сей беженки не бери под кров.
Да здравствует левогрудый ков
Немудрствующих концов!

Но может, в щебетах и счетах
От вечных женственностей устав —
И вспомнишь руку мою без прав
И мужественный рукав.[50]

My delicate boy! By the gray hair of your ancestors:
Don't take this refugee girl [that I am] under your roof.
Long live the Amazonian conspiracy
Of simple-minded ends!

[50] *Ibid.*, p. 9.

But perhaps, amidst the twitterings and the [household] bills,
Tired of eternal femininities
You will still recall my hand, with its lack of rights
And the masculine [cut of my] sleeve.

О по каким морям и городам
Тебя искать? (Незримого — незрячей!)
Я про́воды вверяю провода́м,
И в телеграфный столб упершись — плачу.[51]

Oh, in what seas and cities
Should I seek you? (The invisible sought by the unseeing!)
I entrust the farewells to the wires,
And stopped by the telegraph pole, I weep.

Перестрадай же меня! я всюду:
Зори и руды я, хлеб и вздох,
Есмь я и буду я, и добуду
Губы — как душу добудет Бог[52]

So suffer me through and survive me! I am everywhere:
I am dawns and ores, bread and breath;
I am and I shall be and I shall obtain
[Your] lips the way God will obtain [your] soul

Меч, терзай нас и, меч, прознай нас,
Меч, казни нас, но, меч, знай,
Что бывает такая крайность
Правды, крыши такой край . . .[53]

Bruise us, sword, and pierce us, sword,
Kill us, sword, but know, O sword,
That there exists such an extremity
Of truth, such an edge of the roof . . .

In an unpublished letter to Salomea Halpern (June 11, 1929),
Cvetaeva points out an unexpected similarity she had found
between George Balanchine's choreography for Prokofiev's *The*

---

[51] *Ibid.,* p. 67.
[52] *Ibid.,* p. 69.
[53] *Ibid.,* p. 110.

Prodigal Son and her own poetry: "I've been to see the Diaghilev [company]; in *The Prodigal Son* there are several intelligent gestures which resemble verse (they remind me of my own): a cloak is transformed into a sail and thereby the carousers are transformed into oarsmen" (cf. Cvetaeva's commentary on her *poèma* "Pereuločki" in Chapter VIII). This kind of sudden, clever shifting from one plane of perception to another, the economy of means by which this is achieved, and the revelation of a new and subtle inner truth thus accomplished is a typically twentieth-century contribution to artistic sensibility. The poetry of Cvetaeva's *Posle Rossii* is as genuine an aspect of this contribution as are the paintings of Picasso, the music of Webern and Stravinskij, the stage direction of Vaxtangov and Mejerxol'd, and the choreography of Balanchine.

Posle Rossii is a rich and varied book. Much of Cvetaeva's past poetic experience has contributed to its variety. The Gypsy poems of *Versty II* are continued in the two poems of *Posle Rossii* that can be described as Gypsy rhapsodies: "Ruč'i" ("Brooks") and "Plač cyganki" ("A Gypsy Girl's Lament"). The Eurasian-oriented, colloquial cycle "Xanskij polon" in *Remeslo* is the point of departure for the cycle "Skifskie" in *Posle Rossii,* with the important difference that now the ancient nomadic tribes have no current political associations. The idealistic romantic outlook of Cvetaeva's first two collections is also present in *Posle Rossii:* the poet still expects and demands from life more than she knows it can possibly give. But the most important thing about *Posle Rossii* is that in this book, as nowhere else, Marina Cvetaeva found a completely new and original way of looking at life, evolved a successful personal idiom in which to express this view, and did so in a poetry of unique metrical freshness and verbal beauty.

Later Lyric Poems: 1926–1939

After the publication of *Posle Rossii,* the short lyric poems written by Cvetaeva sharply decrease in number. The apparent reason for this decrease is that much of her later work is in other literary forms. In the nineteen-twenties Cvetaeva wrote mostly long verse narratives and lyrical *poèmy* and in the thirties her literary output was largely devoted to prose. There may be a body of unpublished lyric poetry dating from the years 1926–1941, but it cannot be very large. When given the opportunity to publish short poems in *Poslednie Novosti* in the late nineteen-twenties and in *Russkie Zapiski* in 1937, Cvetaeva submitted poems dating from her pre-emigration period, many of them published earlier in other periodicals. This leads one to suppose that she did not have any new short lyrics to offer. The known lyric poetry from the period after *Posle Rossii* appeared for the most part in *Sovremennye Zapiski,* with a few separate works in this form appearing in *Volja Rossii, Vstreči,* and *Čisla.* These are all either comparatively long poems or developed cycles—in the late Cvetaeva we find almost no separate short poems of several stanzas. Some of these poems continue the trend of philosophical poetry initiated in *Posle Rossii.* Such is, for example, "Nereida" ("Nereid"), the only poem of Cvetaeva's published in *Čisla,*[54] in which what at first seems to be a defense of swimming in the nude is developed into an extended metaphor of the impossibility of having any direct unencumbered experience:

> Нереида! Волна!
> Ничего нам не надо
> Что не я, не она,
> Не волна, не наяда.
>
> Узнаю тебя, гроб,
> Как тебя ни зови:
> В вере — храм, в храме — поп.
> Вечный третий в любви.

> Nereid! Wave!
> We need nothing
> That is not I, is not she,
> Not a wave, not a naiad.
>
> I recognize you, coffin,
> Whatever you may be called:
> In faith — a temple, in the temple — a priest.
> The eternal third [one] in [any] love.

The theme of rejecting humanity in favor of communion with the plant world, expressed in the cycle "Derev'ja" of *Posle Rossii,* is

---

[54] *Čisla,* Paris, II–III (1930), 6.

taken up in the poem "Kust" ("A Shrub") written in 1936.[55] A number of Cvetaeva's later poems express the poet's fatigue, weariness, need for solitude, desperate desire to withdraw from daily life. A poem written in 1926 and published for the first time posthumously in *Izbrannoe* ends as follows:

Богом мне — тот	My God shall be he
Будет, кто даст мне	Who shall give me
(Не времени!	(Tarry not!
Дни сочтены!)	The days are numbered!)
Для тишины —	Four walls
Четыре стены.[56]	For [peace and] quiet.

Connected with the theme of tranquillity and withdrawal is the one that Cvetaeva shares with such major twentieth-century poets as Majakovskij, Zabolockij, and Julian Tuwim: the fear and dislike of the complacent, faceless philistine. In one poem after another of the nineteen-thirties we find this contempt, to which Cvetaeva keeps returning as Puškin kept returning to his closely related concept of *čern'*. Among the most vivid expressions of this attitude are "Rolandov rog" ("Roland's Horn"),[57] in which the poet pursues her lonely fight to the accompaniment of a fool's derisive whistle and the laughter of the philistine; "Toska po rodine! Davno . . ." ("Homesickness"),[58] in which the poet, whose origin is "before any century," cannot hope to be understood by the twentieth-century reader who is a "swallower of tons of newspapers, a gossip-milker"; the poem about these newspaper-readers; and the violent "Oda pešemu xodu" ("Ode to Walking"), which indicts the present century for sacrificing all other interests to a pursuit of mechanical speed, with the result that humanity ("parasites of space / Alcoholics of mileage") is on its way to becoming mollusks.[59]

Cvetaeva's invective, very prominent in her poetry after the 1930

---

[55] *Sovremennye Zapiski,* LXII (Paris, 1936), 188–189. Reprinted in *Novyj mir,* III (1965), 156–157.

[56] *Izbrannoe,* p. 177.

[57] *Ibid.,* p. 199.

[58] *Ibid.,* pp. 206–207. English translation by Lydia Pasternak Slater, *Tri-Quarterly* (Spring, 1965), 62–63.

[59] *Izbrannoe,* pp. 187–191. A manuscript copy of this poem, rejected by *Sovremennye Zapiski,* is in the Houghton Library collection, Harvard University.

cycle of poems to Majakovskij, stems from her realization that she is hopelessly at odds with her century and her epoch. This realization, strongly and unequivocally stated in her correspondence with Ivask,[60] is central to such works of the thirties as the cycle "Ici-Haut" in memory of Vološin,[61] the cycle "Stol" about her writing desk,[62] and the poem "Čitateli gazet" ("Newspaper Readers").[63] In some of the poems of the thirties the invective turns into sheer and violent hatred of everyone who is smugly prosperous (the fourth poem of the cycle "Stol" and the poem which begins "Nikuda ne uexali").[64] Against the background of these violent denunciations, the cycle "Stixi sirote" addressed to Štejger appears as a brief interlude of human affection and personal happiness.

The poems addressed to other poets that reappear in the later poetry of Cvetaeva are by now mostly poems *in memoriam* ("Majakovskomu," "Ici-Haut," the poem in memory of Nikolaj Gronskij). The Puškin cycle is basically a debate against the distortions of the poet's life and work by tendentious scholarship, while the historical poem "Pëtr i Puškin" ("Peter and Puškin") [65] examines the role of Peter the Great in the development of the Russian culture which produced Puškin. The amphibrachic trimeter which Cvetaeva uses in this poem irresistibly and rather unfortunately brings to mind the meter of Nekrasov's "Moroz Krasnyj Nos," which does not seem appropriate to the subject of the poem. Another historical poem, which Cvetaeva wrote in 1930, is "Sibir' " ("Siberia"),[66] a long tribute to the eighteenth-century pioneer settlers of Siberia, apparently inspired by the reading of some historical accounts of the period. The poem "Čeljuskincy," written in honor of the successful Soviet North Pole expedition, brings to Cvetaeva's poetry a new dimension which it usually lacked earlier, but which is also apparent in her prose of the thirties—that of gentle humor:

[60] Letters to Ivask, *passim*, but especially pp. 214–215.
[61] *Vstreči* (Paris, 1934), IV, 160–161, and V, 210–211.
[62] *Izbrannoe*, pp. 200–204.
[63] *Ibid.*, pp. 214–216.
[64] *Ibid.*, pp. 217–218.
[65] *Ibid.*, pp. 183–186. Here, Cvetaeva's admiration of the historical role of Peter the Great is at variance with her attack on him in *Lebedinyj stan*.
[66] *Volja Rossii*, III–IV (1931), 241–246.

На льдине (не то,
Что — черт его — Нобиле!)
Родили дитё
И псов не угробили —

На льдине!
Эол
Доносит по кабелю:
"На льдов произвол
Ни пса не оставили!"

И спасши (мечта
Для младшего возраста!)
И псов и дитя
Умчали по воздуху.[67]

On an ice floe (unlike
What the hell's his name — Nobile!)
They gave birth to a kid
And did not do their dogs in

On the ice floe!
Aeolus
Reports by cable:
"Not a single dog has been left
To the mercy of the ice!"

And after rescuing them ([what] a dream
For junior readers!)
They sped both the dogs and the infant
Away by air.

What may be termed political poetry was temporarily abandoned by Cvetaeva after *Remeslo*. She made two major returns to political subjects in her later poetry. In 1928, in connection with her work on "Perekóp," Cvetaeva's interest in the October Revolution was revived, as is witnessed by the poem "Krasnyj byčok" ("The Red Bull-Calf"),[68] in which the dream of the poet's daughter about being pursued by a red calf and the memory of a similar adventure

[67] *Izbrannoe*, pp. 208–209.
[68] *Volja Rossii*, XII (1928), 35–38.

Cvetaeva and Mandel'štam had in 1916 are developed into the
symbol of Revolution, seen as blind animal violence. The Majakovskij cycle of 1930 may also be termed political poetry, if only for its
sweeping attack on any kind of political approach to the evaluation
of literature. The final invasion of Cvetaeva's poetry by politics and
world affairs occurs in her two cycles on Germany's take-over of
Czechoslovakia, written in 1938–39 and published posthumously.
This time the object of political invective is Nazi Germany and, as
in *Lebedinyj stan,* Cvetaeva brings to her topical poetry all of her
passion and imagination and her poetic craft:

> Полкарты прикарманила,
> Астральная душа!
> Встарь — сказками туманила,
> Днесь — танками пошла.

> Пред чешскою крестьянкою
> Не опускаешь вежд,
> Прокатываясь танками
> По ржи ее надежд?

> Пред горестью безмерною
> Сей *маленькой* страны —
> Что чувствуете, Германы:
> Германии сыны?[69]

> You've put half the map in your pocket,
> [You] ethereal soul!
> Of old, you spread the fairy tale mists,
> Now you send [your] tanks.

> Before the Czech peasant girl
> You do not lower your eyes,
> While rolling [your] tanks
> Over the rye of her hopes?

> Before the immeasurable sorrow
> Of that *little* country
> What do you feel, Hermanns:
> Sons of Germany?

[69] *Izbrannoe,* pp. 235–236.

The meaning and the language of much of Cvetaeva's lyric poetry are extremely concentrated. This poetry is intended for the reader who will take the trouble to read it attentively, and it is designed to frighten away—possibly deliberately—anyone in search of familiar poetic formulae and facile, expected emotions. In her effort to achieve a concentration of expression, the poet occasionally makes her poetic language cryptic to the point where even the most attentive study cannot yield the meaning of the poem without a further clue or commentary. One such extreme case is the haunting poem in *Posle Rossii* ("Promenjavši na stremja . . ."),[70] in which the subject of the developed series of beautiful comparisons eludes the reader even after numerous readings, yet an allegory of some sort is obviously implied. Such extreme examples are rare. More frequent are poems whose meaning is vastly enhanced by comparison with passages that correspond to them in Cvetaeva's prose works and published letters. For example, the poem "Xvala bogatym" ("Eulogy of the Rich") has been interpreted by Cvetaeva's Soviet editor Orlov as ironic and satirical.[71] A comparison of the poem with a passage in "Zemnye primety,"[72] which is beyond any doubt its point of departure, immediately excludes any such reading of "Xvala bogatym"—Cvetaeva's sentiments about the wealthy that are stated in the poem represent her earnest and serious convictions. The parallels that we find in Cvetaeva's letters to Baxrax to the poems addressed to him in *Posle Rossii* are too numerous to be quoted. It is obviously one of the tasks of future Cvetaeva scholarship to examine such parallels and to use Cvetaeva's prose and letters as sources for explicating her lyric poetry.

The body of lyric poetry written by Cvetaeva is vast and varied. It has become customary in criticism, when mentioning this fact, to comment on the uneven artistic worth of this body of poetry.[73] This is probably the place to take issue with this majority opinion. The

---

[70] *Posle Rossii*, pp. 151–152.

[71] *Izbrannoe*, p. 13.

[72] *Volja Rossii*, I–II (1924), 100.

[73] E.g., A. Baxrax, "Zvukovoj liven'," p. 184 ("Her failures and misses were innumerable . . . "); V. Orlov's introduction in *Izbrannoe*, p. 16 ("There is much in it [Cvetaeva's work] that has become obsolete or was dictated by incidental considerations, by the topical interests of days long gone. There are also plainly unsuccessful pieces, and these are by no means few.")

interpretation of Cvetaeva's poetry presents difficulties; one of these, perhaps the greatest, stems from her tremendous versatility and variety within what may at first appear as a unified manner. Her specific "poetic voice," the individual and unmistakable timbre that is so entirely her own, is apparent in everything she wrote from *Versty I* on. But her constant evolution continually added new dimensions to her basic manner. This accounts for the recurrent phenomenon of the critics' enthusiasm for one work and their violent rejection of some later one that is of equal and often superior artistic value. Appreciation of *Remeslo,* for example, in no way prepared one for a grasp of *Posle Rossii,* while a familiarity with Cvetaeva's later poetry could at times prevent one from realizing the poetic value of *Lebedinyj stan.* The critics often looked for the qualities that had charmed them in a previous poem or collection of Cvetaeva's, and, not finding them in a later work under examination, they pronounced it poor. A comparable phenomenon is taking place to this day in the musical criticism of the work of Igor' Stravinskij. Music critics who valued his early ballets often saw a sharp decline in his work of the nineteen-twenties, while a later generation of critics, who saw in "Oedipus Rex" and "Symphony of Psalms" the towering musical accomplishments of our age, are quite incapable of appreciating "Threni" or "Agon." The basic mistake is always in looking in a given work for values that are typical of quite another work by the same artist, and thereby missing other, equally important values that are present.

An unprejudiced and sympathetic examination of Cvetaeva's lyric poetry, conducted with the factors outlined above in mind, will dispel the idea that there is a large number of inferior works in her output. Like all poets, even the greatest, Cvetaeva has her weaker moments, in which the work she produces is less successful than her very finest. This applies to her prose and dramatic works to a greater extent than to her lyric poetry. Nonetheless, the percentage of really weak poems by Marina Cvetaeva among those published is really quite small, and the amount of dross in the pure poetic gold of her verse is certainly lower than that in the work of such undoubtedly first-rate Russian poets as Lermontov and Blok.

VIII 🖋
Longer Poems

In Russian literary terminology, the term *poèma* is used to designate an extended narrative in verse. In the eighteenth century the term usually indicated an epic poem; in Puškin's day it was applied to the Byronic tale in verse. The eighteenth- and nineteenth-century *poèma* presupposed a developed fictional or historical plot. Russian Symbolists applied the name to a somewhat different genre. Such works as Vjačeslav Ivanov's "Mladenčestvo," Blok's "Vozmezdie," and Belyj's "Pervoe svidanie" are called *poèmy,* but instead of the well-constructed plot of the epic and the romantic *poèma,* these works deal with fragmentary autobiographical episodes. Futurist poets practiced the genre of *poèma* more widely than the Symbolists and brought it to a greater flowering than it had enjoyed since the time of Puškin and Lermontov. Both the fictional and the autobiographical varieties were current during the Futurist period, and the *poèma* figures importantly in the work of Xlebnikov, Majakovskij, Pasternak, Aseev, and their lesser contemporaries. While the three Symbolist poets, Ivanov, Blok, and Belyj, were apt to abandon their typical style in their extended verse narratives (and, in the three works named above, to turn to the example and influence of Puškin), the Futurists made the *poèma* one of the basic vehicles of their literary expression at its most advanced and individual stage. The *poèmy* of Marina Cvetaeva are closest to the practice of her Futurist contemporaries. She wrote no extended or narrative works in verse prior to the Revolution, and her entire output in this form encompasses one single decade, 1920–1930. We know no completed work by Cvetaeva in this form that dates from the nineteen-thirties and V. Orlov, who evidently had access to the Cvetaeva archives in the U.S.S.R., lists twelve *poèmy,* which would account for all the published ones.

The narrative poetry of Cvetaeva can be classified in two basic categories: the *poèmy* which follow the Symbolist tradition in narrating episodes from the poet's life and describe her subjective experiences; and the group of epic and satirical poems which are based on plots borrowed from literary sources. For all her tremendous talent as a poet and prose writer, the one thing Marina Cvetaeva (like Shakespeare) never attempted to do was to invent a plot. This did not prevent her from creating works of undoubted originality, whether based on folk motifs, diaries of others, or her personal life. In this chapter we shall examine the two basic types of Cvetaeva's verse narratives according to the derivation of their subject matter, since this is the factor that contributed most to the form of the works. The lyrical-autobiographical *poèmy* are closer in subject and form to Cvetaeva's lyric poetry considered in the preceding chapter and will accordingly be discussed first.

On a Red Steed (*Na krasnom kone*)

The first extended narrative work in verse by Cvetaeva, the epic folk tale *Car'-devica* (1920), was soon followed by another long poem, "Na krasnom kone" ("On a Red Steed"), written in January of 1921.[1] This is basically a personal and lyrical work, although, alone among Cvetaeva's lyrical *poèmy,* it shows marked features of epic poetry and folk tradition. The violent and turbulent poem falls into three principal sections with an introduction and an epilogue. Against the background of some natural calamity, the heroine, who is the poet, is exposed to three temptations and is rescued each time by a symbolic figure of a winged knight riding a red steed, who, as the epilogue first makes clear, represents her poetic genius. During

[1] *Razluka,* pp. 19–38; *Psixeja,* pp. 85–94.

the first temptation, the heroine is a little girl caught in a house on fire and concerned with saving her favorite doll.[2] The Knight of the Red Steed saves both the girl and the doll and orders the heroine to break the doll he has rescued in order to "liberate Love." In the second section, the heroine, caught in a violent snowstorm and freezing, finds refuge in a deserted church. She is about to offer herself to Christ in gratitude, but her guardian genius descends from heaven and orders his horse to step on her chest. In the third section, the mature heroine, on a battlefield which symbolizes erotic love, understands in desperation that the man of her choosing does not love her. Amidst the imagery of a military battle, the guardian genius finds her and offers himself as a replacement of all the things he made her renounce:

И шопот: Такой я тебя желал!
И рокот: Такой я тебя избрал,
Дитя моей страсти — сестра — брат —
Невеста во льду — лат.

Моя и ничья — до конца лет.
Я, руки воздев: Свет!
— Пребудешь? Не будешь ничья, — нет?
Я, рану зажав: Нет.[3]

And the whisper: "[Now] you are as I desired you!"
And the murmur: "[Now] you are as I elected you,
Child of my passion — [my] sister — [my] brother —
[My] bride in the ice of armor.

My own and no one's — till the end of years."
I, with arms raised: "[My] light!"
"You will remain so? You will not be anyone's? No one's?"
I, clutching my wound: "No."

[2] The image of the doll in "Na krasnom kone" has strong autobiographical significance for Cvetaeva. As her other writings show, a Paris doll she had adored as a child came to be a symbol of loving an unresponsive or indifferent object, chosen only for its physical appearance, into which the lover reads qualities that are not there (see, especially, Letters to Baxrax, *Mosty,* VI, 339, and "Moj Puškin," *Proza,* p. 34).

[3] *Psixeja,* p. 93.

"Na krasnom kone" is a poem about the terrible and demanding nature of art. All the three temptations have complex symbolic overtones, but at their basic level they stand for the renunciation of love, religion, and pride—a rather unexpected sequence of life's essential elements. The introduction and the epilogue are based on the trope of "Slavic antithesis," or comparison by negation, usual in Slavic folk poetry. In the introduction the poet denies having any communion with the Muse. This negation is taken up in the epilogue and leads to the explanation that her inspiration comes not from the usual Muse but from a personal genius: the Knight of the Red Steed of the episodes just narrated, who will ultimately claim her and speed her towards heaven.

Three literary associations strongly suggest themselves in connection with "Na krasnom kone." When initially published in the volume *Razluka,* the poem was dedicated to Anna Axmatova (this dedication does not appear in the version of the poem printed in *Psixeja*). The name of Axmatova, whose poetry frequently describes her Muse as a young foreigner who visits her, explains the Muse of the introduction and the epilogue and raises the possibility that one of the meanings of "Na krasnom kone" is Cvetaeva's answer to the critics who were constantly comparing her with Axmatova. The insistence on the absence of a Muse would then be Cvetaeva's way of pointing to the essential and basic difference between her poetry and that of her contemporary whom she both tremendously admired and felt to be a constant hindrance and rival.[4] The framework of the poem, in which the poet communes three times with a supernatural guardian (the first time as a child), bears a considerable, possibly accidental, resemblance to the structure of the mystical poem "Tri vstreči" ("Three Encounters") by the nineteenth-century philosopher Vladimir Solov'ëv. Finally, the scene of the conflagration in the first episode, with its comment that the heroine's soul is what is really on fire, is one of the few obvious instances in which the influence of another poet led Cvetaeva to borrow imagery. The model for this scene is, without doubt, the scene of the metaphoric fire in Majakovskij's "Oblako v štanax" ("A

---

[4] The sense of rivalry with Axmatova is expressed in the eleventh poem to her of the 1916 cycle ("Ty solnce v vysi mne zastiš' "), *Versty I,* p. 89, and in the brief fragment "No val moej gordyni pol'skoj" in *Remeslo,* p. 64.

Cloud Wearing Trousers") (where the poet's heart was on fire) with its fire brigade and the caving in of the roof.[5]

Metrically, "Na krasnom kone" is a poem of great verve and inventiveness. In it Cvetaeva made one of her earliest extensive uses of meters based on the choriamb, including the already mentioned choriambic dimeter. In keeping with the turbulence of the imagery, the meter is frequently changed. In addition to choriambic meters, there are long stretches of mixed iambic tetrameter and trimeter; there is also an interesting sequence of seventeen quatrains in which the odd-numbered lines are in amphibrachic trimeter with a metrical pause that turns one of the feet (most frequently the first one) into an iambic, while the even-numbered lines are in iambic dimeter.

Stylistically, "Na krasnom kone" is related to the lyric poetry of *Remeslo*. In this poem, the subjective experiences of the poet have found an adequate symbolic representation, and the narrative elements derived from Slavic folklore (the triple temptation, the introductory trope) are organically blended with elements of personal and emotional biography to result in a work of art that is both clear and sophisticated.

Poem of the Hill (*Poèma gory*) and
Poem of the End (*Poèma konca*)

The next two lyrical *poèmy* describe a personal emotional experience, but in them the poet's manner is greatly objectivized in comparison with "Na krasnom kone." "Poèma gory" ("Poem of the Hill") and "Poèma konca" ("Poem of the End") were both written in Prague in 1924, and they both deal with the same emotional event in Cvetaeva's life: the end of her love affair with the former White army officer she had met in Prague. There is very little narration in "Poèma gory." It is simply a series of descriptions or evocations, told in what is basically a sequence of ten interconnected lyric poems followed by an epilogue, of the Prague hill on which the lovers met

---

[5] Cf. Majakovskij, "Oblako v štanax," *Polnoe sobranie sočinenij* (Moscow, 1955), I, 180–181, and *Psixeja,* pp. 87–89.

in the days of their happiness. In the ninth and tenth sections, the poet imagines this hill in later years becoming part of the city of Prague, built over with houses and shops. She expects the love and misery that she is experiencing on the hill to lay a curse on it and foresees that this curse will work havoc with the lives of the complacent philistines who will reside there in the future. The poem ends in complete bitterness, directed both at the world and at the former lover. Although written simultaneously with *Posle Rossii,* "Poèma gory" is in the line of Cvetaeva's poetry of anti-philistine invective in the thirties. There is great pain in this poem, and its hatred and destructive urge produce a frightening impression. One wonders whether it was Cvetaeva's dissatisfaction with such an epitaph to her love affair that made her treat the same subject all over in "Poèma konca" only a few months later.

"Poèma konca" is considerably longer than its predecessor. It describes the last evening the lovers spent together. The reader follows them through their appointed meeting somewhere near the railroad tracks, their decision not to go home, a stroll by the river, a visit to a café and their discussion there during which the man gently communicates his decision not to continue the affair, their subsequent conversation, another stroll during which they pass a dairy shop where they once met. Late at night, they wander to the suburbs of the city, still unable to take final leave. In the last two sections, the man is unable to hold back tears, causing some merriment on the part of three prostitutes who happen to witness the final farewell. The events of the evening are told in minute detail, with the lovers' conversations alternating with descriptions of heroine's emotions. The method is that of a stream of consciousness, and "Poèma konca" is one of the great psychological poems in the Russian language. Every word, glance, and action of her departing lover is analyzed by the desperate heroine, with the constant conflict between her imagination and what her reason and senses tell her to be facts. The imagery is bold and varied, and there are numerous digressions, such as the antiphilistine diatribe during the visit to the café and the meditation on the similarity between poets and Jews when the lovers walk past the Jewish quarter of Prague. Brief recollections of past happiness occasionally change the gloomy and desperate tone of the work into a sunny or gently humorous one.

Cvetaeva is an unusually word-conscious poet, and in "Poèma konca" she organized her emotionally-charged material into verbal structures of considerable complexity, making wide use of suggestive word-root similarities:

Корпусами фабричными, зычными
И отзывчивыми на зов . . .
Сокровенную, подъязычную
Тайну жен от мужей, и вдов

От друзей — тебе, подноготную
Тайну зева от чрева, — вот:
Я не более чем животное,
Кем-то раненное в живот.[6]

[We walk] past factory workshops, sonorous
And responsive to [shouted] calls . . .
[Here is] the innermost, the sublingual
Secret that wives keep from husbands, and widows

From their friends; for you, the most intimate
Secret that the maw keeps from the venter,—here it is:
I am no more than an animal
That someone has wounded in the guts.

Metrically, the poem shows great variety and imagination in its selection of appropriate meters to express the shifts of the heroine's mood. The meter of the eighth section is a startling invention: the dividing dashes after the first syllable of the odd-numbered lines turn what would otherwise have been an iambic dimeter into a four-syllable line in which *all* syllables but the third are stressed. This alternates with an amphibrachic trimeter, with a metrical pause on the second unstressed syllable of the second foot of the line:

Во-да и твердь.
Выкладываю монеты.
День-га за смерть.
Харонова мзда за Лету.

---

[6] *Izbrannoe,* p. 276.

Мо-неты тень
В руке теневой. Без звука
Мо-неты те.
Итак, в теневую руку —[7]

Water and firmament.
I lay out the coins.
A copper piece [as price] for death.
Charon's fee for Lethe.

The coin's shadow
In the shadowy hand. Soundless
Are those coins.
And so, into the shadowy hand —

"Poèma konca" is one of Cvetaeva's finest accomplishments. This poem and "Poèma gory" (which is somewhat marred by the excessive self-pity and the blind hatred of its tone) show us the poet at the peak of her originality and poetic stature. The advanced and even revolutionary means of expression used in these two poems explain the derision and incomprehension with which they were met by such important older writers as Bunin, Gor'kij, and Zinaida Gippius.[8] However, both poems are finding a new and appreciative audience in the Soviet Union since they were included in the collection *Izbrannoe* in 1961.

From the Seacoast (*S morja*), *An Attempt to Construct a Room* (*Popytka komnaty*), and *The Staircase* (*Lestnica*)

The next group of lyrical *poèmy* are the three works Cvetaeva wrote while staying at the seashore at St. Gilles-sur-Vie in the spring and summer of 1926: "S morja" ("From the Seacoast"), "Popytka komnaty" (contextually, "An Attempt To Construct a Room" rather than "Essay of the Room") and "Lestnica" ("The Staircase"). The first two works are records of dream experience. In "S morja," the poet, asleep on the French coast, steps into a dream of another poet who is at the same time sleeping in Moscow. During

---

[7] *Ibid.*, p. 273.
[8] See Chapter III notes 24, 39, and 40.

this dream encounter, the two poets saunter along the beach,
describing the objects found there and assigning to them various
symbolic significance. The tone is that of a casual conversation, even
badinage. Interspersed with the symbolic comments on the objects
found on the beach are occasional pointed references to the Soviet
literary scene of the nineteen-twenties:

Только песок, между пальцев, плеский.
Стой-ка: гремучей змеи обноски:
Ревности! Обновясь
Гордостью назвалась

И поползла себе с полным правом.
Не напостовцы — стоять над крабом
Выеденным. Не краб:
Славы кирпичный крап.[9]

Only sand between the fingers, plashing.
Wait: [here's] the castoff garb of [that] rattlesnake,
Jealousy! Renewing itself
It called itself pride

And off it crawled, self-righteously.
[We're] not [like those] *On Guard* types, who guard a discarded
Crabshell. [This is] not a crab
[But] brick-red specks of fame.

Toward the end of the poem, there comes an outburst against the
state of things that keeps two mutually admiring poets apart and
separates Russians from each other by artificially promoted class
hatred. The metrical pattern of "S morja" is that of free *dol'niki*
with a basic underlying pattern of either the amphibrach or the
dactyl. Certain personal allusions in the poem make one suspect that
it is actually a cryptic epistle to Boris Pasternak. It is to be
considered as a *poèma* only because Marina Cvetaeva herself
designated it as such.[10]

---

[9] "S morja," *Versty*, III (Paris, 1928), 10. "Napostovcy" (*"On Guard
types"*)—from *Na postu*, the Soviet publication of Communist literary
vigilantes of the nineteen-twenties which published a scurrilous denunciation
of *Versty I*, qualifying the book as religious propaganda and stating that for
Cvetaeva "the cult of the Virgin and the church is a primary task" (S. Rodov,
"Grešnica na ispovedi u Gosizdata," *Na postu*, II–III [1923], 148–150).

[10] In the list of her *poèmy* appended to *Posle Rossii*, p. 160.

"Popytka komnaty," written one month after "S morja" (in June 1926), describes a similar dream encounter, but it is a far more complex piece of poetry. In this work, the poet tries to take advantage of the dream world to overcome the limitations of both time and space. She is trying to control her own dream in order to construct, laboriously, a dream-room at the time of the last Tsar's abdication, in which she expects to meet a friend who in 1917 was eight years old (in biographical terms, this could possibly refer to Nikolaj Gronskij). While the dream imagery in "S morja" is in the main realistic and even satirical, "Popytka komnaty" conveys a hallucinatory dream logic that allows us just this once to apply to Cvetaeva's poetry the adjective "surrealistic." The poet plays with the notions of time, space, and gravity and emphasizes beyond all expected proportion certain details, such as her doubt whether the fourth wall of the room (the one behind her back) really existed. At one point, there are complex references to the circumstances of Puškin's duel with D'Anthès, which in their unexpectedness reinforce the surrealistic mood. Before the guest for whom the dream-room was conjured up can appear, reality intervenes and destroys the dream-world piece by piece in a manner that is greatly reminiscent of some dream scenes in the fiction of Vladimir Nabokov:

Оттого-ль, что не стало стен —
Потолок достоверно крен
Дал. Лишь звательный цвел падеж
В ртах. А пол — достоверно брешь.
А сквозь брешь, зелена как Нил . . .
Потолок достоверно плыл.[11]

Whether it was because the walls were no longer there . . .
The ceiling clearly listed.
Only the vocative case flourished
In mouths. And the floor clearly cracked.
And through the crack, green like the Nile's . . .
The ceiling was clearly floating.

Like "S morja," "Popytka komnaty" is written in *dol'niki,* but this time the basic metrical pattern is anapest.

[11] "Popytka komnaty," *Volja Rossii,* III (1928), 39.

"Lestnica," written during the same summer of 1926, is, together with "Poèma konca," one of Cvetaeva's finest accomplishments in the genre of lyric-narrative poetry. It is a philosophical and satirical work, written in the technique that is in part reminiscent of "Krysolov." The separate sections are not numbered, unlike the ones in "Poèma konca," but one can distinguish them by the changes of pace and mood. The opening section is a satirical and biting description of the staircase of the title—the back-stairs of a large apartment house inhabited by the poor. Cvetaeva depicts the sights, sounds, and smells of this dingy setting, using a syncopated jazzy style, with an economy of images and a reliance on metonymy (a violinist is represented only by his violin, his sheet music, and the tails of his coat) that remind one of the dissolved and reduced images and forms in certain paintings of the period of Synthetic Cubism. The kaleidoscopic shuffling of bits of images is used to convey an atmosphere of social oppression and a sort of hopeless cynicism. As Cvetaeva herself says in this section, the result achieved is a "Marxist sermon in the manner of Stravinskij, by means of a multitude of patches" ("Bol'-šinstvom zaplat/Marksa propoved'/na stravinskij lad").[12] This section only sets the stage. The hubbub on the backstairs is succeeded by the stillness of the night. In the next section, the objects and substances which make up the paraphernalia of human civilization attempt to regain and to reassert their original nature and purpose. The section (an adagio that follows the boisterous allegro of the beginning) reads like a paradoxical combination of Tjutčev, Colette's libretto for Ravel's opera "L'enfant et les sortilèges," and the revolt of objects in Xlebnikov's *poèma* "Žuravl' " ("The Crane"). It begins:

Ночь — как бы высказать?
Ночь — вещи исповедь.
Ночь просит искренности,
Вещь хочет высказаться —

Вся! Все унижены
Сплошь, до недвижимых
Вплоть. Приступ выспренности:
Вещь хочет выпрямиться.

[12] "Lestnica," *Volja Rossii,* IX (1926), 32.

Винт черной лестницы —
Мнишь — стенкой лепится?
Ночь: час молитвенностей:
Винт хочет вытянуться.[13]

Night: how to express it?
Night: the object's confession.
Night begs for sincerity.
The object wants to unburden itself —

Totally! [They] all are humiliated,
Every single one, the immovable
Included. An access of eloquence:
The object wants to straighten up.

The spiral of the back stairs —
Do you [really] think it cleaves to the wall?
Night: the hour of prayerfullness —
The spiral wants to stretch out.

The objects and substances refuse to serve the humiliating uses to which they are put by man. For several pages Cvetaeva, the inveterate romantic, develops her Rousseauist conception of material civilization. In images that would have met with the approval of Gerard Manley Hopkins, she condemns man ("that visible spirit, that ailing god") for leaving his smudge on the original paradise of nature by inventing the "inanimate object—that most false of all slanders." The filthy, evil-smelling staircase of the beginning thus becomes the summit achievement of this material civilization, its most typical, most basic symbol. To understand the true nature of the artificial object, says Cvetaeva, one has to examine the objects used by and belonging to the poor. There follows the shattering digression on these belongings of the poor ("Vešči bednyx"), the one section of "Lestnica" that has found favor in the Soviet Union and was printed there twice as a separate excerpt.[14] The objects are

---

[13] *Ibid.*, p. 35. Other treatments of the theme of the "revolt of things" are mentioned in V. Markov, *The Longer Poems of Velimir Khebnikov*, p. 61.

[14] Quoted almost entirely in A. Ležnëv and D. Gorbov, *Literatura revolucionnogo desjatiletija* (Xar'kov, 1926), pp. 141–148, and reprinted in *Tarusskie stranicy*, 1961.

humanized by Cvetaeva in this section and take on the properties of their owners' miserable existences. The digression is interrupted by a brief section comparing the threadbare objects to disembodied human souls. The last section of the poem proposes the ideal solution to the squalor described: the magnificence and nobility of destruction by fire. But the poet realizes that this solution is un-realizable, and at the end, the staircase resumes its morning activities, while the poet puts the just-completed poem to rest.

"Lestnica" is a strong and passionate statement of a poet's resentment directed against artificial ugliness and the conditions which force human beings to live in it. The circumstances of her own life have forced her to have a closer look at such things, as she herself makes clear several times in brief asides. Yet, there is no hatred or bitterness in "Lestnica" of the kind Cvetaeva had expressed in "Poèma gory," only a violent protest and a sense of injustice, which makes the poet's voice all the more effective. The solution of the problems raised—the destruction of material civiliza-tion by purifying fire—is obviously meant to take place on an ideal plane, though the image of fire has always been closely connected with Cvetaeva's ideal of revolt. The idea that uncontrolled growth of technology not only breeds ugliness but may lead to an eventual destruction of mankind has an uncanny prophetic ring about it, now that we know more about such things than Cvetaeva could have known in 1926. The conclusion of the poem, which in the terminology of Russian Formalist critics could be described as "laying bare the device" (*obnaženie priëma*), emphasizes the poet's realization that her only effective way of dealing with the questions she has raised is to create a work of art about them. Structurally and metrically, "Lestnica" is an inventive and varied as "Poèma konca." The dividing dashes and explanatory footnotes in this particular poem do not refer to unusual position of stresses, as they almost always do elsewhere in Cvetaeva, but rather to unexpected or emphatic caesurae, and in this particular case Cvetaeva could have avoided the footnotes by using a Majakovskij-like, ladder-shaped breakdown of her verse.

New Year's Greetings (*Novogodnee*) and
Poem of the Air (*Poèma vozduxa*)

"Novogodnee" ("New Year's Greetings"), also called "Pis'mo k Ril'ke" ("A Letter to Rilke"),[15] was written in February 1927. It is in couplets of trochaic pentameter and thus the only one of Cvetaeva's *poèmy* couched entirely in a conventional Russian meter. Again we have a personal experience of the author forming the basis of the verse narrative. At the very end of 1926, Marina Cvetaeva is told by an unnamed editor or journalist of the death of Rainer Maria Rilke. She is requested to write an article on Rilke and reminded of her promise to attend a ball given to celebrate New Year's Eve. She refuses to write the article, feeling it would constitute a betrayal of her friendship with Rilke, and instead of going to the ball remains at home, spending New Year's Eve alone, meditating on Rilke and on death:

Что мне делать в новогоднем шуме
С этой внутреннею рифмой: Райнер — умер.
Если ты, такое око смерклось,
Значит жизнь не жизнь есть, смерть не смерть есть.
Значит — тмится, допойму при встрече! —
Нет ни жизни, нет ни смерти, — третье,
Новое. И за него (соломой
Застелив седьмой — двадцать шестому
Отходящему — какое счастье
Тобой кончиться, тобой начаться!)
Через стол, необозримый оком,
Буду чокаться с тобою тихим чоком
Стекла о стекло?[16]

What am I to do amidst the New Year's hubbub
With this internal rhyme: Rainer — dead.
If you, such an eye, could be extinguished,
Then life is not life, death is not death.
Then [things are] dark, I will [truly] understand when we meet:
There is neither life, nor death, but a third [thing],

---

[15] In the list mentioned in note 10 above.
[16] "Novogodnee," *Versty,* III (Paris, 1928), 17.

[Something] new. And to it (packing away in straw
The [nineteen-twenty] seventh — happy the departing twenty sixth,
Having begun with you, to end with you!)
Shall we touch glasses with a quiet clinking
Across a table, unsurveyable to eye,
Glass to glass?

The lament for Rilke and the meditation on the pure and disembodied nature of her relationship with the poet leads Cvetaeva to conjure up a whole idealized poetic cosmogony in which the creation of poetry is the main motive force. This poetic universe is ruled by a Creator who grows and expands like a baobab tree and over whom there is another Creator and so on *ad infinitum*. The complex and original cosmogony outlined toward the end of "Novogodnee" is one of the strongest expressions of Cvetaeva's continuous driving urge to escape from bounds of time and of human condition.

"Poèma vozduxa" ("Poem of the Air") was written in Meudon "in the days of Lindbergh," i.e. in June, 1927. It is in form a sequel to "Popytka komnaty" and in essence a synthesis between that poem and "Novogodnee." The starting point is again a dream experience, and the introductory section (printed in *Volja Rossii* with several obvious misprints and with one crucial line missing) takes us back to the dream room of "Popytka komnaty." This time the encounter and the unity with another person, of which the poet dreamed in "Popytka komnaty," are realized:

> Сню тебя иль снюсь тебе, —
> Сушь, вопрос седин
> Лекторских. Дай вчувствуюсь [:]
> Мы, а вздох один.[17]

> Whether I dream you or am dreamed by you, —
> Is a barren issue, a question for grey-haired
> Lecturers. Let me sense this fully [:]
> We [are two], yet [there is but] a single breath.

[17] "Poèma vozduxa," *Volja Rossii*, I (1930), 19.

The poem is a set of variations, with the physical and acoustical properties of air as the basic metaphor, which describe the ideal conditions of freedom for the poet and the unity and harmony with another human being for which all persons yearn. "Poèma vozduxa" is connected with the poem "Sivilla mladencu" ("Sibyl to an Infant") in *Posle Rossii,* in which death was depicted as falling into the firmament; with Cvetaeva's later poem "Nereida," in which the impossibility of an ideal union with another is lamented; and with some of the imagery of Rilke's "Elegie" dedicated to Cvetaeva (which was also echoed in "Novogodnee"). It is curious that just as the staircase in "Lestnica" symbolized the worst in human civilization, Lindbergh's epochal flight is made to stand for what is best and purest in the human condition. Verbally, this poem is more inventive and daring than other lyric *poèmy* as is shown in the following passages, which describes the ability of air to hum:

> Рыдью, медью, гудью,
> Вьюго-Богослова
> Гудью — точно грудью
> Певчей — небосвода
> Нёбом или лоном
> Лиро-черепахи?[18]

Most of "Poèma vozduxa" is in trochees (tetrameter and trimeter), but there are also passages in amphibrach-based *dol'niki.*

Epic Poems:
The Tsar-Maiden (Car'-devica)

The lyrical *poèmy* of Cvetaeva are subjective and introspective poems, in which the author at all times has the center of the stage. This is their main difference from another set of *poèmy* which we have chosen to call epic for the sake of convenience. The earliest of these chronologically is *Car'-devica (The Tsar-Maiden),* which Cvetaeva wrote between July and September 1920 and published in 1922 as a separate book. Although the subject of the warrior maiden,

---

[18] *Ibid.,* p. 23. Neologisms and extreme compression of meaning make this passage, clear enough in the original Russian, impossible to translate without the surrounding context.

taken from popular folklore, was treated in a sort of ballad by
Deržavin in 1812 [19] (the title has also been used in a song by Ja.
Polonskij, which has nothing to do with the folk tale on the
subject), Cvetaeva's basic source for her long narrative tale is
Afanas'ev's collection of popular Russian magic tales.[20] She combined the elements of the two tales on the subject of the Tsar-
Maiden found in Afanas'ev's collection to form her own plot and
added to it a situation from the Greek myth that fascinated her most
of all—that of Phaedra and Hippolytos. In folklore diction, developed and perfected in *Versty I, Car'-devica* tells of the drunken old
Tsar, his frail musician-son, and the amorous stepmother (barely
hinted at in the Afanas'ev version) who resorts to witchcraft to win
the love of her stepson. The heroine of the title is that strange
female character recurrent in Russian folklore and epics: the
warrior-maiden, a powerful Amazon who usually falls in love with
a weak, delicate man. She wins the musician prince by the use of
white magic, while the desperate stepmother and her accomplice,
the prince's lecherous tutor, fight against the Tsar-Maiden with
black arts. Up to a certain point, Cvetaeva's tale follows the folk
tradition as well as the literary tradition of *skazki* in verse as they
were practiced during the first half of the nineteenth century by
Žukovskij, Puškin, Jazykov, and Eršov. But the embellishments that
Cvetaeva brings to the material taken from Afanas'ev, and particularly the strong erotic overtones in such descriptions as the stepmother's strip-tease in front of the Tsar, her payment with her body
for the magical assistance of the tutor, or the old Tsar's offer of his
wife to his son, take *Car'-devica* far out of the literary genre and
tradition of the nineteenth-century verse *skazka*. However, such
descriptions are quite common in the authentic Russian folk tales of
this type, which, unlike some of their literary adaptations, are meant
for an adult audience.

The style and language of *Car'-devica* merit a special study. The
authentic folklore tone of this tale is a marvel of its kind. By turning

[19] G. R. Deržavin, *Stixotvorenija* (Moscow, 1957), pp. 352–358.
[20] A. N. Afanas'ev, *Narodnye russkie skazki* (Moscow, 1958), tales 232 and
233 (Vol. II, pp. 227–234). Cvetaeva's three-volume edition of Afanas'ev was
given to her in 1915–1916 by the editors of *Severnye Zapiski* ("Nezdešnij
večer," *Proza*, p. 280).

to the genuine Russian folklore tradition, Cvetaeva puzzled her Russian readers, accustomed to nineteenth-century stylizations of folktales, stylizations which were frequently based on Western European models. Similiarly, Russian listeners, accustomed to Rimskij-Korsakov's arrangements of folk tunes for a Lisztian-Wagnerian orchestra and believing these arrangements to be genuinely Russian, were puzzled by Stravinskij's settings of folklore melodies for pianos and percussion instruments in "Svadebka." A comparison between Cvetaeva's language in *Car'-devica* and transcriptions of unvarnished authentic Russian folklore tales should prove most instructive. The most Cvetaeva-like feature of this work, however, is the musical gift of the hero. It is the artist in him that makes him respond to the better and purer of the two contending women. The reversal of the sex roles in almost all the situations of this work is also interesting and significant when viewed within the whole of Cvetaeva's work and in terms of her personal biography.

Sidestreets (Pereuločki)

"Pereuločki," finished in Moscow in April 1922 and included by Cvetaeva in the collection *Remeslo,* is the most striking result of Cvetaeva's interest in the poetry of magic chants and incantations, which is also manifest in some of the poems of *Versty I* and of *Remeslo.* Other women poets of the twentieth century have shown an interest in this type of poetry,[21] but few have used it as a basis for an extended narrative work. On first reading, "Pereuločki" is a puzzling piece of poetry, and the critics who reviewed *Remeslo* at the time of its publication preferred to pass this *poèma* over in silence. A work of dazzling verbal virtuosity, it strikes the reader as one vast incantation, in which the narrative elements are drowned in the continuous flow of verbal display and are not easily perceived as a coherent whole. Fortunately, this *poèma* puzzled Ivask and he questioned Cvetaeva about its contents. In her letter to him of October 11, 1935, she wrote: " 'Pereuločki' (didn't you know it?) is

---

[21] On elements of magic incantations in the work of Gertrude Stein and Edith Sitwell, see William Seabrook, *Witchcraft* (New York, 1940).

a story of the ultimate seduction. . . ." [22] Apparently, Ivask was still not satisfied by the explanation, and in Cvetaeva's letter of January 25, 1937, we find a long commentary on "Pereuločki":

. . . you have simply understood nothing in "Pereuločki." Open your *byliny* and find the *bylina* about Marinka who lives in the Ignat'ev sidestreets and practices magic behind the bed-curtain, turning young swains into aurochs, getting them drugged. In my poem, she does it by words, by chatter, everything is done while one is lulled by it: suddenly, the bed-curtain is no longer a bed-curtain but a sail, and here is the river and here is the little fish, and so on. And the one leitmotif is temptation: at first, by apples, then by the river rainbow, then by the fiery abyss, then by the seventh heaven. She is *deceit* and she is playing with what is the most frightening.

And the horse (the voice of his horse) is his valor, calling and neighing, trying to destroy the spell and, as always, in vain, because she is the one who is victorious [in the end]: there are footprints of an aurochs by the gate, that is, one more aurochs and one more fool [*tur — i dur*]. This work of all my works (*Mólodec* did not yet exist then) was loved most of all in Russia, it was understood, everyone was stunned by it, every half-educated technical school student. But to you this ability was not given.[23]

Cvetaeva greatly overrates the perceptive abilities of her Russian audience by assuming that "Pereuločki" could be that easily accessible. Her statement provides us not only with an indispensible key to this *poèma* but directs us to the proper literary address for its source. The unnamed heroine turns out to be the sorceress Marina Ignat'evna, who appears in the *bylina* of the Dobrynja Nikitič cycle.[24] Historically, this is one of the several avatars in the Russian oral epic tradition of the Polish wife of the False Dmitrij, Marina Mnišek (Maryna Mniszchówna, ca. 1587–1614), always one of Cvetaeva's favorite historical personages, who after being anathema-

---

[22] Letters to Ivask, p. 226.

[23] *Ibid.*, pp. 230–231.

[24] The standard version of this *bylina* appeared in the eighteenth-century collection of Kirša Danilov (*Drevnie rossijskie stixotvorenija sobrannye Kiršeju Danilovym* [Moscow-Leningrad, 1958], pp. 52–59). Certain minor details in "Pereuločki" suggest that Cvetaeva used not the Danilov version but the less bloody and sadistic version of this folk poem which appeared in the collection of *byliny* edited by M. Speranskij (M. Speranskij, ed. *Byliny*, I [Moscow, 1916], 38–42).

tized by the Orthodox church entered the folk tradition as sorceress
and heretic. The hero of "Pereuločki," however, is not the epic hero
Dobrynja from whom Marina Ignat'evna traditionally gets her
punishment for sorcery, but rather one of his predecessors whom
this Slavic Circe drugs and turns into an aurochs. With the
narrative canvas provided by the *bylina,* we can follow the action of
"Pereuločki" which is developed alternately from the point of view
of the heroine and of her victim. Numerous details are retained
from the *bylina:* the doves who work the erotic suggestion, the
references to the hero's mother as a possible source of his salvation,
and the important image of the curtain. The role of the hero's horse
as the symbol of his masculine integrity and the apotheosis the hero
imagines at the very moment he is being turned into a beast are
Cvetaeva's own inventions, and, most importantly, so is the unique
language in which the tale is told. One can easily believe that half-
educated students were stunned by Cvetaeva's recitation of "Pereuločki" in Moscow of 1922—the poem, for all its obscurity and need
of commentary, is one of the most colorful explosions of verbal
fireworks in the whole of Russian poetry. But the reference to the
bylina is quite indispensable for grasping the meaning and the
essence of this work: the only possible key in the text itself is the
name of the street in which the heroine resides. We cannot be
grateful enough for the commentary in the Ivask correspondence
and cannot recommend too strongly the addition of this commentary to any future printings of "Pereuločki."

The Swain (*Mólodec*)

The next folk epic of Cvetaeva, *Mólodec,* finished in Prague in
December, 1924 and dedicated to Boris Pasternak, is again based on
a story from the Afanas'ev collection. While *Car'-devica* and
"Pereuločki" took only their basic elements from folklore, *Mólodec*
follows its source, the folk tale "Upyr'" ("The Vampire") [25] with
utmost fidelity, even to the point of including into its verse texture
quotations from Afanas'ev's version. The story, which is a combina-

[25] Afanas'ev, *op. cit.,* tale 363 (Vol. III, pp. 124–127).

tion of two popular wandering motifs (the fiancé who turns out to be a vampire and the flower which turns into a young girl), tells of a village maiden Marusja who goes to a dance, meets a handsome young swain who turns out to be a vampire and, instead of denouncing him and saving herself, keeps silent while her mother, her brother, and finally herself, in a scene of mixed horror and tenderness, are killed by the vampire. She is buried in accordance with certain magic instructions suggested by the vampire (in Afanas'ev, by her grandmother) and is reincarnated in a flower that grows upon her grave. In the second part of *Mólodec,* a local nobleman finds the flower, brings it to his castle, and surprises it at midnight when it turns into a woman. To prevent Marusja from turning back into a flower, the nobleman puts the sign of the cross on her. Listless and apathetic, she remains with him, marries him, and bears him a son. After five years, taunted by friends that his wife is unbaptized, the nobleman forces her to attend a church service. At this point, Cvetaeva's plot becomes radically different from her source in Afanas'ev. In that version, the heroine was confronted by the vampire in the church, threw some holy water on him destroying him forever, and lived happily ever after with her new husband. In *Mólodec,* against the background of solemnly intoned fragments from the Church Slavic liturgy and quotations from the psalms, Marusja becomes aware of the presence of her first love, the vampire, and, forsaking her husband and son, flies with him toward heaven in a burst of scarlet light.

After several critics offered varied interpretations of *Mólodec,* Cvetaeva replied to their critiques with her own commentary. In "Poèt o kritike" she wrote:

Mme C. wanted to give us a folk tale, utilizing for it such and such elements. . . . I (stress on I) wanted this? No. *This* was what I wanted? But no, not at all. I read "The Vampire" and was puzzled why Marusja, who feared the vampire, kept so stubbornly refusing to admit what she had seen, knowing that to name it was to be saved. Why no instead of yes? Fear? But from fear one not only buries oneself in bed, one even jumps out the window. No, not fear. Granted, fear, but something else, too. Fear and what else? When I am told: do this and you are free and I do not do it, that means that I do not want freedom, that un-freedom is more precious to me. And what is this precious un-freedom between people? Love. Marusja loved the vampire and therefore would not name him and kept losing, one after another, her mother, her brother, her life. Passion and crime, passion and sacrifice. . . .

Such was my task when I started working on *Mólodec*. To uncover the essence of the folk tale, implicit in its skeleton. To release it from its spell [*Raskoldovat' vešč'*]. And not at all to create some "new form" or "folk tale form." [26]

On a deeper level, all three of Cvetaeva's Russian folklore epics can be read as allegories of the problem that was central in much of her writing: the amoral nature of art. In *Car'-devica,* the artist-hero is a pawn in a game between the good and the evil forces. The good, personified by the Tsar Maiden actively takes him over, while the lustful stepmother is shown with all the sympathy that Cvetaeva was later to lavish on the Phaedra of her tragedy. If the hero of *Car'-devica* was claimed by both good and evil, the one in "Pereuločki" tempts the dark forces with which he cannot cope and which vanquish him at the moment he believes himself to be accomplishing something genuine and great. The apotheosis, imagined by the hero of "Pereuločki," links that *poèma* with the genuine apotheoses experienced by the heroines of *Mólodec* and, most importantly, of "Na krasnom kone." The sudden unexpected twist Cvetaeva gives to the plot of the folk tale in *Mólodec* reveals it as a re-telling, in epic terms, of "Na krasnom kone," her lyric *poèma* about the demanding nature of art. The image of physical ascension, common to "Na krasnom kone," "Pereuločki," and *Mólodec* (with the destination designated by the key words *lazur'* [the azure], its dialectal equivalent *lazor',* and *sin'* [blue skies], which is personified in "Pereuločki" and which begins and ends *Mólodec*), is related to similar imagery in the later *poèmy* "Novogodnee" and "Poèma vozduxa," demonstrating the close connection in the poet's mind between the notions of artistic creativity and of total union or fusion with another being or, possibly, with the universe (both of these notions being implicit in the apotheoses and ascensions).

The folklore style of *Mólodec* is again a new invention in comparison with the two earlier epic poems. It is permeated with

[26] "Poèt o kritike," pp. 123–124.

popular Russian dance rhythms which start throbbing from the very
first lines,

Синь да сгинь — край села,
Рухнул дуб, трость цела.
У вдовы у той у трудной
Дочь Маруся весела.[27]

The azure [. . .] And begone [!] At the village edge,
The oak has toppled, the reed is standing.
That hard-working widow yonder
Has a merry daughter, Marusja.

and keep recurring throughout the entire long poem. Cvetaeva's
own choriambic meters blend themselves organically into the
folklore-influenced verse structure. "By some miracle," wrote one
critic of *Mólodec,* "a plume of the fabled Bird of Russian folksong
has been stolen and this plume is being used to write 'civilized'—in
terms of plot and form—poems. Instead of congratulating civilization (or at least being offended on behalf of epos), some of our
critics merely shrug their shoulders." [28]

The three Russian folk epics of Cvetaeva appear original and
independent when compared to the folklore stylization tradition in
Russian poets from Mej to Bal'mont. They fit the pattern of interest
in folklore which we can observe immediately before and after the
Revolution in Russian literature (cf. the folk tales of Remizov), in
painting (Gončarova, Larionov, Chagall) and music (Stravinskij's
"Pribautki," "Bajka pro lisu [*Renard*]," and "Svadebka [*Les Noces*]"
and Prokof'ev's "Šut," also based on Afanas'ev). While in painting
and in music such twentieth-century reinterpretations of Russian
folklore found appreciative foreign audiences, their literary counterparts had trouble finding any public at all. The average Russian
reader, who prefers the *Igor Tale* in a "modernized" verse translation, was simply not interested, while critics as sophisticated as
Ajxenval'd and Adamovič were unable to see the basic and startling
differences between *Mólodec* and the cloying, sugar-coated *style*

[27] *Mólodec,* p. 9.
[28] Review of *Mólodec,* signed Š. (D. Šaxovskoj?) in *Blagonamerennyj,* I
(1926), 160—161.

russe of the late nineteenth century, and complained about the few differences they did manage to perceive. Cvetaeva's folk epics are an odd example of valid works of art suspended in a vacuum, still waiting for their right audience. It would be curious to see the impression they make when and if they are published in the Soviet Union.

The Pied Piper (*Krysolov*)

For her next epic-based work in verse, Cvetaeva turned to German folklore. Her "lyrical satire" (as she called it), "Krysolov," is of course based on the medieval German legend of the Pied Piper of Hameln (*Der Rattenfänger von Hameln*), familiar in numerous popular versions and literary adaptations, the best known of the latter being the poem by Robert Browning and Goethe's song "Ich bin der wohlbekannte Sänger." While most of the adaptations of this legend are romantic in style, Cvetaeva uses it for a devastating social and political satire. Cvetaeva wrote "Krysolov" in Všenory and Paris between March and November, 1925, and it was serialized in *Volja Rossii* in 1925 and 1926.[29] It was admired by Pasternak, by G. P. Fedotov, and by such younger poets as Aleksej Èjsner.[30] Mirskij devoted to it an enthusiastic article.[31] Yet it never became known in the Soviet Union and was comparatively rapidly forgotten by the Russian literary critics abroad.

"Krysolov" is in six cantos. The first canto is a description, both bitter and humorous, of a provincial German town. Cvetaeva, who loved Germany deeply and in her earlier poetry saw it as a country of poets and philosophers, here found biting and sarcastic words for German philistinism—not the Russian and international varieties, which she had attacked elsewhere, but the specific German phenomena of *Borniertheit* and *Spiessigkeit.* The German locale is asserted not only by the proper names and the mores described, but also by occasional macaronic passages (which occur throughout the poem) of mixed Russian and German:

[29] See bibliography for publication data on "Krysolov."

[30] For opinions of Èjsner and Fedotov, see E. P. Fedotova, introduction to Cvetaeva's letters to Fedotov, p. 162.

[31] D. Svjatopolk-Mirskij, " 'Krysolov' M. Cvetaevoj," *Volja Rossii,* VI–VII (1926), 99–100.

Juri и *Rührei* и *Rühr uns nicht*
An (в словаре: не тронь нас!)[32]

Juri and *Rührei* and *Rühr uns nicht*
An (in the dictionary: touch us not!)

A special feature of the first canto is the middle section described in the text as "digression about a button." This is Cvetaeva's strongest statement about the similarity between the creative artist, the pauper, and the criminal. The idea, also stated in "Lestnica" and in several of the shorter poems (especially "Xvala bogatym"), bears a strong resemblance to the anti-bourgeois statements of the French *poètes maudits,* particularly Baudelaire. Cvetaeva's disgust with the material well-being of the bourgeoisie combined with its spiritual poverty is here conveyed in humorous and sarcastic terms, cleverly driven home by such ironic devices as the sly paraphrase of the famous Maksim Gor'kij motto:

| Города Гаммельна гражданин, — | A citizen of Hameln town, — |
| Это выходит гордо.[33] | That sure sounds proud. |

The second canto reinforces the impression left by the first in describing the prosaic and materialistic dreams of the burghers. The third canto opens with a description of the food market. A romantic and anti-materialistic poet, Cvetaeva could have never followed the examples of Deržavin and Puškin, who have devoted poetic passages to food and gastronomy. In "Krysolov," the monstrous abundance of food is equated with moral decay and is seen as the direct cause of the rat plague. The rats get organized for a concerted attack, using a language compounded of Communist jargon and Soviet-type murine abbreviations: *glavxvost, glavsvist, narkomčort, narkomšiš,* and the like. This particular feature of the poem of course ruined any chance of its being appreciated by the Soviet critics (who would have otherwise undoubtedly liked it very much). The main weapon of the rats is their irreverence and lack of respect for the conventions which the burghers assume to be eternal and unassailable. This enables the rats to take the town over, rapidly

[32] *Volja Rossii,* IV (1925), 27.
[33] *Ibid.* Cf. Satin's famous remark in Act IV of Gor'kij's play *Lower Depths:* "A human being! That has a proud sound."

and efficiently. In the fourth canto, a flutist garbed in green, whose "only Mistress is Music," enters Hameln. Learning that the mayor has promised to give his adolescent daughter Greta in marriage to the person who delivers the city from the rat plague, he uses his flute to lure the rats into a swamp, where they drown. The rats, victims of overfeeding and of creeping *embourgeoisement* (this part of the poem owes something to Majakovskij's satires on Soviet *meščan- stvo*), follow the flute in the false belief that they are on their way to India, where they intend to start a world revolution. When the flutist tries to claim his prize in the fifth canto, the entire city council lectures him on the impossibility of a marriage between the mayor's daughter and the impoverished artist. In the slighting and con- temptuous speeches of the city officials about the nature and uses of art, Cvetaeva's satirical war on philistinism achieves its most vivid expression. For pages the city officials hold forth on the uselessness and impracticality of artistic creation and vent their suspicions and irritation with the artist. In the sixth canto, the musician has his revenge by luring all the children and adolescents in town, including the fair Greta, into a lake, where they drown.

Commenting on the finale of "Krysolov," Mirskij wrote of the "dry and, as it were, cruel tone" of the description of the children's drowning. But a careful reading of the final canto shows that it is not a simple murder that we have here. The real revenge of the Pied Piper is luring the children into an anarchy of freedom and opening to them a world of the spirit and of the imagination, which their parents are unable to perceive. The death of the children by drowning is as seductively attractive as the death of Rilke in "Novogodnee" and is represented as the ultimate deliverance from everything transient and petty:

> В царстве моем — ни свинки, ни кори,
> Ни высших материй, ни средних историй,
> Ни расовой розни, ни Гуссовой казни,
> Ни детских болезней, ни детских боязней:
>
> Синь. Лето красно.
> И — время — на все.[34]

[34] *Volja Rossii,* I (1926), 69.

> In my kingdom there is no mumps, no measles,
> No higher matters, no middle histories,
> No racial strife, no execution of [John] Huss,
> No children's illnesses, no children's fears:
>
> The azure. A fair summer [eternally].
> And — time — for everything.

The crucial word *sin'* convinces us that the finale of "Krysolov" is another of Cvetaeva's apotheoses—the children escape into an eternal childhood like the heroine of Cvetaeva's first two books of verse, into the life of the spirit like Rilke and the heroine of "Na krasnom kone," into their own private paradise like Marusja in *Mólodec.*

In "Krysolov" Cvetaeva once more found a new language and metrical structure to fit her subject. Her verbal and structural imagination is prodigious in this poem and so is the variety of refrains, syntactic variations, and echo effects used. In terms of metrics, there is a whole series of particularly felicitous *trouvailles.*

One can agree with Mirskij, who wrote: "Undoubtedly, 'Krysolov' is not only what it appears to be at first glance; it is not only a verbal structure that is astounding in its richness and harmony, it is also a serious 'political' (in the broadest meaning of this term) and ethical satire which is perhaps destined to play a role in the growth of consciousness of all of us." [35] That Mirskij's prediction did not come true is a reflection not on the work itself but on Cvetaeva's literary fate and on the situation of twentieth-century Russian poetry.

Perekóp

"Krysolov" is the last of Cvetaeva's epic poems that was published. In 1928, Cvetaeva remembered her self-appointed role as "the chronicler of the White Army." [36] Between August, 1928 and May, 1929 she wrote the epic poem "Perekóp," named after the isthmus

[35] See note 31 above.
[36] *Lebedinyj stan,* p. 53.

separating the Crimea from the mainland. This was the last area held by the White Army, and the taking of it by the Red Army marked the end of the Russian Civil War. The Soviet poet Nikolaj Tixonov wrote a poem under the same title in which he celebrated the liberation of the Soviet Union from its White foes. Cvetaeva's "Perekóp" was based on her husband's diaries, which for some reason were no longer available to her at the end of her work. Cvetaeva considered this poem unfinished, and she described it as follows: "The *poèma* is about the hundred-day siege of Perekóp. Life at the fort, fortification work, air raid, a visit by Vrangel', and finally, the celebrated breakthrough, when at night they said the mass, turned off the lights and started. They broke through and entered Russia. Some Latvians were drowned. At this point I ended, but I wanted to show the very end of Perekóp, the last two or three days, the end of everything." [37]

Deprived of her husband's diary, Cvetaeva sought other sources for the continuation of "Perekóp": "I cannot find an eyewitness. They offered me to have a talk with a general from the headquarters. But it is not a general I need, but a line officer: the details are important, what sort of weather they had, what words were said. Finally, they found me a man who was in the Drozdovskij unit—he is now working at a factory. I wrote him. The reply I received was to the effect that on Saturdays they drink and on other days they have no time. And inasmuch as it would be embarrassing to drink in front of you, this would mean that we lose our one free day. . . . So nothing came of it." [38] Cvetaeva recited "Perekóp" at several of her public appearances in the nineteen-thirties, but it was rejected by every émigré journal and has not been published to this day. [39]

The *poèma* is broken into short sections with descriptive titles like "Turncoats," "Brusilov," "Air Raid." The authentic military imagery and terminology are new in Cvetaeva's poetry and so is the

---

[37] Gorodeckaja, "V gostjax u M. I. Cvetaevoj," *Vozroždenie* (Paris), March 7, 1931.

[38] *Ibid.*

[39] The author is grateful to Professor Gleb Struve for the opportunity of examining a photostat of the manuscript of "Perekóp." In Cvetaeva's letter to Salomea Halpern of March 3, 1931, we read: " 'Perekóp' lies idle, rejected by *Čisla*, by *Volja Rossii*, by *Sovemennye Zapiski*."

syncopated, slangy language, the closest parallel to which is provided by the anti-Soviet poems in *Remeslo*. The episodes of military
daily life are contrasted to the romantic-sentimental episode
"Siren' " ("Lilacs"), in which a poetic young girl offers a bouquet of
lilacs to a White officer (Sergej Èfron, according to a footnote) who
later feeds the flowers to his famished horse. The style is casual,
occasionally coarse, deliberately matter-of-fact (Cvetaeva's variant of
style dépouillé of certain contemporary composers). The occasional
Slavonicisms are of the modest variety, in keeping with the poem's
austerity, and so, curiously, is the wide use of soldiers' slang. In its
hopeless and loyal glorification of the lost cause, unpopular even
among many of the Paris émigrés, and written in a style utterly
incomprehensible to the ex-officers whose exploits it celebrates,
"Perekóp" typifies Cvetaeva's singlemindedness and independence
of spirit.

In the early nineteen-thirties, Marina Cvetaeva wrote an unfinished *poèma* on the subject of the assassination of the Russian
imperial family. She mentioned her intention to write this *poèma* in
the interview she gave Nadežda Gorodeckaja in March, 1931.[40]
Elena Izvol'skaja recalls being present at readings of this *poèma* and
says that it expressed "a profound note of doom, which neither the
monarchists nor the anti-monarchists were able to understand." [41]
The Great Soviet Encyclopedia of 1934 denounces Cvetaeva for
having written a recent work which glorifies the Romanov family.
In her statement to Gorodeckaja, Cvetaeva indicated that this work
was to be based on the study of sources, and this would lead one to
expect that it was another epic poem. However, there is no record of
this work having been published, and if a manuscript has survived
its whereabouts are not known.

This chapter has given only a cursory survey of the lyric and epic
poèmy of Marina Cvetaeva. To later scholars they will undoubtedly
be rewarding and fascinating subjects for detailed study and

[40] Gorodeckaja, *op. cit.*
[41] Izvol'skaja, "Ten' na stenax," p. 157. Cvetaeva's letters to Salomea
Halpern (letters of June 15 and August 20, 1929) outline her research for the
poem about the Romanovs; she was particularly interested in factual
information about the youth of the Empress Aleksandra Feodorovna. Letter
of March 3, 1931 indicates that she was still working on this *poèma*, although
she saw no chance of getting it accepted by any of the émigré journals.

exegesis. The genre occupies an important place in the work of Cvetaeva, and such unique and varied works as "Krysolov," "Poèma konca," "Lestnica," and "Pereuločki" demonstrate the remarkable versatility of this poet and constitute major and basic contributions to twentieth-century Russian poetry.

IX ✌
Dramatic Works

Marina Cvetaeva was fascinated by the theater since her childhood
—possibly since the unforgettable impression made on her at the age
of six by a concert performance of a scene from Čajkovskij's *Eugene
Onegin* (described in "Moj Puškin"). In her youth, as we have seen,
she was deeply involved with the verse dramas of Edmond Rostand;
according to Pavel Antokol'skij,[1] Cvetaeva did a verse translation of
L'Aiglon while still in her teens. Her own efforts as a playwright,
however, date only from the years after the October Revolution.
They came at the time when Cvetaeva, separated from her husband
and many of her earlier friends, formed a number of close
friendships and associations with members of the Moscow theater
world: the director Vaxtang Mčedelov, the actor Jurij Zavadskij,
Zavadskij's sister Vera, Sonečka Holliday, the appealing young actor
identified only as Volodja A. who is the hero of the second part of
"Povest' o Sonečke," and several others. Unlike her poetry of the
post-revolutionary years, with its frequent concern for current
realities, the plays of Cvetaeva are largely her main means of
escape into the Romanticism of the past. In her earlier, "romantic"
plays, this past is the eighteenth century; in the later, "classical"
ones, it is the world of Greek mythology. At the same time the

[1] Pavel Antokol'skij, postscript to Cvetaeva's "Dva Lesnyx Carja" in
Masterstvo perevoda (Moscow, 1964), p. 290.

237

escapist tendency of the settings and treatment did not always prevent contemporary and even topical concerns from finding their expression in her plays, as is revealed, for example, by a closer analysis of "Fortuna."

The plays written by Marina Cvetaeva fall into two well defined categories, distinguishable both chronologically and thematically. The four romantic plays in verse (five, if we consider *Konec Kazanovy* a separate work) were all written in Moscow between 1918 and 1921. They are all connected with Cvetaeva's interests and preoccupations which we know from her verse and her memoirs of that period, and they reflect her connections in the Moscow theater world and her friendships with the actors and actresses for whom specific roles in those plays were intended. The two classical tragedies written in the nineteen-twenties are based on an entirely different conception of the theater than the earlier plays and reflect the poet's interest in classical myths which also manifested itself in many of the poems in *Posle Rossii*.

Snowstorm (*Metel'*)

The earliest of Cvetaeva's published plays is entitled "Metel'" ("Snowstorm"). In "Povest' o Sonečke," Cvetaeva tells the story of writing this play, which she originally intended to dedicate to Jurij Zavadskij and his sister Vera, and describes her reading of the play to Evgenij Vaxtangov and the members of his Third Studio. It was after this reading that Cvetaeva first met her friend Sonečka Holliday. According to "Povest' o Sonečke," plans were made to have "Metel'" produced at the Third Studio, but they were never realized. The play was published in 1923 in the Paris journal *Zveno*[2] with the note that it was written in Moscow between December 3 and 12, 1918, during a snowstorm. Relations with Zavadskij having become less friendly by the time of publication, there was no dedication.

[2] The author expresses his gratitude to Mrs. E. I. Eleneva (Catherine Elène) for providing him with a typewritten copy of "Metel'," which is a duplicate of the one she made earlier from a copy of *Zveno* in the New York Public Library. That copy of *Zveno* has been stolen, and no information on the pagination or the exact issue of the journal is therefore available.

"Metel'" is subtitled "Dramatic scenes in verse." It is a very short play. The scene is an inn in Bohemia, in which, on New Year's Eve, 1830, a group of travelers is caught during a snowstorm. The Innkeeper, a Huntsman, and a Trader, described as "personifications of their trades," an Old Woman said to personify "the entire eighteenth century," and a Lady in a Cape are gathered around the fireplace. The Old Woman reminisces about her youth, the Lady is aloof and waiting for something, and the three men are being obvious, vulgar, and materialistic, drinking toasts to security, to the present age, and to Vienna, "the good city of pink angels and sausages." The Lady refuses to join them, is gossiped about by the men and defended by the Old Woman. In the second scene, the Old Woman, for a mysterious reason they both seem to understand, offers the Lady a diamond ring that was once given to her by the king, while the insolent Innkeeper makes sarcastic comments. There is a sound of sleighbells, which begins at the time the ring is given, and then a Gentleman appears who introduces himself as Prince of the Moon, Chevalier of the Rotonde, and Knight of the Rose. The Lady in a Cape, it turns out, is Countess Lanska who has realized that morning she does not love her husband and, obeying an incomprehensible urge, has started out into the snowstorm:

Сегодня утром, распахнув окно,
Где гневным ангелом металась вьюга . . .
Вы будете смеяться — все равно!
Я поняла — что не люблю супруга.
Мне захотелось в путь — туда — в Метель . . .

This morning, flinging open the window,
Where the blizzard raged like a wrathful angel . . .
You may laugh — I don't care!
I understood that I do not love my husband.
I wanted to be off — away — into the Snowstorm . . .

She suddenly finds herself talking to the Gentleman with great frankness and intimacy, feeling sure that she has met him before. As the dialogue grows more fantastic, he admits that they knew each other in a previous existence, and that this is their last pre-ordained encounter. He puts a spell on her, forcing her to forget the encounter, hints that he will visit her every time the moon looks into her room, and departs while she sleeps, with the "ringing of sleighbells, disappearing forever."

At the time she was writing "Metel'," Cvetaeva was an experienced and independent poet, the author of *Versty I* and of subsequent poems that were later included in *Lebedinyj stan* and *Psixeja*. As a dramatic author, however, she was a beginner who had to recapitulate the long apprenticeship which as a lyric poet she had long ago left behind her. "Metel'," a work of great charm despite its brevity, is also one of her less original works. The basic situation of the play—that of a mysterious bond between an astral being and a chosen, unique mortal, depicted against a background of vulgarity and incomprehension—is clearly taken over from Aleksandr Blok's play "Neznakomka." The sex of the protagonists is reversed, but even so, Blok's fallen star Maria is the close and evident model for Cvetaeva's Prince of the Moon. The soliloquy of the Old Woman about her youth in the eighteenth century is very similar to the monologue of the Countess in the libretto based on "The Queen of Spades" which Modest Čajkovskij wrote for his brother's opera (this is a comparison that would have outraged Cvetaeva, who as an adult detested adaptations of Puškin for the operatic stage). The charm of the play lies unquestionably in the great beauty of its verse, but even here Cvetaeva abandons much of her own style and falls under the very strong spell of Blok and, to a lesser degree, Anna Axmatova:

> — Юная женщина, вспомни!
>
> Крылья слетались на пир,
> И расставались в лазури
> Двое, низринутых в мир
> Тою-же бешеной бурей.
>
> И потому — раньше всех —
> Мой бубенец издалече . . .
> Это не сон и не грех,
> Это — последняя встреча.

— Young woman, recall [how it was]!

Wings were gathering for a feast;
And the two, cast down into the world
By the same frenzied storm,
Were parting in the azure.

And this is why — before anyone else —
[You heard] my sleighbell[s] from afar . . .
This is no dream and no sin,
This is the final encounter.

The mysticism of the short prayer recited by the Gentleman is quite untypical of Cvetaeva and also brings Axmatova to mind. The play as a whole is a work in the tradition of Russian Symbolism, and although the concept of escaping from the unbearable present into the world of aristocratic and exclusive imagination is in no way alien to Cvetaeva's thinking, the way it is presented here is closer to the poetics of Blok, Belyj, and Vjačeslav Ivanov than to those of Marina Cvetaeva.

The Casanova Plays

While we know that "Metel'" was the earliest play written by Cvetaeva during the last years before her emigration, the chronology of the remaining plays of this group is by no means certain. All of these plays date from the period of Cvetaeva's intense friendship with Sonečka Holliday and all contain roles—principal or subordinate—written especially for her actress-friend, who specialized in portraying unpredictable and unruly teen-age girls.[3] We can begin the consideration of these plays with the one-act play in verse *Konec Kazanovy* (*Casanova's End*), published in a separate little volume in Moscow in 1922 but undoubtedly written considerably earlier.

---

[3] "Povest' o Sonečke," p. 59, identifies these roles: Rosanetta in "Fortuna," the Street Girl in "Priključenie," and Francesca in *Konec Kazanovy* (and therefore also in "Feniks").

Although the historical Giacomo Casanova de Seingalt died on June 4, 1798, the action of the play takes place on New Year's Eve (as so often in Cvetaeva) of 1799—the last hour of the eighteenth century (or, rather of the *settecento*)—during a snowstorm. The famous adventurer, said to be seventy-five, is shown in the castle of Dux in Bohemia, where he actually spent the last years of his life as the librarian of Count Waldstein. At the beginning of the play, Casanova is shown burning old love letters, recalling in a long and humorous soliloquy his amorous adventures. He begins to pack to leave the castle where he has suffered indignities, when he receives a sudden visit from Francesca (Franciska in Russian), the adopted daughter of the forest warden, who has come to declare her love and admiration. The rest of the play if a long whimsical dialogue between the two. The gallant, experienced man of seventy-five does not quite know how to turn down the amusing, straightforward, and precocious girl of thirteen who is insistently offering herself to him. The scene is interrupted by the visit of an aged butler who is the only person in the castle to treat Casanova with respect and who brings him a New Year's Eve dinner. With food and wine, Francesca becomes even more deliberately seductive. Casanova counters her blandishments with reminiscences of Venice and with the story of Paolo and Francesca from Dante. Finally, feeling his resolve weaken, he sings the girl to sleep with a whispered lullaby and at the final curtain is about to depart (like the Prince of the Moon in "Metel'," to the sound of sleighbells), leaving the old butler to deliver Francesca to her adopted father.

Konec Kazanovy is an effective piece of theater. One of the least likely and potentially most embarrassing situations is treated in it in a convincing way, and the tone found by Cvetaeva seems to be the only right and possible one for the improbable situation. The role of Francesca, conceived for the talents of Sonečka Holliday, is a particularly well realized characterization, and in the hands of suitable actors the play may come off on the stage without seeming ridiculous to the audience because of the unusual basic situation. A careful reading of "Povest' o Sonečke" convinces one that *Konec Kazanovy* is a reenactment of a daydream of Cvetaeva about her friend. Cvetaeva felt that Sonečka, scorned by the handsome actor she loved and given to casual affairs with men who did not appreciate her, would be best off if she had a courtly and experienced older protector, and in her reflections Cvetaeva cast A. A. Staxovič in the role of such a man.[4] Nothing like this ever occurred in real life, but *Konec Kazanovy* may be read as a subdued and stylized realization of the idea of such a relationship.

Some time after writing *Konec Kazanovy,* Cvetaeva expanded it into a three-act play called "Feniks" ("Phoenix"), in which the original *Konec Kazanovy* became, with additions and alterations, the third act.[5] The first act of this version is called "Dvornja" ("The Servants"). It is set in the kitchen of the castle of Dux. The large household staff of Count Waldstein, mostly hostile to the librarian Casanova, discusses him and his strange ways. The Major-domo, the Chaplain, and the court poet Viderol conspire to humiliate Casanova by hanging his portrait in a toilet. The second act, entitled "Znat'" ("The Nobility"), shows a gala dinner at Dux. Prince de Ligne, the celebrated warrior and writer who is the uncle of the host, Count Waldstein, is the center of attention. He tries to show courtesy and consideration for Casanova, while the host, the Major-domo, and the elegant aristocratic ladies of various nationalities all treat the aged adventurer with boorish disrespect. A poetry contest is held between Viderol and Casanova. The young poet, after determining the tastes of his patrons, recites a mannered rondeau which delights everyone. Casanova retorts with a macabre sonnet about the horrors of old age, which disgusts the guests. After a lyrical dialogue

[4] "How many times—I am not ashamed to say this—I regretted during my brief time with her that she did not have an old, affectionate, enlightened protector, who would hold her in his old hands as in a silver setting. . . . And at the same time would direct her like an experienced helmsman. . . . " ("Povest' o Sonečke," p. 58). "Why didn't you, Aleksej Aleksandrovič, you who knew how to value women—and pearls—and souls, why didn't you fall in love with my Sonečka, did not love her more than your soul?" (*Ibid.,* p. 80.)

[5] "Feniks" was published in *Volja Rossii,* VIII–IX (Prague, 1924), 17–84. The date July–August, 1919 at the end may possibly refer only to the last act, which is almost identical with *Konec Kazanovy.* The later date of publication of the expanded version and the fact that it draws on a larger number of sources than did *Konec Kazanovy* inclines one to believe that the shorter version was written earlier (it is less likely for an author to abridge a work, publish it, and follow a few years later with the publication of an unabridged earlier version). The final solution of this question would require the examination of Cvetaeva's drafts and manuscripts.

between Prince de Ligne and Casanova about the splendors of earlier days, and a disgraceful quarrel between Casanova and Viderol, the ladies, to pacify the cantankerous old man, urge him to recite the story of his adventures. He tells of his lowly birth, of his early illnesses, of how a sorceress dedicated him to Aphrodite and how that goddess, descending from the evening star over Venice, appeared to him in person to instruct him in his first amatory experience. The gathered company finds his recital shocking and, in a scene reminiscent of Griboedov's *Gore ot uma* (*The Misfortune of Being Clever*), the guests gradually leave the stage. Left alone, Casanova is informed by an old servant of the prank with his portrait. The last act of "Feniks" is subtitled "Konec Kazanovy," and it is substantially the play of that name, the main difference being the added episode, just before the appearance of Francesca, in which Prince de Ligne visits Casanova and, after listening to the enumeration of the indignities suffered by the adventurer at Dux, approves his intention to leave.

As a dramatic work, the expanded play is a considerably weakened one in comparison with *Konec Kazanovy*. The profusion of minor roles (a feature typical of the plays of Rostand) causes the interest to waver. The chatter of the servants in the first scene is often well realized, especially in the speeches of the Laundress (couched in the dialectal Russian idiom, which Cvetaeva always handles well), but it bears little relation to the main action. The weakest point of the added first two acts is characterization. Except for the sympathetic figure of Prince de Ligne, Casanova is surrounded by a horde of rude and inhuman puppets, and the conflict between them and the hero they persecute is really no contest at all. The work is somewhat more successful if regarded as a poem intended to be read and not to be performed on the stage.

A comparison of "Feniks" with the sources on which Cvetaeva based it is extremely interesting for the comprehension of her transformation of historical material and her deliberate distortion of reality for poetic purposes. While *Konec Kazanovy* was very loosely based on Casanova's memoirs, drawing on these memoirs to any appreciable extent only in the soliloquy of Casanova when he burns his letters, the first two acts of "Feniks" rely very heavily on two curious documents that were appended to Volume VIII of the 1880

Paris edition of these memoirs: two fragments on Casanova from the memoirs of Prince de Ligne [6] and Casanova's "Lettres écrites au sieur Faulkircher." [7] According to later Casanova scholars, the letters were written (but never sent or shown to the addressee) by the aged librarian at Dux to vent his irritation with Count Waldstein's steward Feltkirchner and the butler-courier Wiederholt, who in the absence of the Count treated the Italian without the respect he thought was his due and who persecuted him with petty and stupid pranks. [8] The letters to Feltkirchner (Casanova spells the name "Faulkircher") are embarrassing reading—crude, bombastic, forever flying into violent rages and denunciations over petty, insignificant incidents. Both the letters and the excerpts from the memoirs of Prince de Ligne (who writes of Casanova's last years with affectionate humor) show the famous memoirist as a difficult, vindictive, and selfish old man. Cvetaeva chooses to turn him into a hero and, while making extensive use of factual detail contained in her two sources, imposes her own poetic interpretation on historical facts.

The reasons for Cvetaeva's re-interpretation of her sources become clear once we realize why she was so particularly attracted to the final period of Casanova's life. The famous memoirs, which captured the sweep, the gaiety, and the flavor of the eighteenth century, were written shortly after the French Revolution, which tried to end everything that that century as understood by Marina Cvetaeva stood for. While trying to achieve his life's work, Casanova was pestered by petty vulgarians but encouraged by grand aristocrats like the Duke of Weimar and the Prince de Ligne. His life's work lived on, bringing to succeeding generations a romantic and seductive image of the past which Casanova's contemporaries

[6] *Mémoires de J. Casanova le Seingalt écrits par lui-même* (Paris, 1880), VIII, 445–472. It is possible that Cvetaeva had also consulted the original edition from which these two fragments were taken (Le Prince de Ligne, *Mémoires et mélanges historiques et littéraires,* 4 volumes, [Paris, 1828]; the quoted excerpts on Casanova are in Vol. IV, pp. 3–42 and 291–294).

[7] Casanova, *op. cit.,* pp. 473–504.

[8] For a historical account of Casanova's conflict with Feltkirchner and Wiederholt, see Charles Samaran, *Jacques Casanova, Vénitien* (Paris, 1914), pp. 428–429. This and other historical reconstructions of the events described in Casanova's letters to Feltkirchner were available at the time of Cvetaeva's writing of "Feniks," but she was apparently unaware of their existence.

were doing their best to revile. This conception of Casanova's role
and significance, perhaps not entirely accurate historically, had an
immediate and direct relevance for Marina Cvetaeva in 1918–1919
and made the shady adventurer, whose book she had once indig-
nantly refused to read,[9] a powerful symbol of current and topical
matters. Casanova and Prince de Ligne of "Feniks," standing head
and shoulders above their brainless junior contemporaries in vision
and imagination, reflect Cvetaeva's awe and admiration for Volkonskij and Staxovič. The sycophantic and opportunistic court poet
Viderol is Cvetaeva's answer to the younger Futurists and the new
Proletarian poets who in the early years of the Revolution clamored
for the overthrow of Bal'mont, Blok, and Brjusov.[10] Cvetaeva makes
her hero a poet (obviously a distortion of historical fact, despite
Casanova's minor contribution to one of Da Ponte's librettos for
Mozart and some dreary dramatic works of his old age). This has
relevance not only for his poetic duel with Viderol in the second act
of "Feniks," but also brings new and topical significance to the last
act, which the original *Konec Kazanovy* did not have. While both
the aristocrats and the plebeians at Dux prefer the facile and
opportunistic poetry of Viderol, the independent poet Casanova is
loved and admired by Francesca, a daughter of the people and a
child, and hence the voice of the future.

To express these conceptions in dramatic terms, Cvetaeva resorts
to the curious procedure of splitting many of the persons mentioned
in her two historical sources into two or more dramatic characters.
Thus, the disreputable butler-courier Wiederholt (Cvetaeva's retain-
ing of Casanova's Gallicized spelling Viderol is strong evidence that
she consulted no other sources beyond the two mentioned above) is
the point of departure for both the insolent young butler in the first
act and the historically nonexistent court poet. Casanova's patron,
Count Waldstein, who, according to both Prince de Ligne and
Casanova's letters, treated his librarian with great kindness and
consideration, appears in the play as a brash young boor. However,
the character of the Count in the play is derived not from the Count

---

[9] At the age of eighteen, Cvetaeva received Casanova's memoirs from
Vološin and returned them immediately without reading the book. See "Živoe
o živom," *Proza,* p. 147.

[10] Cf. "Geroj truda," *Proza,* p. 211.

of the letters, but rather from the character of the steward to whom these letters were addressed, so that the "Faulkircher" of the letters is split into Count Waldstein and the Major-domo of the play. The two aristocratic ladies, Princess de Clary and Princess Jablonowska, whose visit at Dux is mentioned in the letters several times, are multiplied by Cvetaeva into five minor female characters: the two young princesses and the French, Polish, and Viennese visiting ladies. The castle laundress Caroline, a promiscuous young flirt according to Casanova's letters to Feltkirchner, appears in the first act not only as the elderly Russian *baba* of a laundress, but also as a whole array of younger female servants. Cvetaeva completely ignores any aspect of Casanova's old age, as revealed in her sources, which might contradict her image of him or be personally distasteful to her, such as his preoccupation with mathematics, his anti-Semitism, and his disgraceful intrigues against Goethe and Wieland.[11] Casanova's recitation of the wrongs he suffered at Dux is a faithful rendition in verse of a passage from the memoirs of Prince de Ligne, with the important difference that in the original the tone was ironic and the offenses were shown to be mostly imaginary, while in "Feniks" the same offenses are taken most seriously and the reader feels sympathy for the proud old man subjected to cruelty and indignities.[12] All in all, the comparison of "Feniks" with its sources not only demonstrates Cvetaeva's ability to color reality in ways suitable to her poetic purposes, but also emphasizes the difference between historical and poetic truth which Cvetaeva herself was to demonstrate convincingly many years after writing "Feniks" in her critical study of Puškin and Pugačëv.[13]

If in "Feniks" the life of Casanova served Cvetaeva as a pretext for current topical commentary, her other play about him, written at

[11] Prince de Ligne, in Casanova, *op. cit.,* p. 469; "Lettres écrites au sieur Faulkircher," *ibid.,* p. 491.

[12] Cf. Prince de Ligne, in Casanova, *op. cit.,* pp. 467–468 (this passage is also the source of some of the servants' dialogue in the first act of "Feniks") and Casanova's long speech in "Feniks," pp. 51–52.

[13] Although the poetic Francesca of "Feniks" and *Konec Kazanovy* appears to be Cvetaeva's own invention, one might mention that in Casanova's "Lettres écrites au sieur Faulkircher" there appears a certail "pauvre fille de l'honnête maître des forêts," who according to Casanova contracted "une vilaine maladie" from Wiederholt and died as a result (Casanova, *op. cit.,* p. 482).

approximately the same time, is an undisguised escape into the romance of the past. Unlike "Feniks" and *Konec Kazanovy,* "Priključenie" ("An Adventure"),[14] which may be described as a romantic comedy in verse in five scenes, is based directly on Casanova's memoirs. From the vast panorama of the book, Cvetaeva selected what is probably its most appealing episode: Casanova's brief love affair at the age of twenty-three with the mysterious Frenchwoman known only as Henriette.[15] As Casanova tells it, he met Henriette when she was traveling in Italy in man's clothing, accompanied by an aged Hungarian army captain who spoke to her and everyone else only in Latin. With the captain's consent, Casanova established Henriette as his mistress, bought her an elegant wardrobe, and for a few months was sublimely happy with her, although he knew nothing of her origin or true identity. On one occasion, when Casanova prevailed on the shy and secretive Henriette to attend a private concert given by one of his wealthy French friends, she quite suddenly replaced the soloist and performed a difficult violoncello concerto with great virtuosity and without any previous rehearsal. This proved to be the undoing of the idyll, for rumors of her performance enabled Henriette's noble family, from whose care she had escaped, to locate her. After receiving a mysterious letter through the local French ambassador, Henriette left Casanova. Returning later to the hotel where their final farewell had taken place, Casanova found the message which Henriette had scratched out with her diamond on the window pane in their room: "Vous oublierez aussi Henriette."[16] This, essentially,

[14] Published in *Volja Rossii* (Prague, 1923), XVIII, 1–18, and XIX, 1–22, but written, as "Povest' o Sonečke" indicated, during the friendship with Sonečka Holliday, i.e. ca. 1919.

[15] Cvetaeva cites Vol. IV of Casanova's memoirs as her source for "Priključenie." If the volume number is not a misprint, this would indicate that she used one of the abridged late nineteenth-century editions of the memoirs, for in the complete twelve-volume editions the episode of Henriette is told in Chapters One to Five of Volume III (e.g. *Mémoires de J. Casanova de Seingalt,* [Paris, 1922], III, 11–74). For speculations about the possible historical identity of Casanova's Henriette, see the 1960 edition of the memoirs (Jacques Casanova de Seingalt, *Histoire de ma vie,* VI, note on p. 357) and Charles Samaran, *op. cit.,* the chapter "Une 'inconnue' de Casanova," pp. 14–24.

[16] This phrase also serves as an epigraph for the entire play. Cvetaeva completely disregards the subsequent encounters with Henriette which

is the canvas used by Cvetaeva as a plot for "Priključenie." However, she changed and adapted not only this plot but also Casanova's characterizations, particularly that of Henriette. Casanova's Henriette was a sweet, modest creature who wore male attire through necessity and allowed herself an occasional off-color joke to show off her wit and because such was the spirit of the age. Her counterpart in Cvetaeva is a marvellously ambiguous creature called Henri-Henriette who initially appears dressed as a hussar, speaks of herself (and is spoken of by her Hungarian traveling companion) in the masculine gender, fights a duel over another woman, and forces her company on Casanova. Later in the play Henri-Henriette changes into female attire and at once becomes the most seductive and admired woman in Parma, driving all men wild not only with her beauty, but with her erudition, wit, and musical talent. She remains a woman for the rest of the play, yet when Casanova reminisces about her after losing her, he does it with the words: "My Love! My moonlit boy!" [17] This ambiguous, almost hermaphroditic character is the most frank embodiment of Cvetaeva's indistinct dream of love and intimacy based on personal worth, which would exceed the limitations of one particular sex. The same tendency can be discerned in the cycles "Učenik" in *Remeslo*, "Brat'ja" in *Psixeja*, the poem "Klinok" in *Posle Rossii*, and in some of the episodes of "Povest' o Sonečke." In line with this transformation of Casanova's heroine, several basic relationships in the play become different from their prototypes in the memoirs. The relation between Henriette and her Latin-speaking captain was obviously erotic in Casanova, but it is that of comrades-in-arms in "Priključenie."

"Priključenie" is an unconvincing play when read, and it must be almost impossible to perform on the stage with any degree of success. The dramatic structure is more dependent on Rostand than in any other play by Cvetaeva: the work is full of dramatic

---

Casanova mentions elsewhere in the memoirs, particularly his encounter with the married Henriette who had put on so much weight that he failed to recognize her (Casanova, *Histoire de ma vie,* VI, 172). In the romantic universe of Cvteaeva's plays, phenomena of this nature simply do not happen.

[17] "Priključenie," second installment, p. 20.

confrontations, sudden revelations, unexpected developments, all of them very much in the style of the obvious *coups de théâtre* which crowd every scene of *L'Aiglon*. The role of Henri-Henriette is in all probability unplayable, and may have possibly been intended for a transvestite actor, as certain roles are in the plays of Jean Genêt. The single most unconvincing aspect of the work is the staggering contrast between Henri-Henriette and all the other characters in the play, including Casanova. In "Feniks" the hero moved in an environment of churls and villains; in "Priključenie," the heroine is entirely surrounded by worshippers. Everything she does and says is enthusiastically appreciated by everyone: her lover, his friends, servants, seamstresses. This heady aura makes one suspect, perhaps unfairly, that "Priključenie" is less a play than a reenactment of another very special and personal daydream of the poet. The last scene of "Priključenie" is a serious departure from Casanova's account, for instead of returning to the hotel to find Henriette's message, Casanova waits thirteen years and discovers the inscription while in the company of a mercenary Street Girl (another custom-tailored role for Sonečka Holliday) whom he had picked up for the night. Two other points may be mentioned in connection with "Priključenie": a passage from Henriette's farewell speech in scene four also occurs as the text of the letter the aged Casanova reads in *Konec Kazanovy* and "Feniks"[18] (which makes the respective dating of these plays even more complex); and there is an odd echo of Majakovskij's "Oblako v štanax" in Casanova's speech at the end of scene two:

> Ты не веришь, верно думаешь — я грубый,
> Буду нежным, буду страшно осторожным.[19]

> You don't trust [me], you must think me rough;
> I'll be gentle, I'll be terribly careful.

Fortuna

Cvetaeva's infatuation with Jurij Zavadskij in the winter of 1918 was different from any other involvement in her life, for in this

---

[18] Cf. *Konec Kazanovy*, pp. 21–22, "Feniks," p. 55, and "Priključenie," second installment, p. 13.

[19] "Priključenie," first installment, p. 18.

particular case she was attracted mainly by the actor's appearance
and personal charm. In "Povest' o Sonečke," Cvetaeva tells us that
she described Zavadskij in her "spray of poems" in the cycle
"Komediant" and in two plays: "Fortuna" and "Kamennyj angel"
("The Stone Angel").[20] Cvetaeva's diary entries and the letters
written during her friendship with Zavadskij were later reworked
into a part of her memoir "O ljubvi" ("On Love"), in which he
figures under the name Lauzun and is described with cruel
objectivity which occasionally verges on malice. The whole episode
left Cvetaeva puzzled about the power that mediocre but physically
attractive people have over the complex, creative, and humanly
superior persons who fall in love with them and thereby lose the use
of some of their most distinctive faculties. The problem continued to
preoccupy Cvetaeva in her later writings, for example in her
speculations on how two elegant blank pages in human form,
Natalija Gončarova and Georges d'Anthès, could bring about the
death of Russia's greatest poet, or how their counterparts in the
Iliad, Paris and Helen, could cause the Trojan War.[21]

The plot of "Kamennyj angel," which has not been published to
this day, is described as follows: "A stone angel in the village square
on account of whom brides leave their bridegrooms, wives—their
husbands, all lovers give up love, on account of whom everyone
drowned themselves, took poison, entered monasteries, while he just
stood there. It seems there was no other action." [22] "Fortuna," which
survived and was published,[23] had an equally devastating hero and
Cvetaeva found him in the memoirs of Armand Louis de Gontaut
Biron, duc de Lauzun (1747–1793). Cvetaeva could have read those
memoirs as part of her deliberate escape into the eighteenth century
during the first years after the October Revolution, yet there is a

---

[20] "Povest' o Sonečke," p. 97.

[21] "Natalija Gončarova," *passim;* "Moj Puškin" in *Proza,* p. 34; Letters to
Baxrax, *Mosty,* VI, 322, where we read: "I have a huge German volume, there
is much about Helen there, I finally wanted to know just who she was and it
turns out—no one. She merely allowed herself to be abducted. Paris is a
seductive nonentity, something like my Lauzun. And how charming that
precisely because of them there were wars."

[22] "Povest' o Sonečke," p. 97.

[23] In *Sovremennye Zapiski,* XIV (1923), 145–167, and XV (1923), 128–156.
According to "O ljubvi," "Fortuna" was written in 1918–1919, although
Zavadskij is mentioned in that memoir under the name Lauzun in entries
ascribed to 1917.

definite parallel between the endless succession of Lauzun's con-
quests (enumerated with matchless fatuity in his memoirs and
involving some of the most spirited and brilliant women of his age)
and the reactions of Jurij Zavadskij's contemporaries, including
Marina Cvetaeva, to the young actor, as described in "Provest' o
Sonečke." More recent studies of Lauzun show that there was more
to him than the smug and complacent lover that he himself
portrayed in the memoirs,[24] and the subsequent career of Jurij
Zavadskij likewise indicates that he was more than the glamorous
nonentity Cvetaeva has depicted. Yet, for a proper understanding of
"Fortuna," we have to equate the Russian actor and the eighteenth-
century French statesman.

The first scene of "Fortuna" is entitled "Rog izobilija" ("Cornucopia") and takes place at the time of Lauzun's birth. By the use of
a particularly unoriginal device, that of a revealing conversation
between the Majordomo and the Nurse, the reader is told of the
circumstances of the Gontaut Biron family and of the death of
Lauzun's mother soon after his birth. When the Nurse dozes off,
Fortuna, the goddess of fortune, "flies in like a rosy silken
whirlwind" in the guise of the Marquise de Pompadour.[25] Covering
the cradle with roses from her cornucopia, Fortuna names the child
fortune's son and lover and bestows on him "the most fearful of
gifts—seductiveness." In the next three scenes, preceded like all the
scenes of the play by appropriate quotations from Lauzun's memoirs, Lauzun is shown with three of the women who have loved
him, selected by Cvetaeva from the vast number described in the
first half of his memoirs. In the second scene, the Marquise

[24] R. de Gontaut Biron, *Le duc de Lauzun* (Paris, 1937), amasses an
impressive documentation to show that Lauzun did his subsequent reputation
a disservice by concentrating only on his amorous adventures in his memoirs
(written to be read by his last love, Aimée de Coigny, and apparently never
intended for publication). In the book of M. de Gontaut Biron, his ancestor
emerges as a military and political figure of considerable scope who played an
important role during the American Revolutionary War. Cvetaeva's view of
Lauzun is close to that of nineteenth-century French criticism, as exemplified
by Sainte-Beuve and the Goncourts.
[25] "Fortuna," first installment, p. 149. The father of the historical Lauzun
was in fact a courtier much in favor with the Marquise de Pompadour, and
part of Lauzun's childhood was spent in her boudoir, where among other
things he copied her correspondence. See Duc de Lauzun, *Mémoires* (Paris,
1928), pp. 42–43.

d'Esparbès, who has casually seduced the young Lauzun, just as casually informs him that their affair is over while the two are playing chess in her rose-strewn boudoir. The boy's despair at the news is shrugged off by the fickle Marquise:

> Пока мы юны —
> Все — хорошо, все — пустота, все взмах
> Слепого колеса Фортуны![26]

> While we're young,
> All is fine, all is empty, all is [but] a swing
> Of Fortuna's blind wheel.

The third scene of "Fortuna" shows Lauzun's secret visit at Powązki,[27] the Trianon-like country estate of the Czartoryski family near Warsaw, to see Princess Izabela Czartoryska (1746–1835), famous in Polish history as the mother of the nineteenth-century statesman Adam Czartoryski. As Lauzun's memoirs tell it and as is recollected in the course of this scene, the two had met in London during Lauzun's affair with Lady Sarah Bunbury, were drawn to each other, had a child together [28] after Lauzun forced Izabela to break off her liaison with the former Russian ambassador to Warsaw, Prince Nikolaj Repnin, and were eventually separated by circumstances.[29] At the time of the visit, Izabela, in poor health, is being looked after by Lauzun's nurse from the first scene, another of Cvetaeva's folksy nurses, based this time not so much on Zavadskij's nurse described in "Povest' o Sonečke" as on Tatjana's from Puškin's *Eugene Onegin*.[30] In the conversation of the two lovers during the visit it becomes clear that while Izabela's love is one

[26] "Fortuna," first installment, p. 156. The sources in the memoirs for this scene are Lauzun, *op. cit.,* pp. 51–56.

[27] Cvetaeva's reading of this name as "Povanskoe" reflects the spelling of Lauzun, corrected in the more recent editions of the memoirs but still occurring in Gontaut Biron, *op. cit.,* p. 37, who spells it "Powonski."

[28] Lauzun's paternity of one of Izabela Czartoryska's children, prominently mentioned in his memoirs (and in "Fortuna"), is usually left unmentioned in her Polish biographies, e.g. *Polski słownik biograficzny* (Cracow, 1937), pp. 241–250, the article "Izabela Czartoryska" by Helena Waniczkówna, which only mentions that Lauzun was in love with Izabela and wished to be an ambassador to Warsaw in order to be near her.

[29] Lauzun, *op. cit.,* pp. 117–132, 156–174, and *passim.* The visit in the play is described by Lauzun on pp. 161–162.

[30] This nurse apparently corresponds to Mme Parisot, a French chambermaid Lauzun had placed in Izabela's service (*ibid.,* p. 162).

endless, selfless sacrifice, that of Lauzun for her is merely gallant and somewhat naive. Izabela's offer to make Lauzun king of Poland seems to be Cvetaeva's own invention (dramatically justified), for in the memoirs the lovers only hoped that he might become the French ambassador to Warsaw.

The fourth scene is based on Lauzun's often disputed account of his relations with Queen Marie-Antoinette. According to his memoirs, Lauzun dreamed of being an intermediary between Marie-Antoinette and Catherine II of Russia in order to form in the union of these two female monarchs the greatest world power in existence. But Marie-Antoinette was bored and frightened by politics and was far more interested in Lauzun personally. As interpreted by Cvetaeva, this situation has a great personal relevance to her relations not only with Zavadskij, but with several other men. There is more than an echo of the fourth scene of "Fortuna" in a passage from one of Cvetaeva's letters to Baxrax where she describes such relationships: "Please understand, the other is drawn to my wealth, while I am drawn—through him—to become a pauper. He wants to exist through me, I want to disappear in him. In any case, I suffer too much. . . ."[31] The personal significance of this scene, despite all the details and almost verbatim quotations from Lauzun's memoirs, is driven home when Marie-Antoinette dismisses Lauzun with a quotation from the beginning of Cvetaeva's love poem to Zavadskij from "Komediant":

Вы столь забывчивы, сколь незабвенны![32]

You are as forgetful as you are unforgettable!

In the fifth and final scene, Lauzun, after having gone over to the side of the Revolution and fought against the aristocratic insurgents of the Vendée, has been condemned to the guillotine during the terror and is awaiting his execution.[33] He completely charms the

[31] Letters to Baxrax, *Mosty,* VI, 337.

[32] Cf. "Fortuna," second installment, p 140, and "Komediant," *Sovremennye Zapiski,* XIX (1924), 170.

[33] The details of Lauzun's last hours in "Fortuna" come from the *Mémoires* of Mallet du Pan ([Paris, 1851] II, 492) as quoted by Sainte-Beuve in his article on Lauzun in *Causeries du lundi* ([Paris, 1858] IV, 287–308). Cvetaeva knew Sainte-Beuve's work well and spoke of him with great admiration in "Poèt o kritike."

jailer's daughter Rosanetta—again Sonečka Holliday—who brings
him his last meal. The girl's name, based on the Russian word *rozan*
rather than on any French form of the name, is the final
development of the image of the rose that persisted throughout the
play as the symbol of Lauzun's fortune. The center of this scene is
Lauzun's long soliloquy which draws an unmistakable parallel
between the events of the French Revolution and the recent Russian
one and evokes the many noble liberals who were put to death by
the very revolutions they had helped to bring about.

И я, Лозэн, рукой белей чем снег,
Я поднимал за чернь бокал заздравный!
И я, Лозэн, вещал, что полноправны
Под солнцем — дворянин и дровосек!

Чем я рожден? — Усладой королев,
Опорой королей. — Цветком лилеи
Играл ребенком. — Что-ж мой юный лев,
За что умрешь сегодня? За Вандею?
— Нет я останусь в Луврской галлерее:
Против Вандеи генерал-ан-шеф.

Да, старый мир, мы на одном коне
Влетели в пропасть и одной веревкой
Нам руки скрутят, и на той стене
Нам приговор один — тебе и мне:
Что взвешен быв, был найден слишком легким . . .[34]

I, Lauzun, with my hand whiter than snow,
Also used to raise the cup to the health of the mob!
I, Lauzun, also used to proclaim
That the nobleman and the woodchopper have equal rights
    under the sun!

What was I born? Delight of queens,
Support of kings. As a child, I played with the *fleur de lys*.
Well then, my young lion,
For what will you die today? For the Vendée?

[34] "Fortuna," second installment, pp. 145–146.

— No, I shall have my place in the Louvre Gallery:
A *général-en-chef* [who fought] against the Vendée.

Yes, [my] old world, we rushed into the abyss
On the same steed, and they will bind our hands
With the same rope, and on yonder wall
Is the single verdict on you and on me:
Weighed and found wanting [*lit.:* too light] . . .

In her subsequent memoir "Moi služby," Cvetaeva quotes this
passage when she tells of reading "Fortuna" on July 7, 1919, during
a program in which she shared the platform with Lunačarskij who
at the time was the Soviet Commissar for Education. "A nobleman's
soliloquy right into the commissar's face—this is life! Too bad it was
only to Lunačarskij and not to . . . I was about to write 'Lenin,'
but Lenin would not have understood any of it—well then, not to
the entire Lubjanka prison." [35] After sharing his last meal with
Rosanetta and offering a glass of wine to his executioner, Lauzun
goes to his death holding high the rose given to him by the jailer's
daughter and saluting the goddess who had guided his life with the
words: "Vive la Reine!"

"Fortuna" is the most impressive of Cvetaeva's romantic plays.
The Soviet critic who dubbed this play a "ladylike esthetic bon-
bon" [36] had simply overlooked the great personal and political
significance that the poet invested into the framework borrowed
from Lauzun's memoirs. It is also superior in language and
versification to the other plays dating from the same period.
"Metel'," as we have seen, is entirely faithful in this respect to the
practices of later Russian Symbolism, while the Casanova plays are,
as far as style and diction are concerned, a case of retreat to the
Cvetaeva of her first two published collections. The Casanova plays
are written in the kind of iambic tetrameter and pentameter that
was launched by Griboedov and imitated by Lermontov in his
"Maskarad." In all the plays of this period, Cvetaeva set aside the
metrical and linguistic innovations she had pioneered in *Versty I*. In

---

[35] "Moi služby," *Proza*, pp. 132–133.
[36] D. Gorbov, "10 let literatury za rubežom," *Pečat' i Revoljucija,* VIII
(Moscow, 1927), 24.

the Casanova plays particularly, her linguistic inventiveness is held in rigid check, only rarely bursting out in the stage directions, such as the description of Casanova in "Priključenie" as "Ostryj ugol i ugol'." [37] The dialectal forms of language are sparingly used by the servants, while the Pedant in "Priključenie" speaks in an archaic diction which sounds like an imitation of Trediakovskij:

> Когда-б
> Сам Цицерон, через летейски воды
> Обратный путь свершив, древесный свод
> Сей огласил прекрасными речами, —[38]

> Had Cicero himself, retracing his steps
> Across Lethean waters, made resound
> This leafy canopy with beauteous discourse, —

Taken as a whole, the romantic plays are timid in language and versification compared to Cvetaeva's lyric poetry of the same period. "Fortuna" is metrically the most varied of them and the usual linguistic inventiveness of Cvetaeva is felt, for example, when Izabela Czartoryska calls Lauzun "Ubóžestvo moe i božestvó" ("My poverty and my deity").[39]

The plays so far discussed are important for the understanding of Cvetaeva's poetry as a whole. When considered in conjunction with *Večernij al'bom, Volšebynj fonar',* and *Versty II,* these plays represent a further development of a definite aspect of Cvetaeva's poetry—that aspect which we have termed romantic and idealistic. Compared with her other work—her lyric poetry, her *poèmy* and her tragedies—these plays, even at their best as in *Konec Kazanovy* and "Fortuna," appear less significant and less original. For all the charm of their verse, "Metel'," "Feniks," and "Priključenie" are simply not the achievements which Cvetaeva's other work leads us to expect. It is interesting to note that a commentator like Osorgin, who valued the romantic trait in Cvetaeva above all others, was

---

[37] "Priključenie," first installment, p. 1.

[38] *Ibid.,* second installment, p. 2.

[39] "Fortuna," first installment, p. 166. The same verbal play occurs in "Tezej" (p. 63), in the speech of Bacchus to Theseus: "Božestvu li s ubožestvom/Sporit'?"

quite incapable of appreciating her infinitely greater accomplishments in "Krysolov" and *Posle Rossii.*

Theseus (Tezej) and *Phaedra (Fedra)*

About five years separate the last of Cvetaeva's romantic plays from her first tragedy on a classical subject, "Tezej," written in 1924.[40] Her second tragedy, "Fedra," was written in 1927 and at the time of its publication was designated as the second part of a trilogy.[41] However, we do not know the third tragedy of the cycle; it is not clear whether Cvetaeva never wrote it or whether she refrained from publishing it in view of the extremely adverse reaction in the émigré press to the first two tragedies. The genre of classical tragedy was introduced into Russian literature in the eighteenth century and was prominently revived early in the twentieth century by Sologub and Brjusov, but above all by two poets of the Symbolist generation whom Cvetaeva greatly admired: Innokentij Annenskij and Vjačeslav Ivanov.[42] Annenskij and Vjačeslav Ivanov were two of the most erudite Greek scholars in the whole history of Russian literature, and their attempts to revive Greek tragedy in modern terms were supported by a deep knowledge of its origins and development. Cvetaeva was not a scholar, and when compared to these two predecessors, her use of sources appears naive to the point of absurdity. "The sources of my 'Fedra' and of my mythics (*moej mifiki*) in general are the juvenile adaptations of the myths by Gustav Schwab. More correctly (since I myself am my sources, the sources are within me), these are my materials in the same way as the materials for *Car'-devica* and *Mólodec* were the corresponding tales in Afanas'ev," she wrote.[43] Cvetaeva must have

---

[40] Published in *Versty*, II (Paris, 1927), 5–83. The title of this tragedy was later changed by Cvetaeva. It appears as "Ariadna" in *Izbrannye proizvedenija*, 1965.

[41] Published in *Sovremennye Zapiski*, XXXVI (1928), 121–162, and XXXVII (1928), 114–146.

[42] Of Annenskij's several tragedies, the posthumously published "Famira Kifared" belongs among the finest accomplishments of Russian Symbolist poetry. Vjačeslav Ivanov's two tragedies on ancient classical subjects are "Tantal" (1905) and "Prometej" (1919). Cvetaeva used a line from Annenskij's poem "Nevozmožno" as an epigraph for "Priključenie" and expressed her admiration for him in "Geroj truda" (*Proza*, p. 213). On Cvetaeva and V. Ivanov, see Chapter II, note 22.

[43] Letters to Ivask, p. 209.

come in contact with the popular German paraphrases of Schwab (1792–1850) in her childhood. These didactic, moralizing, and frequently bowdlerized versions of the Greek myths, first published in 1837–39 and still reprinted to this day in the German-speaking countries, were Cvetaeva's sole source for her tragedies, and they account for some of her more startling departures from the traditional stories of Theseus, Ariadne, and Phaedra.

The romantic plays Cvetaeva wrote after the Revolution often echo the style of her earliest poetry. "Tezej" was written at the time Cvetaeva was working on her finest collection, *Posle Rossii,* and from the very beginning of the speech of the Herald with which the tragedy opens, we are in the presence of Cvetaeva at the peak of her creative and inventive powers. The language of the tragedy is the same perfected blend of the poet's own diction with archaisms and colloquialisms that we admire in *Posle Rossii.* The Cretan adventure of Theseus is told in the traditional five acts of the neo-classical tragedy. In the first act, Poseidon, disguised as a wanderer, arouses the Athenian population and forces King Aegaeus to include his son among the youths and maidens sent to feed the Minotaur in the Labyrinth. In the second act, Theseus is at the palace of Minos, where he meets Ariadne, and after some hesitation accepts her aid in the form of the famous ball of yarn. The third act consists of Ariadne's long soliloquy as she waits for Theseus outside the Labyrinth, and their dialogue after the victory over the Minotaur, during which Theseus overcomes Ariadne's misgivings about following him to Athens. In the fourth act, while Ariadne is asleep on Naxos, Bacchus, here the god of divine inspiration, appears to Theseus as a beam of light and claims Ariadne for his own. The protesting Theseus is told by the god that his abandonment of the sleeping Ariadne is the only way for her to attain the higher fate for which she was destined. The fifth act shows the suicide of Aegaeus after sighting the black sail and believing his son dead. At the end of the tragedy Theseus realizes that this suicide was an act of revenge of Aphrodite, the goddess of physical love, for his abandonment of Ariadne to her higher destiny.

Structurally and poetically, the scene at Naxos is the center of the tragedy. Gustav Schwab, in trying to set Theseus up as an example for German children of the Victorian era, dispensed with the ignominious abandonment of the sleeping Ariadne and replaced it with a prophetic dream in which Bacchus claimed Ariadne as his own bride.[44] What is usually represented as an act of betrayal thus became an act of piety. Cvetaeva interpreted Schwab's silly moralizing in an entirely personal way and made her interpretation the axis of the tragic situation in "Tezej." By renouncing Ariadne, whom he loves, to her divine destiny, Theseus acquires the stature of a tragic hero, a stature that is higher than his original one of a fearless warrior and impetuous lover. Ariadne, who believes herself abandoned and betrayed, is instead moving to a superior level of existence, and her suffering and humiliation are the price of the already familiar Cvetaevan apotheosis, more universal in this case, but not different in kind from the ones experienced by the heroines of "Na krasnom kone" and *Mólodec*. The death of his father is the price Theseus has to pay for allowing the ideal considerations to triumph over the immediate and material ones.

In this tragedy Cvetaeva makes a wide use of structural and narrative techniques typical of the seventeenth-century French and eighteenth-century Russian neoclassical tragedy. In the first act, the Water Carrier recites to the disguised Poseidon the troubles of the ruling houses of Athens and Crete which antedate the main action; the Water Carrier's speech amounts to a traditional *récit* in the tragedies of Corneille and Racine. There are heralds announcing off-stage events and choruses of youths, maidens, and Athenian citizens who recite comments on the action of the tragedy. The slaying of the Minotaur, in a device typical of French tragedy, occurs behind the scene while the waiting Ariadne is expressing her anxiety to the audience. Despite all this, "Tezej" is more than a re-telling of a baroque tragedy in twentieth-century terms, just as the Greek-Italian goddesses of Picasso are more than a re-telling of Ingres and the music of *Oedipus Rex* is more than a re-telling of Haendel. As in the best of Cvetaeva's lyric poetry, the distinction of "Tezej" lies in an organic fusion of philosophic and verbal

---

[44] Gustav Schwab, *Die Schönsten Sagen des klassischen Altertums* (Basel, 1948), I, 259. ("Da erschien ihm der Gott Bakchos im Traum, erklärte, dass Ariadne die ihm vom Schiksal bestimmte Braut sei, und drohte ihm alles Unheil, wenn Theseus die Geliebte nicht ihm überlassen würde. Theseus war von seinem Grossvater in Götterfurcht erzogen worden; er scheute den Zorn des Gottes, liess die wehklagende, verzagende Königstochter auf der einsamen Insel zurück und schiffte weiter.")

originality, in structural ingenuity and in a remarkably fresh and sonorous versification. In "Tezej" more than anywhere else, Cvetaeva uses the choriamb-based meter with the hyperprosodic stress on the first syllable. This meter is used in the speeches of both Ariadne and Theseus and occurs in moments of particular emotional stress, as for example when Ariadne hears the fall of the Minotaur's body but does not know which of the contenders has been victorious:

> Пал! — С молотом схожий
> Звук, молота зык!
> Пал мощный! Но кто же:
> Бо—ец или бык?
>
> . . . .
>
> Так — рухают царства
> В прах— брусом на брус!
> Не—бесный потрясся
> Свод, — реки из русл!
>
> На — лбу крутобровом
> Что: кровь или нимб?
> Ве—кам свое слово
> Ска—зал лабиринт![45]

He has fallen! A hammerlike
Sound, a hammer's roar!
The mightly one has fallen! But which one:
The warrior or the bull?

. . . .

Thus do kingdoms topple
To dust, beam upon beam!
The heavenly vault is shaken,
The rivers [overflow] their beds!

On the steep-browed forehead,
What? Blood or a nimbus?
The Labyrinth has spoken
Its word to the centuries!

[45] "Tezej," p. 41.

The versification of "Tezej" widely uses Cvetaeva's refrains, anaphora, and parallel constructions that we know from *Posle Rossii*. A particularly rich use of these techniques is made in the echoing choruses of youths and maidens in the first act. The language is expressive and concentrated, and the expressive quality of certain speeches is further emphasized by the recurrent stage direction "napevom" ("in a sing-song manner").

The sequel of "Tezej," "Fedra," is also based on one complete episode in Schwab.[46] Again a moralizing distortion of Schwab resulted in a drastic reinterpretation of a classical myth. In Schwab, the incestuous passion of Phaedra for her stepson and its outcome were blamed on the influence of Phaedra's depraved and permissive nurse. The figure of the nurse in Cvetaeva, derived from Schwab's conception, dominates the tragedy and becomes a powerful Mother Nature figure, forcing the child she loves to seek carnal pleasure without regard for the consequences to herself and others. "Fedra" is in four acts, the first of which begins with a long chorus of Hippolytos' hunting companions in praise of Artemis, which is in itself an extended *poèma* about forests, hunting, and celibacy. The headlong rhythms of this chorus vividly suggest galloping hooves and hunting-horn calls, and the whole long passage may be regarded as a literary counterpart to the *concerts champêtres* in the music of seventeenth-century French composers. The rest of the tragedy tells the familiar story of the encounter between stepmother and stepson, her attempt at seduction and his rejection, her suicide, the false accusation of the innocent Hippolytos by the furious nurse, his death, and the final revelation of the truth. The role of Phaedra ends in the third act with her rejection by her stepson. At the beginning of the fourth act she is already dead and the nurse, until then the dark motive force of the action, becomes the main protagonist and remains the principal character throughout the fourth act. In Schwab, the guilty Phaedra sought repose under a myrtle tree.[47] In Cvetaeva's tragedy, this tree becomes a myrtle branch, a persistent image which stands both for Phaedra's irresistible attraction to Hippolytos and the deadly nature of this attraction. The image, reappearing in various contexts throughout the tragedy,

[46] Schwab, *op. cit.,* pp. 269–274.
[47] *Ibid.,* p. 270.

becomes at the end a symbol of the unity of death and desire, when
the forgiving Theseus orders Phaedra and Hippolytos to be buried
together under a myrtle tree. The plant imagery in the fourth act of
"Fedra" is similar to Cvetaeva's use of plants in the cycle of poems
"Derev'ja" in *Posle Rossii*. Two other cycles of poems from the same
collection, the Hamlet and the Phaedra cycles, are even more
basically and profoundly connected with "Fedra." The chorus of
Phaedra's friends in the fourth act of the tragedy tells of her death
in images that rather unexpectedly recall the death of Ophelia in
Hamlet. In *Posle Rossii,* the Phaedra and Hamlet cycles, written by
Cvetaeva in February and March of 1923, are printed on adjacent
pages and one of the Hamlet cycle poems, "Ofelija v zaščitu
korolevy" ("Ophelia in the Queen's Defense") mixes the two myths
in comparing the guilt of Gertrude to that of Phaedra.[48] In the light
of these poems and of the imagery of the friends' chorus, we can see
that the character of Phaedra in Cvetaeva is in a way a fusion of
Shakespeare's rejected Ophelia and rejected Queen. Equally reminiscent of Hamlet is Hippolytos' denunciation of women and his
blind idealization of his Amazon mother Antiope at the beginning
of act three.[49] The mature Cvetaeva remains the disciple of George
Sand, the idol of her youth, in championing and justifying the
women's right to love, and the figure of Hippolytos-Hamlet in
"Fedra" continues the line of the poems in *Posle Rossii* which point
to the self-sufficient, virginal, and callous male as a natural source of
female suffering.

The language of "Fedra" is more experimental than that of
"Tezej." In both tragedies, archaic Russian and Church Slavic forms
are widely used to convey the atmosphere of Greek antiquity
(Church Slavic being traditionally used in Russian poetry to suggest
Greek, Latin, or Hebrew). Cvetaeva's use of archaic forms reaches
its extremes in the two tragedies, with systematic use of the vocative
case in the masculine, attributive use of short-form adjectives and
participles and, in one case, an attempt to employ the aorist tense in
modern Russian ("Èto sxodstvo! Ad li prizraku povele?").[50]
Cvetaeva's knowledge of archaic forms, derived from the liturgical

[48] *Posle Rossii,* pp. 59–63; "Ofelija v zaščitu korolevy," p. 60.
[49] "Fedra," second installment, pp. 114–118.
[50] "Tezej," p. 33.

language and the practice of eighteenth-century poets, is usually adequate to her purposes, although one can point out two clearly erroneous usages: the confusion between *zrěti,* "to see," and *zrěti,* "to ripen," in the chorus of the youths and maidens liberated from the Labyrinth in "Tezej" ("Brata uzreju! Mater' uzreju! Žatvu uzreju! Slava Tezeju!"[51] where she clearly means "uzrju"); and the indiscriminate use of the dative suffix *-ovi* for inanimate nouns in "Fedra" ("Vzdox—mirovi, krasu—praxovi, zrak—svetovi"),[52] something which occurs rarely in a few Church Slavic prayers, hardly ever in Old Russian, but corresponds instead to the usage of modern Polish. In "Fedra," the language of carnal passion is made deliberately earthy and salty by an extensive use of colloquial and dialectal forms, so that certain passages suggest nineteenth-century Russian countryside rather than ancient Greece. The colloquial language is most prominent in the speeches of the nurse, of the serving maids, and of Phaedra herself in moments of stress and emotion.

The deliberate stylistic mixture in "Fedra" was received by the émigré critics with a veritable howl of outrage. Xodasevič wrote of an "inexcusable and tasteless confusion of styles."[53] Adamovič wrote that "Fedra" is "howled and screamed rather than written,"[54] and Vladimir Vejdle complained of a "total absence of feeling for words as responsible and meaningful *logos."*[55] The critics compared "Fedra" to Racine's tragedy and to "Penthesilea" by Kleist and found Cvetaeva verbose, inelegant, and incoherent by comparison.

[51] *Ibid.,* p. 52.

[52] "Fedra," second installment, p. 115.

[53] V. Xodasevič, "Sovremennye Zapiski, kn. 36-aja," *Vozroždenie* (Paris), September 27, 1928.

[54] G. Adamovič, "Sovremennye Zapiski, XXXVI," *Poslednie Novosti* (Paris), October 4, 1928. Adamovič followed this extremely unfavorable criticism of "Fedra" by one of his typical reversals and in *Poslednie Novosti* of January 10, 1929, after the appearance of the second installment, had a number of complimentary and favorable things to say about Cvetaeva's tragedy. In 1957, Adamovič came out in print with a thoroughly demagogical attack on "Fedra" (which he persistently called "Tezej" throughout the article), based on the patently false premise that this tragedy is an unsuccessful adaptation of Racine's "Phèdre" ("Neskol'ko slov o Marine Cvetaevoj," *Novoe Russkoe Slovo* [New York], July 9, 1957).

[55] V. Vejdle, "Sovremennye Zapiski, XXXVII," *Vozroždenie* (Paris), January 10, 1929. See also N. Kul'man's violent objection to Cvetaeva's use of archaisms in "Tezej" in his review of *Versty* (*Vozroždenie* [Paris], February 10, 1927).

The reception of "Fedra" by the émigré criticism is the most obvious example of a condemnation on the basis of irrelevant comparisons and inapplicable criteria. Even as astute a critic as Xodasevič failed to see that the essential intention of Cvetaeva was considerably different from either classical or romantic poets and that the unfamiliar "mixed" style was adequate for conveying her conception of the myth. The reception of "Fedra" demonstrates how the tyranny of what is considered the current good taste can seriously impede a comprehension of valid forms of artistic expression which happen to be outside such current definition.

We know of no attempt to produce any of Cvetaeva's dramatic works on the stage. With the possible exception of *Konec Kazanovy,* they would offer considerable difficulties both in terms of staging and interpretation. In her preface to *Konec Kazanovy,* Cvetaeva pointed out that anything she might write for the theater should be considered a poem in dramatic form rather than a play.[56] Read as poems, many of her plays make exciting and rewarding reading. "Fortuna," the best of the early plays, is an elegant piece of ripe romanticism, while "Tezej" is not only a magnificent poetic accomplishment but an impressive philosophical conception as well. On the whole, Cvetaeva's plays, while not being the striking and unique contributions to Russian literature that her lyric poetry and *poèmy* are, remain a significant and respectable part of her total literary accomplishment.

[56] *Konec Kazanovy,* pp. 6–7.

X ✒

Prose

The prose of Marina Cvetaeva belongs entirely to the period after her emigration. Before she left Russia, she had published translations of prose works, most notably of the novel *La Nouvelle espérance* by Anna de Noailles,[1] and two brief prose prefaces, to *Iz dvux knig* (1913) and to *Konec Kazanovy* (1921). Within a year after emigrating Cvetaeva wrote two long critical articles, "Kedr" ("A Cedar") about the memoirs of Prince Sergej Volkonskij[2] and "Svetovoj Liven'" ("A Cloudburst of Light") about Pasternak's book of poetry *Sestra moja žizn'*,[3] and was at work on her first book of prose which she intended to call *Zemnye primety* (*Terrestrial Indicia* is closer to Cvetaeva's meaning than other possible translations, such as "signs" or "omens"). These early works map out the subsequent path of Cvetaeva's prose work, which is all in the form of memoirs, literary criticism, and philosophical-ethical meditations. Cvetaeva continued to write prose throughout her residence abroad and, during the nineteen-thirties, as has already been mentioned, her prose works became the major portion of her literary output. Although some of her later prose works are referred to in criticism

[1] *Severnye Zapiski* (Saint-Petersburg, 1916), IX–XII. B. P. Koz'min (*op. cit.*, Chap. I, note 45) mentions Cvetaeva's translation of Romain Rolland which the present writer has been unable to locate.

[2] "Kedr," *Zapiski nabljudatelja* (an anthology) (Prague, 1924), pp. 138–164. Written in January, 1923.

[3] See Chapter III.

and bibliographies as short stories or novellas, she actually wrote no fiction.

"Works of fiction do not attract us," Cvetaeva wrote in one of her earliest pieces of original prose. "The reason is clear: after the great phantasmagoria of the Revolution with its first-shall-be-last and last-shall-be-first, after a four-year-long waking nightmare, after the blackened Kremlin cupolas and red banners over the Kremlin, after the yard-wide 'Give birth to a calf, O Lord!' [4] scribbled on the walls of the Strastnoj Monastery, after coffins issued upon presentation of the thirty-third coupon of the consumers' goods ration card and the laurel wreaths of the late composer Skrjabin sold by his family on the market place by the pound [as bay leaf]—nothing, it would seem, can thrill us, except possibly the simple human truth: the unified, indivisible human essence." [5] In her rejection of fictional prose forms, Cvetaeva, as in many other areas, had independently arrived at a formulation of one of the basic new trends in the Russian literature of the nineteen-twenties. The trend toward the nonfictional was given a strong impetus even before the Revolution by the popularity of the work of Vasilij Rozanov, whose aphoristic style is remotely comparable to certain features of Cvetaeva's prose. By the time Viktor Šklovskij and the theoreticians of the Soviet Futurist group *Lef* formulated their theories of documentary literature and "factography" (*literatura fakta*) [6] in 1926, Cvetaeva had already written her *Zemnye primety* and published a number of sections from it in the periodical press. In connection with this book of Cvetaeva's, we have to mention again the name of Aleksej Remizov, who in his book *Vzvixrennaja Rus'* (*Russia in a Whirlwind*), published in Paris in 1927 but written at approximately the same time as *Zemnye primety* and like it based on diaries kept during the Revolution, also attempted to present a personal and subjective account of the factual side of the revolutionary years.

Cvetaeva's published correspondence with Roman Gul' and A. Baxrax outlines the history of *Zemnye primety*—the inception, the

---

[4] "Gospodi, otelis'!" is a quotation from an early blasphemous poem by Sergej Esenin.

[5] "Kedr," p. 138.

[6] On theory and practice of *literatura fakta,* see Victor Erlich, *Russian Formalism* ('s-Gravenhage, 1955), pp. 98–99, and Gleb Struve, *Soviet Russian Literature, 1917–1950* (Norman, 1951), pp. 204–207.

writing, and the subsequent failure to publish it. In December, 1922, Cvetaeva informed Gul' of her diaries kept in 1917–1920, adding that they were "neither personal nor social in character: thoughts, observations, conversations, the daily life under the Revolution—all sorts of things. Gelikon was very anxious to have them for a separate book." [7] The relations between Cvetaeva and the publisher A. G. Višnjak, whom she usually called Gelikon after the name of his publishing firm, apparently cordial at the time of Cvetaeva's stay in Berlin, worsened after her departure for Czechoslovakia, and in February, 1923 she asked Gul' to act as an intermediary in her negotiations with the publisher. "By April I will have ready a book of prose (of prose notations). Something in the nature of a spiritual (and in part workaday) diary. Certain preliminary inquiries have to be made—who will take it? Gelikon, who has read my notebooks, was ready to tear them out of my hands. If you see Gelikon, drop a few words without letting out the secret. For me to offer him anything is unthinkable. I hope to finish it early in April. If one were to find a reliable publisher, I could come to Berlin early in May." [8] The intercession of Gul' at first brought results: there were telegrams from Višnjak, financial negotiations involving the unstable exchange of the German mark, and Cvetaeva's trip to Berlin appeared quite settled. Then, early in March, the axe fell, and Cvetaeva's letter informing Gul' of this deserves to be quoted at length.

A few words about my affairs. Gelikon has answered, offering splendid terms . . . but: *leave out politics.* I answered in my turn. Moscow of 1917–1919—does he think I was being lulled in a cradle? I was twenty-four to twenty-six years old, [9] I had eyes, ears, hands, feet: with these eyes I saw, with these ears I heard, with those hands I chopped (and wrote!), with those feet I walked from morning till night to marketplaces and through roadblocks—oh, the places they had to carry me to!

There are no *politics* in my book: there is an impassioned truth: the

---

[7] Letters to Gul', p. 171.

[8] *Ibid.,* p. 173.

[9] Cvetaeva's age, as stated here, is at variance with her own chronology. See Chapter I, note 2.

prejudiced truth of cold, of hunger, of anger, of *That Year!* My younger girl died of starvation in an orphanage—this, too, is 'politics' (the orphanage was Bolshevik-operated).

Oh, Gelikon and Co! The aesthetes, who do not want to soil their little hands! I am writing to him for the last time, asking him to accord me this one final grace: I am writing that I am sorry that he will not publish it, but I *cannot* disfigure the book.

The 'politics' in my book consist of: 1) a trip to a requisitioning center (*a Red one*)—Jewish officers, Russian Red Army men, peasants, a railroad car, pillaging, conversations; 2) my job at the People's Commissariat of Nationalities (all very humorous and slightly macabre); 3) a thousand little scenes: in breadlines, in city squares, in marketplaces (e.g., the impression the tsar's execution made in the streets), black market prices—the whole of day-to-day living in revolutionary Moscow. And besides, encounters with White officers, impressions of the October anniversaries (the first and the second ones), meditations in connection with the attempt to assassinate Lenin, memoirs about a certain Kannegiser (assassin of Urickij). I am now speaking of 'politics.' And beyond that—there is everything: dreams, conversations with Alja, meeting people, my own soul—the whole of me. This is not a *political* book, not for a second. This is a living soul in a hangman's noose, and nevertheless, living. The background is morbid, it was not I who invented it.[10]

The negotiations with Višnjak gradually broke down, and Gul' offered the book to another Berlin publishing house, Manfred. In the meantime, Cvetaeva conceived the idea of publishing *Zemnye primety* in two volumes, the second volume to consist of some 250 pages of the diary entries of her daughter Alja. This insistence on her daughter as co-author must have been one of the reasons for the reluctance on the part of publishers, but the main issue remained politics, or perhaps Cvetaeva's insistence that morals come before politics. "This is a book of living life and truth," she wrote to Gul' after learning of his negotiations with Manfred, "which politically (i.e., from the angle of lies!) is a failure in advance. In it, there are charming Communists and irreproachable White Guards, the first will see only the latter, the latter—only the first." [11] In June, 1923,

[10] Letters to Gul', pp. 176–177.
[11] *Ibid.*, p. 182.

Cvetaeva was still optimistically trying to get *Zemnye primety* published as a separate book. In one of her first letters to Baxrax, she requested him to try and find a publisher for it:

. . . please find me a publisher for my book in prose *Zemnye primety*— Moscow impressions between 1917 and the end of 1919. Here is Moscow, Revolution, day-to-day life, my daughter Alja, my dreams, observations, encounters—a sort of a diary of the soul and of the eyes. It is a large book: some 450 foolscap pages [. . .]. The danger shoals of this book are: counter-revolution, hatred of the Jews, love of the Jews, glorification of the rich, vilification of the rich; despite an undoubted White Guard attitude, certain irreproachable living Communists are given their full due of admiration. Yes, and also a fierce love of Germany and a ridicule of the bull-like patriotism of the Russians during the first year of the war.

In a word, the publisher, like my own ribcage, should be able to encompass EVERYTHING. Here, everyone is involved, everyone stands accused, everyone is acquitted. This is a book of TRUTH. There.

. . . Everyone will tear this book to pieces (with their teeth!), everyone . . . except for a few genuine unprejudiced persons, who know that TRUTH IS A TURNCOAT.[12]

Cvetaeva's multiple point of view turned out to be more than any émigré publisher could take. When the hope of seeing the complete book published dwindled, Cvetaeva fashioned from it a series of essays and memoirs which were published in various émigré periodicals.[13] The description of the contents of *Zemnye primety* in Cvetaeva's letters to Gul' and Baxrax enables us to establish that all the shorter prose pieces she published between 1924 and 1927 are in fact excerpts from that book. In addition to the prose pieces thus identified, passages from the book must have been subsequently incorporated (possibly in altered form) into such later memoirs as "Geroj truda," "Nezdešnij večer" (the sections on Kannegiser), and "Povest' o Sonečke."

The prose pieces derived from *Zemnye primety* are linked to each other by the author's strongly felt personality and by the individuality of her prose style rather than by the unifying theme of the

---

[12] Letters to Baxrax, *Mosty,* V, 305.
[13] See bibliography for titles and publication data of memoirs which were originally a part of *Zemnye primety*.

Revolution. In certain smaller pieces ("O ljubvi," "O blagodarnosti," "O Germanii"), the upheavals of the period are not felt at all,
and the author's interest is devoted to meditations on the eternal
themes—love, the nature of gratitude, the attractive sides of German
art and of German national character. The larger episodes, described
in Cvetaeva's letter to Gul', were published as separate, long
memoirs, "Vol'nyj proezd" and "Moi služby." The imaginative
approach of Cvetaeva to the art of memoir writing always leads her
to transform remembered factual experience into a work of art.
Without detracting from its veracity, this method results in narration that borders on the fictionalized, as one of the earliest critics to
write on Cvetaeva's prose, M. Cetlin, has pointed out. Reviewing
"Moi služby," Cetlin wrote that Cvetaeva's memoirs are "vivid to
the point of hurting the eye. Everyone she encountered comes to life
under her pen, as under that of a real artist, although she depicts
them perhaps slightly larger than life-size" [14] Cvetaeva's vision is not
that of a Russian realist, a *bytovik,* but is rather a combination of
telescopic and microscopic views (in this, she is comparable to such
writers as Remizov and Zamjatin): a detached, generalized view
combined with a sudden focusing of attention on individual vivid
details of scene and speech. Occasionally, the method verges on
caricature, as in the portraits of the rigid and intolerant Jewish
Communists Kaplan and Levit in "Vol'nyj proezd" and of Kaplan's
profiteering, vulgar wife, whom Cvetaeva nastily hoodwinked at the
end of their encounter into believing that she herself was a Jewess
named Mal'vina Ciperovič. The acid and contemptuous tone of the
episodes with the Kaplans must have caused the editors of *Sovremennye Zapiski* to print Cvetaeva's 1916 poetic eulogy of the Jews,
"Evrejam," in the same issue as "Vol'nyj proezd" at the time of its
original publication, possibly to forestall any charges of anti-
Semitism.

The two long critical articles by Cvetaeva which date from the
twenties, "Svetovoj liven'" and "Kedr," are both frank panegyrics, as
Cvetaeva herself admitted, with the reservation that she dislikes the
sound of that word; [15] the former is to a remarkable new poet, the

---

[14] M. Cetlin, "Sovremennye Zapiski XXVI," *Dni* (Paris), January 24,
1926.

[15] Letters to Gul,' p. 185.

latter to a remarkable human being. The subtitle of "Kedr" is "an apologia" and this term describes a considerable portion of Cvetaeva's critical writings. While in "Svetovoj liven'" the critical method is subjective and impressionistic, with a wide use of rather Merežkovkij-like explication-by-contrast (which Cvetaeva was to use in many other essays), "Kedr" shows that Cvetaeva could use the more conventional methods of literary criticism—textual and stylistic analysis, for example—when she chose to. Her personal friendship and admiration for Volkonskij led Cvetaeva to overestimate his ability and importance as a writer, but her concept of his human and historical role makes interesting and absorbing reading. In her prose, Cvetaeva did not bother to separate her own memories and impressions from literary criticism: in "Geroj truda" literary judgments on Brjusov and Cvetaeva's personal and literary reminiscences are freely intermingled; similarly, in "Kedr" and in "Svetovoj liven'" we find an arbitrary mixture of prose genres, artfully woven into a unified whole by the author's individuality.

The stylistic peculiarities of Cvetaeva's prose are all manifest in her earliest prose works of the nineteen-twenties. In them we already observe her personalized and varied use of syntax—from staccato one-word phrases to long developed periods, with a frequent tendency to terse, aphoristic formulations and asides. "O blagodarnosti" is in fact a collection of brief anecdotes and aphorisms. In poetry, Cvetaeva was always a mistress of balanced and clearly organized verse structure, but in her early prose the architecture of the whole tends toward the amorphous, and it is possibly this shortcoming that led Svjatopolk-Mirskij to launch his unexpected and odd attack on Cvetaeva's prose style in his otherwise highly complimentary section on her in his English history of Russian literature.[16] An example of this deficiency of organization may be

[16] "As Marina Tsvetayeva is alive (and one is even tempted to add 'and kicking'), the rule *aut bene aut nihil* does not apply to her, and it is only fair to say that the prose she has hitherto written is the most pretentious, unkempt, hysterical and altogether worst prose ever written in Russian." (D. S. Mirsky, *Contemporary Russian Literature: 1881–1925* [London, 1926], p. 263). As Professor Struve points out (*Russkaja literatura v izgnanii,* p. 156), at the time this evaluation was written, Cvetaeva had not yet produced her best works in prose. However, Mirskij's severity about Cvetaeva's prose may also have had a face-saving motivation as a kind of partial justification of his earlier negation of the value of her poetry.

seen in Cvetaeva's long memoir "Geroj truda," which she began writing shortly after Brjusov's death in 1924. While the separate sections of this piece are full of interest, the respective arrangement of the reminiscences and the numerous critical digressions on Brjusov's role in Russian literature result in a structure that is far less satisfactory than the respective arrangement of sections in such later memoirs as "Plennyj dux" or "Moj Puškin." What was conspicuously added to Cvetaeva's more mature prose works of the nineteen-thirties is the ability to organize her material into more balanced and coherent structures, a better command of overall form.

In her prose, Cvetaeva retained the viewpoint of a lyrical poet. She could only write about herself, about life as *she* saw it, about the people she knew, and about literature. This did not necessarily lead to narrowness of vision, because Cvetaeva was enough of a creator to conjure a convincing universe of her own. Her one attempt to break out of the boundaries of this universe was her book [17] about the painter Natalija Gončarova. Writing about an artist whose importance she fully realized, whose work she admired, and with whom she was personally on friendly and cordial terms, Cvetaeva was unable to sustain her main subject for more than a few pages at a time. Opening with a marvelous extended prose poem about ancient buildings, Paris and its stones, "Natalija Gončarova" devotes less than one half of its pages to the painter of the title. There are lengthy digressions on Puškin's marriage and death (on the flimsy pretext that Puškin's wife was also named Natalija Gončarova and that the painter descended from one of her brothers), on Cvetaeva's own childhood, on the nature of the creative process, on the role of the machine in modern life, on the poetry and personality of Tixon Čurilin, on the origin of "Krysolov," and a few other subjects. Like all of Cvetaeva's prose, "Natalija Gončarova" makes absorbing reading, and it contains some of her most basic and significant pronouncements, especially in the sections on Puškin and in the Rousseauist digression on the machine, where Cvetaeva restates in prose some of the ideas we find in her *poèma* "Lestnica." Regarded

[17] In the text of "Natalija Gončarova," Cvetaeva refers to this work variously as a book and as *živopisanie,* i.e. a portrait. It was published only in a serialized form in *Volja Rossii.*

as a monograph on a painter, however, the work is undoubtedly a failure.

The single most successful and valuable piece among Cvetaeva's prose writings of the twenties is in all probability her essay on the art of criticism, "Poèt o kritike." [18] The essay is remarkable not only for its fresh and well-argued views, its obvious and passionate sincerity, and its witty use of unexpected parallels and comparisons, but also for its striking and enormously original prose style in which Cvetaeva managed to transpose the syntactic and lexical innovations of her poetry of the nineteen-twenties into adequate prose equivalents. "Poèt o kritike" is not only a work of literary criticism; it also is concerned with the problems of personal and literary ethics and thus belongs in a sense together with such later essays on ethical problems as "Isskustvo pri svete sovesti." In "Poèt o kritike," as she often does, Cvetaeva uses a multiple vantage point, in this case that of an innovating creative artist and that of an intelligent and inquisitive reader. The alternation and occasional combination of these vantage points makes Cvetaeva's statements on criticism forceful and convincing.

The meditations on the nature of art and of the creative process that began in "Poèt o kritike" are continued in her articles of the early nineteen-thirties. If Cvetaeva's longer prose works had been published in book form, as she originally planned, Cvetaeva's third book of prose would have been called "Isskustvo pri svete sovesti." This plan was never realized, and we have only a few fragments that were published in *Sovremennye Zapiski* under that title with the numerous editorial deletions of Vadim Rudnev and with the note that they are part of a book.[19] In these fragments, as in "Poèt o kritike" and in the subsequent "Poèt i vremja," Cvetaeva elaborates her theory of literature and art. Art, according to Cvetaeva, is a natural organic process like life itself. As such, it is completely amoral in essence. The illusion of the basic moral quality of art and of beauty is based on a misunderstanding: people mistake strength

---

[18] *Blagonamerennyj*, II (Brussels, 1926), 94–125. For the story of publication and reception of "Poèt o kritike," see Chapter III.

[19] *Sovremennye Zapiski*, L (1932), 305–326, and LI (1932), 251–264. Reprinted in *Proza* (also with the note that it is an excerpt from a book), pp. 372–409.

for truth and magic for saintliness. This position is illustrated in Cvetaeva's analysis of Puškin's "Feast During the Plague" and of a poem by an unknown Russian nun, admirable and even profound from the moral point of view but inept and trite as art. Her own creative activity is regarded by Cvetaeva as an organic, cosmic, and (she never uses this adjective) Platonic process, in which the work of art already exists in an abstract state in another universe; the role of the artist is to reproduce that work to the best of his ability by using his talent and craftsmanship. The poet may be taken over by subjects he would prefer to reject, and Cvetaeva cites as examples Majakovskij's involuntary homage to the White leader Vrangel' and her own epic poems on subjects from Russian folklore, the rhythms of which expressed the spirit of revolutionary changes to which the author was actively hostile. The passive role of the poet is described in a vividly exaggerated manner: "Certain aspects of Russia wanted to be expressed, I was selected. And they would convince, they would seduce me—by what? By my own strength: only you! Yes, only I. And yielding—at times seeingly, at times blindly, I would obey, would search with my ear some previously assigned aural lesson. And it was not I who out of a hundred words (not rhymes!) possible in the middle of a line would select the hundred and first one, but it (the poem!) would reject those hundred epithets: no, that is not my name." [20] In "Poèt i vremja," Cvetaeva meditates on the relation of the poet to the time in which he is living and concludes that the really important poets are affected by the spirit of their time whether they want to be or not. This, she makes clear, is quite the opposite of accepting the command of any given party or creed: the poet is creatively attuned to his time and the spirit of the future and needs no intermediaries. Polemicizing with Ivan Bunin (not named, but easily identifiable as "the main trump card of the émigré literature"), Cvetaeva pointed out that Bunin's inability to accept any of the more recent poetry stemmed from the fact that for him both time and art had stopped some thirty years earlier. The concept of art and the artist as related to time, elaborated by Cvetaeva in this 1932 essay, possibly had a belated echo in Boris

---

[20] Quoted from *Proza,* p. 399. A remarkably similar description of the literary creative process is given by Vladimir Nabokov in a recent interview. See *Playboy* (January, 1964), p. 39.

Pasternak's forceful statement of the same idea in the last lines of his 1956 poem "Noč" ("Night"):

Не спи, не спи, художник,	Do not sleep, do not sleep, artist,
Не предавайся сну, —	Do not yield to sleep, —
Ты — вечности заложник	You are Eternity's hostage
У времени в плену![21]	In Time's captivity!

In her critical prose, Cvetaeva frequently returned to the poetry of Pasternak—he impressed her more than any other of her contemporaries. Altogether, she devoted three separate article to Pasternak: "Svetovoj liven'" in 1922, and two in 1933—"Èpos i lirika sovremennoj Rossii: Vladimir Majakovskij i Boris Pasternak," which appeared in the journal *Novyj Grad,* and the article which we know only from its Serbo-Croatian translation, "Poets with History and Poets without History." The beginning of this last article suggests that the new wave of interest in Pasternak came after Cvetaeva's reading of the volume of his collected poetry that was published in that year. The article on Majakovskij and Pasternak was commissioned by G. P. Fedotov as an article on Pasternak alone, but in the course of writing the article Cvetaeva preferred to compare and contrast him with Majakovskij. None of the Pasternak articles represent Cvetaeva's critical writing at its best. Her impression of Pasternak is too unique and personal, and while the spectacle of Marina Cvetaeva reading Pasternak is intriguing, her remarks on his poetry and her conception of Pasternak as a poet completely without ancestors and outside all tradition are not as convincing as one would wish. A person not familiar with Pasternak's poetry would fail to derive any coherent conception of it from reading Cvetaeva's articles—but such a person would undoubtedly learn a few things about Cvetaeva herself.

With the series of personal and family memoirs which Cvetaeva began to publish in various periodicals in 1933,[22] we are at the opening of the period of Cvetaeva's finest accomplishments as a prose writer. These articles follow no definite chronology, but each concentrates on a particular aspect or a particular event of Cve-

---

[21] Boris Pasternak, *Stixi 1936–1959* (Ann Arbor, 1961). p. 82.

[22] See bibliography for a listing of Cvetaeva's personal and family memoirs and their publication data.

taeva's childhood or youth—her dream of meeting a devil in "Čort," her first acquaintance with Puškin's poetry in "Moj Puškin," her ordeal by piano practice in "Mat' i muzyka," a summer trip of the Cvetaev family to Tarusa in "Xlystovki," or a single memorable day during young Marina's stay at the boarding school in the Black Forest in "Bašnja v pljušče." Yet one can imagine arranging these memoirs in an approximate chronological sequence—beginning with "Dom u Starogo Pimena," which deals with some events in the Ilovajskij and Cvetaev families that occurred before Marina was born and in which she appears as a very small child, and ending with "Otkrytie muzeja," in which the recently married Marina witnesses the crowning event in her father's life—and publishing them as a separate book. Such a book would be a moving and often profound record of a remarkable childhood and adolescence in turn-of-the-century Russia; the quality of its writing would allow one to place this book unhesitatingly alongside such classical Russian records of childhood and adolescence as Sergej Aksakov's *Childhood Years of Bagrov-Grandson* and Lev Tolstoj's early autobiographical trilogy.

Even more impressive than the fine series of personal memoirs of 1933–1937 are the three literary memoirs of the same period: "Živoe o živom," "Plennyj dux," and "Nezdešnij večer." These memoirs can be considered as the high point of Cvetaeva's prose writing. All three contain the mixture of genres peculiar to Cvetaeva's prose—personal experience, reminiscences of literary life, and literary criticism. In "Živoe o živom," Cvetaeva's loyalty to Maksimilian Vološin's memory and her affection for him may have resulted in a certain exaggeration of his literary and human stature (as was the case with Volkonskij in "Kedr"). This was noted by Xodasevič, who wrote of this memoir: "Cvetaeva's memoir on Vološin is incomparably more significant than Vološin himself: therein lies its remarkable literary value and its undoubted deficiency as a memoir."[23] The literary portrait of Andrej Belyj in "Plennyj dux" is almost overwhelming in its vividness, while "Nezdešnij večer" evokes not only Mixail Kuzmin but the entire brilliant St. Petersburg literary coterie of the last years before the Revolution. The tone

[23] Vladislav Xodasevič, "Knigi i ljudi. Sovremennye Zapiski, kn. 53," *Vozroždenie* (Paris), November 9, 1933.

of these three memoirs is unusually relaxed for Cvetaeva and, as in a few of her poems of the mid-thirties, there is an unexpected gentle humor. This applies in particular to "Plennyj dux": Cvetaeva admired Belyj and "loved him tenderly," [24] but this did not prevent her from observing certain eccentricities and absurdities in his behavior. In the course of reading "Plennyj dux" one laughs a great deal, and a few episodes, such as the reaction of patrons of a Berlin literary café to Belyj's manners or his conversation with a small boy about a toy pig, are downright hilarious.

"Nezdešnij večer" makes an interesting comparison with the book of literary memoirs *Peterburgskie zimy* (*St. Petersburg Winters*) by Georgij Ivanov,[25] one of the younger Acmeists, who became prominent as an émigré poet, writing his finest poetry in the nineteen-fifties, shortly before his death. Certain passages of *Peterburgskie zimy* describe some of the same persons (Kuzmin, Leonid Kannegiser, the publishers of *Severnye Zapiski*) and places (the Kannegiser home) as Cvetaeva's memoir of St. Petersburg in 1916. Ivanov writes of the period with nostalgia, but his approach to the people he describes is ironic, at times openly sarcastic. The loyal Cvetaeva remembers the same people with fondness, admiration, and gratitude. The contrast is especially marked in the respective treatment of Sof'ja Isaakovna Čackina, the publisher and financial sponsor of *Severnye Zapiski,* shown as a kindly and cultivated woman by Cvetaeva and as a hysterical and capricious liberal millionairess by Ivanov.[26] Skepticism, rather than praise, is often more likely to inspire confidence, and yet, Cvetaeva's recollections are far more believable than Ivanov's. Gleb Struve has compared Cvetaeva, the memoir writer, to Andrej Belyj, adding that "for all of her undoubted subjectivity, one believes her more." [27] The significance of Cvetaeva's literary memoirs for the history of Russian literature has been affirmed by Xodasevič, and such biographers of

[24] "B. N. [Borisa Nikolaeviča Bugaeva-Belogo] nežno ljublju." Letters to Baxrax, *Mosty*, V, 311.
[25] Georgij Ivanov, *Peterburgskie zimy* (New York, 1962; originally published in Paris in 1928).
[26] Cf. in particular "Nezdešnij večer" in *Proza*, pp. 280–281, and G. Ivanov, *op. cit.,* p. 226.
[27] Gleb Struve, *Russkaja literatura v izgnanii*, p. 157.

Belyj as Konstantin Močul'skij [28] and Oleg Maslenikov [29] have used passages from "Plennyj dux" as factual biographical material.

Of the critics who reviewed Cvetaeva's personal and literary memoirs of the nineteen-thirties at the time of their original publication, Vladislav Xodasevič came closest to describing their particular literary form and quality. He considered "Mat' i muzyka" as coming close to being a work of fiction: "In subject matter, this is part of an autobiography, but in execution, in the solution of problems which the author has undoubtedly set up for herself, these are not memoirs." [30] Xodasevič went on to compare Cvetaeva's personal memoirs to Tolstoj's *Childhood* and Andrej Belyj's *Kotik Letaev,* pointed out that "in the foreground we have a psychological pattern which is of interest in itself, without regard to the historical and literary personality of the memoirist," and concluded that "in this [prose] fragment of Cvetaeva's there is such literary brilliance and mastery that one is obliged to hail her henceforth not only as a poet but as a prose writer." [31] Xodasevič described Cvetaeva's portrait of Belyj in "Plennyj dux" (which dovetailed with his own memoir on Belyj, published before Cvetaeva's and dealing with a later period in Belyj's life) as "not a photograph, but a painting, in which the personality of the painter is distinctly felt." [32] In connection with Cvetaeva's dedication of "Plennyj dux" to him, Xodasevič ended his review with a declarative statement in which he claimed for himself and Cvetaeva a literary independence and integrity that was no longer known or understood in the Russian literary Paris of the thirties.

Cvetaeva's last published memoir, "Povest' o Sonečke," relies on her post-revolutionary Moscow diaries and as a work of prose represents a throwback to the manner of the memoirs of the early nineteen-twenties. Here again we have a structure based on free

[28] K. Močul'skij, *Andrej Belyj* (Paris, 1955), pp. 233–239.
[29] Oleg A. Maslenikov, *The Frenzied Poets* (Berkeley and Los Angeles, 1952), p. 107.
[30] Vladislav Xodasevič, "Knigi i ljudi. Sovermennye Zapiski, kn. 57," *Vozroždenie,* April 4, 1935.
[31] *Ibid.*
[32] Xodasevič, "Knigi i ljudi. Sovremennye Zapiski, kn. 55," *Vozroždenie,* May 31, 1934.

association, with frequent self-interruptions, unexpected or unmotivated digressions, quotations from Alja's diary, and even passages in French, which supposedly quote Cvetaeva's conversations about Sonečka with a French friend she knew much later. This time the disheveled texture of the prose is meant as a deliberate effect, as the author makes clear in several asides to the reader: "I know, I know that by my love I weaken the effect, that the reader himself wants to feel love, but I want to love all alone . . .";[33] "I know that I am breaking the unity of the narrative at this point, but honor is higher than art."[34] The impression of utter intimacy, of being let in on the author's emotional experience and mental processes is thus achieved, but as a work of literature (as opposed to a memoir or a "human document") "Povest' o Sonečke" is inferior to the other memoirs of the mid-thirties.

Of Cvetaeva's remaining prose pieces published during the thirties, her essay on Gronskij is another panegyric, or perhaps a posthumous ode in prose, while "Puškin i Pugačëv" and the brief "Dva lesnyx carja" ("The Two Erlkönige")[35] are unique in Cvetaeva's prose in being two successful pieces of authentic literary criticism of unquestionable scholarly value. "Dva lesnyx carja" is a piece of textual analysis which compares Goethe's celebrated ballad with the popular Russian rendition of it by Žukovskij. By demonstrating the lexical differences of the two versions and pointing out the resulting difference in imagery, Cvetaeva proves that Žukovskij's "Lesnoj car'," while ostensibly a translation of Goethe's "Der Erlkönig," should in fact be considered a separate poem on the same subject. In "Puškin i Pugačëv," Cvetaeva discusses Puškin's realistic and historically exact account of Pugačëv's activities in *History of the Pugačëv Rebellion* as opposed to his romantic concept of the rebel leader in the novel *The Captain's Daughter* and comes to far-reaching conclusions about the difference between historical and poetic truth.

Cvetaeva is one of the most interesting Russian letter writers of the twentieth century. Only a portion of her correspondence has been published so far, yet the letters that are available are an

[33] "Povest' o Sonečke," *Russkie Zapiski,* III (1938), 58.
[34] *Ibid.,* p. 77.
[35] See bibliography for publication data.

invaluable aid in understanding her personality and her literary production. Many of these letters open up aspects of Cvetaeva which we could not know from her poetry and published prose. Not necessarily written for subsequent publication, many of those letters are, nevertheless, works of art. Cvetaeva was too much of a literary artist for her skill not to have been reflected in her private correspondence. The very first of Cvetaeva's letters to Ivask begins with the following confession: "To write you a comprehensive letter in reply to yours would mean to give up writing any letter at all: I know myself, I would have tried, as I always do when I write, whatever I write, to find the right formula, and time would pass, and I have no time at all for anything, and in the end—a very remote end of remote ends—I would have ended up with a lyrical essay. . . ." [36] Heightened emotion was inevitably connected with literary creativity for Cvetaeva, and the most imaginative letters of the ones we know are addressed to persons with whom she was emotionally involved—Baxrax and Štejger in particular. As is the case with Puškin, we find some of Cvetaeva's most penetrating and imaginative literary criticism in her private letters. This is to be found largely in the letters addressed to Ivask, but among the letters to Štejger, Letter XIX (unfortunately not published in *Opyty*) [37] is of great interest for understanding Cvetaeva's *credo* as a poet. In criticizing a pessimistic poem which Štejger sent her, Cvetaeva admitted a poet's right to express personal bitterness but took strong objection to the tendency of younger Paris poets to express a universal, cosmic despair, combined with a contemptuous attitude toward those émigré intellectuals who refused to recognize or profess the fashionable existential disgust and boredom. Cvetaeva went to the point of invoking the younger poets' responsibility to the émigré reader, calling on Štejger either to stop disillusioning those who are already disheartened or, as an alternative, to become like Nietzsche and to champion the destruction of the intolerable world openly: "Nietzsche is one of the ultimate

[36] Letters to Ivask, pp. 208–209.

[37] The author is grateful to Professor Ivask for providing him with a photostat of Cvetaeva's letters to Štejger released for publication by Štejger's family, but not published in *Opyty* because of the discontinuation of that journal.

incarnations of human (of inhuman!) suffering. And if I said: then be like him—this only meant: learn to suffer with his *purity*. Kill (first of all, your own self) *without quotation marks*. But also love without quotation marks." [38]

Cvetaeva's memoirs, literary criticism, and letters, are an essential part of her total work. As Xodasevič has pointed out, she really found herself as a prose writer only during the last decade of her life.[39] Her best prose pieces—"Plennyj dux" or "Moj Puškin," for instance—can compare in sheer originality of conception and execution with anything produced in Russian prose during the present century. Her untimely death and the tragic circumstances of the last years of her life prevented Marina Cvetaeva from a further exploration and development of the unique prose manner she had discovered.

[38] Quoted from the photostat provided by Professor Ivask.
[39] Xodasevič, "Knigi i ljudi. Russkija Zapiski, kniga 3-ja," *Vozroždenie,* March 25, 1938.

Conclusion

The Significance Of Marina Cvetaeva: Song And Formula

Wäre denn alles ein Spiel, Wechsel des Gleichen, Verschiebung,
nirgends ein Name und kaum irgendwo heimisch Gewinn?
Wellen, Marina, wir Meer! Tiefen, Marina, wir Himmel.
Erde, Marina, wir Erde, wir tausendmal Frühling, wie Lerchen,
die ein ausbrechendes Lied in die Unsichtbarkeit wirft.
                                        —Rainer Maria Rilke*

Twenty years after her death, the poet Marina Cvetaeva became a
legend—a legend potentially as rich as the personal legends of a
Rimbaud, of an André Chénier, of a Lermontov. Considered at the
distance of almost a quarter of a century, she appears as an
archetype of a struggling artist, eternally and tragically at odds with
society and her environment, extracting from her very isolation the
substance of a unique and revolutionary artistic creation. This
widespread nineteenth-century cliché is applicable to Marina Cvetaeva's life and art to an uncanny extent, but there are significant
aspects in which it is inapplicable or at least insufficient.

Cvetaeva knew and understood the darker sides of existence as
well as any of the French *poètes maudits* or the Russian turn-of-the-
century Symbolists.[1] But through both her life and her work there

---

* Rainer Maria Rilke, "Elegie an Marina Zwetajewa-Efron," *Sämtliche
Werke*. Insel Verlag, Frankfurt am Main.
[1] A difference between Cvetaeva's notion of evil and that of certain Russian
Symbolists can be perceived by comparing her memoir "Čort" to the book
Tragičeskij zverinec (*The Tragic Menagerie*) by Lidija Zinov'eva-Annibal

runs a strong current of vitality and affirmation. At its most elementary level, this current is expressed in Cvetaeva's answer to the wife of the former mayor of Moscow, who remarked that she did not know whether to pity or envy those who died before the Revolution. Cvetaeva's reply to this woman who had lost everything and everyone in the post-revolutionary Moscow of 1918 was: "Live. And try to help others to live. May God help you!"[2] Through all the tragedy that is the substance of much of her work, through all the pain that throbs in some of her personal correspondence, there is this thread of refusal to yield to darkness, to tragedy, to death.

Another basic difference between Cvetaeva and the poet-pariah as conceived in the nineteenth century is her absence of destructive attitudes, her constant strain of pity and compassion: ". . . anything that is being hurt regains its innocence. It gathers all of its forces and straightens out, it regains all of its rights to exist and stands up. Note the effectiveness of persecuted ideas and men."[3] From this, there follows logically Cvetaeva's refusal to align herself with any specific literary program or political creed—a refusal that brought her the hostility of adversaries as different as Brjusov[4] and Adamovič, Miljukov and Majakovskij.[5] To Russian critics and writers conditioned to the tyranny of ideas, Cvetaeva's anarchic independence was unbearable, and when one reads Mark Višnjak's

---

(St. Petersburg, 1907), the wife of Vjačeslav Ivanov and a minor prose writer of the Symbolist period. The book, to which Cvetaeva was introduced by Vološin and which she has called "an enchanting woman's book" ("Živoe o živom," in *Proza*, p. 147), contains a section, also called "Čort," which is similar to Cvetaeva's memoir in setting and in some of the details. The significant difference is that while for Zinov'eva-Annibal the devil of the title represents a pure, metaphysical evil force which is an integral part of human nature and existence, Cvetaeva's devil is a symbol of escape and possibly revolt.

[2] "Moi služby," *Proza*, p. 109.

[3] "Otryvki iz knigi 'Zemnye primety,'" *Volja Rossii*, I–II (1924), 89.

[4] In 1920, Brjusov did not include either Cvetaeva or Xodasevič in a planned recital of "all contemporary literary movements" he was sponsoring simply because he could not assign them to any of the existing literary groups. See "Geroj truda," *Proza*, p. 238.

[5] Cvetaeva continued admiring and championing Majakovskij even after his attacks on her poetry (see Chapter III). It is not clear whether she was aware of those attacks.

charges of Cvetaeva's irresponsibility,[6] one is vividly reminded of similar accusations against Anton Čexov, so frequently leveled by the Populist and other "progressive" critics of the eighteen-eighties.

Her independence was expressed in many and varied ways. She had all the respect in the world for work, and she herself could and did work prodigiously; yet she could write that "labor becomes repellent, even the labor of others, when love for it is imposed and its glorification is made compulsory."[7] She refused to subscribe to the cherished Russian notion that good art is always ethical and always edifying and that therein lies its value. In "Iskusstvo pri svete sovesti," Cvetaeva exposed this idea for the quasi-mystical illusion that it is. Her Goethe-derived respect for the sources of life in all of their manifestations, her preference for the exalted and the lofty rather than for the lowly and the humble went against the grain of the greater part of the Russian nineteenth-century literary tradition after Puškin. "Humanity is not only depth, it is also height," Cvetaeva wrote. "A tree does not grow in the air, I respect the roots, but is it not a mistake on the part of the Russians that for the sake of the roots (the inner core) they not only neglected the crown (the

----

[6] M. V. Višnjak, *op. cit.*, p. 148, note 9, where Cvetaeva's mentality is likened to "either the consciousness of an anarchist or that of an irresponsible and capricious poetess." The fact that Višnjak, a man who in some ways represents the finest liberal and democratic traditions of pre-revolutionary Russian intelligentsia, could see irresponsibility and caprice in Cvetaeva's deep-going ethical concern points to the same basic flaw in Russian culture that had at various times alarmed A. K. Tolstoj and Čexov, Blok and Pasternak: the precedence of political and economic theories over moral considerations and elementary human compassion. This attitude, much in evidence in the nineteenth century, became an official dogma in Soviet times. How well Cvetaeva understood this can be seen from a prophetic statement she wrote in 1931, when discussing the possibility of returning to the Soviet Union: "I would not survive there, for indignation is my passion (and there is a great deal to be indignant about!)" (unpublished letter to Salomea Halpern, September 7, 1931). But her conflict with Miljukov (discussed elsewhere) and Višnjak's censure show that Cvetaeva's disagreement with some of the basic attitudes of her fellow Russians went deeper than a quarrel with Soviet or émigré policies or mentality. "If I lived outside the river-bed of [this] culture, it was because it did not traverse me" (Letter to Ivask, April 4, 1933).

[7] *Lebedinyj stan*, p. 42; the same idea is also expressed in 'Povest' o Sonečke," p. 72.

blossoms), but even considered it a sort of impermissible luxury. It is easy to get bogged down in the roots. There are roots and wellsprings, yes, but there are also roots and worms. And how often, when one begins with the roots, one ends up with the worms. And I also want to say that the roots (the inner core) are never the ultimate aim. The roots are the foundation, the stem is a means, the blossom (the light) [in Russian: cvet (svet)] is the aim. The roots are always for the sake of something else." [8]

The aim of this figurative tree of life in Cvetaeva's own case was undoubtedly poetry, her own and that of other poets. As the editor of the Soviet edition of her selected poems wrote: "That was what she was: a poet, only a poet, a poet totally, a poet from head to foot. Her difficult, impoverished, insecure life of a pariah was filled to the brim with unceasing work of thought and imagination." [9] The tragedy of Marina Cvetaeva's personal destiny, her exile, her lack of audience, her failure to find love, the hounding by her fellow émigrés, and the brutal encounter with the Soviet realities which within two years drove her to suicide—all these become immeasurably more significant when seen as parts of the biography of a unique and remarkable poet. Cvetaeva's independence, her loyalty to the past, her *à rebours* quality place her within a small group of significant Russian writers of the present century, totally different in most other respects, but united in their championing of the rights of the individual and of literature. These are Vladislav Xodasevič, Vladimir Nabokov, and, in *Doctor Zhivago,* Boris Pasternak; behind them loom the shadows of Puškin and Čexov. It is almost impossible to separate Cvetaeva the woman from Cvetaeva the poet, but it can be said that the first is automatically on the side of the individual and of human suffering, while the second is on the side of poetry, the hard bedrock of poetry that she admired, quite beyond considerations of politics or the current idea of literary taste, in poets as divergent as Majakovskij and Kuzmin, Mandel'stam and Bal'mont, Axmatova, Čurilin, and the unknown Russian nun.

Cvetaeva had the fortune to live in one of the most brilliant and significant periods that Russian or any other poetry has ever known. Her tragedy and that of poetry was that it was also a period when

[8] "Kedr," pp. 138–139.
[9] *Izbrannoe,* p. 12.

the lot of all significant poets was isolation, persecution, and violent physical annihilation. The additional tragic aspect of Cvetaeva's poetic fate was the apparent (but only apparent) dichotomy between the substance and the manner of her poetry. If the content of her poetry often took her to the poetic vicinity of such important but non-innovating poets as Axmatova or Xodasevič, the form of her poetry, her language, and her subject matter often lead us to place her into an entirely different literary configuration. Cvetaeva never took part in the Futurist movement in Russian poetry, but if we go beyond the limitations of literary politics and apply to this movement the term "verbalism" (*verbizm*), as Remizov and certain émigré critics have done to describe the whole phenomenon of the verbal-phonetic preoccupations in the Russian poetry of the twentieth century, we can recognize Cvetaeva as one of the four great verbal innovators in that poetry, alongside Xlebnikov, Majakovskij, and again Pasternak.

The temporal and spiritual outlook of these four poets was varied. One can define the difference by pointing out that Xlebnikov's spiritual home was in a past so remote that it almost touched an inconceivably remote future; Majakovskij believed in and yearned for the immediate future in which everything would be solved by industrializing and communizing the earth; Marina Cvetaeva longed for a dimly perceived Romantic past of the eighteenth century and the Napoleonic age, while Boris Pasternak was a rare case of a poet firmly anchored in the immediate present. Yet, for all the divergence of their outlook, these four poets brought about a new and exciting conception of poetry, and together with a host of lesser contemporaries (Aseev, Čurilin, Kamenskij, Guro, Kručenyx, and Sel'vinskij all contributed in their own way), forged a new language for this poetry, inaugurating a magnificent tradition that was totally smashed and annihilated in both Soviet and émigré poetry in the thirties and forties.

There are other literary configurations into which one could place Cvetaeva in one's effort to understand her poetry and to assess its value. Going outside of Russian literature, one could bring up Virginia Woolf, who was also interested in new ways of putting words together to convey new meanings and who also died by her own hand at approximately the same time. Future scholars may find thematic affinities with the poetry of Emily Dickinson and stylistic and personal parallels with Arthur Rimbaud. Cvetaeva's other-worldly orientation (to use Lovejoy's terminology), which persists in her writing throughout, betrays her lasting affinity with the Russian Symbolist poets, under whose impact her own poetic language first began to evolve. However, both the analytical and the comparative methods can take us only so far. After examining the obvious connections between the poetry of Marina Cvetaeva and the work of Remizov or Majakovskij, or analyzing the more remote, yet subtle ties that unite her to Rilke, after describing her vocabulary or her versification, we are obliged to put all the pieces back where we found them so as not to blur the initial and the final picture of what Marina Cvetaeva is first and foremost.

The moral strength implicit in Marina Cvetaeva's life is impressive and exhilarating. The story of this life and her role in the history of Russian literature is absorbing. What ultimately remains after all is said and done, however, is her poetry, which she herself called "my transfigured, my real life." [10] As is the case with most poets, the comprehension of Cvetaeva's poetry is enhanced by what we know of her life, and Cvetaeva is right in saying that "chronology is a key to understanding." [11] The poetry of Cvetaeva is not easy, it requires "imagination and good will." [12] When read with attention and sympathy, it reveals itself as a very great poetry indeed. When Osip Mandel'štam was complaining of the Russian readers' ingratitude to their poets, he did not include Cvetaeva in his list of slighted poets, but like the other poets he named in his list (and to a greater degree than some) Cvetaeva is also a Russian poet "not for today, not for tomorrow, but forever." [13] Like Montaigne, Cvetaeva devoted much of her life to an effort to understand herself. This understanding did not make her wiser or happier; it did not save her from horrible loneliness and final despair. But a by-product of this self-understanding is a body of poetry unlike any other in the world. We, the world, are grateful, for the study of this poetry makes us a little wiser and a great deal happier than we would have been had it never existed.

[10] Letters to Ivask, p. 334.
[11] "Poèt o kritike," p. 97.
[12] Ibid., p. 119.
[13] Osip Mandel'štam, op. cit., p. 327.

As early as 1912, Marina Cvetaeva predicted the course of her poetic fate when she wrote: "The two things I love most in the world: song and formula. (This is my note of 1912: chaos and the victory over it!)." [14] Cvetaeva understood and expressed the natural song (folk song) as well as any poet, and she could also understand and express the elemental chaos, present both in her lyrical *poèmy* and in her personal life. As a human being, Cvetaeva was finally taken over and destroyed by this very chaos. The ultimate victory of Cvetaeva the poet "over both time and gravity" [15] is to have enclosed that song and that chaos in the precise and imperishable formula of her poetic art.

[14] "Otryvki iz knigi 'Zemnye primety,'" p. 97.
[15] "A možet, lučšaja pobeda/Nad vremenem i tjagoten'em—" (first two lines of the poem "Prokrast'sja," *Posle Rossii*, p. 90).

Bibliography

There exist no complete and satisfactory bibliographies of works by and about Marina Cvetaeva. Bibliographical information about her works is appended to two of her published collections of verse, *Posle Rossii* (pp. 161–162) and *Lebedinyj stan* (p. 62). I have also made use of a bibliography of works by Cvetaeva compiled by Professor Tatiana Kosinski. Included here are the published works by Cvetaeva which I have been able to discover or trace. Among the unpublished works, only those discussed in the present study have been included.

Bibliographies of works about Marina Cvetaeva are to be found in B. P. Koz'min, *Pisateli sovremennoj èpoxi* (Moscow, 1928), p. 262, and in K. D. Muratova, ed. *Istorija russkoj literatury konca XIX-načala XX veka. Bibliografičeskij ukazatel'* Moscow-Leningrad, 1963), pp. 420–421. Both listings are sketchy and incomplete. The present bibliography includes only the works about Cvetaeva which I have been able to examine and use in the course of writing the present study. A few of the items mentioned in Koz'min and Muratova were not available to me and are thus not included. The material about Cvetaeva is included under three sections. The first one includes separate articles of a general nature about Cvetaeva's work or her life; also included in this section are books which contain separate chapters devoted to her. The second section comprises separate book reviews and articles dealing with individual works. The third section is a listing of books and articles which discuss or mention Marina Cvetaeva and which were used as sources for the present study. The material in the first and third sections is arranged alphabetically by author; the second section additionally follows a chronological sequence in accordance with the time the reviewed works were published.

The following abbreviations are used in this bibliography to denote the most frequently mentioned publications:

JOURNALS:

SZ   *Sovremennye Zapiski,* Paris.

VR   *Volja Rossii,* Prague.

B   *Blagonamerennyj,* Brussels.

NEWSPAPERS:

NRS *Novoe Russkoe Slovo,* New York.

PN   *Poslednie Novosti,* Paris.

V   *Vozroždenie,* Paris. (For the period prior to World War II, this title refers to the daily newspaper of that name; after World War II, it refers to the currently published literary journal.)

D   *Dni,* Berlin, and after ca. 1925, Paris.

BIBLIOGRAPHY OF WORKS BY MARINA CVETAEVA

A. POETRY

I. SEPARATE BOOKS OF VERSE

a. Collections of verse:

Večernij al'bom. Stixi. (Detstvo. Ljubov'. Tol'ko teni.) Moscow, 1910.

Volšebnyj fonar'. Moscow, 1912.

Iz dvux knig. Moscow, 1913. (Selections from the first two books.)

Versty I. Moscow (Gosizdat), 1922. Second edition, Moscow ("Kostry"), 1922.

Stixi k Bloku. Berlin, 1922.

Razluka. Kniga stixov. Berlin, 1922. (First section, "Razluka," was later included in *Remeslo;* second section, the *poèma* "Na krasnom kone," was included in *Psixeja.*)

Remeslo. Kniga stixov. Berlin, 1923.

Psixeja (Romantika). Berlin, 1923. (This volume contains selected "romantic" poems from other collections—*Versty I, Stixi k Bloku,*

Remeslo, and possibly *Versty II.* Appended are poems by Cvetaeva's daughter Alja.)
Posle Rossii. 1922–1925. Paris, 1928.
Lebedinyj stan. Stixi 1917–1921 gg. Munich, 1957.

b. Unpublished collections
Junošeskie stixi (1913–1916). Mss in possession of A. Èfron, Tarusa, USSR. Separate poems from this collection have appeared in periodicals, in *Izbrannoe,* 1961, and a larger selection in *Izbrannye proizvedenija,* 1965.
Versty II. (1917–1921).

c. Posthumous selection of poetry
Izbrannoe. Moscow, 1961. (Contains a large selection of lyric poetry, one translated poem, and two *poèmy,* "Poèma konca" and "Poèma gory.")
Izbrannye proizvedenija. Moscow and Leningrad, 1965. (An expanded version of the above volume, which also contains six of the *poèmy,* three plays, alternate readings of texts, and seven portraits of Cvetaeva.)

2. LONG POEMS (POÈMY, SKAZKI, SATIRA)

a. Published as separate volumes
Car'-devica. Poèma-skazka. Moscow (Gosizdat), 1922. Second edition, Berlin (Epoxa), 1922. Included in *Izbrannye proizvedenija,* 1965.
Mólodec. Skazka. Prague, 1924.

b. Included in collections of verse
"Na krasnom kone. Poèma." Included in *Razluka, Psixeja,* and *Izbrannye proizvedenija,* 1965.
"Pereuločki." Included in *Remeslo.*

c. In periodicals, anthologies, or collections of miscellany (in the order of publication)
"Poèma konca" (1924). In *Kovčeg* (an anthology), Prague, 1925, pp. 3–29. Reprinted in *Izbrannoe,* 1961, and *Izbrannye proizvedenija,* 1965.
"Poèma gory" (1924). In *Versty, I* (Paris, 1926), 12–19. Reprinted in *Izbrannoe,* 1961, and *Izbrannye proizvedenija,* 1965.
"Krysolov. Liričeskaja satira." Serialized in *VR.*
   Canto 1: IV (1925), 24–31; Canto 2: V (1925), 41–46;
   Canto 3: VI (1925), 37–48; Canto 4: VII–VIII (1925), 38–56;
   Canto 5: XII (1925), 20–35; Canto 6: I (1926), 60–70.

Cantos 1 and 2 reprinted in *Novyj mir*, III (Moscow, 1965), 158–166. Censored version of the whole poem in *Izbrannye proizvedenija*, 1965.

"Lestnica. Poèma" (1926). In *VR*, XI (1926), 29–44. Reprinted as "Poèma lestnicy" (with deletions) in *Izbrannye proizvedenija*, 1965.

"Popytka komnaty. Poèma" (1926). In *VR*, III (1928), 32–39.

"S morja" (1926). In *Versty*, III (Paris, 1928), 7–13.

"Novogodnee" (1927). In *Versty*, III (Paris, 1928), 14–19.

"Poèma vozduxa" (1927), In *VR*, I (1930), 16–26.

"Avtobus" (1934–1939), first publication in *Izbrannye proizvedenija*, 1965.

d. Unpublished

"Perekóp" (1928–1929). Mss in the Library of University of Basel, Switzerland.

3. SEPARATE POEMS IN PERIODICALS

It is not practicable at the present time to compile a complete bibliography of separate poems by Marina Cvetaeva which have appeared in various journals, newspapers, and anthologies. The most important of these publications have been indicated in the text of the present study. During the period before the Revolution, Cvetaeva's poems were most prominently featured in the literary journal *Severnye Zapiski*, St. Petersburg; after the Revolution, the most important outlet for single lyrical poems was *Sovremennye Zapiski*, Paris. Other émigré journals in which her poems appeared were *Russkaja Mysl'*, Prague-Berlin; *Èpopeja*, Berlin; *Spoloxi*, Berlin; *Volja Rossii*, Prague; *Svoimi Putjami*, Prague; *Studenčeskie Gody*, Prague; *Blagonamerennyj*, Brussels; *Vstreči*, Paris; and *Russkie Zapiski*, Paris. During the nineteen-twenties, her poems also appeared in the émigré newspapers *Dni*, Berlin and Paris, and *Poslednie Novosti*, Paris. A considerable portion of poems published in émigré periodicals were included in Cvetaeva's collections of verse, published either previously or subsequently to the periodical publication.

B. DRAMATIC WORKS

1. PUBLISHED AS A SEPARATE VOLUME

Konec Kazanovy. Dramatičeskij ètjud. Moscow, 1922.

2. PUBLISHED IN PERIODICALS

"Metel'." In *Zveno* (Paris, 1923). Reprinted in *Izbrannye proizvedenija*, 1965.

"Fortuna. P'esa v 5-ti kartinax, v stixax." In *SZ*, XIV (1923), 145–167;
XV (1923), 128–156.
"Priključenie (v 5 kartinax)." In *VR*, XVIII (1923), 1–18; XIX (1923),
1–22. Reprinted in *Izbrannye proizvedenija*, 1965.
"Feniks (P'esa v 3 kartinax, v stixax)." In *VR*, VIII–IX (1924), 17–84.
(This is an expanded and rewritten version of *Konec Kazanovy*.)
"Tezej. Tragedija." In *Versty*, II (Paris, 1927), 5–83. Reprinted as "Ari-
adna" in *Izbrannye proizvedenija*, 1965.
"Fedra (Tezej, trilogija. Čast' vtoraja)." In *SZ*, XXXVI (1928), 121–
162; XXXVII (1928), 114–146.

C. Prose Works

    1. books in prose
        a. *Zemnye primety* (Diaries of 1917–1921, prepared for publica-
        tion in 1923, but never published in complete form. The fol-
        lowing prose pieces published by Cvetaeva in the periodic
        press are excerpts from this book.)
"Iz knigi 'Zemnye primety'," *VR*, I-II (1924), 85–102.
"Vol'nyj proezd. Vospominanija," *SZ*, XXI (1924), 247–278.
"Moi služby. Vospominanija," *SZ*, XXVI (1925), 258–286.
Reprinted in *Proza*, 1953, pp. 102–134.
"O blagodarnosti (iz dnevnika 1919 g.)," *B*, I (1926), 119–125.
"Iz dnevnika (Smert' Staxoviča)," *PN*, January 21, 1926.
"Oktjabr' v vagone," *VR*, XI–XII (1927), 3–13.
"Čerdačnoe (Iz moskovskix zapisej 1919–1920 gg.)," *D*, December 25,
1924.
"O Germanii (Vyderžki iz dnevnika 1919 g.)," *D*, December 13, 1925.
"O ljubvi (Iz dnevnika 1917 g.)," *D*, December 25, 1925.
        b. *Iskusstvo pri svete sovesti*. Only excepts from this book were
        published. *SZ*, L (1932), 305–326; LI (1932), 251–264. Re-
        printed in *Proza*, 1953.
        c. Posthumous edition of selected prose pieces: *Proza*. New York,
        1953. This bibliography indicates selections included here when
        listing their original publication.

    2. prose works in periodicals
        a. Personal and family memoirs (in the order of publication).
"Tvoja smert'," *VR*, V–VI (1927), 3–27.
"Bašnja v pljušče," *PN*, July 16, 1933.
"Dom u starogo Pimena," *SZ*, LIV (1934), 212–256.

BIBLIOGRAPHY 295

"Otkrytie muzeja," *Vstreči*, II (1934), 69–72. Reprinted in *Proza*, 1953, pp. 96–101. Reprinted under the title "Otec i ego muzej" ("My Father and His Museum") in *Prostor*, October, 1965 (Alma-Ata), pp. 36–42. A new introductory section, not present in the *Proza* version, has been added; the portion of the text that appears in *Proza* has been censored and the final sections, describing the inauguration mass and the appearance of the Tsar almost entirely omitted.

"Xlystovki," *Vstreči*, VI (1934), 243–248. Reprinted in *Tarusskie stranicy*, Kaluga, 1961, under the title "Kirillovny," pp. 252–254. English translation by Collyer Bowen, *Pages from Tarusa* (Andrew Field, ed.), Boston, 1964, pp. 292–300.

"Skazka materi," *PN*, February 17, 1935.

"Mat' i muzyka," *SZ*, LVII (1935), 241–266. Reprinted in *Proza*, 1953, pp. 66–95.

"Čort," *SZ*, LIX (1935), 206–226.

"Moj Puškin," *SZ*, LXIV (1937), 196–234. Reprinted in *Proza*, 1953, pp. 17–65. In abridgement, *Den' poèzii*, Moscow, 1962, pp. 287–291, and *Don*, III (Rostov, 1965), 182–190.

"Povest' o Sonečke," first half only, in *Russkie Zapiski*, III (1938), 36–103. Remainder of the manuscript is in the library of University of Basel, Switzerland.

b. Literary portraits and reminiscences

"Bal'montu," *Svoimi Putjami*, V (Prague, 1925), 13–15.

"Geroj truda (Zapisi o Valerii Brjusove)," *VR*, IX–X (1925), 42–68; XI (1925). Reprinted in *Proza*, 1953, pp. 203–270.

"Natalija Gončarova," *VR*, V–VI (1929), 37–69; VII (1929), 31–44; VIII–IX (1929), 88–121.

"Živoe o živom (Vološin)," *SZ*, LII (1933), 238–261; LIII (1933), 215–250. Reprinted in *Proza*, 1953, pp. 135–202.

"Plennyj dux (Moja vstreča s Andreem Belym)," *SZ*, LV (1934), 198–255. Reprinted in *Proza*, 1953, pp. 286–352.

"Nezdešnij večer," *SZ*, LXI (1936), 172–184. Reprinted in *Proza*, 1953, pp. 271–285.

"Istorija odnogo posvjaščenija," *Oxford Slavonic Papers*, XI (Oxford, 1964), 112–136.

c. Essays and literary criticism

"Svetovoj liven'," *Èpopeja*, II (1922), 10–33. Reprinted in *Proza*, 1953, pp. 353–371.

"Kedr. Apologija (O knige kn. S. Volkonskogo 'Rodina')," *Zapiski Nabljudatelja*, Prague, 1924, pp. 138–164.

"Poèt o kritike," *B*, II (1926), 94–125.

"O novoj russkoj detskoj knige," *VR*, V–VI (1931), 550–554.

"Poèt i vremja," *VR*, I–III (1932), 3–22.

"Èpos i lirika sovremennoj Rossii: Vladimir Majakovskij i Boris Pasternak," *Novyj Grad*, VI (1933), 28–41; VII, 66–80.

"Dva Lesnyx Carja," *Čisla*, X (1934), 212–216. Reprinted in *Masterstvo perevoda. Sbornik 1963*, Moscow, 1964, pp. 283–289.

"O knige N. P. Gronskogo 'Stixi i poèmy,'" *SZ*, LXI (1936), 464.

"Puškin i Pugačëv," *Russkie Zapiski*, II (1937), 155–189. Reprinted in *Voprosy literatury*, VIII (Moscow, 1965), 174–195.

d. Prose works published only in Serbo-Croatian translation

"Pesnici sa istorijom i pesnici bez istorije," *Ruski Arhiv*, XXVI–XXVII (Belgrade, 1934), 104–142.

"Pesnik Alpinist," *Ruski Arhiv*, XXXII–XXXIII (1935), 62–88.

"Reč o Baljmontu," *Ruski Arhiv*, XXXVIII–XXXIX (1936), 58–67.

e. Miscellaneous

"Rodina ne est' uslovnost' territorii . . ." (Reply to a questionnaire about the contemporary state of Russian literature), *Svoimi Putjami* (Prague, August–October, 1925), pp. 7–8.

"Vozroždenščina" (Statement in defense of the journal *Svoimi Putjami* against certain political accusations), *D*, October 16, 1925.

"Cvetnik" (Selection of passages from the critical articles by G. Adamovič, with critical commentary), *B*, II (1926), 126–136.

"Majakovskomu" (A brief statement on the occasion of Majakovskij's visit to Paris), *Evrazija* (a newspaper), November 28, 1928. Quoted in full in V. Katanjan, *Majakovskij. Literaturnaja xronika*, Moscow, 1961, p. 375.

A statement on Proust quoted in *Cahiers de la Quinzaine. Marcel Proust*, Series 20, No. 5 (Paris, 1930).

D. PUBLISHED CORRESPONDENCE OF MARINA CVETAEVA

12 letters (with editorial deletions) to Ju. P. Ivask (1933–1937), in *Russkij literaturnyj arxiv*, pp. 208–237. Edited by Dmitry Čiževskij and Michael Karpovich. New York, 1956. Introductory essay by Ju. Ivask, pp. 207–208.

15 letters to Roman Gul' (1922–1924) (with editorial deletions), *Novyj Zurnal*, LVIII (1959), 169–189.

21 letters to A. Baxrax (1923–1928), the personal journal "Bjulleten' bolezni" of August, 1923, and 8 poems to Baxrax (most of which appear in the collection *Posle Rossii*), with an introductory essay by A. Baxrax. *Mosty*, V (Munich, 1960), 299–318; VI (1961), 319–346.

12 letters to G. P. Fedotov (1932–1933), with an introductory note by E. N. Fedotova. *Novyj Žurnal*, LXIII (1961), 164–172.

1 letter to Vladimir Majakovskij (December 3, 1928), quoted by V. Katanjan, *Majakovskij. Literaturnaja xronika*, Moscow, 1961, pp. 375–376.

13 letters to Anatolij Stejger (1936), in *Opyty*, V (New York, 1955), 45–67; VII, 8–18; VIII, 21–25.

E. TRANSLATIONS BY CVETAEVA

1. INTO RUSSIAN

Anna de Noailles, *La Nouvelle espérance* (Grafinja de Noaj, *Novoe upovanie*), *Severnye Zapiski*, IX (1916), 66–97; X (1916), 42–66; XI (1916), 57–78; XII (1916), 60–106.

Rainer Maria Rilke, a selection from his letters with an introductory note ("Neskol'ko pisem Rajner Marija Ril'ke"), *VR*, II (1929), 25–32.

"The Ballad of Robin Hood," from L. E. Fidgwick, *Popular Ballade of the Olden Time* ("Ballada o Robin Gude i malen'kom Džone"), *Internacional'naja Literatura*, Moscow-Leningrad, 1941, Vol. VI, pp. 101–103.

Icxok Leibuš Perec, "Biblejskij motiv," *Znamja*, V (1941), 245. Reprinted in *Izbrannoe*, 1961, p. 243.

Važa Pšavela (Luka Razikašvili), "Gogotur i Apšina," "Èteri," "Ranenyj bars," in Važa Pšavela, *Poèmy*, Leningrad, 1947, pp. 35–42, 57–73, 74–77.

Julian Przyboś, "Materik," "Gorizont," and "Begstvo"; Lucjan Szenwald, "Scena u ruč'ja. Vstuplenie," in *Pol'skaja poèzija*, Moscow, 1963, Vol. II, pp. 351–353, 441–444.

2. INTO FRENCH

Aleksandr Puškin, Two Poems ("Chanson du Festin en Temps de Peste" and "A Ma Vielle Bonne"), *Les Lettres et les Arts*, Paris, 1937(?), pp. 316–318.

"Les Demons," in *Puškin* (*odnodnevnaja gazeta*), No. 2, Paris, 1937.

3. UNPUBLISHED TRANSLATIONS MENTIONED BY PAVEL ANTOKOL'SKIJ IN
   Masterstvo perevoda. Sbornik 1963, Moscow, 1964, p. 290.

Edmond Rostand, *L'Aiglon* (into Russian).

Alfred de Musset, *On ne badine pas avec l'amour* (into Russian, said to
have been translated in 1919).

Miscellaneous poems by Puškin and Lermontov, old revolutionary songs
and popular songs from Soviet films of the nineteen-thirties (into
French).

Poems by Baudelaire and by unspecified Czech poets (into Russian,
translations done in Moscow in 1939–1941).

BIBLIOGRAPHY OF WORKS ABOUT MARINA CVETAEVA

A. ARTICLES AND SEPARATE CHAPTERS IN BOOKS

Adamovič, G. "Neskol'ko slov o Marine Cvetaevoj," *NRS,* June 9, 1957.

Anon. "Moscow Discovers Tsvetayeva," (London) *Times Literary Supplement,* May 4, 1962, p. 312.

Antokol'skij, Pavel. Short untitled article on Cvetaeva as translator in
Masterstvo perevoda. Sbornik 1963, Moscow, 1964, pp. 290–291.

Bal'mont, K. D. "Marina Cvetaeva," *SZ,* VII (1921), 92.

———. The chapter "Gde moj dom," in *Gde moj dom,* Prague, 1924,
pp. 169–182.

Baxrax, A. "Pis'ma Mariny Cvetaevej," *Mosty,* V (Munich, 1960), 299–
304.

———. "Zvukovoj liven'." *Russkij Sbornik,* I (Paris, 1946), 183–186.

Cvetaeva, Anastasija. "Iz prošlogo" (first installment), *Novyj mir,* I
(Moscow, 1966), 79–133.

Elenev, Nikolaj. "Kem byla Marina Cvetaeva," *Grani,* XXXIX (Frank-furt-Main, 1958), 141–159.

Èfron, A., and Saakjanc, A. "Večno sovremennyj . . . ," *Don,* III
(Rostov, 1965), 180–181.

Èrenburg, Il'ja. "Marina Ivanovna Cvetaeva," in his book *Portrety
russkix poètov,* Berlin, 1922, pp. 150–152 (also Moscow, 1923, pp.
73–74).

———. "Poèzija Mariny Cvetaevoj," *Literaturnaja Moskva,* II (1956),
709–714.

Fedotova, E. N. "Pis'ma M. Cvetaevoj k G. P. Fedotovu," *Novyj Žurnal*, LXIII (New York, 1961), 162–164.

Field, Andrew. "A Poetic Epitaph: Marina Tsvetaeva's Poems to Blok," *Tri-Quarterly* (Evanston, Spring, 1965), 57–64.

G., M. (Modest Gofman?). "Večer Mariny Cvetaevoj," *Rul'* (Berlin), February 12, 1926.

Gorodeckaja, N. "V gostjax u M. I. Cvetaevoj," *V*, March 7, 1931.

Gul', Roman. "Cvetaeva i ee proza," *Novyj Žurnal*, XXXVII (New York, 1954), 129–140.

Ivanov, Vsevolod. "Poèzija Mariny Cvetaevoj," *Tarusskie stranicy*, Kaluga, 1961, p. 251.

Ivask, Jurij (George Ivask). "Cvetaeva," *Nov'*, VI (Tallin, 1934), 61–66.

———. "Popytka nametit' temu. Novye spartancy," *Meč* (Warsaw), March 8, 1936.

———. "Blagorodnaja Cvetaeva," in Marina Cvetaeva, *Lebedinyj stan*, Munich, 1957, pp. 7–15.

———. "O čitateljax Cvetaevoj," *NRS*, June 30, 1957.

Izvol'skaja, Elena. "Ten' na stenax," *Opyty*, III (New York, 1954), 152–159.

———. "Poèt obrečennosti," *Vozdušnye Puti*, III (New York, 1963), 150–160.

Korjakov, M. "Listki iz bloknota. Marina Cvetaeva v Moskve," *NRS*, July 4, 1965 (based on memoirs of Lidija Tolstaja-Libedinskaja, serialized in *Sibirskie ogni*, Novosibirsk, in spring of 1965).

Kubka, František. "Smutná romance o Marině Cvětajevové," in his book *Hlasy od výhodu*, Prague, 1960, pp. 17–25.

Lo Gatto, Ettore. "Marina Cvetaeva," in his book *Storia della letteratura russa contemporanea*, Milan, 1958, pp. 344–347.

Morkovin, Vadim. "Marina Cvetaeva v Čexoslovakii," *Československá Rusistika*, VII (Prague, 1962), 1:42–53.

Orlov, V. "Marina Cvetaeva," in Marina Cvetaeva, *Izbrannoe*, Moscow, 1961, pp. 3–24.

Osorgin, M. "Poèt Marina Cvetaeva," *PN*, January 21, 1926.

Pasternak, Boris. "Tri teni," in "Avtobiografičeskij očerk," *Proza 1915–1958*, Ann Arbor, 1961, pp. 45–50.

Paustovskij, Konstantin. "Lavrovyj venok," *Prostor* (Alma-Ata), October, 1965, pp. 34–35.

300   BIBLIOGRAPHY

Poggioli, Renato. "Marina Tsvetaeva," in his book *The Poets of Russia,* Cambridge, 1960, pp. 312–315.

D.—v. (Daniil Reznikov?). "Večer Mariny Cvetaevoj," *D,* February 6, 1926.

Schakovskoy, Zinaida (Zinaida Šaxovskaja). "Tombeau de Poètes," *L'Age Nouveau,* LXII (Paris, 1951), 12–16.

Shabad, Theodore. "Russians Pay Tribute to a Disputed Poet. Tsvetayeva Is Memorialized Despite Dim View of Her Held by the Party," *New York Times* (Western Edition), December 29, 1962.

Slonim, Mark (Marc Slonim). "Dve pesnikin'e," *Ruski Arhiv,* IV (Belgrade, 1929), 99–110.

Stepun, Fedor. "Predislovie," in Marina Cvetaeva, *Proza,* New York, 1953, pp. 7–16.

Struve, Gleb. "Cvetaeva," in his book *Russkaja literatura v izgnanii,* New York, 1956, pp. 146–157.

Širjaev, Boris. "Izlom i vyvix," *V,* XXXII (1954), 143–146.

Terapiano, Jurij. "Samoubijstvo i Ljubov'," (third installment, devoted to Cvetaeva), *Russkaja mysl',* July 11, 1964.

Veličkovskaja, Tamara. "O Marine Cvetaevoj," *V,* CXL (1963), 45–56.

Vil'čkovskij, Kirill. "Perepiska Mariny Cvetaevoj s Anatoliem Štejgerom," *Opyty,* V (New York, 1955), 40–45.

Volkonskij, Kn. Sergej. "Posvjaščenie," in his book *Byt i bytie,* Berlin, 1924, pp. vii–xvi.

Zabežinskij, G. "Vulkaničeskaja buntarka," *Sovremennik,* VI (Toronto, 1963), 57–67.

Zajcev, Boris. "Drugie i Marina Cvetaeva," in his book *Dalekoe,* Washington, 1965, pp. 128–134.

Žernakova-Nikolaeva, Aleksandra. "Cvetaevskij dom," *Russkaja Mysl'* (Paris), March 23 and 26, 1963.

B. SEPARATE BOOK REVIEWS AND ARTICLES ABOUT A PARTICULAR WORK.

(Titles of articles and reviews are omitted when they are identical with the work by Cvetaeva that is being reviewed. Articles in which Cvetaeva's work is reviewed together with works by other authors are to be found in Section C, below. The date after the title of the reviewed work refers to the year of its publication.)

Volšebnyj fonar' (1912).

Sergeev, B. *Zatva,* III (Moscow, 1912), 269–271.

Iz dvux knig (1913).
  Narbut, V. *Vestnik Evropy*, VIII (St. Petersburg, 1913), 355–356.
Versty I (1922).
  Rodov, S. "Grešnica na ispovedi u Gosizdata," *Na Postu*, II–III
    (Moscow, 1923), 148–150. Also in his book *Žizn' i znanie*, Moscow,
    1926, pp. 150–151.
  Brjusov, V. *Pečat' i revoljucija*, VI (Moscow, 1922), 293.
  Gul', R. *Novaja Russkaja Kniga*, XI–XII (Berlin, 1922), 13.
Car'-devica (1922).
  Bobrov, S. *Pečat' i revoljucija*, I (Moscow, 1924), 276.
    This article is also a review of *Remeslo*.
Konec Kazanovy (1922).
  Bobrov, S. (under pen name E. P. Bik). "Irina Odoevceva [sic].
    Konec Kazanovy," *Pečat' i revoljucija*, II (Moscow, 1922), 363.
Razluka (1922).
  Ant. (Pavel Antokol'skij?). *Nakanune* (Berlin), No. 34, May 7, 1922.
  Èrenburg, I. "Vmesto recenzii," *Novaja Russkaja Kniga*, II (Berlin,
    1922), 17.
  S., M. (Mark Slonim). *VR*, XIII (1922), 24.
Remeslo (1923).
  Bobrov, S. (See under *Car'-devica* above.)
  Lur'e, Vera. *Novaja Russkaja Kniga*, III–IV (Berlin, 1923), 14–15.
Remeslo and *Psixeja* (1923).
  Maslov, S. *Kniga i Revoljucija*, IV (XXVIII) (1923), 72–73.
  Struve, Gleb. *Rul'* (Berlin), June 24, 1923.
Mólodec (1924).
  A., Ju. (Julij Ajxenval'd). *Rul'* (Berlin), June 10, 1925.
  Černova, Ariadna. *B*, I (1925), 151–154.
  Kadašev, Vladimir. *Studenčeskie Gody*, IV (XXI) (1925), 35.
  Svjatopolk-Mirskij, Prince D. *SZ*, XXVII (1926), 569–572.
  ———. "Mólodets. A Fairy Tale," *The Slavonic Review*, VI, No. 12
    (London, 1926), 775–776.
"Poèma konca" (1924).
  Reznikov, D. *D*, January 24, 1926.
"Krysolov" (1925–1926).
  Svjatopolk-Mirskij, Prince D. *VR*, VI–VII (1926), 99–102.
"Novogodnee" (1927).
  Černova, Ariadna. *Stixotvorenie*, I (Paris, 1928), 16.

Posle Rossii (1928).
Adamovič, G. *PN*, June 21, 1928.
S., M. (Mark Slonim). *D*, June 17, 1928.
Xodasevič, Vladislav. *V*, June 19, 1928.
Proza (1953).
Sazonova, Ju. "Prizvanie," *NRS*, May 9, 1954.
Terapiano, Ju. *NRS*, March 7, 1954.
Vejdle, V. *Opyty*, IV (New York, 1955), 73–75.
Lebedinyj stan (1957).
Anon. *Jahrbücher für Geschichte Osteuropas*, Bd. 7, H. 2, 233.
Markov, V. *The Slavic and East European Journal*, XVI, No. 3, 253–254.
Sokol'nikov, S. "Poèzija blagorodstva," *Grani*, XXXVII (Frankfurt-Main, 1958), 236–237.
Wytrzens, Günther. *Wiener Slavistisches Jahrbuch Graz-Köln*, VII (1959), 207–208.
Izbrannoe (1961).
Tvardovskij, A. *Novyj Mir*, I (Moscow, 1962), 281.

C. BOOKS AND ARTICLES WHICH DISCUSS MARINA CVETAEVA and which were used by the author during the work on the present study. (The authors are listed alphabetically; the list of books or articles that appears under each author's name follows the chronological sequence.)

Adamovič, G. "SZ [Sovermennye Zapiski], kn. 36," *PN*, October 4, 1928.
———. "SZ, kn. 37," *PN*, January 10, 1929.
———. "SZ, kn. 46," *PN*, June 4, 1931.
———. "SZ, kn. 50," *PN*, October 27, 1932.
———. "SZ, kn. 51," *PN*, March 2, 1933.
———. "SZ, kn. 53," *PN*, November 2, 1933.
———. "SZ, kn. 54," *PN*, February 15, 1934.
———. "SZ, kn. 57," *PN*, February 21, 1935.
———. "SZ, kn. 58," *PN*, July 4, 1935.
———. "SZ, kn. 61," *PN*, July 30, 1936
———. "SZ, kn. 63," *PN*, May 6, 1937.
———. "Russkie Zapiski," *PN*, April 7, 1938.
———. "Iz zapisnoj knižki," *Novosel'e*, XXXIX–XLI (New York, 1949), 146.

———. "Sumerki Bloka," *NRS*, August 17, 1952.

———. *Odinočestvo i svoboda*, New York, 1955, pp. 23, 154–157, 163, 223, 299.

———. "Poèzija v èmigracii," *Opyty*, IV (New York, 1955), 49.

———. "Temy," *Vozdušnye Puti*, I (New York, 1960), 47.

Ajxenval'd, Ju. "SZ, kn. 21," *Rul'* (Berlin), October 24, 1924 (under the pen name B. K., i.e. Kameneckij).

———. "Literaturnye zametki (SZ, kn. 26)," *Rul'* (Berlin), January 13, 1926.

———. "Literaturnye zametki," *Rul'* (Berlin), May 5, 1926.

Aminado, Don (A. P. Špoljanskij), *Poezd na tret'em puti*, New York, 1954, pp. 136, 293, 304, 346.

Andreyev Carlisle, Olga. *Voices in the Snow*, New York, 1962, pp. 17, 25, 29–30, 105, 115, 189, 199.

Aronson, G. "Tarusskie stranicy," *NRS*, May 13, 1962.

Belyj, Andrej (B. N. Bugaev). *Načalo veka*, Moscow-Leningrad, 1933, pp. 45, 51, 358.

———. *Meždu dvux revoljucij*, Leningrad, 1934, pp. 368–373, 384.

Bem, A. "Pis'ma o literature. V zaščitu čitatelja," *Rul'* (Berlin), July 16, 1931.

———. "Pis'ma o literature. Pravda prošlogo," *Molva*, Warsaw, No. 189 (412), 1933.

———. "Pis'ma o literature. V tupike," *Meč* (Warsaw), April 5, 1936.

Brjusov, V. "Novye sborniki stixov," *Russkaja Mysl'*, No. 2 (Moscow, 1911), second pagination p. 233. Also in his book *Dalekie i blizkie*, Moscow, 1912, pp. 197–198.

———. "Segodnjašnij den' russkoj poèzii," *Russkaja Mysl'*, No. 7 (Moscow, 1912), third pagination pp. 24–25.

———. "Sredi stixov," *Pečat' i Revoljucija*, I (1923), 74–75.

Bunin, I. "Versty," *V*, August 5, 1926.

———. *Vospominanija*, Paris, 1950, p. 43.

Buznik, V. "Liričeskaja poèzija našego vremeni," *Russkaja Literatura*, I (Moscow, 1959), 95.

Cetlin, M. "SZ, XXVI," *D*, January 24, 1926.

Chuzeville, Jean. "Lettres russes," *Mercure de France*, CVI (Paris, 1913), 203.

C., V. "Blagonamerennyj, Kn. 2," *Versty*, I (Paris, 1926), 211.

Čeremnin, G. "N'ju-Jorkskij sbornik materialov po istorii russkoj literatury," *Voprosy Literatury*, VIII (Moscow, 1957), 248.

Eremin, Dm. "Zametki o sbornike 'Literaturnaja Moskva'," *Literaturnaja Gazeta* (Moscow), March 5, 1957.

Èrenburg, Il'ja. *Ljudi, gody, žizn'*, Moscow, 1961, Vols. I–II, pp. 369–380; also pp. 120, 188, 198, 489.

Fedin, K. *Polnoe sobranie sočinenij*, Moscow, 1962, Vol. IX, p. 315.

Fedotov, G. "O parižskoj poèzii," *Kovčeg*, New York, 1942, p. 190.

Gibian, George. *Interval of Freedom*, Minneapolis, 1960, pp. 10, 14, 22, 153.

Gippius, Zinaida (under pen name Anton Krajnij). "O 'Verstax' i o pročem," *PN*, August 14, 1926.

Gorbačev, Georgij. *Sovremennaja russkaja literatura*, Leningrad, 1929, p. 23.

Gorbov, D. "Mertvaja krasota i živučee bezobrazie," *Krasnaja Nov'*, VII (Moscow, 1926), 234–245.

———. "10 let literatury za rubežom," *Pečat' i Revoljucija*, VIII (1927), 10–35.

———. "Zarubežnaja literatura," in A. Ležnëv and D. Gorbov, *Literatura revoljucionnogo desjatiletija 1917–1927*, Kharkov, 1926, pp. 141–148.

Gor'kij, Maksim (A. M. Peškov). Letter to B. Pasternak, in *Literaturnoe Nasledstvo*, LXX (Moscow, 1963), 301–302; letter to K. Fedin, *ibid.*, p. 497.

Gorodeckij, Sergej. "Ženskoe rukodelie," *Rec'*, April 30, 1912.

Granoff, Katia. *Anthologie de la poésie russe*, Paris, 1961, p. 486.

Gumilev, N. "Pis'ma o russkoj poèzii," *Apollon*, V (St. Petersburg, 1911), 78. Also in his book *Pis'ma o russkoj poèzii*, Petrograd, 1923, pp. 113–114.

———. "Pis'ma o russkoj poèzii," *Apollon*, V (1912), 50–51.

Gusman, B. *Sto poètov*, Tver, 1923, pp. 272–273.

Gussejn, Mexti (M. Gusejnov). "Stranicy dnevnika," *Znamja*, III (Moscow, 1962), 110.

Ia-Fet (pseud.). "Svjaščennaja lira," *Nov'*, VIII (Tallinn, 1935), 149–153.

Ivanov, Vjačeslav. *Svet večernij*, Oxford, 1962, pp. 200–201.

Ivanov-Razumnik, R. *Pisatel'skie sud'by*, New York, 1951, p. 21.

Istorija russkoj sovetskoj literatury. Izdatel'stvo Moskovskogo Univesiteta, Moscow, 1963, Vol. II, p. 751.

Kadmin, N. (N. Ja. Abramovič). *Istorija russkoj poèzii*, Moscow, 1915, Vol. II, p. 311.

K., S. "Kovčeg," *D*, December 20, 1925.

Katanjan, V. *Majakovskij. Literaturnaja xronika*, Moscow, 1961, pp. 94, 375–376, 447, 488.

Kodrjanskaja, Natal'ja. *Aleksej Remizov*, Paris, 1959, pp. 29, 145.

Koz'min, B. P. *Pisateli sovremennoj èpoxi*, Moscow, 1928, p. 262.

Kubka, Frantisek. *Básnici revolucniho Ruska*, Prague, 1924, pp. 100–101.

Kul'man, N. "Pjatiletie Sovremennyx Zapisok," *V*, January 21, 1926.

——. "Versty N° 2," *V*, February 10, 1927.

Kułakowski, Sergiusz. *Pięćdziesiąt lat literatury Rossijskiej* (1884–1934), Warsaw, 1939, pp. 219–220.

Ličnye arxivnye fondy v gosudarstvennyx xraniliščax SSSR (Ukazatel'), Moscow, 1963, Vol. II, p. 281.

Majakovskij, V. *Polnoe sobranie sočinenij*, Moscow, 1959, Vol. XII, pp. 10, 79, 391.

Mandel'štam, O. "Literaturnaja Moskva, 1," *Rossija* (Moscow, 1922) No. 2.

Markov, V. "Mysli o russkom futurizme," *Novyj Zurnal*, XXXVIII (New York, 1954), 169–181.

——. "Zametki na poljax," *Opyty*, VI (New York, 1956), 62–66.

Maslenikov, Oleg A. *The Frenzied Poets*, Berkeley and Los Angeles, 1952, pp. 65, 107.

Men'šutin, A., and Sinjavskij, A. *Poèzija pervyx let revoljucii. 1917–1920*, Moscow, 1964, pp. 29, 33, 384–390, 393, 400.

Mirsky, D. S. (See Svjatopolk-Mirskij, Prince D.)

Močul'skij, K. *Andrej Belyj*, Paris, 1955, pp. 233–259.

Moric, Junna. "Pisateli o tradicijax i novatorstve," *Voprosy Literatury*, I (Moscow, 1963), 20–21.

Nabokov, Vladimir. "Sovremennye Zapiski XXVII," *Rul'* (Berlin), January 30, 1929 (under the pen name V. Sirin).

——. *Drugie berega*, New York, 1954, pp. 242–243.

——. *Speak Memory* (also published earlier as *Conclusive Evidence*), New York, n.d., p. 216.

Ocup, N. "Gumanizm v SSSR," *Grani*, XXXIV–XXXV (Frankfurt-Main, 1957), 264–265.

——. *Literaturnye ocerki*, Paris, 1961, pp. 169, 221–224.

———. *Sovremenniki*, Paris, 1961, pp. 134, 147.

Osetrov, E. "Stixi idut v nastuplenie," *Literaturnaja Gazeta* (Moscow), December 15, 1962.

Osorgin, M. (M. A. Il'in). "Djadja i tetja," *PN*, April 29, 1926.

———. "Po poljam slovesnym," *PN*, July 28, 1927.

Pavlovič, Nadežda. "Moskovskie vpečatlenija," *Literaturnye Zapiski* (Petrograd), June 23, 1922.

Parnok, Sofija. "Pasternak i drugie," *Russkij Sovremennik*, I (Moscow-Leningrad, 1924), 311.

Pasternak, B. "Oxrannaja gramota," in *Proza 1915–1958*, Ann Arbor, 1961, p. 284.

———. Letters to Maksim Gor'kij in *Literaturnoe Nasledsvo*, LXX (Moscow, 1963), 298, 300, 307–308.

Pozner, V. "Sžigal'ščiki i sžigaemye," *D*, May 6, 1926.

Reznikova, Natalija. "Knižnye novinki," *Rubež*, Harbin, 1933, No. 26, p. 24.

Ryl'skij, M, "Sčastlivye nasledniki," *Literaturnaja Rossija* (Moscow), April 12, 1963.

Sarnov, B. " 'Novatory' i 'Arxaisty'," *Voprosy Literatury*, X (1962), 56–74. In abridged form under the title "A esli b i bylo" in *Den' poèzii*, Moscow, 1962.

Sedyx, Andrej (Ja. Cvibak). *Dalekie, blizkie*, New York, 1962, pp. 31, 71–72, 74, 102–103.

Slonim, M. "Literaturnye otkliki," *VR*, IV (1924), 58.

———. "Literatura èmigracii," *VR*, II (1925), 177.

———. "Obzor žurnalov," *VR*, II (1927), 119.

———. *Outline of Russian Literature*, New York and London, 1958, pp. 214–215.

Solovejčik, S. "Volja Rossii XI–XII," *D*, January 29, 1928.

Sosinskij, B. "O čitatele, kritike i poète," *VR*, II (1928), 60.

Stepun, F. *Byvšee i nesbyvšeesja*, New York, 1956, Vol. I, pp. 273–276, 310.

Struve, Gleb. "Kovčeg," *V*, January 21, 1926.

———. "Literaturnye 'reakcionery'," *V*, Novmber 25, 1926.

———. *Soviet Russian Literature 1917–1950*, Norman, 1951, p. 5.

———. *Russkaja literatura v izgnanii*, New York, 1956, *passim*.

———. "Ob Adamoviče-kritike," *Grani*, XXXIV–XXXV (Frankfurt-Main, 1957).

Struve, P. B. "Zametki pisatelja," *V*, May 6, 1926.
Svjatopolk-Mirskij, Prince D. *Russkaja lirika*, Paris, 1924, p. xii.
——. "Poèty i Rossija," *Versty*, I (Paris, 1926), 145–146.
——. "SZ, VR," *Versty*, I (Paris, 1926), 206–210.
——. "O nynešnem sostojanii russkoj literatury," *B*, I (1926), 93, 97.
——. *Contemporary Russian Literature, 1881–1925*, London, 1926, p. 263.
——. "Vejanie smerti v predrevoljucionnoj literature," *Versty*, II (Paris, 1927), 253.
——. *A History of Russian Literature*, New York, 1960, p. 492.
Š. (D. Šaxovskoj?). "Kovčeg," *B*, I (1926), 160–161.
Š., V. "Russkie pisatel'nicy za rubežom," *Novoe Slovo* (Berlin), September 15, 1934.
Terapiano, Ju. "Po povodu 'Myslej o russkom futurizme' V. Markova," *NRS*, February 6, 1955.
——. "Sovremennik N° 6," *Russkaja Mysl'* (Paris), December 15, 1962.
——. "Pasternakiana,' *Russkaja Mysl'* (Paris), September 4, 1963.
Trockij, L. (L. Bronštejn). *Literatura i revoljucija*, Moscow, 1923, p. 30 and *passim*.
Txorževskij, I. *Russkaja literatura*, Paris, 1950, Vol. II, p. 506.
Varšavskij, V. S. *Nezamečennoe pokolenie*, New York, 1956, pp. 24, 178, 193, 210, 287–293.
Vejdle, V. "SZ, XXXVII," *V*, January 10, 1927.
Višnjak, M. V. *Sovremennye Zapiski*, Bloomington, 1957, pp. 102, 112, 123, 144–148, 208, 214, 220.
Weidle, Wladimir. (See Vejdle, V.)
Xodasevič, V. "Russkaja poèzija," *Al'ciona*, Moscow, 1914, I, 209.
——. "SZ, kn. 36-aja," *V*, November 27, 1928.
——. "Knigi i ljudi," *V*, April 6, 1933.
——. "Knigi i ljudi," *V*, November 9, 1933.
——. "Knigi i ljudi," *V*, May 31, 1934.
——. "Knigi i ljudi," *V*, April 4, 1935.
——. "Knigi i ljudi," *V*, May 15, 1937.
——. "Knigi i ljudi," *V*. March 25, 1938.
Yale Russian Seminar, The. New Haven, 1963, pp. 12–13.
Zavališin, V. "Trudnyj xleb," *NRS*, July 1, 1962.
Zelinskij, K. *Kritičeskie pis'ma*, Moscow, 1934, p. 147.

Znosko-Borovskij, E. "Zametki o russkoj poèzii," *VR*, III (1924), 95–97.

POEMS BY OTHER POETS, DESCRIBING MARINA
CVETAEVA OR DEDICATED TO HER.

Antokol'skij, Pavel. "Marina," *Den' poèzii*, Moscow, 1962, p. 42.

Axmatova, Anna. "Nas četvero" and "Nevidimka, dvojnik, peres-mešnik . . . ," *Vosdušnye Puti*, III (New York, 1963), 9–10.

Belyj, Andrej. "Marine Cvetaevoj," *Èpopeja*, II (Berlin, 1922), 11. Another version of this poem is in his book *Posle razluki*, Berlin, 1922, p. 123.

Čurilin, Tixon. "Iz detstva dalečajsego. Glavy iz poèmy. Ljubov'" (Marine Cvetaevoj. 5 marta 1916 g.), *Gjulistan*, Mosow, 1916.

Gronskij, N. "Otper dver' ja . . . " and "Iz glubiny morej podnjav-šeesja imja . . . " in his book *Stixi i poèmy*, Paris, n.d., pp. 15–16.

Ivanov, Vjačeslav. "Ispoved' zemle," in his book *Svet večernij*, Oxford, 1962, p. 84.

Knorring, Irina. "Cvetaevoj," *PN*, March 21, 1926.

Mandel'štam, Osip. "V raznogolosice devičeskogo xora . . . ," "Na rozval'njax uložennyx solomoj . . . ," and "Ne verja voskresen'ja čudu . . . ," *Sobranie sočinenij*, New York, 1955, pp. 82–83, 86–87. Also in *Sobranie sočinenij*, Washington, 1964, I, 57–59, 62–63.

Maršak, S. "Marine Cvetaevoj," *Izbrannaja lirika*, Moscow, 1963, p. 144.

Pasternak, Boris. "M.C.," *Stixi i poèmy 1912–1932*, Ann Arbor, 1961, p. 225. Under the full title, "Marine Cvetaevoj," *Stixotvorenija i poèmy*, Moscow and Leningrad, 1965, pp. 200–201. Earlier version of this poem, *ibid.*, p. 646.

———. "Mgnovennyj sneg . . . " (an acrostic on the name Marina Cvetaeva), *Stixotvorenija i poèmy*, p. 552.

———. "Lejtenant Šmidt. Posvjaščenie" (Acrostic dedication to Cveta-eva), *Stixotvorenija i poèmy*, p. 661. Originally, *Novyj Mir*, No. 8–9 (1926), p. 33.

———. "Pamjati Mariny Cvetaevoj," *Stixi 1936–1959*, Ann Arbor, 1961, pp. 39–40; *Stixotvorenija i poèmy* (1965), p. 567. Earlier versions, drafts, and commentary disclosing that Pasternak wrote this memorial poem at the instigation of the poet Aleksej Kručenyx, *ibid.*, pp. 703–705.

Prismanova, Anna. "Karandaš," in her collection *Ten' i telo*, Paris, 1937, p. 20.

Rilke, Rainer Maria. "Elegie an Marina Zwetajewa-Efron," *Sämtliche Werke,* Wiesbaden, 1956, Vol. II, pp. 271–273.

——. "Marina: voici galets et coquillages . . . ," *Sämtliche Werke,* Wiesbaden, 1956, Vol. II, pp. 678–679.

Rudjakov, Genrix. "V gostjax u èstetov," *Oktjabr',* I (Moscow, 1963).

Severjanin, Igor (I. V. Lotarev). "Cvetaeva," in his book *Medal'ony,* Belgrade, 1934, p. 96.

Struve, Gleb. "Černyj kèb," *Rul'* (Berlin), October 10, 1923.

Šaxovskoj, Prince D. "Isxod k polunoči," *Studenčeskie, Gody,* IV/xxi (1925), 6.

Vološin, Maksimilian. "K vam duša tak radostno vlekoma," quoted in Marina Cvetaeva, *Proza,* New York, 1953, p. 143.

Index

This index contains the names of persons relevant to Cvetaeva's personal or literary biography, literary figures, and personalities from the realm of the arts. Literary scholars and critics have been included when there are statements about them in the text or in the notes (but not when they are the subject of the author's references or acknowledgments). Politicians, historical and fictional characters have not been indexed.

Adalis (Adelina Éfron), 50
Adamovič, Georgij, 38n, 66, 70–71, 78, 80, 84, 84n, 85, 85n, 88, 91, 108n, 109, 194, 229, 264, 284
Afanas'ev, A. N., 37, 64, 223, 226, 229, 258
Ajxenval'd, Julij, 70, 229
Aksakov, Sergej, 277
Aldanov, Mark (M. A. Landau), 38n, 80, 97
Aminado, Don (A. P. Špoljanskij), 194n
Annenkov, Jurij, 80n
Annenskij, Innokentij, 2, 5, 110n, 156, 159n, 181, 258
Antokol'skij, Pavel, 46–47, 93, 102–103, 119, 237
Apuxtin, A. N., 125
Aragon, Louis, 76n, 80n
Aseev, Nikolaj, 78n, 105, 157, 207, 287
Axmadulina, Bella, 119
Axmatova, Anna (A. A. Gorenko), 3, 6, 7, 38, 39, 41, 53, 54, 66, 77, 87, 102–103, 112, 117n, 128, 155, 169,

182–183, 189, 210, 240–241, 286, 287

Balanchine, George (G. M. Balančivadze), 198–199
Bal'mont, Konstantin, 2, 5, 6n, 44, 47–49, 50, 53, 60, 66, 74, 85, 88–89, 149, 163, 178–179, 185, 229, 246, 286
Baratynskij, Evgenij, 1, 4, 195
Barghoorn, Frederick C., 111n
Baškirceva, Marija (Marie Baschkirtseff), 27, 31, 174, 180
Batjuškov, Konstantin, 188
Baudelaire, Charles, 27, 28, 231
Baxrax, Aleksandr, 9, 18n, 39, 55n, 58–59, 59n, 75, 91, 106–107, 110, 123, 146, 164, 196, 205, 205n, 254, 267, 270, 281
Belinskij, Vissarion, 4–5
Belyj, Andrej (B. N. Bugaev), vi, 2, 5, 8, 23, 28nn, 29, 29n, 30n, 32, 33–34, 53–54, 55–56, 57, 87, 132, 153n, 156–157, 164n, 176, 181, 191, 207, 241, 277–279

Bem, A. L., 74n, 86, 194
Berberova, Nina, 10, 80, 84n, 97, 111n
Berdjaev, Nikolaj, 49
Blok, Aleksandr, 2, 4–6, 29, 32, 41, 48, 75, 81, 87, 109n, 112, 126, 129, 155, 159, 159n, 169, 178, 181, 182–183, 185, 191–193, 206, 207, 240–241, 246, 285
Bokov, Viktor, 119
Brjusov, Valerij, 2, 5, 6, 8, 18n, 23, 30–32, 33, 34, 45, 50, 54, 66n, 93, 110n, 113, 117n, 147, 176, 177, 193, 246, 258, 272, 273, 284
Brodskij, Iosif, 4, 7
Browning, Robert, 230
Bruni, Lev, 103n
Bunakov-Fondaminskij, I. I., 94–95
Bunin, Ivan, 20n, 66, 69, 70, 80, 214, 275
Bušman, Irina, 169n
Byron, George Gordon, 41, 180, 188

Casanova de Seingalt, Giacomo, 37, 188, 242–250
Cendrars, Blaise, 80n
Cetlin, M. O., 47, 271
Chénier, André, 185, 283
Claudel, Paul, 27
Colette, 217
Corneille, Pierre, 260
Cvetaev, Andrej (Cvetaeva's half-brother), 17, 19–20, 24, 26
Cvetaev, Dmitrij Vladimirovič (Cvetaeva's uncle), 16
Cvetaev, Ivan Vladimirovič (Cvetaeva's father), 16–21, 24, 25, 29–30, 34, 36, 277
Cvetaev, (Father) Vladimir (Cvetaeva's paternal grandfather), 15–16
Cvetaeva, Anastasija ("Asja," Cvetaeva's younger sister), 18, 19–20, 25–29, 38, 65, 102, 106, 174, 176
Cvetaeva, Marija Aleksandrovna

(née Mejn, Cvetaeva's mother), 17, 19–26
Cvetaeva, Marina,
    BOOKS: *Izbrannoe*, 1961 (*Selected Poems*), 17n, 83nn, 92nn, 93n, 112–113, 117n, 187, 195, 201, 204; *Izbrannye proizvedenija*, 1965 (*Selected Works*), 117n; *Iz dvux knig* (*Selections from two Books*), 34, 171, 177–178, 266; *Junošeskie stixi* (*Juvenilia*), 8, 36, 37, 117n, 119n, 125, 155, *179–181*; *Lebedinyj stan* (*Swans' Encampment*), 8, 45, 49, 51, 53, 62, 76–77, 85n, 94, 110, 125, 132, *184–186*, 187, 190, 196, 204, 206, 240; *Posle Rossii* (*After Russia*), 64, 65, 74, 75, 76, 110, 114, 117n, 127, 140, 146, 150, 155n, 158, 161–163, 167, 170, 191, *193–199*, 200, 205, 206, 212, 215n, 222, 238, 249, 258, 259, 262, 263; *Proza* (*Prose*), 17n, 83n, *108–110; Psixeja* (*Psyche*), 9n, 60, 67, 125, 186–187, 210, 240, 249; *Razluka* (*Separation*), 9n, *53*, 56, 210; *Remeslo* (*Craft*), 8, 9n, 45, 49, 51, 53, 60, 66, 68n, 74, 85n, 128, 149, 151, 153, 158, 163, 185, *189–191*, 193, 194, 199, 203, 206, 211, 224, 235, 249; *Stixi k Bloku* (*Verses to Blok*), 9n, 53, 54, 66, 127, *191–193; Večernij al'bom* (*Evening Album*), 17n, 18, 33, 144, 154, 166, *171–179*, 182, 257; *Versty I* (*Versts I*), 37, 39, 41, 53, 54, 56, 64, 66, 74, 76, 105, 125–128, 130, 155–157, 158, *181–184*, 188, 189, 190, 191, 194, 196, 206, 215n, 224, 240, 256; *Versty II* (*Versts II*), 45, 76, *184–189*, 194, 199, 257; *Volšebnyj fonar'* (*The Magic Lantern*), 33, 114, 146, *171–179*, 257; *Zemnye primety* (*Terrestrial Indicia*), 38n, 43, 49–50, 60, 266–271.
    LONG POEMS (*poèmy*): "Avtobus" ("The Bus"), 117n; *Car'-de-*

vica (*Tsar-Maiden*), 46, 53, 56, 58, 129, 130, 163, 208, 222–224, 226, 228, 258; "Krysolov" ("The Pied Piper"), 64, 67, 69, 116, 118n, 139, 150, 157–158, 217, 230–233, 236, 258, 273; "Lestnica" ("The Staircase"), 114, 117, 118n, 214, 217–219, 231, 236, 273; *Mólodec* (*A Swain*), 60, 67, 79–80, 96, 129, 225, 226–229, 233, 258, 260; "Na krasnom kone" ("On a Red Steed"), 18, 53, 85n, 132, 160, 189, 208–211, 228, 233, 260; "Novogodnee" ("New Year's Greetings"), 69, 73, 220–222, 228, 232–233; "Perekóp," 76, 78, 79, 11n, 116, 203, 233–235; "Pereuločki" ("Side Streets"), 51, 86, 129, 130, 149, 153, 191, 199, 224–226, 228, 236; "Poèma gory" ("Poem of the Hill"), 57, 59, 64, 69, 117n, 128, 211–212, 214, 219; "Poèma konca" ("Poem of the End"), 9, 59, 64, 65, 69, 78, 110n, 117n, 137, 145, 167, 211–214, 219, 236; "Poèma vozduxa" ("Poem of the Air"), 221–222, 228; "Popytka komnaty" ("An Attempt to Construct a Room"), 214, 216, 221; "S morja" ("From the Seacoast"), 69, 148, 214–215.

PLAYS: "Ariadna," see "Tezej;" "Fedra" ("Phaedra"), 130, 258, 262–265; "Feniks" ("Phoenix"), 60, 67, 243–247, 257; "Fortuna," 60, 67, 238, 250–257, 265; "Kamennyj angel" ("The Stone Angel"), 251; *Konec Kazanovy* (*Casanova's End*), 53, 238, 241–243, 257, 265, 266; "Metel'" ("The Snowstorm"), 60, 238–241, 257; "Priključenie" ("An Adventure"), 60, 120, 247–250, 257; "Tezej" ("Theseus"), 69, 86, 162, 164–165, 258–262, 265

Cvetaeva, Valerija (Cvetaeva's half-sister), 17, 19, 20, 24, 26, 36

Cvetaeva, Varvara Dmitrievna (née Ilovajskaja, I. V. Cvetaev's first wife), 17

Čackina, S. I., 37–38, 278
Čajkovskij, Modest, 240
Čajkovskij, P. I., (P. I. Tschaikowsky), 237, 240
Čarskaja, Lidija (L. Čurilova), 104, 125, 174
Červinskaja, Lidija, 84, 85n
Čexov, Anton, 285, 285n, 286
Čurilin, Tixon, 40, 47, 183, 273, 286, 287

Dali, Gala (Galja D'jakonova), 176
Dali, Salvador, 176
Danilov, Kirša, 225n
Dante, 242
Deržavin, Gavriil, 131n, 186, 223, 231
Desbordes-Valmore, Marceline, 174
Dickens, Charles, 188
Dickinson, Emily, 288
Dobroljubov, Nikolaj, 5
Doroševič, Vlas, 30
Dostoevskij, Fëdor, vi, 47n, 72, 82, 98, 120

Elenev, Nikolaj, 36–37, 59
Eleneva, E. I. (Catherine Elène), 10, 72n, 111n, 238n
Eluard, Paul, 176
Erlich, Victor, 267n
Esenin, Sergej, 3, 5, 6, 38, 69, 70, 81, 113, 130, 161, 267n

Efron, Ariadna ("Alja"), 17n, 36, 37, 41, 49–50, 51, 56, 57, 89, 93, 101–102, 112, 114, 117, 118n, 119, 169, 172n, 181, 182, 269, 270, 280

Efron, Georgij ("Mur"), 61, 97, 99, 103, 105–106

Efron, Irina, 41, 42, 45, 269

Efron, Sergej, 18n, 33, 35–36, 40–43, 44, 50–51, 56, 57, 61, 63, 68, 74, 81, 89–90, 95–96, 98–99, 101–102, 112, 176, 190, 234–235

Ejsner, Aleksej, 230
Ellis (Lev Kobylinskij), 28–30, 32
Erenburg, Il'ja, 21n, 31–32, 35, 44, 47, 50, 51n, 52, 53, 54–55, 73, 76n, 80n, 101–103, 106, 111–112, 114, 118, 186, 190

Fadeev, Aleksandr, 113
Fedotov, G. P., 82, 83, 85, 95, 107, 110, 230, 276
Fedotova, E. N., 82, 95, 96–97, 99n, 230n
Fet, Afanasij, 2, 4, 109n, 125, 133, 154, 155

Gasparov, M. L., 161
Genêt, Jean, 250
Gercyk, Adelaida, 32, 53
Geršenzon, Mixail, 32
Gippius, Zinaida, 2, 7, 66, 69, 70,71, 80, 85, 110n, 155, 186, 214
Gobineau, Joseph-Arthur de, 172
Goethe, Johann Wolfgang von, 27, 72, 156, 195, 230, 247, 280, 285
Gogol', Nikolaj, 20, 24, 124, 153
Golovina, Alla, 91, 99
Goncourt, Edmond and Jules, 252n
Gončarova, Natalija Sergeevna, 8, 79–80, 117, 135, 229, 273
Gor'kij, Maksim (A. M. Peškov), 21n, 60, 64–65, 143n, 168, 174, 214, 231
Gorodeckaja, Nadežda, 82, 234n, 235
Griboedov, Aleksandr, 50, 244, 256
Gronskij, Nikolaj, 75, 83, 87–88, 91n, 148, 202, 216, 280
Gul', Roman, 56, 60, 110, 267–271
Gumilëv, Nikolaj, 2, 3, 5, 30–31, 32, 78, 81, 110n, 111n, 113, 117n, 120, 145n, 161, 177
Guro, Elena, 287
Gussejn, Mexti (M. Gussejnov), 113

Habeas (N. Komarova), 110n
Haendel, Georg Friederich, 260
Halpern, Salomea, 10, 74, 81, 82,

89–90, 111n, 115n, 198, 234n, 235n, 285n
Hauff, Wilhelm, 22
Heine, Heinrich, 27, 106, 156
Hoelderlin, Friederich, 27
Holliday, Sof'ja (Sonečka Gollidèj), 46–47, 93, 237, 238, 241–243, 248n, 250, 255, 280
Hopkins, Gerard Manley, 218

Ilovajskaja, Nadja, 20n, 25
Ilovajskij, D. I., 8, 17, 19, 20n, 23, 26, 34
Ilovajskij, Sergej, 23, 174, 176
Ivanov, Georgij, 3, 5, 38n, 39–40, 278
Ivanov, Vjačeslav, 2, 5, 7, 32, 48, 50, 76n, 207, 241, 258, 284n
Ivanov, Vsevolod, 114, 118
Ivask, George (Jurij Ivask), 9, 10, 17n, 55n, 65, 66n, 69, 72, 73, 75nn, 78, 82, 83, 85, 86, 88, 92, 96–97, 108, 110, 111n, 125, 131, 155, 164n, 202, 224–226, 281
Izvol'skaja, Elena (Helene Iswolsky), 63, 67n, 72n, 74, 95–97, 102n, 235

Jazykov, Nikolaj, 223

Kadmin, N. (N. Ja. Abramovič), 179
Kallin, Anna, 10, 26, 176
Kamenskij, Vasilij, 188, 287
Kannegiser, Leonid, 38, 269, 270, 278
Kjuxel'beker, Vil'gel'm (Wilhelm Küchelbecker), 131–132
Kleist, Heinrich von, 264
Kljuev, Nikolaj, 3, 6, 7, 129
Knorring, Irina, 62
Knut, Dovid, 85n

Kobylinskij, Lev, see Ellis
Kogan, P. S., 45, 192
Kol'cov, Aleksej, 156
Korjakov, Mixail, 103n
Kručenyx, Aleksej, 72n, 103n, 145, 149, 287
Kul'man, Nikolaj, 164, 264n

Kuprin, Aleksandr, 80
Kuzmin, Mixail, 2, 6, 7, 29, 32, 38, 87, 124, 155, 177, 178, 189, 190, 277–278, 286

Ladinskij, Antonin, 85n
Lamotte-Foucqué, Friederich de, 27
Larionov, Mixail, 80n, 229
Lauzun, Duc de, 251–256
Léger, Fernand, 80n
Lermontov, Mixail, 1, 125, 155, 206, 207, 256, 283
Leskov, Nikolaj, 124
Levertov, Denise, 140
Levinson, Andrej (or André), 80
LoGatto, Ettore, 110n
Lomonosov, Mixail, 75

Majakovskij, Vladimir, 3, 5, 6, 47, 66, 70, 71, 76–78, 80–81, 85, 88, 105, 108, 109n, 112, 118n, 124, 127, 130–131, 143, 150, 158, 161, 167, 169, 186, 194, 201, 202, 204, 207, 210, 219, 232, 250, 275, 276, 286, 287, 288
Malraux, André, 80n
Mandel'štam, Osip, 3, 6, 7, 38–40, 71, 74, 81, 84, 87, 88, 94, 112, 115, 117n, 125, 126, 155, 171, 182, 183, 204, 286, 288
Markov, Vladimir, 10, 84n, 96, 109nn, 188n, 218n
Maršak, Samuil, 116
Maslenikov, Oleg, 279
Matveeva, Novella, 7
Mčedelov, Vaxtang, 47n, 237
Mej, L. A., 229
Mejerxol'd, Vsevolod (Meyerhold), 199
Mejn (Meyn), Aleksandr Danilovič, 17, 19
Mejn, Marija Lukinična (née Bernacka), 21n
Merežkovskij, Dmitrij, 80, 85, 272
Miljukov, P. N., 76–78, 81, 87, 94, 284, 285n

Močul'skij, Konstantin, 71, 80, 279
Moldavskij, Dmitrij, 115
Montaigne, Michel de, 195, 288
Mozart, Wolfgang Amadeus, 109n, 153, 246

Nabokov, Vladimir, 4, 57, 80, 84n, 94, 97, 108, 216, 275n, 286
Nekrasov, Nikolaj, 2, 130, 202
Nemirovič-Dančenko, V. N., 49
Nerval, Gérard de, 18
Nesmelov, Arsenij, 86
Nietzsche, Friederich, 281–282
Nilender, Vladimir, 29, 30, 32–33, 38n, 176
Noailles, Countess Anna de, 37, 266
Nolle-Kogan, Nadežda, 192

Ocup, Nikolaj, 66, 109
Orlov, V., 103, 112–113, 117n, 119, 205, 205n, 208, 286
Osorgin, Mixail (M. I. Il'in), 61n, 67, 70–71, 257

Parrain, Brice, 80
Pasternak, Boris, 3, 6, 7, 8, 21n, 23, 35, 42n, 47, 53, 55–56, 61, 64, 66, 67, 68, 69, 70, 71, 72–73, 77, 78, 84, 85, 85n, 87, 90, 97, 101, 103, 105, 106, 110n, 112, 113, 115, 117n, 120, 125, 126, 147, 168n, 169, 181, 190, 196, 207, 215, 226, 230, 266, 275–276, 285, 286, 287
Pasternak, Leonid, 73n
Pavlova, Karolina, 193–194
Picasso, Pablo, 80, 194, 199, 260
Pisarev, Dmitrij, 4
Platen, August von, 34
Poggioli, Renato, 110n
Polonskij, Jakov, 125, 223
Poplavskij, Boris, 84, 85n, 91
Pozner, Vladimir, 71n, 80n
Prokof'ev, Sergej, 74, 198–199, 229
Proust, Marcel, 18, 72, 80n
Puškin, Aleksandr, v, 1, 2, 4, 8, 19, 20, 23, 24, 27, 28n, 41, 93, 104,

Puškin, Aleksandr (continued) 109n, 110n, 117, 127, 152, 159n, 172, 180, 186, 201, 202, 207, 216, 223, 231, 240, 247, 253, 273, 275, 277, 280, 281, 285, 286

Racine, Jean, 71, 169, 260, 264, 264n
Ravel, Maurice, 158, 217
Reis, Ignatij (Ignace Reiss), 95–96
Remizov, Aleksej, 55, 67, 68, 70, 124, 127, 131, 132, 141, 143, 144, 229, 267, 271, 287, 288
Reznikova, Natalija, 86, 87–88
Rilke, Rainer Maria, 23, 25, 27, 59, 72–73, 100n, 111n, 119, 220–222, 232–233, 288
Rimbaud, Arthur, vi, 9, 27, 32, 283, 288
Rimskij-Korsakov, Nikolaj, 224
Rostand, Edmond, 27, 31, 125, 172–174, 180, 237, 244, 249
Rozanov, Vasilij, 124, 267
Rubinstein, Anton, 17
Rudnev, Vadim, 83, 116, 274

Sainte-Beuve, C. A., 252n, 254n
Saker, Ja. L., 37
Salieri, Antonio, 109n
Samojlov, David, 119
Sand, George, 33, 263
Schiller, Friederich, 98
Schwab, Gustav, 258–260, 262
Sel'vinskij, Il'ja, 77, 78n, 287
Serebrovskaja, Elena, 115
Setchkarev, Vsevolod, 159n
Severjanin, Igor' (I. V. Lotarev), 115
Shakespeare, William, 71, 169, 196, 208, 263
Sitwell, Dame Edith, 224n
Skrjabin, Aleksandr (Scriabine), 267
Slonim, Mark (or Marc), 10, 58, 67, 74, 79, 108, 111n
Sologub, Fëdor (F. K. Teternikov), 2, 6, 48, 81, 110n, 186, 258
Solov'ëv, Sergej, 29

Solov'ëv, Vladimir, 210
Staël, Germaine de, 183
Staxovič, A. A., 48–49, 125, 185, 243, 246
Stein, Gertrude, 224n
Stepun, Fëdor, 17n, 29n, 32, 44, 108
Stravinskij, Igor', 64, 199, 206, 217, 224, 229
Struve, Gleb, 10, 62n, 68n, 98n, 99n, 131, 234, 267n, 272n, 278
Struve, P. B., 53, 66, 69, 110
Surkov, Aleksej, 115–116
Suvčinskij, Pëtr (Pierre Souvtschinsky), 68, 74
Svjatopolk-Mirskij, Prince D. A., 66, 67, 68, 74, 85, 230, 232–233, 272
Šaginjan, Marietta, 30
Šaxovskaja, Zinaida (Zinaïda Schakovskoy), 96, 99
Šaxovskoj, Prince D. A., later Archbishop John of San Francisco, 10, 67n, 69, 111n, 230n
Šestov, Lev (L. I. Svarcman), 68, 69
Širjaev, Boris, 110, 115
Šiškov, A. S., 131–132
Šklovskij, Viktor, 267
Štejger, Anatolij, 59, 84, 90–93, 99, 110, 140, 202, 281

Tairov, Aleksandr, 36–37
Taranovski, K., 10, 161n, 166n
Terapiano, Jurij, 66n, 80, 84, 99, 109, 164
Tereškovič, Konstantin, 80n
Tesková, Anna, 58
Tèffi, N. A., 80
Tixonov, Nikolaj, 77, 234
Tjutčev, Fëdor, 1, 5, 155, 195, 217
Tolstaja-Libedinskaja, Lidija, 103n
Tolstoj, A. K., 2, 23, 156, 285n
Tolstoj, A. N., 186
Tolstoj, Lev, vi, 72, 143n, 277, 279
Tomaševskij, Boris, 158
Trediakovskij, Vasilij, 4, 131, 142, 150, 153, 195, 257

Triolet, Elsa, 76n, 194
Turgeneva, Anna ("Asja"), 10, 33–34, 176
Tuwim, Julian, 201
Tvardovskij, Aleksandr, 118
Twain, Mark, 174–175
Txorževskij, Ivan, 107

Unbegaun, Boris, 159n, 165

Vaksmaxer, M., 119
Valéry, Paul, 80n
Vastangov, Evgenij, 46–47, 199, 238
Vejdle, Vladimir (Wladimir Weidlé), 80, 108, 264
Verlaine, Paul, 150n
Vil'čkovskij, Kirill (Cyrille Wilczkowski), 91, 92
Villiers de l'Isle Adam, Auguste, 172, 175
Vinokurov, Evgenij, 118, 119
Višnjak, A. G., 55, 60, 69n, 189, 196, 268–269
Višnjak, Mark, 42n, 66n, 68n, 83, 284–285
Volkonskij, Prince Sergej, 37, 44, 45, 49, 79, 88, 96, 189, 246, 266, 272, 277
Vološin, Maksimilian, 6n, 18n, 30, 32, 33, 38, 43, 49, 83, 87, 88, 108, 110n, 113, 117n, 174, 175, 176, 202, 246, 277, 284n

Vološina, Elena Ottobal'dovna ("Pra"), 33, 36, 38, 43, 83
Voznesenskij, Andrej, 7

Webern, Anton von, 199
Weidlé, Wladimir, see Vejdle
Woolf, Virginia, 288
Wytrzens, Günther, 72n

Xlebnikov, Velimir, 3, 5, 7, 66, 72n, 115–116, 124, 145–146, 147, 149, 152, 167, 169, 188, 197, 207, 217, 287
Xodasevič, Vladislav, vii, 3, 5, 32, 54n, 69, 71–72, 74, 84, 85, 111n, 130, 156, 158n, 194, 264–265, 277–279, 282, 284n, 286, 287

Zabolockij, Nikolaj, 6, 78, 201
Zamjatin, Evgenij, 60, 271
Zavadskaja, Vera (Vera Arenskaja), 237, 238
Zavadskij, Jurij, 46–47, 93, 169, 237, 238, 250–254
Zdanevič, Il'ja ("Il'jazd"), 80n
Zinov'eva-Annibal, Lidija, 283–284n

Žernakova-Nikolaeva, Aleksandra, 10, 20nn, 26
Žirmunskij, Viktor, 156n
Žukovskij, Vasilij, 1, 5, 27, 125, 154, 223, 280